Lois Merid

Gift from my
son + family —
Birthday 1979

EARLY FAMILIES
OF
WALLINGFORD, CONNECTICUT

BY

CHARLES HENRY STANLEY DAVIS

WITH A NEW INDEX BY

THOMAS L. HOLLOWAK

Baltimore

GENEALOGICAL PUBLISHING CO., INC.

1979

Excerpted from *History of Wallingford, Conn., from its Settlement in 1670 to the Present Time,*
Meriden, Connecticut, 1870
Reprinted with a new Index and a Guide to Families
Genealogical Publishing Co., Inc.
Baltimore, 1979

Library of Congress Catalogue Card Number 78-71272
International Standard Book Number 0-8063-0834-6
Made in the United States of America

PUBLISHER'S NOTE.

THIS work is excerpted from Charles Davis's *History of Wallingford, Conn., from its Settlement in 1670 to the Present Time* and originally constituted pages 611-941 of that work, appearing under the heading "Genealogies." For the economy it offers we have elected to reprint only this section of genealogies. We have therefore retitled the work, renumbered the pages, revised the errata list to conform to the new pagination, and added a Guide to Families and an Index (the genealogies were not indexed in the original publication). The excerpted matter thus takes on a new character, assuming, we trust, the unity and coherence of a finished work.

To the Connecticut Society of Genealogists, Inc., who commended the work to our attention, we offer our heartfelt thanks; to Thomas Hollowak for his work on the index, and to Patti Matulonis for typing the index, we offer our gratitude.

GUIDE TO FAMILIES.

GENEALOGIES.

"To trace lineage — to love and record the names and actions of those without whom we could never have been, who moulded and made us what we are, and whom the very greatest of us all must know to have propagated influences into his being, which must subtly but certainly act upon his whole conduct in this world — all this is implied in ancestry and the love of it, and is natural and good." *Westminster Review, July*, 1853.

INTRODUCTION.

FEW know the amount of time, patience and labor, that is required in compiling genealogies, and no one can estimate the difficulty of collecting these materials, who has not had experience in similar undertakings. It has been said, that it was useless to tell antiquaries anything about the cost of such works, for they understood it; and it was equally useless to tell others, for they could not comprehend you. It is probable that this work would not have been printed for several years had not the services of Mr. ELIHU YALE been called into requisition. He has spent many years in examining town, church and family records, and in an extensive correspondence with the descendants of the families noticed in this work. Every one who has had any experience in labors of this kind, knows that errors are unavoidable. The neglect of parents in having the births, deaths, and marriages in their respective families recorded, renders it imposssible in many cases, to collect from the town records a correct list of a family. I have carefully compared these records with those of the neighboring towns, the published genealogies of some of the families, and also the records of the Probate office, and the office of the Register of deeds for the county. Thus in some instances I have supplied the record of whole families, not found upon the town records at all. It was my intention to bring the record of each family down to the present generation, but the work has grown to such a size that it will be impossible except in a few instances. Of the Parker, Street, and Brown families I have the record of several thousand names of collateral branches, and also the records of numerous Meriden families, since the incorporation of the town. These Meriden pedigrees I had hoped to have incorporated in this work, but perhaps sufficient inducement may be offered to print them separately ; they would occupy about two hundred pages. Any corrections or additions to the families mentioned in these genealogies will be thankfully received by the author.

ABERNATHY.[1]

WILLIAM.

WILLIAM ABERNATHY came to Wallingford from Branford. He was a native of Scotland, and was an active man among the settlers. The name of his 1st wife was Sarah. His 2nd wife was Elizabeth.

Children: 1 *Elizabeth*, b Oct. 15, 1673; 2 *William*, b Jan. 23, 1675; 3 *Sarah*, b Oct. 10, 1677; 4 *Mary*, b Mar. 27, 1679; 5 *Samuel*, b Jan. 10, 1683, d Mar. 14, 1723; 6 *Daniel*, b Sept. 3, 1686; 7 *Susannah*, b July 18, 1689.

2. WILLIAM.

WILLIAM AND MARY ABERNATHY. He died Feb., 1728. She died Jan. 1, 1757.

Children: 8 *Mary*, b April 30, 1700; 9 *Jemima*, b Aug. 20, 1702; 10 *Sarah*, b Dec. 15, 1705; 11 *Ann*, b June 7, 1706; 12 *John*, b Feb. 27, 1708, killed by lightning May 12, 1727, æ 19; 13 *Caleb*, b Feb. 11, 1710, m. to Lois Gaylord by Capt. Yale, Sept. 26, 1733; 14 *Susannah*, b April 28, 1712, m. Samuel Yale.

5. SAMUEL.

SAMUEL ABERNATHY married Elizabeth Peck Nov. 21, 1711.

Children: 15 *Abraham*, b March 1, 1712; 16 *Samuel*, b Dec. 28, 1718, d July 28, 1724; 17 *Jasper*, b Feb. 24, 1721, d Dec. 2, 1741.

13. CALEB.

CALEB and LOIS ABERNATHY, of Wallingford, married, 1733.

Children: 18 William, b July 1, 1734; 19 *Mary*, b Nov. 23, 1736; 20 *John*, b July 2, 1738; 21 *Mary*, b Dec. 9, 1797; 22 Jared, b Oct. 31, 1741.

---

1 Hinman's Letters of Conn., 17, 18.

ALLING AND ALLEN.

JAMES.

JAMES ALLING is the first of this name that I find in Wallingford, with his wife Abigail, before 1700. The name has not been numerous.

Children: 1 *Abigail*, b. June 23, 1701; 2 *James*, b. Nov. 15, 1702; 3 *Stephen*, b. Oct. 13, 1704; 4 *Mary*, b. March 3, 1708; 5 *Samuel*, b. Jan. 15, 1710, m. Mary Blakeslee, June 23, 1726; 6, *Ebenezer*, b. April 8, 1713.

2. JAMES.

JAMES and MARY (Beadles) ALLING were married Sept. 23, 1731.

Children: 7 *Marshal*, b. Aug. 1, 1732; 8 *Rebecca*, b. Feb. 7, 1734; 9 *Abigail*, b. Dec. 1, 1735; 10 *Josiah*, b. Feb. 19, 1738.

6. EBENEZER.

EBENEZER ALLING married Sarah Atwater, Dec. 19, 1742. He died Nov. 3, 1760.

Children: 11 *Sarah*, b Feb. 8, 1745; 12 *Daniel*, b. Oct. 22, 1747, d. July 11, 1746; 13 *Abel*, b. Jan. 30, 1749; 14 *Enos*, b. Jan. 17, 1752; 15 *Damaris*, b. March 15, 1755; 16 *Abigail*, b. July, 6, 1757; 17 *Eunice*, b. Dec. 19, 1760.

EPHRAIM.

EPHRAIM ALLING married Hannah ———.

Children: 18 *Daniel*, b. Nov. 18, 1743; 19 *Esther*, b. Jan. 24, 1744.

ANDREWS.[1]

WILLIAM.

WILLIAM ANDREWS, of Hampsworth, England (carpenter), was one of the fifty-three persons besides women and children who shipped at Hampton, 15 miles west-south-west of London,

1 Andrews' Hist. New Britain; Bubson's Hist. of Gloucester, 57, 58;

about the 6th of April, 1635, on board of the *James* of London, of 300 tons, Wm. Cooper, Master. Several of the 53 passengers had their wives and children with them, but no record of their names was kept. They landed at Boston, where Wm. Andrews was made a freeman in 1635. He was early at New Haven with Eaton and Rev. John Davenport. He built the first meeting-house there in 1644. He is known to have had three sons and one daughter, and is supposed to have had two other daughters whose names are now unknown. The name of his first wife who was the mother of all his children, is also now unknown. He married his 2nd wife, Anna Gibbands, Dec. 7, 1665; she was a daughter of William Gibbands, who was Colonial Secretary in 1657. Mr. William Andrews died at East Haven, March 4, 1676. Mrs. Anna, his wife, died A. D. 1701.

Children: 1 *William*, born in England, died Jan. 3, 1663, left no sons; 2 *Samuel*, born in England, 1632, died Oct. 6, 1704; 3 *Nathan*, born in England, 1638. Ancestor of the East Haven branch. Daughters, supposed three.

Samuel and Nathan were of the original proprietors of Wallingford in 1670. Nathan was one of the twelve selected to lay the foundation for the formation of the Church in Wallingford, and was an active member of the plantation, after giving directions for its government, until they became sufficiently strong to support a minister.

2. SAMUEL.

SAMUEL ANDREWS, son of William the emigrant, married Elizabeth, daughter of Deacon Wm. Peck, of New Haven. He took the oath of fidelity May 2, 1654; settled in Wallingford in 1670. Made his will April 17, 1703, amount of estate

---

Dodd's Hist. of E. Haven, 101, 102; Eaton's Annals of Warren, 376, 377; Eaton's Hist. of Thomaston, 135; Hale's Lawrence Family, 10–13; Hinman's Conn. Settlers, 51–53; Machias, M. Centennial Celebration, 152, 153; Savage's Gen. Dict., I. 51, 57; Walker's Memorials of Walker Family, 215; Ward's Hist. Shrewsbury, 221–5.

£331 2*s.* 6*d.* He died in Wallingford, Oct. 6, 1704, æ. 73 years. She died in Wallingford.

Children: 4 *William*, b. 1658; 5 *Samuel*, b. Feb. 1, 1661, d. 1662, æ. about 1 year; 6 *Samuel*, b. April 30, 1663, m. Anna Hall, Aug. 27, 1686; 7 *William*, b. Feb. 9, 1664, m. to Hannah Parker, by Mr. Moss, Jan. 12, 1692; 8 *John*, b. July 4, 1667; 9 *Nathaniel*, b. Aug 2, 1670, m. Susannah Tyler; she d. June 5, 1721; 10 *Twins*, b. May 30, 1673, d. 1 day after birth; 11 *Elizabeth*, b. July 16, 1674, m. Benjamin Hall; 12 *Mary*, b. March 27, 1677; 13 *Joseph*, b. June 1, 1679, m. Abigail Paine; 14 *Margery*, b. Jan. 15, 1681; 15 *Dinah*, b. July 25, 1684.

3 NATHAN.

NATHAN ANDREWS, son of William the emigrant, married 1st, Elizabeth Miles, July 26, 1686; 2nd, Hannah Gibbons, of New Haven. He went to Wallingford in 1670. Lot 8 on the west side of Main street was assigned him for his house lot. He died in 1712.

Children by 1st marriage: 16 *Elizabeth*, b. April 8, 1688; 17 *Daniel*, b Aug. 15, 1690, d. Aug. 15, 1690; 18 *Tamer*, b. Aug. 15, 1690, d. Jan. 11, 1727; 19 *Samuel*, b. Aug. 15, 1691, d. Jan. 31, 1727; 20 *Daniel;* 21 *Mary;* 22 *Jonathan*, m. Jemima ——; 23 *Abigail;* by 2nd marriage, 24 *William*, b. Sept. 4, 1729.

6. SAMUEL.

SAMUEL ANDREWS, son of Samuel and Elizabeth, married Hannah, or Anna Hall, August 27, 1686.

Children: 25 *Thomas*, b. March 11, 1687, m. Felix ——; 26 *John*, b. April 18, 1692, d May 6, 1693; 27 *John*, b. May 5, 1693, m. Hannah Merriman, July 19, 1714; 28 *Elizabeth*, b Nov. 27, 1695, d July 19, 1697; 29 *Samuel*, b 1697, m Abigail ——; 30 *Elisha*, b. Apr. 28, 1701; 31 *William*, b July 6, 1702, m. Mary Foster; 32 *Anna*, m. Joseph Roys of Wallingford.

7. WILLIAM.

WILLIAM ANDREWS, son of Samuel and Elizabeth, married to Hannah Parker, by Mr. Moss, Jan. 12, 1692. He died July 8, 1726. (Estate £291.)

Children: 33 *Thankful A.*, m. Matthias Hitchcock.

8. JOHN.

JOHN ANDREWS, son of Samuel and Elizabeth, married Sarah ———.

Children: 34 *Ruth*, b. Oct. 1, 1723.

9. NATHANIEL.

NATHANIEL ANDREWS, son of Samuel and Elizabeth, married Susannah Tyler, Dec. 13, 1705. She died June 25, 1721; and he married Elizabeth Clark, Oct. 16, 1721. He died March 5, 1735. Elizabeth Clark died Sept. 10, 1751.

13. JOSEPH.

JOSEPH ANDREWS, son of Samuel and Elizabeth Andrews, married Abigail Payne Nov. 10, 1704. He made his will Oct. 12, 1741, and died Nov. 20, 1741, æ. 62 yrs., 6 mos., 11 days. She died June 25, 1721.

Children: 35 *Caleb*, b. June 23, 1701; 36 *Caleb*, b. March 12, 1706, d Nov. 20, 1741; 37 *Joseph*, b March 3, 1708, d 1741; 38 *Giles*, b March 19, 1710, m Abigail Curtiss, April 7, 1731; 39 *Mercy*, (twin) b June 15, 1714; 40 *Mary*, (twin), b June 15, 1714, m John Hulls of Wallingford; 41 *Nathaniel*, b March 16, 1717, d 1741; 42 *Andrew*, b Aug. 16, 1719, d. 1792, m Hester ——, she d Sept. 6, 1750; 43 *Stephen*, b May 24, 1722, d 1775, æ. 73.

20. DANIEL.

DANIEL ANDREWS, son of Nathan and Elizabeth, married 1st Mehitable ——, she died. He married 2d, Sarah ——, she died of small pox, 1712.

Children by first wife: 44 *Nathaniel*, b. July 12, 1714; 45 *Elnathan*, Sept. 12, 1717. By 2nd wife: 46 *Jehiel*, b. June, 1720, m. Sarah Cook, Jan. 16, 1746; 47 *Hannah*, b.

May 12, 1723; 48 *Mehitable*, b. April 30, 1726; 49 *Ephraim*, b. May 13, 1731. By 3d wife, Deliverance: 50 *Margery*, b. Nov. 6, 1733; 51 *Abigail*, b. May 1, 1736; 52 *Lydia*, b. June 16, 1740.

22. JONATHAN.

JONATHAN ANDREWS, son of Nathan and Elizabeth; married Jemima Hotchkiss April 11, 1727.

Children: 53 *Abel*, b. Jan. 28, 1728, m. Lettis Williams Feb. 10, 1757, and settled in Cheshire; 54 *Esther*, b. May 9, 1730; 55 *Mary*, b. Jan. 14, 1734; 56 *Daniel*, b. June 4, 1737; 57 *Jemima*, b. Nov. 24, 1740.

25. THOMAS.

THOMAS ANDREWS, son of Samuel and Elizabeth, married 1st Felix ———. He died in 1756, leaving widow Elizabeth.

Children: 58 *Elizabeth*, born April 23, 1717, m. R. Strong of Waterbury, Conn.; 59 *Benjamin*, b. Nov. 26, 1718; 60 *Enos*, b April 13, 1719, m. Content——; 61 *Sarah*, b. July 15, 1720; 62 *Lois*, b. July 15, 1722, m. Leverius Carrington; 63 *Martha*, b. Sept. 25, 1730; 64 *Thankful*, m. Jason Hitchcock.

26. JOHN.

JOHN ANDREWS, son of Samuel and Elizabeth, married Hannah Merriman, July 23, 1714. She died Sept. 28, 1738.

Children: 65 *Ephraim*, b. Oct. 14, 1714; 66 *Phebe*, b. Sept. 11, 1716; 67 *Denizen*, b. May 14, 1718, d. April 13, 1725; 68 *Eben*, b. Jan. 15, 1720; 69 *Anna*, b. Nov. 17, 1721; 70 *Hannah*, b. Jan. 13, 1722; 71 *Peter*, b. Dec. 6, 1723; 72 *John*, b. Nov. 23, 1727; 73 *Hannah*, b. Oct. 24, 1729; 74 *Mary*, b. Sept. 15, 1732, m. Joseph Parker in 1758; 75 *Elizabeth*, b. Aug. 20, 1736.

29. SAMUEL.

SAMUEL ANDREWS, son of Samuel and Anna, married Abigail Tyler, daughter of John and Abigail. He died Oct. 5, 1784, aged 87 years. She died Feb. 13, 1786, aged 89 years. Interred in Meriden.

Children: 76 *Elon*, b Nov. 26, 1721, m. Sarah ——. He died

Sept. 22, 1784; 77 *Jacob*, b. Nov. 18, 1723; 78 *Nicholas*, b. Dec. 27, 1725, died Dec. 21, 1784, æ. 26 years; 79 *Laban*, b. Apr. 25, 1728, m. Prudence Stanley, Apr. 5, 1758; 80 *Denizen*, b. Aug. 27, m. Abigail Whiting, May 11, 1757; 81–2 *Moses* and *Aaron*, twins, b. Aug. 29, 1734; the former was a physician in Meriden; 83 *Samuel*, b. April 27, 1737.

30. ELISHA.

ELISHA ANDREWS, son of Samuel and Annah, married Mabel Andrews.

Children: 84 *Zuba*, b. April 1, 1721, m. John Couch of Meriden, Conn.; 85 *Elisha*, b. Dec. 25, 1727, d. young; 86 *Elisha*, b. Jan. 5, 1728; 87 *Dinah*, b. Mar. 23, 1729, m. Silas Merriman; 89 *Mabel*, b. May 24, 1731, m. Benjamin Tyler of Farmington; 90 *Bartholomew*, b. Jan. 30, 1735, m. Sarah Andrews; 91 *Noah*, b. Feb. 4, 1737, d. in the old French war; 92 *Anna*, b. Dec. 15, 1738, d. in childhood; 93 *Lucy;* 94 *Anna.*

31. WILLIAM.

WILLIAM ANDREWS, son of Samuel and Anna, married Mary Foster, Nov. 1, 1727. He died July 8, 1756. Will dated Oct. 6, 1736.

Children: 95 *Samuel*, b. Aug. 21, 1727, m. Lydia ——; 96 *Anna*, b. Feb. 15, 1729; 97 *Eunice*, b. Feb. 18, 1750; 98 *Titus*, b. June 3, 1732; 99 *William*, b. Feb. 13, 1724; 100 *Thankful;* 101 *Mary;* 102 *Rhoda;* 103 *Titus*, b. March 7, 1751.

35. CALEB.

CALEB ANDREWS, son of Joseph and Abigail (Payne), married, 1st, Esther Beecher, May 22, 1727. She died Oct. 25, 1729. He married 2nd, Mary Culver, July 5, 1733. He died Nov. 20, 1741. Estate £1314.

Children by first marriage: 104 *Sarah*, b. Aug. 22, 1729; by 2nd marriage: 105 *Lament*, b. July 28, 1730, d. December 6, 1736.

38. GILES.

GILES ANDREWS, son of Joseph and Abigail, married Abigail Andrews. They settled in Sheffield, Mass.

Children: 106 *Amos*, b. Jan. 19, 1732; 107 *Joseph*, b May 2, 1743, d. Nov. 8, 1744.

41. NATHANIEL.

NATHANIEL ANDREWS, son of Joseph and Abigail, married 1st, Esther ——; 2nd, Ruth ——; He died July 2, 1756.

Children by Esther: 108 *Amos*, b. April 15, 1733. Children by Ruth: 109 *Rhoda*, b. Feb. 1, 1743; 110 *Nathan*, b. Feb. 2, 1750; 111 *Daniel*, b. May 29, 1751; 112 *Moses*, b. April 8, 1752.

42. ANDREW.

ANDREW ANDREWS, son of Joseph and Abigail, married 1st, Esther ——. She died. He married 2nd, Elizabeth Dunbar. He died Feb. 22, 1772, æ. 72 years, 6 months, and 6 days.

Children: 113, 114, *Johanna* and *Sarah*, b. July 31, 1740, twins; the latter married Bartholemew Andrews; 115 *Margery*, b. March 23, 1742, d. in 1751; 116 *Esther*, b. Feb. 24, 1743; by 2nd wife: 117 *Eunice*, b. Dec. 6, 1746; 118 *Caleb*, b. Dec. 9, 1748; 119 *Margery*, b Nov. 23, 1751; 120 *Margery*, b. June 14, 1752; 121 *Andrew*, b. Aug. 9, 1756; 122 *Joseph*, b. Nov. 26, 1758, died on board of the old prison ship, Jersey; 123 *Nathaniel*, b. May 20, 1761; 124 *Elizabeth*, b. June 20, 1763; 125 *Mary*, b. May 20, 1766, m. Joseph Blakeslee; 126 *Abigail*, b. April 26, 1770, m. Charles T. Jackson, of Litchfield, Conn.

43. STEPHEN.

STEPHEN ANDREWS, son of Joseph and Abigail, married twice; 1st, Mabel ——, she died. 2nd, Hannah ——. He died in Meriden.

Children: 127 *Mary*, b. April 5, 1747, m. a Mr. Bailey; 128 *Abigail*, b Oct. 29, 1749; 129 *Benjamin*, b. Oct. 16, 1751; *Abigail*, b. Oct. 16, 1753; 130 *Mabel*, b. Sept. 23, 1761; 131 *Sarah; Content.*

46. ELNATHAN.

ELNATHAN ANDREWS, son of Daniel and Mehitable, married Hannah ——.

Children: 132 *Bela*, b. March 16, 1740, d. in Cheshire; 133 *Amasa*, b. Sept. 22, 1742–3; 134 *Damaris*, b. March 23, 1745; 135 *Hannah*, b. Jan. 10, 1746; 136 *Elizabeth*, b. June 21, 1758; 137 *Mary*, b. Aug. 29, 1761.

47. JEHIEL.

JEHIEL ANDREWS, son of Daniel and Sarah; married Sarah Cook

Children: 138 *Mabel*, b. July 19, 1746; 139 *Thankful*, b Dec. 9, 1748; 140 *Lois*, b. Aug. 8, 1750; 141 *John*, b. Nov. 12, 1752; 142 *Ebenezer*, b. May 4, 1754; 143 *Sarah*, b. Dec. 29, 1756; 144 *Eunice*, b. March 14, 1759; 145 *Chloe*, b. Dec. 16, 1760.

53. ABEL.

ABEL ANDREWS, son of Jonathan and Jemima, married 1st, Sarah ———; she died, and he married, 2nd, Lettis Williams, Feb. 10, 1757, and settled in Cheshire, where they both died.

Children: by 1st marriage; 146 *Sarah*, b. Feb. 1, 1744. By 2nd marriage; 147 *Samuel;* 148 *Mamre;* 149 *Abel*, m. twice; 150 *Chauncey*, d. in Cheshire; 151 *Esther*, d. in Cheshire.

59. BENJAMIN.

Benjamin Andrews, son of Thomas and Felix, married Susannah ———.

Children: 153 *Samuel*, b. Sept. 21, 1741.

60. ENOS.

Enos Andrews, son of Thomas and Felix ———, married Content———.

Children: 154 *Thomas*, b. Aug. 8, 1744; 155 *Bede*, b. April 2, 1746; 156 *Asahel*, b Nov. 13, 1747; 157 *Huldah*, b. Nov. 3, 1751; 158 *Thankful*, b. Mar. 1, 1754; 159 *Enos*, b. Oct. 12, 1760.

65. EPHRAIM.

EPHRAIM ANDREWS, son of John and Hannah, married Hannah ———.

Children: 160 *Asahel*, b Nov. 5, 1736.

68. EBEN.

EBEN ANDREWS, son of John and Hannah, married Elizabeth Andrews, Dec. 13, 1739.

Children: 161 *Joel*, b Aug. 11, 1740.

72. JOHN.

JOHN ANDREWS, son of John and Hannah, married Abigail ———.

Children: 162 *Abigail*, b Sept. 21, 1740; 163 *Lydia*, b Nov. 13, 1741.

76. ELON.

ELON ANDREWS, son of Samuel and Abigail, married Sarah ———. He died Sept. 22, 1784, aged 63 years. She died April 30, 1797, aged 60.

Children: 164 *Isaac*, d Oct. 24, 1754; 165 *Eunice*, b July 23, 1758; 166 *Isaac*, b March 8, 1762.

77. JACOB.

JACOB ANDREWS, son of Samuel and Abigail, married Ruth ———.

Children: 167 *Abigail*, b Oct. 29, 1749; 168 *Benjamin*, b Oct. 16, 1751; 169 *Abigail*, b Oct. 16, 1753.

78. NICHOLAS.

NICHOLAS ANDREWS, son of Samuel and Abigail, married Lydia ———, March 31, 1761. He died Dec. 21, 1784, æ. 50 years. He when living owned land now owned by Charles E. Yale.

Children: 170 *Amos*, b July 24, 1762.

79 LABAN.

LABAN ANDREWS, son of Samuel and Abigail, married Prudence Stanley.

Children: 171 *Abigail*, b Sept. 21, 1740; 172 *Lydia*, b Nov. 13, 1741.

80. DENIZEN.

DENIZEN ANDREWS, son of Samuel and Abigail, married Abigail Whiting, May 11, 1787. He died at Meriden, June, 1807, æ. 77 years. She died Oct. 1, 1796, æ. 60 years.

Children: 173 *Sarah*, b March 16, 1758; 174 *Abner*, b August 25, 1759. He was paralyzed, died in Meriden, during the Revolutionary war; 175 *Abigail*, b March 23, 1671; 176 *Whiting*; 177 *Samuel*; 178 *Aaron*; 179 *Denizen*; 180 *Oliver*, was a farmer in Meriden, and died there; 181 *Loyal*; 182 *Harvey*; 183 *Sarah*; 184 *Philomelia*.

81. MOSES.

Dr. MOSES ANDREWS, son of Samuel and Abigail, married Lucy ——. He died in Meriden, Oct. 2, 1811, æ. 77. She died June 13, 1832, æ. 86 years.

82. AARON.

DR. AARON ANDREWS, son of Samuel and Abigail, married Sarah Whiting of Stamford, Dec. 18, 1771, and settled in the old village of Wallingford. He owned and occupied the house now owned and occupied by Samuel B. Parmelee Esq., during his life-time. She died Aug. 28, 1836, æ. 92 years, 5 months and 19 days.

Children: 185 *Sherlock*, b. Oct. 19, 1772, d. at Geneva, N. Y., Aug. 28, 1795, m Selina, dau. of Samuel Tyler, of Wallingford; 186 *Betsey*, b. Dec. 11, 1774, m. Oliver Clark, and d. Sept. 10, 1828, at Oswego, N.Y; 187 *John*, (M. D.) b. June 13, 1777, m. Abigail Atwater; 188 *William*, b. Dec. 26, 1779, d. in St. Bartholomew, Nov. 9, 1809; 189 *Drake*, b. Dec. 27, 1781, m. Lucy Whittelsey, and d. in Illinois, May 21, 1841; 190 *Aaron*, b. Dec. 20, 1784, d. in the West Indies, July, 30, 1837.

89. BARTHOLOMEW.

BARTHOLOMEW ANDREWS, son of Elisha and Mabel, married Sarah Andrews, of Wallingford. They both died at Wallingford.

Children: 191 *Elisha*, b Jan. 5, 1761; went to Ballston Spa, N. Y.; 192 *Thomas*, b. May 17, 1762; d. in Wallingford, left Betsey and Orrin; 193 *Esther*, m. Ezra Reid; 194 *Sally*, b. April 17, 1774, d. in Wallingford; 195 *Noah*, b. April 17, 1744, d. in Wallingford; 196 Eunice, b. Sept. 8,

1776, m. Asaph Merriman, of Wallingford; 197 *Lyman*, settled at Ballston Spa, N. Y.; 198 *Caleb*, b. Nov. 11, 1782, went to Nova Scotia, N. B.; 199 *Margery*, m. Constant Abbot.

94. SAMUEL.

SAMUEL ANDREWS, son of William and Mary, married Lydia ———.

Children: 200 *Christopher*, b. Oct. 29, 1752; 201 *Lydia*, b. Dec. 29, 1757

123. NATHANIEL.

NATHANIEL ANDREWS, son of Andrew and Esther, married Lois Blakeslee, May 7, 1781. He died Nov. 21, 1836, aged 75 years, 8 months and 1 day. Mrs. Lois his wife died, March 8, 1823, aged 61 years, 1 month and 29 days.

Children: 202 *Ira*, b Aug. 30, 1781, m. Julia, dau. of Jeremiah Hull; 203 *Andrew*, b Sept. 6, 1783; 204 *Salmon*, b April 3, 1788; 204 *Joseph*, b. Feb. 9, 1791; 205 *Polly*, b May 18, 1793, m Nathan Hull; 206 *Viney*, b Sept. 7, 1795; 207 *Orrin*, b. Dec. 4, 1797, m. —— Cook, dau. of Chester Cook; 208 *Nathaniel*, b 1800; 209 *Aaron*, b April 18, 1803; 210 *Ives*, b March 28, 1805.

GIDEON.

GIDEON ANDREWS, married Hannah ———, and had at his decease the following

Children: 212 *Caleb*, m. 1st, Esther Benham, May 22, 1727. She d. Oct. 25, 1727. Married 2d, Mary Culver, July 5, 1735; 213 *Jedediah;* 214 *Lydia;* 215 *Sarah;* 216 *Phebe;* 217 *Esther;* 218 *Samuel.*

170. AMOS.

AMOS ANDREWS, son of Nicholas and Lydia ———, married Content ———.

Children: 219 *Abigail*, b Feb. 17, 1752; 220 *Sybil*, b July 6, 1754; 221 *Lois*, b April 13, 1756; 222 *Mary*, b Mar. 18, 1758; 223 *Amos*, b Jan. 16, 1760.

TIMOTHY.

Timothy Andrews married Temperance Griswold, Aug. 23, 1741. She died Nov. 25, 1743, æ. 23. He married a second wife, Rachel. She died Jan. 11, 1756, aged 33. He settled at Newark Valley, near Oswego, N. Y.

Children by 1st wife: 224 *Lydia*, b Oct. 27, 1743; by 2d wife, 225 *Elisha*, b Dec. 12, 1746; 226 *Timothy*, b. April 27, 1749; 227 *Phineas*, b Nov. 25, 1752; 228 *Benjamin*, b Dec. 18, 1755.

185. SHERLOCK.

Sherlock Andrews, son of Doctor Aaron and ——, married Salina, daughter of Samuel Tyler, of Tyler's Mills, now Yalesville, Wallingford. He died at Geneva, N. Y., in 1795. She died at Columbus, Ohio, aged 94 or 95.

Children: 229 *Samuel*, was a lawyer at Columbus, Ohio; 230 *Sarah*, m. —— Wilcox, a lawyer at Columbus, Ohio.

187. JOHN.

Dr. John Andrews, son of Dr. Aaron and ——, married Abigail, daughter of Caleb Atwater, by whom he had all his children. His 2d wife was Anna, daughter of Rev. James and Anna Noyes.

Children: 231 Hon. *Sherlock J.*, b Nov. 1801, graduated at Yale, and a lawyer at Cleveland, Ohio; 232 *Jane*, b Dec., 1803, m John M. Wolsey, Esq., of New Haven; 233 *William*, b 1806, a farmer at Elyria, Loraine Co., Ohio; 234 *John Whiting*, b 1809, graduated at Yale. A lawyer at Columbus, Ohio.

189. DRAKE.

Drake Andrews, son of Dr. Aaron and ——, married Lucy Whittelsey, Oct. 12, 1812. He died in Illisia, May 21, 1841. Of his family I have no further information.

229. IRA.

Col. Ira Andrews, son of Nathaniel and ——, married Julia Hall, daughter of the late Jeremiah Hall of Wallingford. He died Jan. 14, 1861, aged 79 years, 4 months, 15 days. She was born the 5th of March, A. D. 1788, and is living Jan., 1870.

Children: 235 *Janet*, b June 9, 1806, m Miller; 236 *Ali*, b Mar. 6, 1800, resides in Bridgeport, Conn; 237 *Gad*, b Nov. 19, 1803; 238-9 *Burr* and *Sarah* (twins), b Oct, 14, 1806; 240 *Lee*, b April 2, 1809; 241 *Joseph D.*, b March 9, 1824; 242 *Jane*, b June 24, 1830.

ATWATER.[1]

JOHN.

JOHN, son of Daniel Atwater of New Haven, settled in Wallingford in 1682 on a lot in the village designated as No.— on the east side of the Main street, being forty rods long and twenty rods wide, and was first settled by Daniel Atwater for his son Joshua, who died before taking possession of it in 1680. He was married to Abigail Mansfield, Sept. 13, 1682, and was a weaver by trade. She died Sept. 24, 1717.

Children: 1 *John*, b. Aug. 17, 1683, m. Elizabeth Mix, Aug. 4, 1713; 2 *Abigail*, b Oct. 17, 1685; 3 *Mercy*, b Feb. 6, 1687; 4 *Hannah*, b Dec. 17, 1690; 5 *Joshua*, b Sept. 18, 1693, m. Mary Peck and Sarah Yale; 6 *Moses*, b July 17, 1696, m. Sarah Merriman and Mary Hotchkiss; 7 *Phineas*, b Sept. 23, 1699, m. Mary Ward; 8 *Ebenezer*, b Feb. 6,1703, m. Jane Andrews; 9 *Caleb*, b Oct. 9, 1705, m. Mehitable Mix; 10 *Benjamin*, b Dec. 8, 1708, m. Elizabeth Porter.

1. JOHN.

JOHN, son of John and Abigail Atwater of Wallingford, married Elizabeth, daughter of ——— Mix, August 4, 1713.

Children: 11 *Elizabeth*, b Nov. 17, 1721, m ——— Ives; 12 *Enos*, b Dec 3, 1717; 13 *Stephen*, b Sept. 8, 1714; 14 *John*, b Jan. 27, 1718; 15 *Sarah*; 16 *Hannah*, b Dec. 28, 1722, m Bela Hitchcock of Cheshire; 17 *Ebenezer*, b 1723, d. Oct. 21, 1755; 18 *Stephen*, b Feb. 2, 1720, m Elizabeth Yale,

---

1 Atwater's Gen. Reg. of Atwaters, 30; Hinman's Conn. Settlers, 76; Savage's Gen. Dict., I. 75, 76.

June 6, 1739; 19 *Titus*, b 1724, d. Dec. 26, 1758; 20 *Amos*, died without issue.

5. JOSHUA.

JOSHUA, son of John, m Mary, dau. of John Peck, 17 Jan. 1723; m 2nd, Sarah, dau. of Theophilus Yale, Sept. 4, 1740. He died Nov. 29, 1757.

Children: by 1st marriage; 21 *Joshua*, b Mar. 8, 1724, d 1747; 22 *Mary*, b Feb. 12, 1727. By 2nd marriage; 23 *Caleb*, b Sept. 5, 1741; 24 *Sarah*, m ——— Hall.

6. MOSES.

MOSES, son of John Peck, m Sarah Merriman, Dec. 28, 1722. She died Feb. 1733, and he married 2nd, Mary Hotchkiss, Apr. 22, 1734.

Children: by 1st marriage; 28 *Abigail*, b Sept. 13, 1725; 26 *Sarah*, b Oct. 29, 1727; 27 *Moses*, b Nov. 22, 1729; 28, *Mercy*, b Aug. 15, 1731. By 2nd marriage; 29 *Elihu*, b Jan. 18, 1735; 30 *David*, b Feb. 23, 1736; 31 *Mary*, b Aug. 1, 1734; 32 *Hannah*, b May 1, 1739.

7. PHINEAS.

PHINEAS, son of John Atwater, m Mary Ward Nov. 9, 1727, and died Oct., 1781. He resided in Cheshire.

Children: 33 *Reuben*, b Oct. 13, 1728; 34 *William*, b 1730; 35 *Thomas*, b Aug. 14, 1733; 36 *Phineas*, b Dec. 12, 1735; 37 *Damaris*, b 1738, m Samuel Tyler of Wallingford; 28 *Menab*, b July 8, 1741, d Sept. 13, 1754; *Ambrose*, b Dec. 19, 1743, m Sarah Tryon.

8. EBENEZER.

EBENEZER, son of John Atwater m, Jane Andrews, Dec. 30, 1737.

Children: 40 *Caleb*, b Sept. 8, 1738, m Phebe Talmage; 41 *Samuel*, b January 30, 1740, m Hannah Bristol; 42 *Ebenezer*, b July 13, 1742; 43 *Ephraim*, b Nov. 27, 1743, m Abigail Rowe; 44 *Esther*, b Feb. 4, 1746; 45 *Elizabeth*, b April 13, 1748; 46 *Abigail*, b Sept. 19, 1754; 47 *Comfort*, b March 16, 1757.

9. CALEB.

CALEB, son of John Atwater, married Mehitable Mix, Nov. 10, 1726.

Children: 48 *Sarah*, b Nov, 28, 1727; 49 *Eunice*, b Sept. 10, 1786, m Phineas Cook.

10. BENJAMIN.

BENJAMIN, son of John Atwater, married Elizabeth Porter, Nov. 28, 1739. She died January 13, 1774, æ. 66 years.

Children: 50 *Elizabeth*, b April 25, 1780; 51 *Mary*, b Dec. 20, 1735; 52 *Comfort*, b Sept. 19, 1749, d January 22, 1789; 53 *Benjamin*, b January 9, 1750, d January 19, 1781.

12. ENOS.

ENOS, son of John 2nd, married Hannah Moss, July 9, 1740.

Children: 54 *Heman*, b March 4, 1743, d Sept. 27, 1752; 55 *Asaph*, b Aug. 1, 1745; 56 *Mehitable*, b July 23, 1747, m Eli Bronson of Waterbury; 50 *Enos*, b Oct. 25, 1748, m Hannah Moss, July 3, 1741; 58 *Eunice*, b Sept., 1750; 59 *Heman*, b Aug. 29, 1752, went to Southington; 60 *Kezia*, b Oct. 10, 1754; 62 *Anna*, b Nov. 17, 1756; 63 *Titus*, b Jan. 6, 1761.

14. JOHN.

JOHN, son of John 2d, m Hannah Thompson, Feb. 22, 1744.

Children: 63 *Jeremiah*, b Nov. 10, 1744; 64 *Phebe*, b Aug. 11, 1747, m ——— Dutton; 65 *Hannah*, b Feb. 17, 1749, m Samuel Hull of Cheshire; 66 *John*; 67 *Jesse*; 68 *Mary*, m ——— Peck of Waterbury.

18. STEPHEN.

STEPHEN, son of John 2d, m Hannah Hotchkiss, Feb. 23, 1744.

Children: 69 *Elizabeth*, b Sept. 12, 1746; 70 *Lois*, m John Upson; 71 *Stephen*, b Sept. 4, 1749, d Aug. 25, 1750; 72 *Sarah*, b Nov. 25, 1751, m Enos Johnson; 73 *Hannah*, b Nov. 27, 1754, m John Hall; 74 *Naomi*, b Aug. 17, 1756, m Enos Bushnell; 75 *Ruth*, b Aug. 17, 1756, m Jonathan Hall; 76 *Stephen*, b May 13, 1758.

19. TITUS.

TITUS, son of John 2nd, m Margaret Scott, Dec, 14, 1758,

Children: 77 *Chloe*, b Sept, 29, 1750, m Samuel Cook; 78 *Amos*, b June 12, 1752, m Mary——, his wife d Oct, 2, 1799, æ 38; 79 *Miriam*, b 1754, m Calvin Cowles; 80 *Rhoda*, b May 15, 1756.

23. CALEB.

CALEB, son of Joshua and Sarah, m Abigail Jones for his 1st wife, and Ruth Wadsworth, Jan. 22, 1776, for his 2nd wife.

Children: 81 *Sarah*, b July 19, 1767; 82 *Mary*, b April 23, 1769; 83 *Lucy*, b Dec. 8, 1770; 84 *Joshua*, b Feb. 8, 1773, m Elizabeth Cook, dau. of Aaron; 85 *James W.*, b June 30, 1777; d Oct. 30, 1777; 86 *Abigail*, b Dec. 13, 1778, m Doct. John Andrews; 87 *Catharine*; 88 *Ruth*.

27. MOSES.

MOSES, of Wallingford, son of Moses, m Emma Newton, Dec. 18, 1755.

Children: 89 *Sarah*, b Nov. 16, 1755; 90 *Lyman*, lived in Broad Swamp, Cheshire.

29. ELIHU.

ELIHU, of Wallingford, son of Moses, married Abigail Tryon.

Children: 91 *Freeman*, b Feb. 16, 1766, went to Canandagua, N. Y.; 92 *Mary*, b March 2, 1767; 93 *Abiah*, b Nov. 3, 1769; 94 *Sally*, b Jan. 23, 1773; 95 *Elihu*, b June 9, 1776, went South; 96 *Jesse*, was Postmaster at New Haven, m Widow Hudson, left no children.

30. DANIEL.

DANIEL, son of Moses of Wallingford, was an apothecary at New Haven, m Eunice Thompson of Stratford, Nov. 15, 1770, and was killed in a skirmish with the British troops at Compo Hill, April 28, 1777.

Children: 97 *Chester*, b Dec, 21, 1772, d Mar. 30, 1773; 98 *Chester*, b April 14, 1774, no issue; 99 *Sylvester*, b Feb. 17, 1776, d Sept, 9, 1776; 100 *David*, b 1777, graduated at Yale 1797, d 1805.

33. REUBEN.

REUBEN, son of Phineas of Wallingford, m Sarah Hall

April 29, 1752, and Mary Russel January 28, 1755. He died Aug, 19, 1801.

Children: 101 *Sarah*, b June 14, 1753; 102 *Merab*, b June 19, 1757; 103 *Phineas*, b Nov. 25, 1758; 104 *Elizabeth M. A.*, b Sept., 1760, m Andrew Hull of Cheshire; 105 *Russel*, b June 20, 1762, went to Blandford, Mass.; 106 *Nabby*, b April 2, 1764, m Dr. Elnathan Beach of Cheshire; 107 *Amaryllis*, b April 2, 1764, m Titus Street of Wallingford, Cheshire, and of New Haven; 108 *Reuben*, b May 18, 1767.

34. WILLIAM.

William, son of Phineas, of Wallingford, married Esther Tuttle.

Children: 109 *Rufus*, b Nov. 29, 1754, m 1st, Mary Tuttle of Wallingford, Dec. 18, 1777. He removed to Nova Scotia; 110 *Lyman*, b Feb. 8, 1757; 111 *William*, b Feb. 16, 1759, went to Nova Scotia; 112 *Chloe*, b Sept. 21, 1763; 113 *Ira*, b June 21, 1765, d April 4, 1738, in Wallingford; 114 *Asenath*, b Oct. 30, 1768; 115 *Esther*, b Oct. 4, 1771; 116 *Ward*, went to Nova Scotia.

36. PHINEAS.

Phineas married Mary ———, and 2nd, widow Hannah Ives, of Goshen, Conn., June 15, 1760.

Child: 117 *Ward*, b 1760.

39. AMBROSE.

Ambrose, son of Phineas, married Sarah Tryon.

Children: 118 *Amelia*, b July 3, 1767, m Thaddeus Tuttle; 119 *Linus*, b July 23, 1769; 120 *Jonathan*, b Oct. 18, 1770; 121 *Ambrose*, b April 5, 1773, d June 23, 1778; 122 *Thomas*, b April 19, 1774; 123 *Sarah*, b April 19, 1775; 124 *Mary*, b Oct, 17, 1778; 125 *Phineas*, b July 12, 1782; 126 *Menab*, b April 17, 1782, m John P. Wetmore; 127 *Clara C.*, b May 6, 1786, m Joshua Tuttle; 128 *William*, b May 9, 1789.

40. CALEB.

Caleb, son of Ebenezer, of Wallingford, m Phebe Tallmage.

Children: 129 *Anne*, b Nov. 17, 1765; 130 *Ebenezer*, b Feb. 16, 1768.

41. SAMUEL.

SAMUEL, son of Ebenezer, m Hannah Bristol, May 5, 1768.

Children: 131 *Sylvia*, b Feb. 21, 1769, m ——— Winchell; 132 *Merab*, b May 11, 1771, m ——— Ives, d 1857; 133 *Samuel*, b Oct. 7, 1773, d in Orange, Conn.; 134 *Joshua*, b Feb. 20, 1779; 135 *Ebenezer*, d in Cheshire.

43. EPHRAIM.

EPHRAIM, son of Ebenezer, m Abigail Rowe, d Oct. 22, 1776, at Danbury, Conn.

Children: 136 *Lowly*, b Oct. 26, 1772, m Noah Andrews, of Wallingford; 137 *Eunice*, b Sept. 18, 1744, m ——— Matthews; 138 *Ephraim*, b March 5, 1777.

STEPHEN.

STEPHEN, son of David, settled in Meriden, then in Wallingford, m Elizabeth Yale. He came from New Haven.

Children: 139 *Ruth*, b June 6, 1740; 140 *Stephen*, b Sept. 16, 1742, settled in Cheshire; 141 *Eunice*, b Sept. 28, 1744; 142 *Daniel*, b Aug. 30, 1747, d unmarried; 143 *Mary*, b June 25, 1750, m ——— Merriam; 144 *Elizabeth*, b July 27, 1752; 145 *Christopher*, b Jan. 6, 1757, d Sept. 10, 1776: 146 *Isaac*, b Dec., 1758.

ABRAHAM.

ABRAHAM, son of Jonathan, the son of Jonathan, the son of Daniel, the son of David, m Mary Bull in May, 1738, and settled in Cheshire, then belonging to Wallingford. He died Jan. 4, 1786, æ 70 yrs. She died May 15, 1811, æ 83 yrs.

Children: 146 *Esther*, b Dec. 19, 1738; 147 *Mary*, b April 28, 1740; 148 *Chloe*, b Oct. 27, 1742; 149 *Isaac*, b June 15, 1746; 150 *Lois*, b June 12, 1749; 151 *Timothy*, b Oct. 30, 1751; 152 *Abigail;* 153 *Samuel*, b 1757, died Jan. 12, 1748; 154 *Esther*, b Dec. 10, 1763.

BENJAMIN.

BENJAMIN, son of Joseph Atwater, the son of Jonathan, m

Phebe ———. She died March 1, 1799, æ 64. He died Feb. 6, 1799, æ 72.

Children: 155 *Joseph;* 156 *Sarah*, b April 26, 1756, m Charles Hull, 2nd, Aaron Hall, of Wallingford; 157 *Benjamin*, b Sept. 26, 1757; 158 *Titus*, b Aug. 29, 1759, d unm. at Cheshire; 159 *Moses*, b May 12, 1765, d at Canandaigua, N. Y.; 160 *Aaron*, b Nov. 10, 1776; 161 *Joel*, b April 22, 1769; 162 *Anna*, b Aug. 23, 1777, d Aug. 29, 1776; 163 *Jeremiah*, d in Canandaigua; 164 *Anna*, m Stephen Jarvis, of Cheshire.

JOSEPH.

JOSEPH, son of Joseph, son of Jonathan, son of Daniel of Wallingford, m Phebe Hall, Aug. 18, 1756. He d Aug. 22, 1769. She d March 23, 1767, æ. 23 yrs..

Child: 165 *Phebe*, b Oct. 15, 1757, d Jan. 19, 1766, æ. 9 yrs.

54. HEMAN.

HEMAN, son of Enos Atwater, settled at Southington, and was the owner of Atwater mills.

84. JOSHUA.

JOSHUA, son of Caleb, of Wallingford, m Elizabeth Cook, dau. of Aaron Cook, Oct. 22, 1793.

Children: 166 *Elizabeth*, b Aug. 4, 1794, m John Barker; 167 *Caroline*, b June 17, 1796, m Dr. Jared P. Kirtland; 168 *Emily*, b Feb. 7, 1798, m Dr. Friend Cook; 169 *Abigail*, b Dec. 28, 1800, d at Durham, Sept. 23, 1823; 170 *Mary*, b Oct. 18, 1802, d July 24, 1804; 171 *Caleb*, b July 11, 1804, m Julia A. Royce, and 2nd, Elizabeth S. Clark; 172 *Joshua*, b Aug. 26, 1806, m Mary H. Day; 173 *Thomas Cook*, b Aug. 20, 1808, m Harriet E. Cook; 174 *Lucretia*, b June 26, 1800, d June 29, 1822; 155 *Edgar*, b Oct 12, 1812, m Sarah S. Yale, d 1860; 176 *John*, b Jan. 19, 1815, m Caroline, and 2nd, Eliza Hall, dau. of Russel Hall; 177 *William*, b Aug. 5, 1817, m Elizabeth Helfenstein; 178 *Mary Ann*, b May 29, 1819, m Lieut. Garrit Barry.

105. RUSSELL.

RUSSEL, son of Reuben Atwater, of Cheshire (then Wallingford), m Clarissa Chapman, Oct. 24, 1790, and died Oct. 3, 1798. She was born Nov. 22, 1762.

Children: 179 *Phineas*, b Nov. 10, 1791; 180 *Merab*, b April 28, 1793, d March 19, 1794; 181 *Russell*, b Jan. 8, 1795, d Dec. 22, 1823; 182 *Frederick*, b Nov. 6, 1796; 183 *Henry*, b Sept. 21, 1798; 184 *Thomas*, b Sept. 21, 1798, d April 15, 1803.

108. REUBEN.

REUBEN, son of Reuben Atwater, m Eliza Willard, and 2d, Sarah Lamb. He died February, 1831.

Children: 183 *Catharine;* 184 *Clinton Edward.*

113. IRA.

IRA, son of William Atwater, m Lois ——. He was a shoe-maker, and lived and died at what is now Yalesville.

Children: 185 *Mary*, m and went to Bethany; 186 *Martha*, m Henry Hough; 187 *William*, d March, 1828; 188 *John*, d South; 189 *Luman*, of Fair Haven, Conn.; 190 *Esther;* 191 *Lois;* 192 *Chloe.*

116. WARD.

WARD, son of Phineas, m Abigail Atwater. She died in New Haven in 1822.

Children: 193 *Rebecca*, b Sept. 23, 1787, d Sept 22, 1788; 194 *Harriet*, b Feb. 23, 1789, d May, 1795; 195 *James*, b May 1, 1790, d Oct. 21, 1791; 196 *James Ward*, b Feb. 11, 1794, d Dec. 8, 1820; 197 *William*, b June 20, 1795, d Jan. 1810; 198 *Harriet*, b March 14, 1797, d Sept., 1798; 199, *Abigail*, b Sept. 4, 1798, d Nov. 11, 1799; 200 *Richard*, b March 25, 1802, d Oct. 3, 1848; 210 *Edward*, b June 29, 1803; 202 *Charlotte*, b Sept., 1804.

120. AMBROSE.

AMBROSE, son of Phineas Atwater, m Sarah Tryon.

Children: 203 *Amelia*, b July 3, 1767, m Thaddeus Tuttle; 204 *Linus*, b Feb. 22, 1769; 205 *Jonathan*, b Oct. 18, 1770; 206 *Ambrose*, b April 5, 1773, d June 23, 1778; 207 *Thomas*, b April 19, 1775; 280 *Sarah*, b Feb. 11, 1777, m Asa Lyon;

209 *Mary*, b Oct 17, 1778, m Peter B. Smith; 210 *Phineas*, b July 12, 1770; 211 *Merab*, b April 17, 1782, m John P. Wetmore; 212 *Clara*, b May 6, 1786, m Joshua Fuller; 213 *William*, b May 9, 1789.

137. STEPHEN.

STEPHEN, son of Stephen and Elizabeth Yale Atwater, m Anna Moss, March 23, 1780. Settled in Cheshire.

Children: 214 *Hannah H.*, b Feb. 8, 1781; 215 *Richard*, b Feb. 10, 1783; 216 *Tempa*, b Sept. 11, 1787; 217 *Anna Maria*, b Aug. 28, 1789; 218 *Betsey*, b Dec. 9, 1794; 219 *Merab*, b June 22, 1797; 220 *Matilda*, b June 5, 1805.

147. ISAAC.

ISAAC, son of Abraham Atwater, son of Jonathan of Cheshire, settled in Columbia, now Prospect, m Eunice ——, May 16, 1771. He died Sept. 13, 1776, at New York.

Children: 221 *Pamelia*, b March 28, 1772; 222 *Abraham*, b March, 6, 1774; 223 *Hannah*, b Oct. 15, 1775.

149. TIMOTHY.

TIMOTHY, son of Abraham Atwater, son of Jonathan of Cheshire, m Lucy ——.

Children: 224 *Deborah*, b May 28, 1773; 225 *Lucy*, b Aug. 8, 1775; 226 *Cato*, b Oct. 18, 1777; 227 *Isaac*, b Oct. 5, 1779; 228 *Lucinda*, m March 4, 1782; 229 *Timothy Glover*, b July 20, 1784, d in Cheshire; 230 *Charlotte*, b July 22, 1786; 231 *Phineas*, b Jan. 20, 1789; 232 *Esther*, b July 1, 1791; 233 *Aaron*, b March 11, 1793, m Betsey Atsom.

151. SAMUEL.

SAMUEL, son of Abraham Atwater, son of Jonathan, settled in Cheshire, m Patience ——.

Children: 204 *Flamen*, b March 30, 1783; 235 *Roxanna*, b Jan. 15, 1785; 236 *Nancy*, b May 15, 1789; 237 *Nancy*, 2d, b Sept. 13, 1789; 238 *Mary Ann*, b Jan. 4, 1792; 239 *Patience*, b March 13, 1794; 240 *Nabby Ann*, b Dec. 13, 1797, 241 *Abigail Ann*, b Oct. 19, 1800; 242 *Lois*, b July 15, 1803; 243 *Lois Maria*, b Feb. 13, 1806, m Joseph Hitchcock of Cheshire.

153. JOSEPH.

JOSEPH, son of Benjamin of Cheshire, m Hannah Hitchcock, Sept. 17, 1783.

Children: 244 *Joseph Hall*, b Feb. 29, 1784, m, had *Joseph H.*; 245 *Phebe*, b Nov. 25, 1786; 246 *Almon*, b March 5, 1788; 247 *Hannah*, b April 20, 1790, m Belina Clark of Cheshire; 248 *Freeman*, b April 17, 1796, m —— Beach.

BEAUMONT.

DEODATE.

DEODATE BEAUMONT was born in Wallingford as early as the commencement of the present century, and perhaps earlier. He was a mechanic and farmer, and owned and occupied the house and lot now owned by his son Elijah Beaumont in Wallingford.

Children: *John*; *Elijah*; *Elizabeth*.

BARKER.[1]

JOHN.

JOHN and SARAH BARKER were in Wallingford previous to 1739, from Branford, where he was born. He built the large brick house now owned by Samuel C. Ford, Esq. His farm was a large one, and one of the best in the county of New Haven. Of his history very little can now be learned.

Children: 1 *Sarah*, b July 22, 1739; 2 *John*, b May 2, 1741; 3 *Mary*, b March 10, 1742, m Solomon Johnson; 4 *Edward*, m Rachel, dau. of Constant Kirtland; 5 *Eunice*, m John Beadles, Jan. 18, 1764.

---

1 For collateral branches, see Abbott's Hist. Andover, Mass., 20–1; Barry's Hist. Hanover, Mass., 206–7; Blood's Hist. Temple, N. H., 203; Bolton's Hist. Westchester Co., N. Y., 501; Deane's Hist. Scituate, Mass., 216; Eaton's Hist. Thomaston, Me., 139; Goodman's Foot family Gen., 189; Hanson's Hist. Gardner, Me., 156; Savage's Gen. Dict., I. 115, 116.

4. EDWARD.

Edward Barker, son of John and Sarah Barker, m Rachel, dau. of Constant and Rachel Kirtland of Wallingford, and remained on the old homestead until his death.

Children: 6 *John*, m Elizabeth Atwater, of Wallingford; 7 *Sarah*, m Wm. H. Jones, New Haven.

BEACH.[1]

Genealogists have been somewhat divided and in doubt regarding the earliest families of this name. Hinman assigns John of Stratford, to Thomas of Milford; but John of Stratford had two children born to him before John the son of the Milford Thomas was born. Savage thinks John of Stratford was probably son of Richard of New Haven, if not his brother. Savage also thinks Benjamin of Stratford was son of Richard of New Haven. But if so, he would have been only fifteen years old when first announced in Stratford, which is out of the question. The probabilities seem to indicate that John, Benjamin and Richard, who all appear in Stratford, and Thomas of Milford, were brothers. The latter had a home lot in Milford in 1648. The Beaches of Litchfield, and George Beach Esq. of Hartford, are said to be of this stock. Richard Beach of New Haven I take to be the man who was in Stratford in 1663, and as keeper of the ordinary or tavern, desired a grant of land from the town, and also exemption from military duty. He bought of Thomas Wheeler, who bought from Robert Rice, the lot where Mr. Meacham now lives. Wheeler moved to Pagusset (Derby), and sold to R. Beach, who sold to Mr. Fenn of Milford, and he sold in 1667 to Rev. Israel Chauncey, the second pastor of the Congregational church in Stratford, part of this land, with part of the land owned by John Brinsmade, one of the first settlers (on the river side), and

---

1 For collateral branches, see Hinman's Conn. settlers, 163, 164; Littell's Passaic Valley Gen., 35–7; Savage's Gen. Dict., I. 144.

the land owned by William Beardsley, with a piece of Nicholas Knell's lot on the back street and now (1868) owned by Alfred E. Beach, son of the late Moses Yale Beach of Wallingford, a lineal descendant of John, brother of Richard.

Benjamin Beach, a brother also of John, as I suppose, was in Stratford in 1659. From him descended Benjamin Beach, the merchant and owner of vessels, who was a man of property and built the old house that was taken down by Mr. Patterson some years ago, and which stood where Mr. Dutcher, in 1863, lived. Benjamin Beach senior's descendants settled in part in Trumbull. The year of John Beach's birth is now unknown: he died suddenly, intestate, in 1667, and the names of his ten children are given on the probate records, but not that of his wife. He became one of the original proprietors of Wallingford, and is represented in the inventory of his estate as having property in Wallingford to the amount of £92 19*s.*; and in Stratford to the amount of £312 13*s.* He seems to have bought in Wallingford with a view to the settlement of his sons there. John Jr., Isaac and Thomas removed to Wallingford, but the first two died in Stratford. Indeed, Isaac in 1694 united with Stratford church, and is entered as of Wallingford. His grave-stone with that of his brother Nathaniel's and also of Nathaniel's wife, yet remain in the old cemetery at Stratford. As John Beach senior's estate was administered in Fairfield county probate court, he evidently had not transferred his residence to Wallingford.

References in the Stratford Records establish the identity of the Wallingford Beaches with the family of John Beach of Stratford, through his son Thomas principally, as will be seen.

Children of John Beach of Stratford: 1 *Elizabeth*, b March 8, 1652, m Eliasaph Preston, went to Wallingford; *John*, b April, 1654, m Hannah, dau of Thomas Staples of Fairfield, 1679; 3 *Mary*, b Sept., 1656; 4 *Thomas*, b May, 1659, m Ruth Peck of Wallingford, and 2nd, Phebe, dau. of Timothy Willcoxen; 5 *Nathaniel*, b March, 1662, m Sarah Porter, April 29,

1693, went to Wallingford; 6 *Hannah*, b Dec., 1665, m Zachariah Fairchild, Nov. 3, 1681, after his decease she m John Barrit; 7 *Sarah*, b Nov., 1667; 8 *Isaac*, b June 27, 1659, m Hannah Birdsey, was a tailor in Stratford; 9 *Joseph*, b Feb. 5, 1671, m Abiah, dau. of Ebenezer Booth; 10 *Benjamin*, b March, 1674, m Mary ———.

John Beach's house lot extended from Main-st, to Back-st, originally called Front street, and covered the present lots now occupied by the Masonic Lodge, Alfred Barnet and Mrs. Hubbell, with a part of Mrs. Linsley's and Miss Poor's grounds.

I will now attempt to trace, so far as I can by existing records, the settlement and increase of the above named ten children of John Beach of Stratford:

1. ELIZABETH.

ELIZABETH m Eliasaph Preston. He was born with his twin brother Hackaliah, April 9, 1643: was a son of William Preston, one of the first settlers of New Haven. Their mother was probably William Preston's 2d wife, and a daughter of Robert Seabrook, another of whose daughters was the wife of Thos. Fairchild, and an original proprietor in Stratford. Eliasaph Preston removed to Wallingford soon after its settlement in 1674, and was the first Deacon of the Congregational church in that place. He died in 1705, æ. 62 years. Elizabeth was his second wife. His first wife Mary Kimberly died in 1674, April 28. She was the widow of Thos. Kimberly, and died in 1672.

The children of Eliasaph and Elizabeth Preston were: 11 *Elizabeth*, b Jan. 29, 1676; 12 *Hannah*, b July 12, 1678; 13 *Eliasaph*, b Jan. 26, 1679–80; 14 *Joseph*, b March 10, 1681–2; 15 *Esther*, b Feb. 28, 1683–4; 16 *Lydia*, b May 25, 1686; 17 *Jehiel*, b Aug. 25, 1688, d Nov., 1689.

2. JOHN.

JOHN BEACH m Hannah, dau. of Thomas Staples of Fairfield, 1679.

Their children recorded at Stratford were: 18 *Mary*,

b July 14, 1683, m Archibald Dunlap, June, 1704, and 2nd, ——— Smith; 19 *Ruth*, b about 1685, m Samuel Fairchild, 1704; 20 *Mehitable*, b Sept. 30, 1690; 21 *Ebenezer*, b Sept. 14, 1692; 22 *Hester*, b May 3, 1694. John Beach 2nd d in Stratford, 1712.

4. THOMAS.

THOMAS BEACH, married 1st, Ruth Peck, a sister of John Peck, and settled in Wallingford May 12, 1680; 2nd, Phebe, dau. of Timothy Willcoxen of Stratford. She was born in 1669. Her father was son of William, an original proprietor of Stratford, whose house-lot was situated about where Mrs. Turk's home-lot now lies (1863), and probably covered Mr. Wm. Benjamin's lot besides. Phebe's mother was Johannah, dau. of Deacon John Birdsey, an original proprietor of Stratford.

Children: 23 *Hannah*, b Feb. 26, 1680, d Sept. 18, 1683; 24 *Ruth*, b Oct. 24, 1684, died young; 25 *Thomas*, b Dec. 9, 1685, d Dec. 13, 1685; 26 *Benoni*, b Oct. 20, 1686, d Dec. 5, 1686. Mrs. Ruth Beach died Dec. 5, 1686. Children by 2nd marriage: 27 *Timothy*, b Jan. 11, 1689, m Hannah Cook, Nov. 25, 1713; 28 *Nathan*, b Aug. 18, 1692, m Jemima Curtiss, Sept. 29, 1713; 29 *Moses*, b Feb. 19, 1695, m Esther Tyler, Sept. 21, 1722, 2nd, Susannah ——; 30 *Gershom*, b May 23, 1697, m Deliverance How of Wallingford; 31 *Caleb*, m Eunice ——; 32 *Thankful*, b Sept. 20, 1702; 33 *Phebe*, b May 23, 1710; 34 *Joanna*, b Oct. 9, 1705, m Mr. Royce. Mr. Thomas Beach died in Meriden, where he was buried in the old cemetery, May 13, 1741, æ 82 years.

5. NATHANIEL.

NATHANIEL BEACH m Sarah Porter, daughter of Nathaniel Porter. She was born 1667. Her mother was a daughter of Philip Groves, the first and only ruling elder in Stratford church. She died in 1738, and her grave-stone yet stands with that of her husband, who died in 1747.

Children: 35 *Ephraim*, b May 25, 1687, m 1712, Sarah, dau. of Andrew Patterson, d Oct. 30, 1717; 36 *Elizabeth*, b

Nov 11, 1689; 37 *David*, b May 15, 1692, m 1717, Hannah Sherman, dau. of Matthew, son of Samuel Sen.; 38 *Josiah*, b Aug. 18, 1694, m 1722, Patience Nichols; 39 *Nathaniel*, b Dec. 22, 1696, m 1720, Sarah, dau. of Solomon Burton, d 1734; 40 *Sarah*, b Nov. 12, 1699; 41 *Daniel*, b Jan 15, 1700, m 1724, Hester, dau. of Benj. Curtiss, son of John, son of William Curtiss; 42 *Anna*, b March, 1704, m Elnathan Beers, Jan. 25, 1728; 43 *Israel*, b May, 1705, m 1731, Hannah Barrett, dau. of Joseph, son of John, son of William; 44 *James*, b Aug. 13, 1709, m Sarah Curtiss 1710, dau. of John, son of Benjamin, son of John.

8. ISAAC.

ISAAC BEACH, married Hannah Birdsey, daughter of John, in 1693. Mr. Birdsey was a son of John, an original settler in Stratford. Her mother was Phebe, daughter of William Willcoxen, also among the first settlers of Stratford. Hannah was born February, 1671. Isaac Beach settled in Wallingford on land given him by his father John Beach, but in 1694 was received into the church at Stratford as from Wallingford. He died in Stratford in 1741, and his grave-stone still remains. Hannah his wife died Oct. 15, 1750, in her 79th year, and was buried in the Episcopal burying-ground, Stratford. He sold land in Wallingford to Joseph Rice in 1699.

Children: 45 *William*, b July 7, 1794, m Sarah Hull of Derby, dau. of Joseph Hull; 46 *Elnathan*, b July 7, 1698, m Abigail Uffont, 2d, Hannah, dau. of Samuel Cook; 47 *John*, b Oct. 6, 1700, Episcopal clergyman at Newtown, Ct., d Mar. 19, 1782; 48 *Mary*, b Dec. 16, 1703; 49 *Hannah*, b May 26, 1709; 50 *Dinah*, b Oct. 14, 1713.

9. JOSEPH.

JOSEPH BEACH, son of John No. 1, married Abiah, dau. of Ebenezer Booth, son of Richard, an original settler in Stratford. He died in 1737, æ. 66. His grave-stone yet remains.

Children: 51 *Sarah*, b July 13, 1697; 52 *Agar*, b April 8, 1699; 53 *Abraham*, b April 29, 1701; 54 *Hannah*, b Feb. 12, 1702, m Zachariah Tomlinson, grandson of Henry and great grandfather of Gov. Gideon Tomlinson, d in 1812; 55 *Joseph;* 56 *Abiah*, b Jan. 12, 1712–13, m Samuel Judson in 1737. His first wife in 1734 was Bethiah Beach.

10. BENJAMIN.

BENJAMIN BEACH of Stratford, m Mary ——.

Children: 57 *Bethia*, b April 23, 1674; 58 *Peter*, b Sept. 14, 1696; 59 *Eunice*, b Aug. 3, 1699; 60, 61, *Benjamin* and *Mary*, b May 19, 1702, the former went to Durham, Conn.

46. ELNATHAN.

ELNATHAN BEACH, son of Isaac and Hannah Beach, was a merchant settled in Wallingford, in the southerly part of what is now Cheshire, and for several years was engaged with Captain Samuel Cooke, in foreign trade, in which they were very successful. Mr. Beach soon became a man of great wealth and high standing in the community. He presented the Congregational society of Cheshire with a bell for their meeting-house, and by his last will left a bequest of several pounds as a fund for the relief of the poor of the parish of Cheshire. He married first Miss Abigail Ufford of Stratford, May 9, 1720. She died Dec. 2, 1738. He married second, Hannah, daughter of Capt. Samuel Cooke, Feb. 8, 1742. She died May 18, 1754, æ. 21 years. He died Aug. 16, 1742, æ 45 years.

Children by first marriage; 79 *Isaac*, b April 7, 1721, d Jan. 27, 1724; 80 *Elnathan*, b July 21, 1723, at Cheshire, d May 18, 1754, æ 31; 81 *Isaac*, b March 3, 1725, d Oct. 13, 1471, æ 16 years; 82 *John*, b 1733, a farmer at Cheshire; 83 *Hannah*, b Nov. 12, 1728; 84 *Abigail*, b Dec. 17, 1730; 85 *Samuel*, b Dec 26, 1737, Dea. of the church, graduated at Yale, 1757; 86 *Sarah*, b March 25, 1727, m Jonathan Atwater of New Haven; 87 *Lois*, b Aug 18, 1732, m Col. Thaddeus Cook of Wallingford, d April 4, 1753; 88 *Esther*.

Child by second marriage: 89 *Abraham*, b Aug. 29, 1743, graduated at Yale, 1757, and was a distinguished clergyman of the Protestant Episcopal Church in the city of New York. He died 1828, æ. 85 years.

45. WILLIAM.

WILLIAM BEACH, eldest son of Isaac and Hannah Beach of Stratford, married Sarah Hull, daughter of Joseph Hull of Derby (ancestor of Com. Isaac Hull), in 1725. Her mother was Mary Nichols, dau. of Isaac 2d of Stratford and Derby.

Children: 62 *Isaac*, b and bap. Oct., 1726, bap. in the Cong. church, Stratford; 63 *Ann*, b April, bap. May, 1729, m Wm. Sam'l Johnson, bap. in Cong. church; 64 *Abel*, b and bap. Nov. 31, 1731, m Mary Lewis 1757, d 1768; 65, 66 *Henry* and *Abijah*, b May, 1734, bap. in the Episcopal church.

63. ANN.

ANN BEACH, daughter of William and Sarah Hull Beach, married in Nov., 1749, at the age of 20 years, Wm. Sam'l Johnson, aged 22 years, son of Rev. Samuel D. D. by his wife Charity, wid. of Benj. Nichols, oldest son of Hon. Matthias Nichols of Islip, L. I. Wm. Samuel Johnson had by wife Ann,

Children: 67 *Charity*, b July, 1750; 68 *Sarah*, b April, 1754; 69 *Gloriance Ann*, b March, 1757; 70 *Mary*, b April, 1759; 71 *Samuel William*, b Oct., 1761; 72 *Elizabeth*, b Dec., 1763; 73 *Robert Charles*, b May, 1766.

71. SAMUEL.

SAMUEL WM. JOHNSON, son of Anna and Wm. Samuel Johnson, married Nov., 1791, Susan, dau. of Pierrepont Edwards Esq., and grand-daughter of Rev. President J. Edwards.

Children: 74 *Anna Frances*; 75 *William Samuel*; 76 *Sarah Elizabeth*; 77 *Edwards*; 78 *Robert Charles*.

85. SAMUEL.

DEA. SAMUEL BEACH graduated at Yale College in 1757. He was an Attorney at Law in his native town, Cheshire, and was a highly respected citizen, and filled with honor many offices of public trust, and was a delegate to the convention which formed the constitution of the United States. He married Mary ——.

Children; 90 *Mary Ann*, b July 31, 1760; 91 *Samuel W.*,

b Feb. 11, 1762, was a farmer in Cheshire, where he died. Sons, Samuel W., Albert and Rufus. By second marriage: 92 *Burrage*, m —— Bowden, was a graduate of Yale College in 1793 and became an Attorney at Law in his native town, where he died æ. 70. He had daughters, Elizabeth, wife of Rev. Dr. Fuller, Augusta, Amelia.

29. MOSES.

MOSES BEACH, son of Thomas and Phebe, of Wallingford, married Esther Tyler, Sept. 26, 1722. She died Sept. 16, 1750, æ 55. He married Susannah ———. She died April 9, 1770, æ 62 yrs. Mr. Beach died in Wallingford. He was a farmer and resided on, and owned the farm called (at the present time) the Wooden Farm, in the southern part of Yalesville.

Children: 93 *Ephraim*, b Aug. 2, 1723, m Lydia ——, d August 29, 1751; 94 *Titus*, b April 4, 1725; 95 *Moses*, b Nov. 8, 1726, m Dinah Sperry, March 19, 1756; 96 *Lois*, b April 29, 1729, d Jan. 4, 1731; 97 *Esther*, b May 16, 1731; 98 *Asahel*, b Jan. 11, 1736, m Keziah Roys, Feb. 11, 1757, and settled in Westbury in Waterbury, previous to 1764.

28. NATHAN.

NATHAN BEACH, son of Thomas and Phebe of Wallingford, married Jemima Curtiss, Sept. 29, 1713. He lived in the house late the property of Jason Beach.

Children: 99 *Joseph*, b June 10, 1764; 100 *William*, b Nov. 18, 1716, m Susannah Holt, Oct. 15, 1739; 101 *Lydia*, b Feb. 26, 1719; 102 *Nathan*, b May 28, 1721; 103 *Stephen*, b April 6, 1729; 104 *Elihu*, b Dec. 14, 1734.

95. MOSES.

MOSES BEACH, son of Moses and Esther, married Dinah Sperry of New Haven, March 19, 1756. She died April 8, 1768, leaving one child, a daughter; 105 *Mary*, b Feb. 14, 1758. She became the wife of Turhand Kirtland of Wallingford. She died Nov. 24, 1792. The 2nd wife of Mr. Beach was Parthenia Tallman of Branford. By this marriage they had one child, a son. She d July 5, 1797, æ 60. 106 *Moses Sperry*, b March 7, 1776, d at Norwalk, Ohio, in 1826, æ 50 yrs., m Lucretia Yale of Wallingford.

104. MOSES.

MOSES SPERRY BEACH, only son of Moses and Parthenia, married Lucretia Yale, daughter of Elihu and Lucretia (Stanley) Yale. She died 1800, and had by this marriage two children: 107 *Sally*, m Horatio Green of Springfield, Mass.; 108 *Moses Yale*, b Jan., 1800, d July 1, 1868, æ 68. He married 2nd, Lois Ives, daughter of Abijah Ives, of Wallingford. She died at New Haven, Huron Co., Ohio.

Children: 109 *Tallman*, b in Wallingford, d at New Haven, Ohio; 110 *Abraham Stanley*, b in Wallingford, d supposed in Canada; 111 *Abijah*, M. D., b in Wallingford, resides in Ohio; 101 *Asahel*, b in Wallingford, d in Kansas.

30. GERSHOM.

GERSHOM BEACH, son of Thomas and Deliverance Howe Beach.

Children: 112 *Ruth*, b Aug. 21, 1722; 113 *Aaron*, b Jan. 14, 1727; 114 *Joanna*, b Aug. 17, 1724, m —— Chittenden; 115 *Gershom*, b Sept. 24, 1729.

CHESHIRE BRANCH.

82. JOHN.

JOHN BEACH, son of Capt. Elnathan and Abigail, married Eunice Eaton in 1744, and settled on a farm left him by his father. His house stood almost opposite the present residence of Edward Andrews, south part of Cheshire, Conn. It was a large two story red house, and was in its day considered a first class house.

Children: 186 *Hannah*, b Jan. 29, 1756, m Samuel Rice, 1776, Feb. 15; 187 *Isaac*, b Aug. 25, 1758, d Dec., 1776; 188 *Elnathan*, b Aug. 30, 1760, m Abigail Atwater; 189 *James Eaton*, b Sept., 1762, m Huldah Sherman of Bridgeport; 190 *John*, b May, 1764, m 1st, Lucy Cornwall, 2d, Lois

Doolittle; 191 *Eunice*, b Jan. 4, 1766, m Dan Bradley; 192 *Abijah*, b 1768, m Jemima Cornwall; 193 *Bildad*, b Sept., 1770, m 1st, Huldah Hotchkiss, 2d, Hannah Cossit; 194 *Abraham*, b 1772, d in 1772; 195 *Lois*, b Dec., 1774, m Calvin Lawrence.

188. ELNATHAN.

ELNATHAN BEACH, M. D., was a physician in his native village, where he married Abigail Atwater. He built and occupied the house now known as the Bronson house, opposite the south-west corner of the public Green in the village. He died in Western N. Y.

Children: 196 *Hannah*; 197 *Narcissa*; 198 *Julia*; 199 *Eliza*.

189. JAMES.

JAMES EATON BEACH married Huldah Sherman of Bridgeport, where he died quite advanced in life, and highly respected by the community generally. A fine marble monument has been erected to the memory of both him and his wife.

Children: 200 *Polly*; 201 *Laura*; 202 *Isaac*, now resides in Bridgeport.

191. EUNICE.

EUNICE BEACH married Dan Bradley, and settled at Marcellus, N. Y.

Children: 203 *Nancy*; 204 *Harriet*; 205 *Augustus*; 206 *William*; 207 *Dan*.

190. JOHN.

JOHN BEACH married Lucy Cornwall, daughter of Abijah Cornwall of Cheshire, and sister of Thomas T. Cornwall, Sept. 20, 1786. She died, and he married Lois Doolittle of Cheshire. He died in western New York, Dec. 23, 1844, æ. 80 years. His wife Lucy died Feb. 14, 1814.

Children: 208 *Abraham*, b Nov. 9, 1787, d March 1, 1788, in his 2d year; 209 *Horace*, b April 11, 1789, m Ann Atwater of New Haven, no issue. His widow m Laban Smith, is living in 1869. He died in 1826; 210 *Isaac*, b June 5, 1792, m

Nancy Cooper of Meadville, Pa., May 15, 1823, she died March 2, 1857; 211 *William*, b Feb. 6, 1797, d Sept., 1820; 212 *John*, b July 16, 1794, m Polly Prescott of New Haven, Feb. 14, 1819, d Oct. 17, 1849; 213 *Matilda*, b Feb. 13, 1799, was the wife of John H. Cooley of New Haven; 214 *Lorraine*, b March 24, 1802, m Minerva Porter of Marcellus, N. Y., Nov. 20, 1823. She dying, he m Sarah Elizabeth Plant of Stratford, Ct., no issue; 215 *Lucy Ann*, b Dec. 15, 1810, d Aug. 17, 1845. She m Samuel Porter Rhodes of Marcellus, April 26, 1829. Her children were: 216 *Edward*, b June 26, 1830, d June 3, 1831; 217 *Edward P.*, b Jan. 14, 1832, d March 31, 1836; 218 *Augusta Comstock*, b Sept. 30, 1833, d Oct. 31, 1859; 219 *William Porter*, b May 2, 1826; 220 *Samuel Porter*, b May 2, 1838; 221 *Ann Elizabeth*, b Nov. 15, 1840; 222 *John Beach*, b Aug. 8, 1843; 223 *Mary Matilda*, b Aug. 12, 1845, d Aug. 22, 1845.

192. ABIJAH.

ABIJAH BEACH married Jemima Cornwall, daughter of Abijah Cornwall of Cheshire, Nov. 6, 1796. He was a merchant, inn-keeper and farmer in his native town Cheshire until his death, which occured Dec. 2, 1821. She died at the house of her son-in-law, Edward A. Cornwall Esq., Dec. 17, 1853. Mr. Beach while living built the house now owned by Burrit Bradley Esq., and also that of Martin Branin in the village of Cheshire, long occupied for a store and hotel by Mr. Beach and others.

Children: 224 *Richard*, b July 14, 1799, m Lucinda Hitchcock, of Cheshire; 225 *Palmina*, b April 19, 1802, m Truman Atwater; 226 *Elnathan*, b Sept. 1, 1804, m Mary Bullard, of Cheshire; 227 *Eunice*, b Feb. 11, 1809, m Edward A. Cornwall Esq., of Cheshire; 228 *Abijah*, b Dec., 1812, d Jan. 9, 1813.

193. BILDAD.

BILDAD BEACH, married for his 1st wife Huldah Hotchkiss, and his 2nd, Hannah Cossit, and removed to Marcellus, N. Y., where the family still reside.

Children: 229 *Emily*; 230 *Laura*; 231 *Hannah*; 232 *Merab*; 233 *Merab*.

224. RICHARD.

RICHARD and Lucinda Beach were married Nov 21, 1824; he resided in his native town, Cheshire, until 1830, as a merchant. He built a store on the canal, at what is now West Cheshire, and gave it the name of Beachport. In 1830 he removed to Burton, Grange Co., Ohio, where he prosecuted the mercantile business with good success, until near the close of his life.

Child: 234 *Ann Palmina*, b July 14, 1826, d Dec. 17, 1848. She married Wm. Tolles, of Burton, Ohio, June 9, 1846, had two children, both deceased.

226. ELNATHAN.

ELNATHAN and Mary Ann Bullard Beach were married Jan 18, 1824. He resided at Cheshire and Hartford, and finally removed to Michigan.

Children: 235 *Lucretia H.*, b Aug., 1824, died 1827; 236 *Elizabeth Eunice*, b Jan. 26, 1826, m Chester S. Steele of Hartford, Conn., Nov. 22, 1852, 3 children; 237 *William A.*, b 1828; 238 *Henry Bullard*, b Oct., 1830; 239 *Mary Ann Beach*, b Sept. 9, 1832, m William Carey, of Pittsfield, Mass. in 1863, and has had three children; 240 *Edward E.*, b Sept. 6, 1834; 241 *Cornelia*, b Sept. 9, 1836; 242 *George*, b July 3, 1840, died Sept. 15, 1842.

WALLINGFORD BRANCH.

27. TIMOTHY.

TIMOTHY, son of Thomas and Phebe Beach, born in Wallingford, married Hannah Cook, Nov. 25, 1713.

Children: 115 *Thomas*, b Aug. 6, 1714, d Sept. 27, 1714; 116 *Thomas*, b Dec. 16, 1751; 117 *Keziah*, b Oct. 18, 1717; 118 *Prudence*, b Oct. 6, 1719; 119 *Hannah*, b April 21, 1722; 120 *Ebenezer*, b Feb. 9, 1724; 121 *Thankful*, b Dec. 19, 1725; 122 *Keziah*, b May 18, 1733.

28. NATHAN.

NATHAN, son of Thomas and Phebe Beach, born in Wallingford, married Jemima Curtis, Sept. 29, 1712.

Children: 123 *Joseph*, b Jan. 10, 1714; 124 *William*, b Nov. 18, 1716, m Susannah ——, she d Sept. 24, 1742; 125 *Lydia*, b Feb. 26, 1719; 126 *Nathan*, b May 23, 1721; 127 *Sarah*, b Oct. 22, 1723; 128 *Enos*, b Jan. 30, 1726; 129 *Stephen*, b Oct. 16, 1729; 130 *Elihu*, b Dec. 17, 1734; 132 *Eunice*, b March 3, 1737.

31. CALEB.

CALEB, son of Thomas Beach, of Wallingford, m Eunice —.

Children: 133 *Sarah*, b Oct. 20, 1728; 134 *Margaret*, b Aug. 28, 1735.

116. THOMAS.

THOMAS, son of Timothy Beach, m Hannah ——.

Children: 135 *Damaris*, b April 5, 1714; 136 *Amzi*, b July 14, 1716; 137 *Abigail*, b Oct. 15, 1718; 138 *Londrey*, b March 5, 1727; 139 *Asa*, b Oct. 3, 1752.

123. JOSEPH.

JOSEPH, son of Nathan and Jemima Beach, of Wallingford, m Experience ——.

Children: 140 *Lydia*, b Sept. 13, 1735; 141 *Mehitable*, b Nov. 2, 1732; 142 *Mary*, b Dec. 22, 1740; 143 *Elizabeth*, b Feb. 24, 1743; 144 *John*, b Jan. 25, 1745; 145 *Joel*, b Sept. 23, 1747; 146 *Sarah*, b Sept. 21, 1749.

128. ENOS.

ENOS, son of Nathan and Jemima Beach, m Anna ——.

Child: 147 *Joanna*, b April 1, 1751, in Wallingford.

124. WILLIAM.

WILLIAM, son of Nathan and Jemima Beach, m Susannah —— for his first wife. His 2nd wife was Martha ——. He built the house in which lived the family of the late Mr. Charles Parker, on Parker's Farms, in Wallingford. He went west with his family. Susanna d Sept. 24, 1742.

Children: by first m, 148 *Benjamin*, b May 21, 1740; by

2nd m, 149 *Solomon*, b March 31, 1744; 150 *Isaac*, b April 16, 1746; 151 *Thankful*, b Sept. 25, 1747.

98. ASAHEL.

ASAHEL, son of Moses and Esther Beach of Wallingford, m Keziah Royce, Feb. 11, 1757. He removed to Waterbury, and from thence to Kingsbury, N. Y., in 1799.

Children: 152 *Esther*; 153 *Keziah*.

JOHN JR.

JOHN Jr., son of John Beach of Stratford, was among the first planters of Wallingford. He died in 1709.

Children: 154 *Nathaniel*; 155 *Lettice*, b Dec. 24, 1679, m Wm. Ward; 156 *Mary*, b Jan. 11, 1681, d Sept. 1, 1688; 157 *Hannah*, b March 17, 1684, m Eliphalet Parker, Aug. 5, 1708; 158 *Thomas*, b Feb. 14, 1686, m Hannah Atwater, May 9, 1711; 159 *John*, b Oct. 15, 1690, m Mary Royce, Feb. 22, 1717; 160 *Samuel*, b Nov. 29, 1696, m Phebe Tyler, April 29, 1718.

160. SAMUEL.

SAMUEL BEACH, son of John Jr., m Phebe Tyler. Family mostly settled at North Haven.

Children: 161 *Beulah*, b March 1, 1719; 162 *Rhoda*, b Nov 26, 1720; 163 *Zopher*, b Feb. 10, 1723; 164 *Phebe*, b Jan. 2, 1725; 165 *Benoni*, d June 5, 1738; 166 *Esther*, b Jan. 6, 1733; 167 *Eunice*, b Jan. 27, 1735; 168 *Pamineas*, b Jan. 15, 1737; 169 *Hannah*, b Nov. 8, 1739; 170 *Daniel*, b. March 24, 1740.

159. JOHN.

JOHN BEACH, son of John, married Mary Royce, Feb. 22, 1718–9.

Children: 171 *Adna*, b Jan. 11, 1718, m Hannah Miles; 172 *Edmund*, b Feb. 18, 1720; 173 *Linus*, b Dec. 5, 1721; 174 *Amos*, b Jan. 3, 1724; 175 *Mary*, b April 28, 1726; 176 *Jacob*, b Dec. 5, 1728; 177 *Royce*, b Oct. 13, 1733; 178 *Samuel*, b Dec. 22, 1729; 179 *Baldwin*, b July 26, 1736.

158. THOMAS.

THOMAS BEACH, son of John, m Sarah Sanford, Feb. 19, 1712. She died, and he married Lois ——.

Children: by 1st marriage, 180 *Barnabas*, b July 1, 1716; 181 *Abel*, b May 12, 1728, d May 7, 1729. By 2d marriage, 182 *Amos*, b Oct. 14, 1747; 183 *John*, b Oct. 15, 1744; 184 *Lois*, b July 1, 1749; 185 *Adna*, b May 17, 1759.

BARTHOLOMEW.[1]

DANIEL.

DANIEL AND SARAH BARTHOLOMEW are the first of the name in Wallingford. Of their origin and subsequent history, nothing has come to my knowledge. The records in relation to this family as well as many others, have been so kept as to render it almost impossible to trace them.

Children: 1 *Samuel*, b April 11, 1735; 2 *Reuben*, b Sept. 19, 1736; 3 *William*, b Feb. 1, 1738; 4 *Jacob*, b June 11, 1740; 5 *Susannah*, b April 11, 1745.

JOSEPH.

JOSEPH BARTHOLOMEW m Mary ——, Jan. 13, 1741; probably a brother of Daniel.

Children: 6 *Hannah*, b Jan. 29, 1742; 7 *Andrew*, b Nov. 24, 1744; 8 *Joseph*, b Sept. 6, 1746; 9 *Jonathan*, b May 6, 1751; 10 *Joseph*, b Aug. 25, 1752.

TIMOTHY.

TIMOTHY BARTHOLOMEW m Mary Hull, July 12, 1737; m 2nd, Abigail Phelps, Jan. 11, 1742.

Child: 11 *Timothy*, b Aug. 11, 1745.

JOHN.

JOHN AND JERUSHA BARTHOLOMEW of Wallingford, had 12 *John Porter*, b Nov. 10, 1740.

1 For collateral branches, see Savage's Gen. Dict., I. 120–130.

BEADLES.[1]

NATHANIEL.

Nathaniel Beadles came to Wallingford, probably soon after the commencement of the last century, and located himself on a farm on the west side of the river, and near the line which divides Cheshire from Wallingford. The house is still standing, and is the first house north of the residence of the late John Cook. He died about 1764. Elizabeth, his wife, died in Wallingford.

Children: 1 *Nathaniel*, b Dec. 15, 1703, m Elizabeth Hitchcock, Nov. 10, 1726; 2 *Mary*, b Sept. 18, 1708; 3 *Josiah*, b Aug. 3, 1711; 4 *Samuel Sharp*, graduated at Yale College in 1757, estate settled in 1763, died Jan. 5, 1762.

1. CAPT. NATHANIEL.

Capt. Nathaniel Beadles, son of Nathaniel and Elizabeth Beadles, married Elizabeth Hitchcock, Nov. 10, 1726. He died Feb. 10, 1762.

Children: 5–6 *Elizabeth* and *Susannah* (twins), b Sept. 17, 1727; 7 *John*, was a captain of the militia; 8 *Hannah;* 9 *Sarah;* 10 *Lois*, b 1743, m John Hull, she died Sept. 6, 1802, æ. 59; 11 *Mehitable;* 12 *Nathaniel*, died March 4, 1763.

7. CAPT. JOHN.

Capt. John Beadles, son of Nathaniel and Elizabeth Beadles of Wallingford, m daughter of John Barker. They had a large family, some of whom settled in the State of New York.

Children: 13 *John;* 14 *Henry*, m —— Blakeslee, dau. of Joseph; 15 *Alfred*, m —— Byington, and settled in Cheshire, a wagon maker.

---

1 For collateral branches see Hinman's Conn. Settlers, 164, 165; Savage's Gen. Dict., I. 144, 145.

BELLAMY.[1]

MATTHEW.

MATTHEW BELLAMY (a weaver), the ancestor of those of the name in Wallingford, appears first at Fairfield, Conn., then at Killingworth, where he married Sarah Wood, Sept. 26, 1705. She died March 8, 1721. He married for his second wife, Mary Johnson, May 31, 1722. He died June 7, 1752, æ. 77 years. Mary died May 10, 1730, æ. 66 years. By 1st marriage;

Children: 1 *Mary*, b Sept. 5, 1706, m Benjamin Gray, May 10, 1731; 2 *Matthew*, b June 1, 1708, m Rachel Clark, Sept. 14, 1754, æ. 46; 3 *John*, b Jan. 26, 1713, m Martha ——; 4 *James*, b Sept. 29, 1716; 5 *Joseph, D. D.*, b Feb. 20, 1719, grad. at Yale; 6 *Samuel*, b Jan. 18, 1721. By 2d marriage, 7, 8, *Sarah* and *Anna*, b Jan. 25, 1722; 9 *Moses*, b June 29, 1725, m Elizabeth Martin, Dec. 8, 1762; 10 *Aaron*, b July 23, 1728, m Desire Parker, Dec. 20, 1753; 11 *Hannah*, b May 17, 1731.

2. MATTHEW.

MATTHEW BELLAMY, m Rachel Clark, Jan. 26, 1734, by Rev. Samuel Hall of Cheshire.

Children: 12 *Thankful*, b Nov. 23, 1734; 13 *Lois*, b Jan. 15, 1737; 14 *Ann*, b Feb. 11, 1738; 15 *Reuben*, b Dec. 31, 1742; 16 *Matthew*, b Feb. 9, 1745; 17 *Asa*, b Dec. 19, 1753; 18 *Silas*, b Jan. 14, 1755.

5. JOSEPH.

JOSEPH BELLAMY, D. D., settled as Pastor over the Congregational church at Bethlem, in 1740; married Frances Sherman of New Haven, April, 27, 1744. She died Aug. 30, 1785. He married 2d, the widow of Rev. Andrew Storrs of Watertown, Conn. He died March 6, 1760.

Children: 19 *Lucy*, b Aug. 1, 1745, m Abijah Gurnsey,

---

1 For collateral branches, see Cothren's Hist. Woodbury, 507; Hinman's Conn. Settlers, 182–5; Savage's Gen. Dict., I. 160–1.

Aug., 1772; 20 *Rebecca*, b Oct. 15, 1747, m Rev. Mr. Hunt, of Preston, Conn.; 21 *Daniel*, b Nov. 10, 1750, d May, 1826; 22 *Jonathan*, b Nov. 18, 1752, d at Oxford, N. J., in 1777; 23 *Samuel*, b March 13, 1756, d Nov. 11, 1802; 24 *Elizabeth*, b Dec. 23, 1759, m Charles Sheldon, of Springfield, Mass.; 25 *William*, b June 28, 1770; 26 *Joseph Sherman*, b 1773.

10. AARON.

AARON BELLAMY, m Desire Parker, Dec. 20, 1753. He resided in the southwest part of Cheshire on the farm late the property of Elias Gaylord Jr., and at this time (1869), the property of Amos Rice.

Children: 27 *Rhoda*, b Oct. 30, 1754; 28 *Desire*, b July 3, 1758; 29 *Mary*, b April 18, 1761.

BENHAM.[1]

1. JOSEPH.

JOSEPH BENHAM came from New Haven to Wallingford in 1670, with the first settlers in the village, and some of his children were born after his removal there. The name of his wife who died in Wallingford was Winifred. He died in 1702.

Children: 1 *Mary*; 2 *Joseph*, b May 25, 1659, m Hannah Ives, Aug. 17, 1682; 3 *Sarah*, b 1660, d 1668; 4 *Johannah*, b July 25, 1762; 5 *Elizabeth*, b Sept. 13, 1664; 6 *John*, b Dec. 28, 1666, d 1670; 7 *John*, b Nov. 3, 1671, in Wallingford; 8 *Mary*, b May 18, 1673; 9 *Samuel*, b May 12, 1673; 10 *Sarah*, b Sept. 6, 1676; 11 *James*, b about 1679, d 1745; 12 *Winifred*, b Aug. 21, 1684.

2. JOSEPH.

JOSEPH BENHAM, Jr. m Hannah Ives, Aug. 17, 1672, and settled in Wallingford.

Children: 13 *Mary*, b May 18, 1683; 14 *Joseph*, b Dec.

---

1 For collateral branches, see Hinman's Conn. Settlers, 195, 196; Savage's Gen. Dict., I. 155.

15, 1685, m Hope, dau. of Samuel Cook; 15 *Abigail*, b April 14, 1688, d 1741.

11. JAMES.

JAMES BENHAM, m Esther Preston, Dec. 9, 1702, in Wallingford. She died a widow July 3, 1764.

Children: 14 *Jehiel*, b Feb. 23, 1703--4, d July 9, 1780, æ. 76; 15 *Sarah*, b April 12, 1706, m Henry Hotchkiss, Nov. 23, 1736; 16 *Esther*, b March 18, 1709; 17 *Samuel*, b Nov. 9, 1711, m Phebe ——; 18 *John*, b Dec. 17, 1714, m Mary ——; 19 *Lydia*, b Jan. 9, 1717; 20 *Mary*, b July 27, 1719; 21 *Eunice*, b Aug. 5, 1723.

14. JOSEPH.

JOSEPH BENHAM, 3d, married Hope, dau. of Samuel and Hope Cook. She died Jan. 31, 1731.

Children: 22 *Hannah*, b Dec. 2, 1708, m Samuel Beach, March 23, 1732; 23 *Esther*, b March 18, 1709; 24 *Joseph*, b April 5, 1711, m Mary ——; 25 *Enos*, b Sept. 8, 1713, m Anna ——; 26 *Thankful*, b Feb. 14, 1716; 27 *Phebe*, b May 20, 1718, m Robert Austin; 28 *John*, b Oct. 4, 1723; 29 *Lois*, b April 30, 1727; 30 *Esther*, b March 22, 1730.

17. SAMUEL.

SAMUEL BENHAM m Phebe ——, she died, and he married Dorothy Hotchkiss, Dec. 27, 1742.

Children: 31 *Esther*, b March 4, 1737; 32 *Oliver*, b July 30, 1743, m Dorothy ———.

18. JOHN.

JOHN BENHAM m Mary Curtis, Sept. 23, 1747.

Children: 34 *John*, b July 15, 1750; 35 *Mary*, b Nov. 6, 1752; 36 *Hope*, b Dec. 21, 1754.

SERG'T JOSEPH.

SERG'T JOSEPH BENHAM, m Mary Curtis, April 5, 1732, and 2d, Mary Bunnell, Aug. 3, 1735. He died April 18, 1754.

Children: 37 *Benjamin*, b May 23, 1733; 38 *Reuben*, b Sept. 30, 1734, m Abigail Clark Sept. 10, 1758; 39 *Asa*, b June 10, 1736; 40 *Shradrack*, b Jan. 14, 1736; 41 *Martha*, b

Aug. 11, 1737, m Benjamin Cook, Aug. 2, 1759; 42 *Nathaniel*, b Jan. 18, 1739; 43 *Abigail*, b Jan. 14, 1740, d Nov. 1, 1743; 44 *James*, b Feb. 1, 1745; 45 *Daniel*, b July 31, 1758, d May 16, 1761.

26. ENOS.

ENOS BENHAM m Anna Hull Aug. 3, 1741.

Children: 46 *Asaph*, b Dec. 23, 1741; 47 *Enos*, b April 6, 1744, d May 2, 1751; 48 *Molly*, b Nov. 16, 1746, d Sept. 8, 1753; 49 *Samuel*, b Oct. 1, 1749, d Jan. 5, 1751; 50 *Polly*, b March 1, 1752; 51 *Theophilus*, d Feb. 1, 1759; 52 *Samuel*, b March 8, 1758; 53 *Molly*, d June 29, 1748; 54 *Anna*, b Aug. 29, 1755, d Sept. 29, 1760; 55 *Enos*, b Nov. 5, 1761, d May 2, 1760.

39. REUBEN.

REUBEN BENHAM m Abigail Clark, Sept. 10, 1758.

Child: 56 *Reuben*, b June 9, 1761.

NATHAN.

NATHAN BENHAM married Mary ——.

Children: 57 *Hannah*, b Jan. 9, 1722; 58 *Patience*, b Dec. 23, 1723; 59 *Ebenezer*, b Oct. 31, 1726, m Elizabeth Hotchkiss Nov. 23, 1750; 60 *Joel*, b March 2, 1730, m Esther Andrews.

JOSEPH.

JOSEPH BENHAM m Em. Curtis Jan. 7, 1735.

Children: 61 *Sarah*, b Oct. 26, 1735, d Dec. 29, 1736; 62 *Isaac*, b Aug 29, 1736; 63 *Samuel*, b June 8, 1755, d April 22, 1759; 64, *Uri*, b Dec. 15, 1751. He settled on a farm near the Honey-pot brook in Cheshire; 65 *Sarah*, b Dec. 25, 1741; 66 *Elizabeth*, b March 23, 1745, d Aug. 10, 1758; 67 *Em.*, b June 5, 1745, d May 20, 1751; 68 *Lois*, b July 13, 1750; 69 *Elisha*, b Nov. 17, 1753.

60. JOEL.

JOEL BENHAM, married Esther Andrews, Dec. 7, 1752, m 2d, Elizabeth——.

Children: 70 *James*, b Oct. 26, 1753; 71 *Elizabeth*, b Mar.

7, 1755; 72 *Ebenezer*, b July 21, 1756; 73 *Lyman*, by 2nd wife, b Oct. 1, 1760.

59. EBENEZER.

EBENEZER BENHAM married Elizabeth Hotchkiss Nov. 23, 1780.

Child: 74 *Sarah*, b Sept. 18, 1763.

62. ISAAC.

ISAAC BENHAM married Lucy Cook, May 11, 1758.

Child: 75 *Elizabeth*, b Oct. 19, 1758.

BLAKESLEE.[1]

The name of Blakeslee, on the early records, is written in twenty-five or more different ways. It is now generally spelled as above.

There is a tradition among the descendants that two brothers of the name of Blakeslee came from the west of England, designing to settle in the Plymouth Colony, and that one of them died on the passage. The other came to Plymouth, where he died in the early days of the Colony, leaving one son, who was placed with a blacksmith in New Haven, Conn., to learn the trade. It is also asserted that the brothers brought an anvil with them, and that it was seen but a few years since in Roxbury, Conn.

SAMUEL.

SAMUEL and Elizabeth Blakeslee appear to be the first of the name in Wallingford; they were in the place about the year 1712; of their history very little now appears.

Children: 1 *Obedience*, b June 13, 1713, m Joshua How; 2 *Jemima*, b Oct. 13, 1717; 3 *Susannah*, b March 15, 1719, m Andrew Parker, April 27, 1736; 4 *Elizabeth*, b July 8, 1721, m Gamaliel Parker; 5 *Abigail*, b Sept. 8, 1723, m Elijah Oakley; 6 *Zeruah*, b Jan. 16, 1726, m Nathaniel Ives, Nov. 8,

---

1 For collateral branches, see Bronson's Hist. Waterbury, 469–77; Savage's Gen. Dict., I. 189–190.

1744; 7 *Phebe*, b Nov. 1, 1728; 8 *Thankful*, b Nov. 26, 1729, m Justus Hoalt, April 26, 1849; 9 *Hannah;* 10 *Joseph*, b April 1, 1732; 11 *Miriam*, b Oct. 4, 1735, m Joshua How Oct. 14, 1756; 12 *Phebe*, b July 1, 1744.

10. JOSEPH.

JOSEPH BLAKESLEE married Lois Ives, April 1, 1757.

Children: 13 *Elizabeth*, b July 14, 1758; 14–15 *Lois* and *Joseph* (twins), b Jan. 9, 1762; 16 *Joseph*, b 1766, d Dec 19, 1831, æ. 65; 17 *John W.*

BRISTOL.[1]

HENRY.

HENRY BRISTOL was in Wallingford in the early part of the last century, and settled in the parish of New Cheshire, where he died, 1750; m Desire Bristol.

Children: 1 *Jonathan*, b Dec. 27, 1725; 2 *Lydia*, b March 16, 1728; 3 *Desire*, m Thomas Brooks, Feb. 12, 1728; 4 *Austin*, d before his father, 1750; 5 *Henry*, d before his father, 1748; 6 *Amos*, m Joanna Parker of Wallingford; 7 *Simeon*, graduated at Yale College; 8 *Gideon*, b 1722, d July 15, 1747, æ. 25; 9 *Augustus*, b 1720, d Feb. 4, 1742, æ. 22.

1 JONATHAN.

JONATHAN BRISTOL m Elizabeth ———, m 2nd, Susannah Peck, Oct. 16, 1761.

Children: 10 *Gideon*, b June 11, 1755; 11 *Lowly*, b Feb. 20, 1753; 12 *Jonathan*, b August 1, 1760, m Thankful ———.

5 HENRY.

HENRY and Lois Bristol, of Cheshire in Wallingford; he died 1748–9.

Children: 13 *Mary*, b March 12, 1742; 14 *Sarah*, b June 10, 1744; 15 *Damaris;* 16 *Henry*.

---

1 For collateral branches, see Redfield's Gen. of the Redfield family, 36.

6. AMOS.

AMOS and Joanna (Parker) Bristol.

Children: 17 *Thomas*, b March 28, 1741; 18 *Augustus*, b July 19, 1743; 19 *Hannah*, b March 20, 1745; 20 *Amos*, b May 6, 1751; 21 *Ezra*, b January 9, 1753; 22 *Reuben*, b Oct. 1, 1755; 23 *Lydia*, b Sept. 15, 1757; 24 *Lucy*, b Sept. 10, 1759.

BROCKETT.[1]

JOHN.

JOHN BROCKETT came to Wallingford with John Moss from New Haven, in 1667 or 1668, and was chosen by the people of New Haven as one of the committee to manage the affairs of the settlement. He was frequently called to fill many of the public offices of the village, and after its incorporation, to represent the town in the General Court. His house lot was No. 1, at the extreme south end of the village, extending from the Old Colony road east toward Wharton's Brook, twenty rods wide and forty rods long; subsequently it was extended to the Brook. The land on which now stands the house of the heirs of the late Edward Hall, is a part of this grant. He died March 12, 1689, æ. 80 years.

Children: 1 *John*, b in England, was a physician, and settled near Muddy river in North Haven; 2 *Benjamin*, b 1648, m Lydia Elcock, he died May 22, 1679; 3 *Abigail*, b March 10, 1649; 4 *Samuel*, b Jan. 14, 1650, m Sarah Bradley, May 21, 1682; 5 *Jabez*, b Oct. 24, 1654, m Dorothy Lyman, Nov. 20, 1691; 6 *Silence*, m Joseph Bradley; 7 *Mary*, m William Pennington of New Jersey.

1. JOHN.

DR. JOHN BROCKETT m Elizabeth ———, and settled at Muddy River as a farmer and physician, and remained there

---

1. For collateral branches, see Savage's Gen. Dict., I. 257, 258.

during his life-time. He died 1720. He settled the estate of his father in 1689–90. At his death he gave all his property to his widow Elizabeth, by will. He had a son Moses, b April 23, 1679.

2. BENJAMIN.

BENJAMIN BROCKETT m Lydia Elcock, Dec. 16, 1720.

Children: 8 *Martha*, b Oct. 2, 1721; 9 *Zilla*, b June 17, 1723, d March 20, 1737; 10 *Alice*, b Feb. 12, 1725; 11 *Hezekiah*, b Dec. 31, 1727; 12 *Lydia*, b March 14, 1729, d Nov. 17, 1729; 13 *Lydia*, d March 7, 1731; 14 *Benjamin*, b May 2, 1733; 15 *Zenieh*, d March 21, 1737; 16 *Lydia*, b March 20, 1737; 17 *Sarah*.

4. SAMUEL.

SAMUEL BROCKETT m Sarah Bradley, Nov. 21, 1682.

Children: 18 *Samuel*, b Feb. 15, 1682, m Rachel Brown, April 15, 1699; 19 *Daniel*, b Sept. 30, 1684; 20 *John*, b Nov. 8, 1685, m Huldah Ells; 21 *Joseph*, b Oct. 25, 1688; 22 *Josiah*, b July 25, 1691; 23 *Alice*, b April 23, 1693; 24 *Josiah*, b July 25, 1698, m Deborah Abbott.

5. JABEZ.

JABEZ BROCKET, m Dorothy Lyman, Nov. 20, 1691.

Children: 25 *Joseph*, b Sept. 17, 1692; 26–27 *James* and *Dorothy* (twins), b March 16, 1695; 28 *Mary*, b March 16, 1699; 29 *an infant dau.*, b May 14, 1696, d June 10, 1696; 30 *Caleb*, b July 5, 1697; 33 *Gideon*, b April 15, 1699, d May 8, 1705; 32 *Andrew*, b July 6, 1701.

18. SAMUEL.

SAMUEL BROCKETT m Rachel Brown, April 15, 1699; she died Jan. 24, 1718. He married Elizabeth How, Aug. 5, 1718.

Children: 33 *Titus*, b June 28, 1700, m Mary Turhand; 34 *Sarah*, b Aug. 26, 1702; 35 *Isaac*, b Sept. 3, 1705, m Mary Sedgwick, June 16, 1733; 36 *Rachel*, b March 20, 1708; 37 *Abigail*, b Feb. 11, 1711; 38 *Samuel*, b June 21, 1714.

20. JOHN.

JOHN BROCKETT married Huldah Ells, March 1, 1711.

Children: 39 *Daniel*, b April 3, 1712, m Rachel ——; 40 *David*, b Nov. 28, 1714; 41 *Anna*, b Feb. 2, 1715, m Gideon Hotchkiss, Jan. 18, 1737; 42 *Christopher*, b April 3, 1718; 43 *Mehitable*, b April 3, 1719; 44 *Elisha*, b May 31, 1726; 45 *John*, b Feb. 14, 1728.

24. JOSIAH.

JOSIAH BROCKETT m Deborah Abbot, Nov. 16, 1725. He m 2nd, Mary ——, who survived him and m Captain Isaac Bronson of Waterbury, Feb. 13, 1755, she d Aug. 1, 1816.

Children by 1st wife: 46 *Hannah*, b Sept. 22, 1725; by 2nd, 47 *Job*, b Sept. 20, 1727, m Martha Ebenathe; 48 *Sarah*, b Dec. 7, 1728, m James Bronson, Aug. 22, 1750; 49 *Abigail*, b July 23, 1732; 50 *Mary*, b Feb. 22, 1735; 51 *Elizabeth*, b April 15, 1736.

33. TITUS.

TITUS BROCKETT m Mary, daughter of Henry Turhand, of Wallingford, Feb. 12, 1728. He was one of the most active Episcopalians in the place, and was one of the four largest contributors toward the erection of the second church edifice, in 1762, which, until within a few years, occupied the lot on the corner opposite the Isaac Peck house, on which a schoolhouse is about being erected, the lot having been given to the town for that purpose by the late Moses Yale Beach Esq. Mr. Brockett died July 29, 1773, æ. 74 years. His wife died May 1, 1777, æ. 64 years.

Child: 52 *Turhand*, b March 7, 1733, d May 23, 1738;

The disease of which Mr. Titus Brockett died was smallpox. He was a member of Parson Andrews' Episcopal church, and a strong Tory. Parties had been formed for and against the British Government. In Wallingford they ran extremely high, and just two years before, Rev. Mr Andrews delivered his celebrated Fast-day sermon, that compelled him to leave for Nova Scotia. At the funeral of Mr. Brockett the Whigs would not have him buried with other members of the family, but compelled Turhand Kirtland and two others, to have the grave dug on a wet, springy place, directly under the east fence of the burying-ground, so that the water immediately filled the grave, though in mid-summer. It was therefore necessary to sink the coffin with two rails till the earth could be returned. For a long time these rails remained standing up out of the grave, and did not decay. Some of the family supposed that the timber was supernaturally preserved, as a testimony against the wicked whigs.

35. ISAAC.

ISAAC BROCKETT married Mary Sedgwick, a daughter of Samuel and Ruth Sedgwick of Hartford, June 16, 1731. She died Jan. 19, 1734. He married Elizabeth Culver, Feb. 25, 1737, who after his death married Daniel Frisbie, May 4, 1748. He died Oct. 18, 1746. He was an ardent churchman.

Child by 1st marriage: 53 *Rachel*, b May 23, 1732, m Constant Kirtland. Children by 2d marriage: 54 *Ruth*, b Feb. 3, 1738; 55 *Esther*, b Oct. 6, 1739; 56 *Hannah*, b Oct. 6, 1741; 57 *Ruth*, b Oct. 26, 1744.

38. SAMUEL.

SAMUEL BROCKETT married Ruth ——. He was a son of Samuel and Rachel Brockett.

Children: 58 *Eunice*, b Jan. 15, 1744; 59 *Zuer*, b Mar. 24, 1746; 60 *Joel*, b June 14, 1749; 61 *Joel*, b July 28, 1750; 62 *Zenas*, b July 12, 1752; 63 *Benjamin*, b Oct. 1, 1760.

39. DANIEL.

DANIEL BROCKETT, son of John and Huldah, m Rachel ——.

Children: 64 *Daniel*, b July 3, 1737; 65 *Daniel*, b April 13, 1740.

45. JOHN.

JOHN BROCKETT, son of John and Huldah Brockett, married Jemima ——.

Children: 66 *Christopher*, b June 2, 1749; 67 *Susannah*, b Nov. 17, 1750.

47. JOB.

JOB BROCKETT, son of Josiah and Deborah Brockett, m Martha Ebernathe.

Child: 68 *Lucretia*, b July 27, 1756.

BROWN.[1]

FRANCIS.

FRANCIS BROWN married Mary Edwards, in England, and came over to America, and to New Haven, in advance of the colony; was one of the company that spent the winter of 1637–8 in a hut which they had erected on the east corner of what is now College and George-sts. He was one of the subscribers to the colony compact, or constitution, in 1639.

Children: 1 *Lydia;* 2 *John;* 3 *Eleazer;* 4 *Samuel;* 5 *Ebenezer.*

4. SAMUEL.

SAMUEL married Mercy Tuttle, May 2, 1667, and was one of the original subscribers for the settlement of the village of Wallingford. Lot No. 7, west side of the Main street, was assigned to him for his encouragement, as a house lot. But it does not appear that he ever built upon it; why he did not is unknown. This lot was subsequently assigned to John Moss, who built a house upon it; and it remained in the family until the death of the late Ebenezer Morse, a few years since. In 1850 Moses Y. Beach purchased this lot, and erected that elegant mansion, now known as the Beach House, upon it. Samuel Brown died in Wallingford, Nov. 4, 1691, æ. 46 yrs.

Children: 6 *Abigail,* b March 11, 1669, d young; 7 *Sarah,* b Aug. 8, 1672; 8 *Rachel,* b April 14, 1677; 9 *Francis,* b Oct. 7, 1679; 10 *Gideon,* b July 12, 1685; 11 *Samuel,* b Oct. 29, 1699.[2]

BUNNEL.[3]

PETER.

PETER BUNNEL came from England in the May-flower, with the Pilgrims, and landed at Plymouth, Mass., in 1620.

1 Durrie refers to 45 works for collateral branches.

2 Bronson in Hist. of Waterbury gives descendants of above.

3 For collateral branches, see Hinman's Conn. settlers, 405, 406.

RICHARD.

RICHARD BUNNEL came from England in 1630, and settled at Watertown, Mass.

BENJAMIN.

BENJAMIN BUNNEL was an early settler in Wallingford; was made a freeman in 1670. He was at New Haven in 1668, and possibly previous to that date. He married Mary Brooks, and had a daughter, 1 *Lydia*, b Aug. 27, 1713.

2. ABNER.

ABNER BUNNEL, born in 1676.

Children: 3 *Abner;* 4 *David;* 5 *Enos*, m Truelove ——, she d May 7, 1717, æ. 22; 6 *Ebenezer*, b 1716.

NATHANIEL.

ENSIGN NATHANIEL BUNNEL was an early settler in that part of Wallingford now Cheshire, where he married Desire, daughter of Benjamin Peck, May 10, 1709. She was born Aug. 26, 1687, and died in 1721. He married Mary Brooks, Feb. 17, 1726, and died of small pox, May 4, 1732, æ. 46 yrs. He appears to have been the ancestor of all who have gone from Cheshire that bear the name of Bunnel.

Children: 7 *Desire*, b March 26, 1711; 8 *Ebenezer*, b May 21, 1713, m Lydia Clark; 9 *Benjamin*, b April 16, 1715; 10 *Parmineas*, b March 1, 1717; 11, 12, *Jared* and *Desire* (twins), b June 25, 1719; 13 *Abner*, b March 24, 1721, m Elizabeth Preston, Feb. 19, 1746; 14 *Joseph*, b Jan. 17, 1723. By 2nd marriage: 15 *Patience*, b Nov. 28, 1726; 16 *Hezekiah*, b Nov. 21, 1727, m Esther ———; 17 *Rachel*, b Nov. 15, 1728, m Samuel Thompson, June 27, 1747; 18 *Rebecca*, b Jan. 6, 1730; 19 *Stephen*, b July 6, 1731.

8. EBENEZER.

EBENEZER BUNNEL m Lydia Clark of Cheshire, 1738.

Children: 20 *Nathaniel*, b June 4, 1739; 21 *Jared*, b Oct. 6, 1741; 22 *Lydia*, b May 4, 1744; 23 *Israel*, b March 17, 1747; 24 *Ebenezer*, b Feb. 15, 1750, d March 1, 1756; 25

Lydia, b Jan. 26, 1753; 26 *Hannah*, b April 11, 1756; 27 *Desire*, b Jan. 7, 1759; 28 *Miriam*, b March 20, 1762.

9. BENJAMIN.

BENJAMIN BUNNEL married Lydia Fox, Dec. 22, 1743.

Children: 29 *Benjamin*, b July 15, 1747; 30 *Samuel*, b Jan. 7, 1750.

10. PARMINEAS.

PARMINIAS BUNNEL m Rachel Curtis, Sept. 20, 1739. After his death she married Samuel Thompson, June 7, 1741.

Children: 31 *Desire*, b May 19, 1740; 32 *Parmineas*, b Jan., 1742; 33 *Mary*, b Jan. 6, 1745; 34 *John*, b April 18, 1746; 35 *Rachel*, b July 2, 1748; 36 *Desire*, b Nov. 7, 1750; 36 *Damaris*, b June 30, 1752; 38 *John*, b July 25, 1754.

13 ABNER.

ABNER BUNNEL m Elizabeth Preston, Feb. 19, 1756.

Children: 39 *David*, b Dec. 2, 1747; 40 *Abner*, b Nov. 18, 1749; 41 *Elizabeth*, b Nov. 20, 1751; 42 *Enos*, b May 15, 1753, m Naomi, dau. of Stephen and Hannah Atwater; 43 *Reuben*, b Feb. 22, 1755; 44 *Samuel*, b May 12, 1757; 45 *Esther*, b March 26, 1759; 46 *Jehiel*, b Oct. 6, 1763

14. JOSEPH.

JOSEPH BUNNEL m Hannah Hotchkiss, Feb. 28, 1745.

Children: 47 *Eunice*, b May 23, 1745; 48 *Miriam*, b May 31, 1747.

16. HEZEKIAH.

HEZEKIAH BUNNEL m Esther ——.

Children: 49 *Nathaniel*, b Jan. 23. 1734, m Lois Rice, June 17, 1759; 50 *Titus*, b Nov. 9, 1735; 51 *Esther*, b Nov. 31, 1737.

19. STEPHEN.

STEPHEN BUNNEL married Mary Hendrick, Sept. 26, 1752.

Children: 52 *Lois*, b July 1, 1754; 53 *Mary*, b March 27, 1756; 54 *Levi*, b July 19, 1759; 55 *Eunice*, b June 10, 1761.

23. ISRAEL.

ISRAEL BUNNEL married Jerusha Dowd, daughter of Benjamin Dowd of Middletown. He was a large landholder in Cheshire, and one of the most prominent and active men in the town, and for many consecutive years served as selectman, and in various other offices in the gift of his fellow-townsmen. His death was greatly lamented by all who knew him, and especially by his neighbors and friends.

Children: 56 *Nathaniel*, d in Cheshire; 57 *Rufus;* 58 *Virgil;* 59 *Israel;* 60 *Jairus*, d in New Haven; 61 *Ebenezer;* 62 *Dennis;* 63 *Hannah;* 64 *Jerusha*, m Doct. Pierre E. Brandon.

CANNON.

LYMAN.

LYMAN CANNON, married ——— , a daughter of the late Elisha Smith, of Wallingford. He carried on the tin business with considerable success during his whole life in Wallingford. He was a Deacon in the Congregational church.

Children: *Burdett*, d in Wallingford; *William*, resided in New Haven; *James*, d in New Haven in 1868; 1 *daughter.*

CARTER.

This name appears in Wallingford before 1738, in the persons of William and Anna Carter. They had a daughter born Nov. 20, 1738, and a son, William, born Nov. 14, 1748, and perhaps others. Dea. Salmon Carter was one of the old inhabitants sixty years ago, in Wallingford. He carried on cabinet making and a small store. He by close application to business and rigid economy in all his affairs, accumulated a very handsome estate. He married ——— Hough, daughter of Joseph and ——— Hough, of Wallingford. In appearance he was a sedate, and remarkably dignified man in his manners and address, but little seen in the public streets, except on business

Children: 1 *Salome,* d unm.; 2 *Betsey,* m Lyman Collins, of Meriden; 3 *William,* m wid. Hiram Yale, of Wallingford, left no children.

CARRINGTON.[1]

This family is one of great antiquity. Sir Michael Carrington, who was a standard bearer to Richard I., 1189, is the first of whom I find any record. His grandson Sir William Carrington was an officer under Edward I., 1272–1307. Sir Edmund Carrington, Kt., was an officer under Edward II., 1307–27. Sir William Carrington, Kt., temp. of Edward III. 1327–77. Sir Thomas Carrington, Kt., Steward (of the household) to Edward III., was the father of John Carrington, who in the beginning of the reign of Henry IV. for his adherence to Richard II. (who was deposed) was compelled to flee from his country, and on returning assumed for disguise the name of Smith. He died 1446, and was father of Hugh (Carrington) Smith, who appears to have been the father of (1445–1500) Sir John Carrington Smith, Baron of the Exchequer, temp. Henry VIII., whose fourth son (1509–47) Francis (Carrington) Smith, of Ashley Tolville, Leicester, was great grandfather of Charles (Carrington) Smith, who was created Oct. 31, 1643, Lord C——, Baron of "Wotton Warren" in Warwickshire, 4th of Nov., following Viscount Carrington in the Peerage of Ireland, was murdered by his valet at Pontoise in France, Feb. 21, 1664, and was succeeded by Francis Carrington Smith, 2d Baron and Viscount. He died in 1705. Charles, his son, died young, in May, 1706. The title and honor thus became extinct.

John Carrington was an early settler in Farmington, and

---

1 For collateral branches, see Andrews' Hist. New Britain, 338; Campbell's Hist. Virginia, 624–625; Foot's Hist. Virginia, 2nd series, 575; Hinman's Conn. Settlers, 491–492; Mead's Hist. of Old Churches and Families of Virginia, II. 29.

one of the "eighty-four proprietors" in 1672. He signed the articles for the settlement of Mattatuck, Waterbury, in 1674, and appears to have joined the new plantation early; for he is named in all the divisions of fences. It appears that for some cause he did not fully comply with the conditions of the new plantation covenant, and was consequently declared to have forfeited his rights, Feb. 6, 1682. But little is known of him. He died in the early part of 1690, leaving a widow who died before the inventory of his effects was rendered, June 30, 1690. His son John was the administrator, and the estate amounted to £120 11*s*. John had £23, and each of the other children had £12; their guardians were instructed to put out the three youngest, and not to be governed or overruled by John the administrator. John's brothers were Ebenezer, Samuel and Ezekiel. John Carrington's house-lot of two acres was on West Main-st., the south side, about where Leavenworth street now runs. It was bounded north and south on the highway, east on Timothy Stanley, west on George Scott. It was sold in 1710, by the heirs to Timothy Stanley and George Scott, for £12.

Children: 1 *John*, b 1667, d 1692 in Farmington, he was a cooper; 2 *Mary*, b 1672, m William Parsons of Farmington, Ct.; 3 *Hannah*, b 1675, m Joshua Holcombe of Simsbury, Ct.; 4 *Clark*, b 1678, m Sarah Higason, and lived in Farmington; 5 *Elizabeth*, b 1682, m John Hoskins of Windsor; 6 *Ebenezer*, b 1687, removed to Hartford, d in Waterbury, had no issue.

1. JOHN.

John Carrington, first of Waterbury, married Miss —— Hunn, from Mass. He married for his second wife Miss ——. He lived on a farm at Red Stone Hill in Farmington, where he died.

Children by 1st marriage: 7 *Nathaniel*, m, had no issue, d on the old homestead; 8 *John*, m Mabel Beach in New York, was a merchant in Goshen, d a young man; 9 *Jeremiah*, b 1746, m Mindwell Cook and settled in Wallingford, where he kept a tavern a great number of years; 10 *Deborah*, m —— Rice, she died at Onondaga, N. Y., a woman of great worth; 11 *Keziah*, m 1st, —— Munson, 2d, Esq. Oliver Stanley of Wallingford; 12 *Martha*, m Fisk Beach of Goshen, brother of Mabel, had 8 children. By 2d marriage: 13 *Jonathan*, b 1748, m Azubah Burns of Bristol, d 1733; 14 *Solomon*, d in the old prison ship New York; 15 *Phineas*, d supposed in the service of the U. States; 16 *David*.

8. JOHN.

JOHN CARRINGTON, son of John and ——— Hunn Carrington, married Mabel Beach, of Goshen, Conn. He was a merchant in Goshen. He died of a fever in New York while a young man.

Children: 17 *Harvey*, m ——— Catlin, children, John and Lucia; 18 *Elisha*, m Judy Thompson, she died leaving 7 daughters and 1 son; 19 *Miles*, resides in Augusta N. Y., is accounted a good man; 20 *Anna*, m a lawyer named Dawes, had 2 children, she died young; 21 *Mabel*, m., and lived in humble circumstances.

JEREMIAH.

JEREMIAH CARRINGTON, son of John and ——— Hunn Carrington, married Mindwell Cook, daughter of Isaac and Jerusha, of Wallingford, and was the keeper of the hotel now kept by Dwight Hall in the village of Wallingford, for a number of years. He died Dec. 17, 1812, æ. 66 years. She died Jan. 7, 1813, æ. 64 years.

Children: 22 *James*, b 1770, d July 6, 1836, æ. 66, m Patty McLean, she died March 12, 1836, æ. 64; 23 *Liverius*, b 1778, d Dec. 22, 1848, æ. 70.

22. JAMES.

JAMES CARRINGTON, son of Capt. Jeremiah and Mindwell Carrington, m Patty McLean of Wallingford. He was an energetic and thorough business man, and for many years was in the employ of Eli Whitney Esq., as superintendent of the Gun Factory at Whitneyville. He was Postmaster at

Wallingford many years, and leader of the singing in the old three-story meeting-house, being a fine musician, and possessed of a remarkably full, well-toned bass voice.

Children: 24 *Miles*, now of Mobile, Ala.; 25 *James Whitney*, Astoria, N. Y.; and several daughters.

23. LIVERIUS.

LIVERIUS CARRINGTON, son of Capt. Jeremiah and Mindwell Carrington, m 1st, Thankful Hall, 2nd, Eliza Kirtland, 3d, Sarah Kirtland Yale, wid. of Selden Yale, and sister to Eliza, his 2nd wife. He studied medicine with Dr. Kirtland of Wallingford. Not liking the professsion he formed a partnership with the late George B. Kirtland, and entered the mercantile business, in which he continued until his decease in 1840.

Children by 1st marriage: 27 *William*, b about 1807, successor to the old firm, C. & K.; 28 *Anna*, and an infant, both of whom died, Anna at the age of 17. Children by 2nd marriage: 29 *Sarah K.*; 30 *Anna*, m Joel Peck, late deceased. Children by 3d marriage: 31 *Kirtland*, business clerk; 32 *Ellen*.

CLARK.[1]

I. EBENEZER.

EBENEZER CLARK, son of James, of New Haven, born Nov. 29, 1651, m Sarah, daughter of James Peck, of New Haven, May 6, 1678; she died May 20, 1696, æ. 37 years. He died April 30, 1721, æ. 70 years. He married Elizabeth Royce for his 2nd wife, Dec. 22, 1696. He was the first of this name in Wallingford.

Children: by 1st m, 1 *Caleb*, b March 6, 1678; 2 *Sarah*, b Aug. 20, 1681, m Isaac Cook, Oct. 11, 1706; 3 *Josiah*, b Feb. 6, 1683, m Mary Burr; 4 *Stephen*, b Dec. 18, 1686; 5

---

1 Durrie refers to fifty-two works containing notices of the Clark family.

Hannah, b Aug. 18, 1689, d before her father; 6 *Sylvanus*, b Feb. 1, 1691–2, m Damaris Hitchcock in 1717; 7 *Obadiah*, b Oct. 17, 1694, d before his father; 8 *Stephen*, b Dec. 7, 1696, d Mar. 25, 1750. By 2nd marriage: 9 *Eliphalet*, b Dec. 28, 1697; 10 *Elizabeth*, b Sept. 24, 1698, d before her father; 11 *Susannah*, b April 29, 1700, d before her father; 12 *Caleb*, b Sept. 26, 1701, m Lois How, Jan. 19, 1722; 13 *Phebe*, b May 20, 1703; 14 *Daniel*, b Feb. 7, 1712, m Elizabeth ——, she d April 17, 1755; 15 *Abigail*, b June 8, 1705; 16 *James*, b Sept. 29, 1713, d before his father; 17 *Susannah*, b Sept. 30, 1717; 18 *Sarah*, b Sept. 24, 1721, d June 18, 1722.

3. JOSIAH.

JOSIAH CLARK, son of Ebenezer and Sarah Clark of Wallingford, m Mary Burr, April 21, 1710.

Children: 19 *Solomon*, b March 6, 1711; 20 *Mary*, b Mar. 22, 1723.

6. SYLVANUS.

SYLVANUS CLARK, son of Ebenezer and Sarah Clark, married Damaris Hitchcock, April 22, 1717.

Children: 21 *Jonah*, b Jan. 31, 1718; 22 *Thankful*, b Dec. 21, 1719, m James Curtis, Nov. 11, 1738.

8. STEPHEN.

STEPHEN CLARK, son of Ebenezer and Sarah Clark, m Lydia Hotchkiss of Cheshire. She died Nov. 1, 1737, æ. 41. He died Nov. 25, 1750, æ. 64 years, at Cheshire. His second wife was Ruth ——.

Children by 1st marriage: 23 *Lydia*, b Nov. 25, 1718; 24 *Sarah*, b Sept. 24, 1721; 25 *Andrew*, b Oct. 24, 1727, m Mehitable Tuttle, Feb. 7, 1748. Children by 2nd marriage: 26 *Desmania*, b Sept. 26, 1751; 27 *Amasa*, b Nov. 25, 1753; 28 *Mary*, b Oct. 4, 1756; 29 *Stephen*, b Dec. 16, 1785, m Mehitable ——; 30 *Levi*, b Jan. 11, 1761.

12. CALEB.

CALEB, son of Ebenezer and Elizabeth Clark, married Lois How, Jan. 19, 1722.

Children: 31 *Margery*, b April 14, 1723; 32 *Eunice*, b Mar. 23, 1725; 33 *Phebe*, b Mar. 1, 1728; 34 *Lois*, b Aug. 31, 1730.

14. DANIEL.

DANIEL, son of Ebenezer and Elizabeth Clark, married Elizabeth Miles, Sept. 17, 1741; she died April 17, 1755. He m again in 1741; he died Aug. 17, 1774, æ. 63 yrs.

Children: 35 *Lois*, b Nov. 12, 1743; 36 *Archibald*, b Sept. 1, 1745-6, m Polly Ives, of North Haven; 37 *Ebenezer;* 38 *Daniel*, was a town pauper for years; 39 *Abigail;* 40 *James.*

25. ANDREW.

ANDREW, son of Stephen and Lydia Clark, m Mehitable Tuttle, Feb. 7, 1748-9.

Children: 41, *Stephen*, b Jan. 16, 1749; 42 *Lydia*, b March 23, 1752; 43 *Mehitable*, b Aug. 21, 1758.

WILLIAM.

WILLIAM CLARK married Mindwell Rowe, Aug. 29, 1749.

Children: 44 *Sylvanus*, b Oct. 4, 1750; 45 *Josiah*, b Aug. 8, 1752.

ABRAHAM.

ABRAHAM CLARK married Martha Tyler, Oct. 5, 1721.

Children: 46 *Mary*, b March 1, 1724; 47 *Lydia*, b March 1, 1726; 48 *Hannah*, b Sept. 12, 1727; 49 *Rufus*, b March 1, 1728; 50 *Keziah*, b Oct. 31, 1731.

COOK.[1]

The ancestors from whom most of the Cooks in New England trace their descent, came from Herefordshire and Kent, in England. The ancestral branch from whom those of the name trace their origin, now resident in various parts of the state, came from Kent, and were of the Puritan stock.

---

1 For collateral branches see Andrews' Hist. New Britain, Conn., 207; Babson's Hist. Gloucester, Mass., 74; Bronson's Hist. Waterbury, 485-7; Cope's Record of Cope family of Penn., 44, 78, 79-82, 157, 175, 176; Fox's Hist. Dunstable, Mass., 242; Freeman's Hist. Cape Cod, Mass., II. 366, 389, 634, 642, 643; Hinmans's Conn. Settlers, 698-703; Hobart's

Henry Cook was at Plymouth, Mass., before 1640. He had sons, Isaac, John, Henry and Samuel. Isaac is supposed to have remained at Plymouth, and John to have settled at Middletown. Henry and Samuel settled at Wallingford, and are the ancestors of most of the name of Cook in Connecticut, and of many in various parts of the country.

SAMUEL.

SAMUEL COOK came to New Haven in 1663, m Hope, daughter of Edward Parker of New Haven, May 2, 1667. They went to Wallingford in April, 1670, with the first planters. He was, perhaps, the first and only shoemaker and tanner of leather in the place. After the decease of his wife Hope, he married Mary Roberts, July 14, 1690. He was regarded as a very good man by his friends and neighbors, and was frequently called to fill offices of responsibility and trust in the village, and in the church of which he was a member. He died March, 1702. He left an estate of £340. His widow m Jeremiah How, sen., April 9, 1705.

Children by 1st marriage: 1 *Samuel*, b March 3, 1667–8, in New Haven; 2 *John*, b Dec. 3, 1669, in New Haven; 3 *Hannah*, b March 3, 1671–2, in Wallingford; 4 *Isaac*, b March 10, 1673, d April 7, 1673; 5 *Mary*, b April 23, 1675, m Nathaniel Ives, April 5, 1699; 6 *Elizabeth*, b August 22, 1677, d young; 7 *Judith*, b Feb. 29, 1679, m Jeremiah How jr., April 20, 1704, she d March 20, 1708; 8 *Isaac*, b Jan. 10, 1681; 9 *Joseph*, b Feb. 25, 1683; 10 *Hope*, b Sept. 27, 1686, m Joseph Benham, Dec. 18, 1706, she d Jan. 30, 1731. By 2nd marriage: 11 *Israel*, b May 8, 1692; 12 *Mabel*, b June 30, 1694; 13 *Benjamin*, b April 8, 1697, d 1717, unmarried, was

---

Hist. Abingdon, Mass., 363–4; Hollister's Pawlet, Vt., 179, 180; Howell's Hist. Southampton, L. I., 210–12; Judd and Boltwood's Hist. Hadley, Mass., 465–471; Kellogg's Memorials of John White, 77; Kidder's Hist. New Ipswich, N. H., 352; Mitchell's Hist. Bridgewater, Mass., 141; Nash's Gen. of Nash Fam., 33, 34; Stiles's Hist. Windsor, Conn., 572–4; Savage's Gen. Dict., I. 445–51; Bond's Hist. and Gen. Watertown, Mass., 163, 164; Jackson's Hist. Newton, Mass., 247–50.

a tanner and currier; 14 *Ephraim*, b April 19, 1699; 15 *Elizabeth*, b Sept. 10, 1701, m Adam Mott, Aug 28, 1717.

1. SAMUEL.

SAMUEL COOK, son of Samuel and Hope Cook, married Hannah Ives, daughter of William of New Haven, March 3, 1692, John Moss Esq. officiating. She died May 29, 1714. He then married Elizabeth Bedel, of Stratford. He died Sept. 18, 1725, æ. 58 years, at Wallingford. His widow married Capt. Daniel Harris, of Middletown, Conn. He was a farmer in the western part of the township, near the line which now divides Cheshire from Wallingford. Some of his descendants are still occupying the same land. Estate, £390.

Children: 16 *Hannah*, b May 28, 1693, m Jeremiah Hull, she died Nov. 22, 1735, æ. 43 years; 17 *Samuel*, b March 5, 1695; 18 *Aaron*, b Dec. 28, 1696; 19 *Lydia*, b Jan. 13, 1699, m Daniel Dutton, d Oct. 12, 1738; 20 *Moses*, b Jan. 4, 1700, d Dec. 25, 1711; 21 *Miriam*, b Nov. 4, 1703, m Benjamin Curtis, Dec. 12, 1727; 22 *Thankful*, b Dec. 24, 1705, d Aug. 19, 1714; 23 *Esther*, b March 8, 1707, m Abel Yale, July 22, 1730; 24 *Eunice*, b Feb. 25, 1709; 25 *Susannah*, b Sept. 5, 1711, m Joseph Cole, Dec. 1, 1735; 26 *Hope*, d Sept. 18, 1728. By 2nd marriage: 27 *Moses*, b Nov. 6, 1716; 28 *Thankful*, b Nov. 14, 1718, m Stephen Hotchkiss, Dec. 31, 1742; 29 *Asaph*, b June 23, 1720; 30 *Hannah*, b Nov. 4, 1721, m Zephaniah Hull, of Cheshire, and settled at Bethlem.

2. JOHN.

JOHN COOK, son of Samuel and Hope Cook, married Hannah Hall, and settled in the western part of the township near Scott's Rock in Cheshire. He died April 30, 1739, æ. 70 years.

Children: 31 *Ezekiel*, b April 20, 1700, d Nov. 7, 1722; 32 *Naomi*, b Jan. 27, 1704, d Nov. 20, 1707; 33 *John*, b Aug. 23, 1707, d Nov. 1, 1722; 34 *Mary*, m John McKay, she d 1763, in Cheshire, Conn.

8. ISAAC.

ISAAC COOK, son of Samuel and Hope Cook, married Sarah Curtis, Oct. 11, 1705. He d Feb. 1, 1712, in Wallingford. His widow married Caleb Lewis, in 1714. Estate, £103.

Children: 35 *Sarah*, b July 20, 1707; 36 *Amos*, d in childhood; 37 *Mindwell*, b May, 1709, m Caleb Evarts of Guilford, Conn.; 38 *Isaac*, b July 22, 1710.

9. JOSEPH.

JOSEPH COOK, son of Samuel and Hope Cook, married Abigail ——. After her death, he married Eleanor Johnson, Oct. 14, 1714, and remained in Wallingford until 1743, when in the autumn of that year, he went to Goshen in Litchfield county, and was among the earliest and most prominent men in the place. He died Nov. 7, 1764, æ. 82 years.

Children by 1st marriage: 39 *Lois*, b April 25, 1700, d in infancy; 40 *Samuel*, b Feb. 18, 1702; 41 *Abigail*, b Jan. 18, 1703. By 2d marriage: 42 *Phebe*, b Oct. 7, 1715, m Eli Pettibone, Feb. 21, 1751, she d about 1767; 43 *Benjamin*, b Jan. 5, 1718; 44 *Daniel*, b Aug. 19, 1720; 45 *Walter*, b Dec. 21, 1722; 46 *Joseph*, b Jan. 18, 1726; 47 *Lois*, b May 23, 1729; 48 *Lambert*, d at Goshen; 49 *Hannah*, b Nov. 15, 1735, m Roger Pettibone, Jan. 25, 1752, she d April 29, 1763.

11. ISRAEL.

ISRAEL COOK, son of Samuel and Mary Cook, married Elizabeth, daughter of Ebenezer Clark of Wallingford, Feb. 22, 1717. He settled in what is now Cheshire, and afterward moved to Vermont with some of his children, where it is supposed he died.

Children: 50 *Catharine*, b July 3, 1718, m Isaiah Smith, of New Haven, May 20, 1750; 51 *Ebenezer*, b Dec. 13, 1719; 52 *Sarah*, b May 5, 1722, m 1st, Jonathan Hall, Dec. 25, 1739, 2d, Jehiel Andrus, Jan. 16, 1745; 53 *Deborah*, b Oct. 1, 1725, m Elisha Perkins, June 20, 1748; 54 *Anna*, b July 4, 1727; 55 *John*, b 1731, bap. in Cheshire, June, 1751; 56

Amos, b Dec. 5, 1734; 57 *Benjamin*, b about 1736; 58 *Ashbel*, b May 6, 1738; 59 *Charles*, doubtless settled in Vermont; 60 *Ezekiel*, b and bap. at Cheshire, June, 1751, supposed settled in Vermont.

14. EPHRAIM.

EPHRAIM COOK, son of Samuel and Mary Cook, married Lydia Doolittle. She died Dec. 25, 1785, æ. 84 years He died March 22, 1774, æ. 75 years. He was licensed by the county court, April 24, 1727, to prosecute the business of tanning and dressing leather in Cheshire.

Children: 61 *Mary*, b Feb. 13, 1723, d same year; 62 *Mamre*, b Dec. 21, 1725, m Daniel Hotchkiss, of Cheshire; 63 *Lydia*, b March 2, 1726, m Jason Hitchcock, Sept. 20, 1741; 64 *Mary*, b April 7, 1728, m John Smith of Cheshire; 65 *Ephraim*, b April 7, 1730; 66 *Tirzah*, b Oct. 3, 1733, m Samuel Smith of Cheshire; 67 *Elam*, b Nov. 10, 1735; 68 *Elizabeth*, b Feb. 10, 1738, m Ebenezer Brown of Cheshire; 69 *John*, b Dec. 27, 1739; 70 *Merriman*, b 1741, d unmarried in Cheshire; 71 *Thankful*, no account of this person recorded; 72 *Phebe*, m Timothy Gaylord, May 4, 1748.

17. CAPT. SAMUEL.

CAPT. SAMUEL COOK, son of Samuel and Hannah Ives Cook, married Hannah Lewis, daughter of Ebenezer and Elizabeth Lewis, of Wallingford, Feb. 8, 1721. He was a wealthy shipping merchant, from the port of New Haven, where he died Nov. 7, 1745 (Thanksgiving Day), leaving an estate of £29103. He was buried at Cheshire, where a fine altar tomb marks his resting place. His benefactions to the church and poor of Cheshire are lasting monuments to his memory and worth.

Children: 73 *Hannah*, b Dec. 22, 1722, m Elnathan Beach. She died May 18, 1754; 74 *Rhoda*, b Oct. 22, 1724, m Benjamin Hitchcock, of Cheshire, Feb. 27, 1745; 75 *Damaris*, b Nov., 1726, m Rev. Ebenezer Boone, of Farmington, Dec. 19, 1750, then removed to Vermont; 76 *Thaddeus*, b Sept. 10, 1728; 77 *Lowly*, b May 10, 1730, m Andrew

Hull of Cheshire, Oct. 17, 1750; 78 *Samuel*, b Nov. 16, 1733; 79 *Eunice*, b June 29, 1735, m Samuel Hull, of Cheshire, b Feb., 1755; 80 *Levi*, b Nov. 10, 1737, m Isaac Benham of Cheshire; 81 *Aaron*, b Nov. 30, 1739.

Elnathan Beach was a partner with Capt. Cook, whose dau. he married. Andrew Hull was the Hon. father of the late Gen. Andrew Hull of Cheshire, and great grandfather of Rear Admiral Andrew Hull Foote, U. S. N. Samuel Hull was brother to Andrew Hull, and grandfather to the late Mrs. Jonathan Law, of Cheshire and Hartford.

18. AARON.

AARON COOK, son of Samuel and Hannah (Ives) Cook, married 1st, Sarah, daughter of James Benham, Nov. 14, 1723. He married 2d, Sarah Hitchcock. She died Aug. 11, 1735, and for his 3d wife he married Ruth Burrage, of Stratford, Feb. 7, 1736. He was a very large landholder in the south-eastern part of Wallingford, Northford survey. He died Oct. 14, 1756, æ. 60 years. Mrs. Ruth Cook died July 2, 1786, æ. 79 years.

Children, by 1st m.: 82 *Samuel*, b Sept. 25, 1725, d before his father; 83 *Stephen*, b Dec. 28, 1727; 84 *Titus*, b Feb. 25, 130; 85 *Abel*, b Feb. 23, 1732. By 2d marriage: 86 *Sarah*, b June 2, 1735. By 3d marriage: 87 *Lydia*, b 1736, m Uriah Collins, she d Jan. 9, 1793; 88 *Ruth*, b Sept. 7, 1738, m William Collins, she d June 9, 1790; 89 *Esther*, b May 14, 1740; 90 *Elizabeth*, b March 16, 1741–2, d Jan. 27, 1751; 91 *Aaron*, b June 5, 1744; 92 *Miriam*, b June 30, 17 46, d Dec. 1, 1750; 93 *Lucy*, b Sept. 20, 1748, d April 29, 1760; 94 *Elizabeth*, b June 7, 1751, d Oct. 19, 1762.

27. MOSES.

MOSES COOK, son of Samuel and Elizabeth Cook, m Sarah Culver, June 18, 1740, and went to Branford. Subsequently he went to Waterbury, where his wife died, Jan. 4, 1760, and he afterwards m Dinah Harrison, widow of Benj., June 7, 1762. He was killed by Moses Paul, an Indian, in the town of Woodbridge, Dec. 12, 1771. (Paul was executed at New Haven in June, 1772). Mr. Cook was æ. 54 years. Mrs. Dinah Cook d Oct. 4, 1792.

Children by 1st m. : 95 *Charles*, b June 3, 1742 ; 96 *Moses*, b May 30, 1744, in Branford, d 1832 ; 97 *Sarah*, b June 13, 1747, d April 5, 1823 ; 98 *Esther*, b June 27, 1750, m Joseph Beebe, she d in Ohio, 1810 ; 99 *Elizabeth*, b May 15, 1752, m Benj. Baldwin, she d 1797 ; 100 *Hannah*, b Jan. 11, 1755, m Titus Bronson, she d 1841 ; 101 *Lydia*, b March 27, 1760, m —— Hickox.

29. ASAPH.

ASAPH COOK, son of Samuel and Elizabeth Cook, m Sarah Parker, of Wallingford, and went to Granville, Mass., where he remained until about the close of the Revolution, when he removed to Granville, N. Y., where he d in 1792 ; she d in 1818, æ. 96 years.

Children: 102 *Samuel*, b Aug. 18, 1744 ; 103 *Amasa*, b 1746, m Miriam Loomis, of Granville, N. Y., subsequently of Essex Co., N. Y. ; 104 *Asaph*, b March 6, 1748 ; 105 *Joseph*, b April 13, 1750 ; 106 *Susannah*, b April 13, 1750, m Ichabod Parker, she d 1770 ; 107 *Sarah*, b 1752, m Wm Meacham, 2nd, Zeruah Everest, she d 1777 ; 108 *Thankful*, b 1754, m Gideon Beebe, of Adams, Mass. ; 109 *Hannah*, b June 5, 1758 ; 110 *Charles*, b May 9, 1764 ; 111 *Lois*, b 1766, m John Merrick, of Granville, N. Y.

38. ISAAC.

ISAAC COOK, son of Isaac and Sarah Cook, m Jerusha Sexton, of Wallingford, Oct. 13, 1733. He died March 16, 1780, æ 80 years. She died Oct. 13, 1795. He was a tanner and currier of leather.

Children: 112 *Amos*, b Dec. 5, 1734 ; 113 *Jerusha*, b Nov. 19, 1736, m Gideon Hosford, Feb. 23, 1757 ; 114 *Isaac*, b July 28, 1739 ; 115 *Caleb*, b Nov. 14, 1741 ; 116 *Mindwell*, b Dec. 9, 1743, d Jan. 26, 1744 ; 117 *Ambrose*, b March 19, 1744, d in infancy ; 118 *Ambrose*, b June 30, 1746 ; 119 *Elihu*, b Aug. 16, 1747, d Aug. 31, 1747; 120 *Mindwell*, b April 20, 1750, m Capt. Jeremiah Carrington, of Wallingford.

43. BENJAMIN.

BENJAMIN COOK, son of Joseph and Eleanor Cook, married Hannah Munson, Jan. 20, 1741. She was celebrated in her day as a skillful midwife in Wallingford, where they lived at the time of his decease, which occurred about 1790. He was a weaver and farmer.

Children: 121 *Benjamin*, b Oct. 8, 1743; 122 *Martha*, m Col. Isaac Cook of Wallingford; 123 *Joel*, b Aug. 31, 1745, d young; 124 *Merriman*, b Oct. 1, 1748; 125 *Lois*, b 1752, m Oliver Doolittle, Jan. 16, 1776; 126 *Phebe*, b May 3, 1756, m Isaac Doolittle of Wallingford.

44. DANIEL.

DANIEL COOK, son of Joseph and Eleanor Cook, m Elizabeth Pond, Feb. 6, 1746. He moved from Wallingford to Goshen, where she died, Sept., 1791.

Children: 127 *Samuel*, b Aug. 2, 1747, in Wallingford, went to Goshen, Conn.; 128 *Amasa*, b Oct. 26, 1749; 129 *Philip*, b Feb. 2, 1752; 130 *Lois*, b Feb. 27, 1754, m Joel Gaylord, of Goshen, Conn.; 131 *Lydia*, b Oct. 29, 1756, m Moses Bartholomew, of Goshen, Conn.; 132 *Daniel*, b Aug. 18, 1761; 133 *Moses*, b April 25, 1764; 134 *John*, b Sept. 8, 1767, no report from him.

45. WALTER.

WALTER COOK, son of Joseph and Eleanor Cook, m Reuema Calling, and went to Goshen, Conn. Subsequently he went to Richmond, Mass. He was a farmer and shoemaker.

Children: 135 *Eunice*, b Nov. 10, 1754, in Wallingford; 136 *Pitman*, b June 28, 1757, in Wallingford; 137 *Walter*, b Sept. 10, 1764, in Goshen; 138 *John*, b Oct. 2, 1767, in Goshen; 139 *Sinai*, b Oct. 12, 1769, in Goshen; 140 *Susannah*, b Feb. 26, 1790, in Goshen; 141 *Lucy*, m Abijah Newton, of Goshen, Conn.

48. LAMBERT.

LAMBERT COOK, son of Joseph and Eleanor Cook, married 1st, Abigail ——, and settled in Goshen, Conn. She died Oct. 8, 1758. He married Mindwell Loomis, for his 2nd wife, Dec. 13, 1759. He died at Goshen, Conn.

Child by 1st marriage: 142 *Mary*, b July 17, 1757. By 2nd marriage: 143 *Abigail*, b Jan. 25, 1760; 144 *Joseph*, b Feb. 25, 1762; 145 *Hannah*, b Dec. 25, 1763; 146 infant, b June 11, 1765, d æ. 1 day.

51. EBENEZER.

EBENEZER COOK, son of Israel and Elizabeth Cook. He married Eunice ——. This family left Wallingford soon after the war of the Revolution.

Children: 147 *Ebenezer*, b May 19, 1760; 148 *Munson*, b March 1, 1762; 149 *Eunice*, b Feb. 28, 1766; 150 *William*, b July 3, 1772.

55. JOHN.

JOHN COOK, son of Israel and Elizabeth Cook, married Naomi Abernathy, and removed to Guildhall, Vermont. She died in 1809, aged about 75 years. He died at Guildhall in 1812, aged 81 years.

Children: 151 *Benjamin*, b Jan. 24, 1764; 152 *Naomi*, b March 12, 1766, m Laban Beach; 153 *John*, b March 16, 1768, d at Guildhall, Vt.; 154 *Ruth*, b Feb. 7, 1769; 155 *Lemuel*, b Feb. 7, 1770; 156 *Enos A.*, b Jan. 7, 1773; 157 *Raphael*, b May 8, 1775; 158 *Abigail*, b May 2, 1777, d at Guildhall, Vt.; 159 *Anna*, b July 4, 1779, m —— Stoddard; 160 *Beulah*, m Eli How, she died in 1810; 161 *Zaccheus*, b Sept. 13, 1781.

57. BENJAMIN.

BENJAMIN COOK, son of Israel and Elizabeth Cook, married Martha Benham, Aug. 2, 1759, and doubtless left Wallingford soon afterwards.

Children: 162 *Martha*, b March 11, 1760, in Wallingford; 163 *Benjamin*, b May 6, 1675.

58. ASHBEL.

ASHBEL COOK, son of Israel and Elizabeth Cook, married Rachel ——. He left Wallingford about 1768, when it is supposed he went to Vermont.

Children: 164 *John;* 165 *Simeon*, d young; 166 *Israel;* 167 *Ashbel;* 168 *Simeon;* 169 *Rice*, b Aug. 12, 1780, in Rutland, Vt.; 170 *Orel.*

65. EPHRAIM.

EPHRAIM COOK, son of Ephraim and Lydia Cook, married Elizabeth Hull, Jan. 1, 1752. He was a farmer, shoemaker, tanner and currier of leather; he died in Cheshire, Conn., Jan. 18, 1789, æ. 59 yrs.

Children: 171 *Lois*, b Jan., 1753, d Nov. 4, 1753, æ. 10 mos.; 172 *Ephraim*, b 1754, d Dec. 2, 1764, æ 10 yrs.; 173 *Lydia*, b Dec. 20, 1756; 174 *Anna*, b Feb. 5, 1764; 175 *Urina*, b 1765, d Dec. 11, 1771, æ. 6 yrs.; 176 *Clarinda*, b 1770, d Dec. 5, 1772, æ. 2 yrs.

67. ELAM.

ELAM COOK, son of Ephraim and Lydia Cook, married Abigail Hall, Jan. 8, 1761. He died in Cheshire, Feb. 3, 1808, aged 73 years. She died in Ohio, Sept. 26, 1816, aged 81 years.

Children: 177 *Merriman*, b Nov. 12, 1761, went to Barton, Ohio; 178 *Samuel*, b 1764, settled in Cheshire, Conn.; 179 *Esther*, b March, 1769, m John Ford of Prospect, and went to Ohio, she was the mother of Gov. Ford of Ohio; 180 *Ephraim*, b Dec. 21, 1775; 181 *Elam*, b 1780, settled in Cheshire; 182 *Joseph H.*, b Feb. 1, 1782; 183 *Abigail*, b July 10, 1784, married Hon. Peter Hitchcock of Ohio, formerly of Cheshire.

69. JOHN.

JOHN COOK, son of Ephraim and Lydia Cook, married Obedience ——; he died in Cheshire, Oct. 2, 1764, æ. 25 yrs. His widow married Daniel Ives, Dec. 7, 1769.

Child: 184 *Ephraim*, b 1763, d Oct. 2, 1765, æ. 2 yrs.

76. THADDEUS.

Col. Thaddeus Cook, son of Capt. Samuel and Hannah Cook, m 1st, Lois, daughter of Capt. Elnathan Beach, of Cheshire, Nov. 28, 1750. She died April 4, 1753, æ. 21 yrs. He m 2nd, Sarah, daughter of Hon. Benjamin Hall, of Cheshire. She died Sept. 5, 1774, æ 44 years. His 3d wife was Abigail ——, she survived him. After having served his country during the Revolution, under the brave Gen. Gates, and his townsmen in almost every office of trust or honor within their gift, he died Feb. 27, 1800.

Child by 1st marriage: 185 *Lois*, b April 1, 1753. By 2d marriage: 186 *Sarah*, b July 23, 1755, m Dr. Gould Gift Norton, of Cheshire, she d Sept., 1838; 187 *Samuel*, b April 19, 1758; 189 *Eunice*, b Jan. 15, 1761, d Feb. 26, 1776, æ. 15 yrs.; 190 *Lucy*, b 1762, m Amos Harrison Ives. She d Feb. 30, 1836, in Cheshire; 191 *Thaddeus*, b May 3, 1764, graduated at Yale, 1783, d Oct. 3, 1789; 192 *Sally*, m Nathan Harrison, of New Branford; 193 *Clarissa*, m —— Hall, and had a dau., Sukey Hall.

78. SAMUEL.

Samuel Cook, son of Capt. Samuel and Hannah Cook, m Jerusha Hollingworth, March 4, 1756. It was the intention of his father that he should receive a liberal education at college, but for some cause now unknown, he gave it up, and settled on a farm in the north part of Cheshire, where he d Jan. 5, 1800, æ. 67 years.

Children: 194 *Hannah*, b April 20, 1758, m a Mr. Wright; 195 *Temperance*, b Aug. 6, 1760; 196 *Perez*, b Dec. 1, 1762; 197 *Jerusha*, b Jan. 7, 1767, d July 29, 1803; 198 *Eunice*, b March 23, 1769; 199 *Damaris*, b Feb. 23, 1772; 200 *Abigail*, b June 27, 1775, m Elkanah Doolittle, of Cheshire. She d Dec. 16, 1800.

81. AARON.

Aaron Cook, son of Capt. Samuel and Hannah Cook, m Mary, dau. of Capt. Cornelius Brooks, of Cheshire. He d Sept. 29, 1776, æ. 37 yrs. She d Sept. 30, 1776, æ. 38 yrs.

He was a farmer, about three and one-half miles south-east of Cheshire meeting-house, where his father formerly lived.

Children: 201 *Jerusha*, b 1757, m Robert Hotchkiss. She d May 19, 1824; 202 *Cornelius*, b Oct. 9, 1763; 203 *Sue*, m Samuel Cook, she d Dec. 24, 1824; 204 *Aaron*, b 1768, d in Cheshire; 205 *Stephen*, b 1771, m Eunice Beadles, of Wallingford; 206 *Mary*, m Shelden Spencer, Esq.

83. STEPHEN.

STEPHEN COOK, son of Capt. Aaron and Sarah Cook, m 1st, Anna Culver, Dec 25, 1751. After her decease he m Thankful Preston, March 2, 1771, and for his 3d wife he married Anna Tyler. Anna his 1st wife died Dec. 10, 1769. Mrs. Thankful his 2d wife died Sept. 20, 1776, and Anna his 3d wife died Sept. 23, 1817, æ. 80 years.

Children by 1st wife: 207 *Samuel*, b Oct. 22, 1752; 208 *Stephen*, b March 25, 1755, went to Vermont; 209 *Anna*, b Oct. 5, 1757; 210 *Elihu*, b July 2, 1760, went to Vermont; 211 *Ruth*, b June 30, 1763, d æ. 90 yrs. By 2d marriage: 212 *Lyman*, b June 30, 1772, went to Ohio; 213 *Jared*, b Aug. 9, 1775. By 3d marriage: 214 *Lemuel*, b Sept. 2, 1779; 215 *Malachi*, b Aug. 28, 1781.

84. TITUS.

TITUS COOK, son of Capt. Aaron and Jerusha Cook, married Sarah Merriman, Jan. 18, 1753. She died Feb. 16, 1795. He died April 4, 1809, æ. 80 years, and was buried in Northford, Conn.

Children: 216 *Sarah*, b Nov. 14, 1753; 217 *Jerusha*, b May 27, 1757; 218, 219 *Lucy* and *Titus*, b April 23, 1761, d in childhood; 220 *Abigail*, b July 19. 1763; 221 *Esther*, b July 21, 1765; 222 *Caleb*, was accidentally killed; 223 *Sally*; 224 *Titus*, b Nov. 7, 1775; 225 *Lydia*, b April 1, 1778.

85. ABEL.

ABEL COOK, son of Capt. Aaron and Sarah Cook, married Mary, daughter of Dea. Benjamin and Elizabeth P. Atwater of Wallingford, Nov. 16, 1757. She was born Dec. 30, 1735, and died Jan. 13, 1774, æ. 39. He died Aug. 10, 1776, æ. 44 years.

Children: 226 *Atwater*, b Nov. 3, 1758; 227 *Porter*, b July 27, 1760; 228 *Elizabeth*, b March 13, 1763; 229 *Abel*, b March 27, 1765; 230 *Chester*, b Aug. 13, 1767, d young; 231 *Daniel M.*, b Feb. 16, 1770; 232 *Mary*, b April 2, 1773, m Col. Eliakim Hall, d Dec. 1, 1839; 233 *Chester*, b Oct. 6, 1775.

91. AARON.

AARON COOK, son of Capt. Aaron and Ruth B. Cook, married 1st, Lucretia Dudley. She died April 16, 1771, æ. 27 years. He married 2d, Elizabeth Taintor. She died April 24, 1816, æ. 65 years. He died Sept. 14, 1825, æ. 80 years, and was interred in Northford grave-yard.

Children; 234 *Oliver Dudley*, b 1766, grad. at Yale College, 1735; 253 *Aaron*, b 1768; 236 *Kilborn*, b 1771, settled in North Guilford, Conn. By 2nd marriage: 237 *Increase*, b 1773, grad. at Yale College, 1793; 238 *Nathaniel*, b 1775, m Susan Baldwin; 239 *Lucretia*, b 1780, d Nov. 14, 1844; 240 *Apollos*, b 1786, settled at Cattskill, N. Y.; 241 *Thomas Burrage;* 242 *Elizabeth*, b 1776, m Joshua Atwater, she d Apr. 4, 1842, æ. 66 years; 243 *Lydia*, m Doct. Amos G. Hull; 244 *Henrietta.*

95. CHARLES.

CHARLES COOK, son of Moses and Sarah Cook, married Sybil Munson, Aug. 1, 1764. He resided severally in New Haven, Waterbury and Watertown, Conn. He died in 1797, æ. 55 years.

Children: 245 *James Munson*, b June 11, 1765, in New Haven; 246 *Sarah*, b Dec. 22, 1766.

96. MOSES.

MOSES COOK, son of Moses and Sarah Cook, married Jemima Upson of Waterbury, March 4, 1766. He was a musician during the Revolutionary war. He died Dec. 25, 1831. She died March 6, 1821.

Children: 247 *Joseph*, b March 4, 1767; 248 *Lucy*, b Sept. 29, 1769, d unmarried, Dec. 8, 1835; 249 *Daniel*, b Sept. 5, 1773; 250 *Hannah*, b March 5, 1775, m Horatio Upson, Waterbury; 251 *Anna*, b March 8, 1778, m Mark Leavenworth; 252 *Elias*, b Dec. 26, 1783, m 2nd, Mrs. Charry Bartholomew.

102. SAMUEL.

SAMUEL COOK, son of Asaph and Sarah Parker Cook, m Chloe Atwater, daughter of Titus and Margarette, of Cheshire. He went with his father to Granville, Mass., and subsequently to Granville, Washington Co., N. Y. He died in 1823, æ. 79 years.

Child: 253 *Moses*, settled at Hartford, Washington Co., N. Y.

104. ASAPH.

ASAPH COOK, son of Asaph and Sarah Parker Cook, married Thankful Parker, June 17, 1776; she was born in Wallingford, April, 1776. They removed to Granville, N. Y. In 1818 they went to Ridgefield, Four Corners, Ohio, where he died in 1826, æ. 78. He was at the battle of Lexington, Mass., as were several of his brothers. His widow died in 1819.

Children: 254 *Elutheras*, b March 21, 1777, d Nov., 1780; 255 *Hannah*, b Feb. 25, 1779, m Lewis Stone, Aug. 3, 1839; 256 *Asaph*, b March 23, 1781, d August 2, 1842; 257 *Rhoda*, b January 7, 1784, d Sept. 30, 1805; 258 *Chloe*, b July 21, 1786, d Oct., 1845; 259 *Elutheras*, b Dec. 25, 1787, d Dec. 27, 1864; 260 *Sarah*, b Jan. 2, 1790, d March, 1829; 261 *Thankful P.*, b April 26, 1792, d unmarried, Aug. 3, 1858; 262 *Erastus*, b Feb. 6, 1795, d July 30, 1849; 263 *Edwin*, b Aug. 25, 1797, d Nov. 3, 1807; 264 *Israel*, b Dec. 4, 1801, d unmarried, Jan. 6, 1854; 265 *Elmira*, b Oct. 15, 1803, d unmarried, Jan. 10, 1852.

105. JOSEPH.

JOSEPH COOK, son of Asaph and Sarah Parker Cook, went early in life with his father and family to Granville, N. Y.;

thence to Hartford, Washington Co., N. Y.; and in 1803 to Adams, Jefferson Co., N. Y.; from there in 1805 to live with his sons in Ohio. He died at Oxford, Erie Co., Ohio, æ nearly 86 yrs. The name of his wife was Rachel Langdon. I have ascertained the names of only two of their children, to wit:

266 *Chauncey*, b 1775, resided in Erie Co., Ohio; 267 *Charles L.*, b 1778.

110. CHARLES.

CHARLES COOK, son of Asaph and Sarah Parker Cook, married Elizabeth Curtis of Granville, N. Y., daughter of David Curtis; he died at Sackett's Harbor, N. Y., May 13, 1855, æ. 91 yrs.

Children: 268 *Betsey*, b Feb. 4, 1791, m Rev. E. Rossiter, she died Nov., 1833; 269 *Daniel C.*, b May 20, 1793, d 1813, was a physician; 270 *Horace*, b Nov. 5, 1775; 271 *Charles*, b May 12, 1778; 272 *Elisha*, b April 12, 1801; 273 *Thecla Louisa*, b Nov. 10, 1802, m B. F. Darrow, 1831, d 1832; 274 *Laura E.*, b Sept. 10, 1804, m Ephraim Read, settled in Ohio; 275 *Hiram E.*, b Jan. 15, 1807, d Aug., 1822, was a physician.

112. AMOS.

AMOS COOK, son of Isaac and Jerusha Cook, married Rhoda, daughter of Gideon Hosford, Feb. 23, 1757; she died May 10, 1810. He died at Wallingford.

Children: 276 *Elihu*, b April 25, 1757; 277 *Rhoda*, b April 16, 1761, m John Davis; 278 *Roswell*, b Dec. 6, 1764; 279 *Uri H.*, b Jan. 19, 1767, supposed to have settled in Norway, Herkimer Co., N. Y., 1789; 280 *Amos*, b Nov. 29, 1768; 281 *Lucinda*, b Oct. 31, 1771, m Stephen Hart in 1790; 282 *Sybil*, b Oct. 10, 1778, m Thomas Welton, Jan. 3, 1797; 283 *Lyman*, b Sept. 21, 1780; 284 *Desire*, b March 5, 1783.

114. ISAAC.

Col. ISAAC COOK, son of Isaac and Jerusha Cook, married Martha, daughter of Benjamin Cook, March 6, 1760; he was in the service of his country during the Revolution, as Colonel. He died June, 1810, æ. 71 yrs.

Children: 285 *Joel*, b Oct. 12, 1760, a distinguished officer in the war of 1812; 286 *Lemuel*, b March 17, 1762; 287 *James*, b Jan 29, 1764, m Chloe Royce, May 4, 1786; 288 *Lucy*, b Jan. 29, 1766; 289 *Isaac*, b July 16, 1768, settled at Chillicothe, Ohio; 260 *Martha*, b June 30, 1770; 291 *Mindwell*, b July 17, 1772, m Asahel Barham, Jan. 6, 1791; 292 *Phebe*, b Feb. 9, 1777, m David Stocking, 1805.

115. CALEB.

Caleb Cook Esq., son of Isaac and Jerusha Cook, married Abigail Finch, Jan. 12, 1764. She died Dec. 22, 1794. He then married Mrs. Lydia Foot. She died May 31, æ. 89. He was a magistrate for many years, and died in his native town, Nov. 17, 1821, æ. 80 years.

Children: 293 *Viney*, b Nov. 26, 1764, m Abel Cook, Dec. 19, 1790; 294 *Augustus*, b Jan. 25, 1767; 295 *Caleb*, b July 27, 1768, d young; 296 *Abigail*, b Nov. 8, 1769; 297 *Nabby*, b April 10, 1777, m Ira Hall, she d 1859; 298 *Betsey*, b Feb. 18, 1779, d unmarried, Jan., 1859; 299 *Mary Ann*, b Aug. 23, 1783; 300, 301, *Caleb* and *Amelia*, b June 4, 1786, the former m Sarah Eaton, the latter d Aug. 31, 1786.

118. AMBROSE.

Ambrose Cook, son of Isaac and Jerusha Cook, married Esther Peck. He died at the age of 78, March 5, 1824. She died Sept. 13, 1822, æ. 78.

Children: 302 *Chauncey*, b Feb. 1, 1767, m Eunice Dutton; 303 *Samuel*, b July 8, 1769, m Martha Cook; 304 *Jerusha*, b April 25, 1771, m Hunn Munson, Esq.; 305 *Abigail*, b Apr. 9, 1773, supposed died young; 306 *Charles*, b April 26, 1775, m Sylvia, dau. of Elihu Yale; 307 *Esther*, b Oct. 9, 1777, m Benajah, son of Stephen Yale; 308 *Lydia*, b Oct. 13, 1779, m Andrew Hall, M. D.; 309 *Nancy*, b Nov. 13, 1782, m Richard Hall; 310 *Orrin*, b Feb. 14, 1784, m Miss —— Stone, of Guilford, Conn.; 311 *Diana*, b Nov. 28, 1786, m Andrew Bartholomew.

121. BENJAMIN.

BENJAMIN COOK, son of Benjamin and Hannah Cook, married April 19, 1770, Esther Rice, dau. of Reuben Rice of Wallingford. He died 1821, ae. 78 years. He was a large, corpulent man.

Children: 312 *Hannah*, m Linus Hall; 313 *Rice*, went west, m a Miss Twiss; 314 *Keziah*, b Jan. 27, 1774; 315 *Munson*, b Aug. 27, 1776; 316 *Daniel*, d about 1860, in western New York; 317 *Betsey*, d unmarried; 318 *Charlotte*, b Oct. 26, 1787, m John Malone.

124. MERRIMAN.

MERRIMAN COOK, son of Benjamin and Hannah Cook, m Mary Osborn, May 2, 1768. He went to Malta, Saratoga Co., N. Y. He died Sept. 27, 1827, ae. 80, and she died May 20, 1832, ae. 83 years.

Children: 319 *Joseph*, b Sept. 1, 1768, m Mary Ann Tolman; 320 *Eunice*, b Dec., 1770, m John Scarrit; 321 *Lydia*, b 1773, m Benj. Hall, d Nov. 8, 1856; 322 *Polly*, b March, 1775, m Samuel Hall; 323 *Elihu*, b May 1, 1777, m Sarah Cooley; 324 *Susannah*, b May 9, 1779, m Isaac Darrow; 325 *Lois*, b May 27, 1782, m Amy Hulin; 325 1-2 *Samuel*, m 1st, Mary Culver, 2d, Sally Galpin; 326 *Lyman*, b Sept. 16, 1783; 327 *Catharine*, b 1786, d 1796; 328 *Marcus*, b 1789; 329 *Sherlock*, b 1781, m Milly Thurston.

128. AMASA.

AMASA COOK, son of Daniel and Elizabeth Cook, married (after his removal to Goshen) Rachel Norton, March 5, 1772. She died Dec. 17, 1819. He died Dec. 4, 1821, æ. 72 years.

Children: 330 *Sally*, b Dec. 28, 1772, m Samuel Chamberlain, she d Aug. 1, 1828; 331 infant, b Oct. 28, 1774, d same day.

129. PHILIP.

PHILIP COOK, son of Daniel and Elizabeth Cook, married Thankful Tuttle, of Goshen, Conn. He removed to Nassau,

N. Y., where she died Jan. 9, 1816, ae. 64. He died March 26, 1825, ae. 73 years.

Children: 332 *Samuel*, b March 4, 1776; 333 *Augustus*, b Jan. 25, 1778, deaf and dumb, d 1843; 334 *Erastus*, b Dec 18, 1779; 335 *Silas*, b Nov. 22, 1781, d Aug. 24, 1811; 336 *Gratia T.*, b Oct. 27, 1784, d unm. Oct. 4, 1840; 337 *Laura H.*, b Jan. 4, 1787, m Samuel McLellan, M. D.

132. DANIEL.

DANIEL COOK, son of Daniel and Elizabeth Cook, married Eliza Porter, of Goshen. He died near the south-west corner of the town.

Children: 338 *Amasa*, he was killed by a cart, 1817; 339 *Phineas*, m Irene Churchill.

133. MOSES.

MOSES COOK, son of Daniel and Elizabeth Cook, married Lydia Thompson. She died Jan. 21, 1821, æ. 72 years. He died Feb. 23, 1841, ae. 77 years.

Children: 340 *George*, b July 24, 1791; 341 *Harriet*, b May 25, 1794, m Samuel Cook; 342 *Betsey*, b March 6, 1797; 343 *Frederick*, b Nov. 9, 1801; 344 *Moses*, b March 2, 1808.

151. BENJAMIN.

BENJAMIN, son of John and Naomi Cook, married Charity Elliott, of Guildhall, Vt. He died May, 1843.

Children: 345 *Elias*, b Sept. 29, 1798; 346 *Naomi*, b May 25, 1800, d unm. June 15, 1818; 347 *Benjamin*, b April 17, 1802; 348 *Charity*, b April 8, 1804, d unm. April, 1820; 349 *Ira*, b Feb. 23, 1806; 350 *Abigail*, b Sept. 16, 1808; 351 *Esther*, b Feb. 12, 1811, m Isaac Brooks; 352 *Anderson*, b March 30, 1813, m Catherine M. Cramer; 353 *Selina*, b April 7, 1816, m Frederick Rich, of Petersham; 354 *Lorenzo*, b April 15, 1819, d unm. June 6, 1855; 355 *Semantha*, b June 18, 1822, m Marshall Twitchell, d Dec. 1, 1854.

155. LEMUEL.

LEMUEL COOK, son of John and Naomi Cook, married Hannah Gustin, and settled at Guildhall, Vt. She died June 1, 1828.

Children: 356 *Thomas*, b May 7, 1802, d at the west; 357 *Mary*, b Aug 6, 1805, m ——— Cheney, May 1, 1831; 358 *Beulah*, b Dec. 22, 1808, m 1831, d June 8, 1846; 359 *Dr. Raphael*, b May 5, 1810, d Aug., 1834, ae. 24 yrs; 360 *Rebecca*, b March 31, 1813, d Feb. 5, 1831, at Guildhall, Vt.; 361 *Lemuel*, b Nov. 20, 1817, d Feb. 12, 1855, ae. 38 yrs; 362 *Adelphia*, b Jan. 13, 1824, m Dec., 1855.

156. ENOS.

ENOS A. COOK, son of John and Naomi Cook, m Susan Palmer, at Granby, Vt. After his decease she went to New Portage, Ohio, with her children, of which the following are a part, viz.:

363 *Raphael*, d in Vermont; 364 *Enos A.*, residence unknown; 365 *Orrin*, m Harriet Cook; 366 *Ambrose*, residence in 1862, Spencer, Medina Co., Ohio.

157. RAPHAEL.

RAPHAEL COOK, son of John and Naomi Cook, m Sally Fox, of Canada. He died at Guildhall, Vt. His widow m Eli Howe, of Guildhall.

Children: 367 *Moses M.*, is a printer by profession; 368 *Naomi*, went to Stanstead, Canada East.

161. ZACCHEUS.

ZACCHEUS COOK, son of John and Naomi Cook, of Wallingford and Guildhall, married Phebe Elliot, and settled at Dryden, N. Y., and probably died there.

Children: 366 *John*, resided at Guildhall, Vt.; 370 *Harriet*, m Orrin Cook, son of Enos.

169. RICE.

RICE COOK, son of Ashbel and Rachel Cook, was born at Rutland, Vt., removed to Stillwater, N. Y. Married Ann ——. He lived in Troy, N. Y., in 1837.

Children: 371 *Mary Ann*; 372 *Sarah Ann*; 373 *Rachel*; 374 *Rebecca*; 375 *Lydia Lorraine*; 376 *Adeline Ann*; 377 *Chas. Rice*, b Aug. 14, 1820, in Stillwater; 378 *Julia Ann*.

177. MERRIMAN.

MERRIMAN COOK, son of Elam and Abigail Hall Cook, m Sally, daughter of Moses and Mary Bradley, Aug. 8, 1781. She died April 11, 1812. He married Betsey Hubbard, May 2, 1815; she died May 7, 1837. He left Cheshire, his native place, in 1809, and settled at Burton, Ohio, where he died Aug. 25, 1858. Betsey, his wife, died May 7, 1857. He was a tanner and currier by trade, shoemaker, &c., &c.

Children: 379 *John*, b Dec. 27, 1782, in Cheshire, Conn.; 380 *Hiram*, b March 21, 1781, in Cheshire, Conn.; 381 *Soalma*, b Feb. 24, 1792, m Adolphus Carlton; 382 *Eleazer*, b Aug. 30, 1799, in Cheshire, Conn.

178. SAMUEL.

SAMUEL COOK, son of Elam and Abigail Cook, married Sue, daughter of Aaron and Mary Cook; he died Oct. 10, 1800, ae. 37; she died Dec. 24, 1843.

Children: 383 *Clara*, b May 12, 1784, m Bellina Plum of Cheshire, she died Oct. 28, 1848; 384 *Samuel*, b 1786; 385 *Samanda*, b Nov. 6, 1788, m Silas Curtis, Dec., 1806.

180. EPHRAIM.

EPHRAIM COOK, son of Elam and Abigail Cook, married Sukey, daughter of Stephen and Susan Ives of North Haven, Oct. 16, 1799; he removed to Burton, Ohio, in 1814, and died there Jan. 29, 1854; she died Dec. 29, 1843.

Children: 286 *Stephen I. C.*, b April 6, 1800; 387 *Marietta*, b March 4, 1802, m John Eldridge; 388 *Harriet*, b Sept. 27, 1804, m Oliver Mastick; 389 *Sally*, b June 4, 1807; 390 *Julia Ann*, b June 27, 1809, died Sept. 12, 1809; 391 *Horace*, b Sept. 11, 1811; 392 *Esther E.*, b Oct. 12 1813, m Asa Carl; 393 *Samuel*, b Dec. 1, 1815, d June 25, 1816; 394 *Lavinia*, b Aug. 11, 1819, d June 24, 1850.

181. ELAM.

ELAM COOK, son of Elam and Abigail Cook, married Rebecca Bradley, Oct. 20, 1799. She died Nov 9, 1829, ae. 51 years. He died March 17, 1830, ae. 51 years.

Children: 395 *Marius*, b July 19, 1800, d Aug. 2, 1804; 396 *Ethelbert*, b Oct. 30, 1801; 397 *Mariah*, b May 28, 1804, m Allen Lounsbury; 398 *Abigail*, b Aug. 29, 1806, m Perez Sanford of Prospect; 399 *Rebecca*, b March 7, 1809, m Orrin Brooks, Meriden; 400 *Emeline*, b Sept. 17, 1811, m Charles R. Miles, Cheshire; 401 *Elam*, b Aug. 15, 1815.

182. JOSEPH.

JOSEPH H. COOK, son of Elam and Abigail Cook, married Lucinda Hitchcock of Cheshire, in 1794. They went to Sharon, Conn., and from thence to Litchfield, Ohio.

Children: 402 *Matilda*, m Rev. Gad Smith; 403 *Lucius*, m Cornelia Sturges.

187. SAMUEL.

SAMUEL COOK, son of Thaddeus and Sarah Cook, married Mary, daughter of Constant Kirtland of Wallingford. He was a thrifty farmer in the western part of the town. He died Sept. 27, 1824, ae. 66. His widow died March 10, 1839, ae. 82 years.

Children: 404 *Russel*, b Sept. 8, 1778, m —— Hall of Cheshire; 405 *Eunice*, b Aug. 24, 1780, m Elias Ford Esq., late of Naugatuck; 406 *Billious*, b Sept. 29, 1782, m Sarah Munson of Wallingford; 407 *Harriet*, b May 17, 1785, m Ira Yale Esq., of Wallingford; 408 *Turhand K.*, b 1787, m Catharine Van Bryan of Catskill; 409 *Samuel*, b Feb. 28, 1788, m Martha Culver of Wallingford; 410 *Thaddeus*, b April 3, 1791, m 1st, Julia Cook, 2d, Sylvia Hall, 3d, Thankful Hall, 4th, Martha Hall; 411 *George*, b April 17, 1794, m Lavinia Culver of Wallingford; 412 *Friend*, b Nov. 1. 1797, m Emily Atwater of Wallingford; 413 *John*, b Dec. 2, 1799, m Mary Munson of Northford.

196. PEREZ.

PEREZ Cook, son of Samuel and Jerusha Cook, married Nancy E. Ely of Saybrook. He died July 23, 1820, ae. 57 years. She married Calvin Ely, and died in New Haven.

Children: 414 *Samuel D. F. S.*, d Jan. 20, 1820; 415 *Virgilius G.*, d in New Haven, Ct.; 416 *Louisa F. S.*, m

Augustus Barnes at New Haven; 417 *Nancy Ely*, m Dr. Miller, she died in 1850.

202. CORNELIUS.

CORNELIUS BROOKS COOK, son of Aaron and Mary (Brooks) Cook, married Louisa Hotchkiss of Cheshire. He died Sept. 1, 1827, ae. 64 years. She died Aug. 4, 1832, ae. 67 years.

Children: 418 *Rufus*, b 1790; 419 *Charlotte*, m 1st, Elam Dickerman, 2nd, Mr. Platt; 420, *Brooks*, b 1798; 421 *Polly*, m Asa Bradley of Hamden.

204. AARON.

AARON COOK, son of Aaron and Mary B. Cook, married Betsey Preston of Wallingford. He died July 16, 1817, ae. 44 years. She died March 26, 1820, ae. 52 years.

Children: 422 *Amasa*, b 1791, d unmarried Dec. 18, 1831; 423 *Hannah*; 424 *Aaron*; 425 *Laura*, m Marshall Ives of Cheshire; 426 *Alfred*; 427 infant, b 1806, d April 23, 1806; 428 *Betsey*, b 1808, d April 6, 1808; 429 *Sedgwick*, d in Windham, N. Y., leaving a family; 430 *Stephen*, d in Cheshire; 431 *Samuel*, b Dec., 1816, d Jan. 29, 1816; 432 infant, d March 14, 1834.

205. STEPHEN.

STEPHEN COOK, son of Aaron and Mary Brooks Cook, married Eunice, daughter of John Bradley, of Wallingford. He died Sept. 4, 1800, ae. 29. She died Oct. 18, 1800, ae. 27 years.

Children: 433 *Sarah*, b 1793, d unmarried; 434 *Julia*, b 1794, m Thaddeus Cook of Wallingford; 435 *Mary*, m 1st, Merrit Tuttle, 2d, Wm. Todd, Jr.; 436 *Stephen*, b June 11, 1800, d in Mass., buried in North Haven.

207. SAMUEL.

SAMUEL COOK, son of Stephen and Anna (Culver) Cook, m —— Smith, and after her death he married Abigail Mallory of East Haven. She died Nov. 4, 1851, aged 91. He died May 12, 1823, ae. 71 years.

Child by 1st marriage: 437 *Rachel.* By 2d marriage: 438 *Lowly*, b May 18, 1782, m Amos Bird, Dec. 13, 1797; 439 *Electa*, b Jan. 11, 1785, m Canfield Downs, Oct., 1822; 440 *Hubbard*, b Aug. 26, 1787, in Wallingford; 441 *Roxanna*, b May 10, 1788, m Newton Hecock, 1814; 442 *Stephen*, b 1790, d ae. 3 yrs.; 443 *Perlina*, b May, 1795, d 1813; 444 *Harriet*, b Dec. 25, 1797, m Samuel Washburn; 445 *Ruth*, b 1802, d May 16, 1826; 446 *Charry*, b 1804, d 1808.

208. STEPHEN.

STEPHEN COOK, son of Capt. Stephen and Anna Cook, m Sylvia Meigs, April 20, 1777. She was born in New Haven, May 27, 1760, and died at Adams' Basin, N. Y., Sept. 7, 1849, ae. 90. He died at Chateaugay, N. Y., Aug. 28, 1829, ae. 75 years.

Children: 447 *Chauncey*, b March 9, 1778, resides in Ottawa, Illinois; 448 *Solomon*, b April 1, 1780, resides in Grand Rapids; 449 *Betsey*, b Sept. 10, 1782, d August 2, 1800; 450 *Rebecca*, b August 2, 1785, d August 7, 1825; 451 *Sylvia*, b Feb. 3, 1788, m J. Morton of Erie, Penn.; 452 *Sally*, b June 5, 1790, m S. M. Moon of ——, N. Y.; 453 *Patty*, b Feb. 5, 1793, resides near Rochester, N. Y., a widow; 454 *Stephen*, b March 15, 1796, res. at Oberlin, Ohio; 455 *Anna*, b Feb. 1, 1799, res. at Plattsburg, N. Y.; 456 *Betsey*, b July 13, 1802, m C. D. Graves, Rochester, N. Y.; 457 *Lyman*, b Mar. 20, 1804, res. at Rochester, N. Y.; 458 *Nelson*, b Sept. 24, 1806, res. at Half Day, Illinois.

210. ELIHU.

ELIHU COOK, son of Stephen and Anna Cook, married Lois Thorp, and removed to New Haven, Vt., afterwards to Illinois. One son only returned to me.

Child: 458 1-2 *Sherlock.*

212. LYMAN.

Dr. LYMAN COOK, son of Stephen and Thankful Cook, m Sarah Lyon, and went to Westchester Co., N. Y. He was aid to Gen. Thomas with rank of Colonel in 1807, and also sheriff of the county of Westchester six years. He died at Painesville, Ohio.

Child: 459 *Caroline*, b Sept. 6, 1797, m Stephen Matthews of Painesville, Ohio, Aug. 11, 1824.

213. JARED.

MAJ. JARED COOK, son of Stephen and Thankful Cook, married Lucy Munson, Feb. 28, 1819. He died Aug. 14, 1828, ae. 53 years. She was burned to death in 1869.

Children: 460 *George Lambert*, b Nov. 21, 1819, d Jan. 2, 1820; 461 *Jared Philos*, b Feb. 1, 1822.

214. LEMUEL.

LEMUEL COOK, son of Stephen and Anna Tyler Cook, married Mrs. Hannah Sears, formerly Bunnel, in 1813. He married, 2nd, Sinai Bunnel, in 1825. He died Sept. 3, 1841, æ. 62, at Northford.

Child: 462 *Augustine*, b 1814, m S. B. Hoadley of New Haven.

215. MALACHI.

MALACHI COOK Esq., son of Stephen and Anna Cook, married Sarah Taintor, Dec. 25, 1802; he died May 27, 1858, æ. 77 yrs. She died Nov. 9, 1852, æ. 69 yrs. He was a side judge of New Haven County Court for several years.

Children: 463 *Emily Cecilia*, b April 21, 1803, m Thomas R. Lindsley; 464 *Homer L. M.*, b April 3, 1805; 465 *Virgil*, b June 22, 1808; 466 *Ossian*, b Nov. 19, 1810; 467 *Hermine C.*, b June 4, 1813, m Gilbert Buck; 468 *Grace T.*, b Sept. 16, 1815; 469 *Henrietta A.*, b Sept. 3, 1817, m George Butler; 470 *Ellen*, b Oct. 21, 1819, m Alexander Brainard; 471 *Sarah Delia*, b Jan. 19, 1823; 472 *Harriet E.*, b Oct. 23, 1827, m Bennet Atwood.

224. TITUS.

TITUS COOK, son of Titus and Sarah Cook, m Lucy Leete of Guilford, Conn.; he died in Wallingford.

Children: 473 *Julia*, m George Bull of Wallingford; 474 *Lucretia*, m ——— Weber of Wallingford; 475 *Jared R.*;

476 *Leverett*, resides in Meriden, m ——— Hotchkiss of Cheshire; 477 *Andrew*; 478 *Louisa*, m Henry Lane.

226. ATWATER.

ATWATER COOK, son of Abel and Mary Atwater Cook, m Mary Bartholomew. He went to Sheffield, Mass.; from thence to Salisbury, Herkimer Co., N. Y., where he died, June 29, 1839, æ. 80 yrs. She died July 2, 1844, ae. 86 yrs.

Children: 479 *Roxilana*, b Sept. 25, 1777, d Sept. 15, 1852; 480 *Rosanna*, b April 14, 1782; 481 *Mary*, b April 3, 1784, d Jan. 13, 1853; 482 *Thaddeus R.*, b July 23, 1786; 483 *Julia*, b July 23, 1788; 484 *Friend*, b Jan. 27, 1792; 485 *Atwater H. W.*, b Dec. 17, 1795, d Feb. 4, 1853; 486 *Betsey*, b April 19, 1798; 487 *Abel*, b Sept. 27, 1801, d ae. 21 yrs; 488 *Delia*, b Sept. 4, 1806.

227. PORTER.

PORTER COOK, son of Abel and Mary Cook, married Sally Jarvis, in 1785; he died Dec. 26, 1848, ae. 89. She died Oct. 31, 1841, ae. 81 yrs.

Children: 489 *Alfred*, b Feb 5, 1786; 490 *Merrick*, b May 18, 1788; 491 *Randall*, b July 19, 1790; 492 *Philo*, b Sept. 30, 1792; 493 *Sally*, b Feb. 22, 1795, d in Ohio; 494 *Franklin*, b April 1, 1797, d in Wallingford.

229. ABEL.

ABEL COOK, son of Abel and Mary Cook, married Mamre Bliss; she died Dec. 19, 1790. He died May 23, 1828, æ. 63 years. His 2d wife, Viney Cook, died Dec. 28, 1848, ae. 83 years, all buried in Northford cemetery.

Children by 1st marriage: 495 *Bliss*, b April 25, 1787, d April 28, 1823, ae. 36. By 2d marriage: 496 *Leverett*, b Jan. 3, 1794; 497 *Cornelia*, b Feb. 21, 1797, m Wm. Everts, of Northford; 498 *Marietta*, b Sept. 8, 1799, m Timothy Bartholomew; 499 *Emily*, b July 23, 1802, m Chas. M. Fowler; 500 *Philander*, b Oct. 13, 1804; 501 *Jennette*, b May 5, 1807, d Nov. 12, 1832.

233. CHESTER.

CHESTER COOK, son of Abel and Mary Cook, married 1st,

Thankful Hall, of Wallingford; 2d, Polly Norton, widow of Jesse Street. Mr. Cook was a farmer and shoemaker.

Children by 1st marriage: 502 *Caroline*, b Sept. 5, 1801, m Orrin Andrews, of Wallingford; 503 *Marilla*, b Nov. 17, 1803, m Sherlock Avery, of Wallingford; 504 *Hiram*, b April 27, 1805, m —— Marks.

231. DAVID.

CAPT. DAVID M. COOK, son of Abel and Mary Cook, married Elizabeth Day Hall; she died Dec., 1855. He died 1857, ae. 91 years. He was frequently a member of the Legislature of the State, and selectman of the town. He was a farmer and shoemaker.

Children: 505 *Betsey*, b May, 1797, m Philo Hall, she d 1858; 506 *Eliakim*, b Nov. 8, 1801, d in childhood; 507 *Elijah*, b Nov. 28, 1804, d in childhood; 508 *Maria*, b June 23, 1805, m Willis Todd, and d in Northford.

234. OLIVER.

OLIVER DUDLEY COOK, son of Aaron and Lucretia Dudley Cook, graduated for the ministry at Yale College, in 1793. He married Sophia Pratt, and settled in Hartford, Conn., where he became an extensive bookseller and binder, accumulated a very large estate, and died April 24, 1833, ae. 67 years. His wife died March 20, 1833, ae 58 years.

Children: 509 *Edward P.*, b 1800, d Sept. 18, 1846; 510 *Oliver D.*, d Oct. 24, 1831; 511 a dau., m Wm. Hammersley.

236. KILBORN.

KILBORN COOK, son of Aaron and Lucretia Dudley Cook, m Emma Williams; she was born March 8, 1771, and died in Illinois, in 1835. He died suddenly at North Guilford, June 9, 1832.

Children: 512 *Eunice*, b Sept. 29, 1796, m Abram Coan, she d May 28, 1859; 513 *Margaretta*, b Dec. 30, 1798, d June 3, 1834; 514 *Aaron Dudley*, resides in Illinois; 515 *Bertha*, m Nath'l Bartlett; 516 *Lucretia Ann*, m Erastus Benton; 517 *Increase W.*, b Feb., 1807, d 1847; 518 *Caroline Jenette*, m Erastus Benton.

240. APOLLOS.

Apollos Cook, son of Aaron and Lucretia D. Cook, married Ruth, daughter of Capt. Caleb Atwater, of Wallingford, Nov. 22, 1813, and settled at Catskill, N. Y. He died July 6, 1832, æ, 46 years.

Children: 519 *Mary A.*, b Dec. 5, 1814, m George Griffing, May 20, 1845; 520 *James*, b July 4, 1817, d Jan. 6, 1842; 521 *Frederick*, b March 19, 1819; 522 *Caroline E.*, b April 5, 1821, m Rev. Frank Olmsted; 523 *John A.*, b Oct. 23, 1823; 524 *Emily H.*, b Feb. 25, 1826; 525 *Edward H.*, b June 24, 1828, d May 28, 1835; 526 *Francis H.*, b March 16, 1831.

241. THOMAS.

Thomas B. Cook, son of Aaron and Lucretia (Dudley) Cook, m Catherine, dau. of Capt. Caleb Atwater, and went to Catskill, N. Y., where he died.

Children: 527 *Frances H.*; 528 *Mary A.*; 529 *Ruth A.*; 530 *John C.*; 531 *Franklin H.*; 532 *Atwater*.

247. JOSEPH.

Joseph Cook, son of Moses and Jemima Upson, married Anna Bronson, Aug. 1, 1792. She was born Dec. 25, 1770, and died Nov. 25, 1855. He died Nov. 26, 1855, æ. 87 yrs., just 10 hours before his wife died.

Children: 533 *Edward B.*, b March 18, 1793; 534 *Samuel*, b Dec. 12, 1794; 535 *Susan J.*, b Oct 25, 1797, m Mark Leavenworth, Dec. 16, 1821; 536 *Sarah L.*, b Oct. 29, 1799, m Salome Austin of Southington; 537 *Nancy*, b Nov. 16, 1801, m Wm. Scoville of Middletown, 1828; 538 *Nathan*, b Jan., 1804; 539 *George*, b April 8, 1806, d July 19, 1815; 540 *George William*, b Feb. 28, 1811.

249. DANIEL.

Daniel Cook, son of Moses and Jemima Cook, married Sally Sperry, of Waterbury, Nov. 25, 1799. He died Dec. 20, 1857, æ. 85 years. She died Nov. 13, 1861, æ. 83 years.

Children: 541 *Marcus*, b Sept. 12, 1800, d Feb. 9, 1831;

542 *Sarah P.*, b Aug. 1, 1804, m Thomas B. Segur, in 1826; 543 *Moses Stiles*, b 1812, resides in Waterbury, Conn.

259. ELUTHEROS.

ELUTHEROS COOK, son of Asaph and Sarah Parker Cook, married Martha Caswell, of Salem, Washington Co., N. Y. He was a lawyer in Washington Co., N. Y., before his removal to Sandusky, Ohio. He was frequently a member of the Ohio Legislature, and was a member of Congress from 1831 to 1833. He died at Sandusky, Ohio, Dec. 27, 1864.

Children: 544 *Sarah E.*, b Jan. 16, 1816, m Wm Morehead; 545 *Pitt*, b July 23, 1819; 546 *Jay*, b Aug. 10, 1821, banker in Philadelphia; 547 *Henry D.*, b Nov. 25, 1825; 548 *Elutheros*, b Dec. 20, 1828, d Oct., 1850, æ. 22; 549 *Catherine E.*, b Sept. 15, 1831, d Oct., 1834, æ. 3.

262. ERASTUS.

ERASTUS COOK, son of Asaph and Sarah P. Cook, married Fanny Anderson, Nov. 10, 1826. He went to Sandusky City, Ohio, and was postmaster there from 1836–41. He died in 1849.

Children: 550 *James W.*, b 1830; 551 *George A.*, b 1840; 552 *Emma E.*, b 1843; they all resided in Sandusky.

270. HORACE.

HORACE COOK, son of Charles and Elizabeth Cook, married Roxanna Thomas, Dec. 20, 1824, and located himself at Sackett's Harbor, Jefferson Co., N. Y.

Children: 553 *Horace Nelson*, b Oct. 26, 1825, d Sept. 17, 1848, æ. 23; 554 *John Spafford*, b June 15, 1828.

271. CHARLES.

CHARLES COOK, son of Charles and Elizabeth Cook, married Harriet Cunningham, and resided at Roberts Corners, N. Y.

Children: 555 *Elizabeth;* 556 *Charles;* 557 *Curtis;* 558 *Harriet.*

272. ELISHA.

ELISHA COOK, son of Charles and Elizabeth Cook, removed from Sackett's Harbor to Huron Co., Ohio., where he died in 1852, æ. 51 years.

Children: 559 *Elizabeth*, b 1835; 560 *Charles*, b 1838, d Feb., 1853; 561 *Elisha*, b 1840.

280 AMOS.

AMOS COOK, son of Amos and Rhoda Cook, married Sabrina Mix.

Children: 562 *Amos*; 563 *Rhoda*; 564 *Orrin*.

283. LYMAN.

LYMAN COOK, son of Amos and Rhoda Cook, married, and left Wallingford in early life.

Children: 565 *Lyman W.*; 566 *Sidney H.*

285. JOEL.

Capt. JOEL COOK, son of Col. Isaac and Martha Cook of Wallingford, m Rebecca Hart, Jan. 1, 1784. He entered the army of the Revolution with his father in 1776, and served through the war. In 1812 he was a distinguished officer under Gen. Harrison, in many hard fought battles with the Indians. He died at (Deer Park) Babylon, L. I., Dec. 18, 1851, ae. 92 years.

Children: 567 *Lucy*, b April 5, 1785, m James Calstead, July 22, 1804; 568 *Minerva*, b June 18, 1789; 569 *Leander*, b March 10, 1792, d at Cincinnati, Ohio; 570 *Patty*, b Nov. 27, 1794; 571 *Rebecca*, b April 5, 1798; 572 *Phebe*, b Jan 5, 1801; 573 *Jennette*, b July 8, 1804; 574 *Joel Wilcox*, b April 28, 1808, res. in Babylon, L. I.

286. LEMUEL.

LEMUEL COOK, son of Col. Isaac and Martha Cook, m Betsey Bates in 1784. He removed to Lewiston, Niagara Co., N. Y., in 1793. She died Sept., 1821.

Children: 575 *Lathrop*, b Nov. 23, 1785, in Wallingford; 576 *Bates*, b Dec. 23, 1787; 577 *Laura*, died in infancy in Wallingford; 578 *Laura*, b May 13, 1792, in Wallingford; 579 *Betsey*, b June 30, 1794; 580 *Amelia*, b Sept. 5, 1796; 581 *Isaac C.*, b 1803; 582 *Amanda M.*, b Nov. 6, 1805.

287. JAMES.

JAMES COOK, son of Col. Isaac and Martha Cook, married Chloe Royce, May 4, 1786 He was a seaman, and is supposed to have been lost or died at sea previous to 1813.

Children, all born in Wallingford: 583 *Miles;* 584 *Melissa;* 585 *Angelina;* 586 *Lucinda;* 587 *Chloe;* 588 *Eliza.*

289. ISAAC.

ISAAC COOK Esq., son of Isaac and Martha Cook, married Margaretta Scott, in 1792. He emigrated to Chillicothe, Ohio, in 1791, and was made an associate judge of the court of Common Pleas. He died Jan. 22, 1844.

Children: 589 *Eliza*, b Oct. 21, 1793, d Aug. 3, 1799; 590 *Martha*, b June 23, 1794, d June 24, 1796; 591 *Isaac T*, b March 6, 1797; 592 *Lucy*, b Feb. 11, 1799, d March 28, 1800; 593 *Marietta*, b March 9, 1801, m James Webb, M. D.; 594 *Matthew Scott*, b April 9, 1803; 595 *Elizabeth*, b March 27, 1805, m John Nelson; 596 *William*, b April 18, 1807; 597 *John Joseph*, b May 28, 1809; 598 *Lucy Hall*, b May 25, 1811; 599 *Phebe*, b Aug. 8, 1813, m Wm. McKell, May 26, 1836; 600 *Margaretta Scott*, b April 9, 1817, m Moses Boggs, Aug. 3, 1841.

294. AUGUSTUS.

CAPT. AUGUSTUS COOK, son of Caleb and Abigail Cook, m Sybel Beach, of Goshen, Sept. 2, 1790; she died Sept. 28, 1792, æ. 22 years. He married Sarah Dutton, June 30, 1793; she died April 28, 1854, ae. 80 years. He died at Middletown, Conn., where he had resided many years, April 18, 1866, ae. 79 years. He was a manufacturer of shoes.

Children: 601 *Luther Dutton*, b June 21, 1794; 602 *Sybil B.*, b June 23, 1797, m Wm. R. Catting, and d Oct. 25, 1825; 603 *Margaretta*, b Jan. 12, 1800, m Wm. S. Camp, Esq., of Middletown; 604 *Sarah*, b May 22, 1811, m Samuel Stearns, Esq., of Middletown; 605 *Catharine*, b May 22, 1813, d Sept. 23, 1813; 606 *Catharine*, b Dec. 30, 1814, m Peter Lanman, she d Jan. 4, 1834.

300. CALEB.

CALEB COOK, Esq., son of Caleb and Abigail Cook, m Amelia, daughter of Jared and Rhoda Lewis, Oct. 16, 1808. He left Wallingford and settled at Richland, Oswego Co., N. Y. He died at Sandusky, Ohio, on his return from a visit to his children at the West, in July, 1852, and was buried in the Oakland cemetery. She died at Pulaski, Oswego Co., N. Y., June 8, 1840.

Children: 607 *Louisa C.*, b July 10, 1809, m Rev. Henry Maltby; 608 *Lewis*, b March 15, 1811; 609 *Henry C.*, b Sept. 11, 1813, d at Sidney, Ohio; 610 *Frederick*, b June 11, 1815; 611 *Juliet*, b June 28, 1817, m C. Preston, she d in 1852; 612 *Edward H.*, d ae. 4 yrs.; 613 *Margaretta*, b May 25, 1819, d Oct. 23, 1820; 614 *Augustus*, b Nov. 3, 1823, d Nov 2, 1848; 615 *William C.*, b July 27, 1825, resides in Richland, N. Y.; 616 *Henrietta*, b 1828, d in Wallingford; 617 *Henry Atwater*, b March 1, 1832, d in infancy.

302. CHAUNCEY.

CHAUNCEY COOK, son of Ambrose and Esther Peck Cook, married Eunice Dutton of Wallingford. He kept a tavern in Wallingford and in New Haven for a long time, and died in the latter place Jan. 22, 1827, ae. 60 years. His widow died at the residence of her son Charles C., in Ohio.

Children: 618 *Laura*, b Oct. 25, 1791, m Orrin Winchell, of New Haven; 619 *Charles C.*, b Jan. 22, 1799, is a physician in Ohio; 620 *Chauncey*, b Nov. 30, 1811, d July 6, 1812.

303. SAMUEL.

SAMUEL COOK, son of Ambrose and Esther Cook, m Martha, daughter of Benjamin Cook, Aug. 1, 1792. He died Aug. 30, 1826, aged 57. He was a shoemaker.

Children: 621 *John Milton*, b Feb. 1, 1795; 622 *Martha A.*, b Oct. 25, 1805, m Elihu Hall, Wallingford; 623 *Lucy A.*, b Oct. 25, 1805.

306. CHARLES.

CHARLES COOK, son of Ambrose and Esther P. Cook, m

Sylvia, daughter of Elihu and Lucretia Yale; she died at Wallingford, Feb. 1, 1825. He died at Cuyahoga Falls, Ohio, June, 1845, aged 70 years.

Children: 624 *Otis*, b April 8, 1797, m —— Butler, of Rocky Hill; 625 *Sinai*, b Sept. 17, 1798, m John Miller White, of Middlefield, Conn.; 626 *Peter*, b July 16, 1800; 627, *Thomas*, b Feb. 1, 1802, d in 1862, æ. 60; 628 *Charles*, b Aug. 13, 1804, res. in Hartford, Conn.; 629 *Orrin*, b May 8, 1808, had no family, d at Cuyahoga Falls, Ohio; 630 *Henry*, b Feb. 12, 1810, d 1865–6; 631 *Isaac*, b Aug. 17, 1813, d at St. Jago, Cuba, W. I.

315. MUNSON.

CAPT. MUNSON COOK, son of Benjamin and Esther Rice Cook, married Thankful Austin, Sept. 4, 1796. They went to Middletown, Ct.; afterwards they came to Cheshire, Ct., where she died, Dec. 24, 1853. He died Aug. 18, 1862, æ. 86.

Children: 632 *Samantha*, b Sept. 4, 1797, d May 31, 1819; 633 *Charles B.*, b Sept. 27, 1799, d Jan. 31, 1850; 634 *Betsey*, b July 4, 1801, d Oct. 3, 1820; 635 *Caroline*, b June 8, 1803, d March 9, 1826; 636 *Hobart*, b Aug. 7, 1805, d Oct. 21, 1807; 637 *Hobart M.*, b July 9, 1807; 638 *Emeline*, b May 8, 1809, d March 1, 1826; 639 *Nathan R.*, b Aug. 10, 1811; 640 *Eliza Ann*, b May 1, 1813, m James R. Hall; 641 *Ozias A.*, b Dec. 18, 1814; 642 *Oliver W.*, b March 21, 1817; 643 *Philander*, b July 3, 1819; 644 *Joel*, b Oct. 15, 1820; 645 *Henry H.*, b April 17, 1823, d July 18, 1825.

316. DANIEL.

DANIEL COOK, son of Benjamin and Esther Cook, married 1st, Mary Thorp, June 13, 1799. After her decease he married Catherine Smith, daughter of Stanton Smith, April 22, 1822. He moved to the State of New York and died there in 1860.

Children by 1st marriage: 646 *Phebe*, b Aug. 14, 1801; 647 *Alma R.*, b June 23, 1805; 648 *Maria*, b May 15, 1807; 640 *Elizur*, b Oct. 9, 1810; 650 *Alexander*, b March 11,

1813. By 2d marriage: 651 *Hiram*, b Feb. 20, 1823. By 3d marriage: *John*, is a sailor.

319. JOSEPH.

JOSEPH COOK, son of Merriman and Mary Cook, married Mary A. Talman, Nov. 30, 1774, and went to Saratoga Springs, N. Y., where he was living a few years since, at the age of 94 years. His wife died April 4, 1860, æ. 86 years.

Children: 652 *Ransom*, b Nov. 8, 1794, in Wallingford; 653 *Marcus*, b Nov. 25, 1796, in Norwich, Ct.; 654 *Andrew*, b Jan. 18, 1799, in Norwich, Ct.; 655 *Mary A.*, b Nov. 23, 1800, in Norwich, Ct.; 656 *Harvey*, b April 15, 1803, at Half Moon, Saratoga Co., N. Y.; 657 *Joseph*, b Nov. 1, 1805, d July 1, 1808; 658 *Nelson*, b Oct. 8, 1808, d in Saratoga Co., N. Y.; 659 *Truman*, b Oct. 25, 1810; 660 *Eli*, b July 15, 1814, d. at Milton, N. Y., April 20, 1816; 661 *Julia E.*, b Aug. 14, 1817, res. at Milton, N. Y.

323. ELIHU.

ELIHU COOK, son of Merriman and Mary Cook, married Sarah Cooley, of Wallingford, in 1798. He died in 1855, æ. 79 years. She died several years since. He was a hatter at Ballston, Saratoga Co., N. Y.

Children: 662 *Eliza*, m Mr. Davis; 663 *Harriet*; 664 *Merriman*, supposed to be now living at Syracuse, N. Y.

325 1-2. SAMUEL.

SAMUEL COOK, son of Merriman and Mary Cook, married Mary, dau. of Charles Culver, of Wallingford. She died in 1838. He married Sally Galpin, and resides at Northumberland, Saratoga Co., N. Y.

Children: 665 *Amanda*, m James Van Byring, d 1854; 666 *Lydia*, m Reuben Wait; 667 *Patty*; 668 *James*; 669 *Charles*, d æ. 24 yrs.; 670 *Samuel*, b March 27, 1819; 671 *Alfred*, b 1824. By 2d wife: 672 *Elizabeth*, m R—— B——, in 1830; 673 *George*.

326. LYMAN.

LYMAN COOK, son of Merriman and Mary Cook, married Amy Hulin, and settled at Malta, Saratoga Co., N. Y.

Children: 674 *Alena*, b Jan. 31, 1809, m 1st, Joseph Gorman, Aug. 17, 1826, 2d, Samuel Hall; 675 *Mary E.*, b April 22, 1811, m Oliver Lockwood, July 3, 1832; 676 *Charles H.*, b July 20, 1813; 677 *Delia A.*, b Nov. 26, 1815, m Henry Warring, Jan. 9, 1839; 678 *Edmond*, b May 3, 1818, d Aug 3, 1818; 679 *Lyman W.*, b June 4, 1820; 680 *Betsey M.*, b May 12, 1822, d Nov. 26, 1826; 681 *Edwin D.*, b July 25, 1824; 682 *Henry M.*, b Feb. 18, 1827, d Dec. 26, 1827; 683 *John C.*, b Feb. 21, 1829, d Feb. 10, 1831; 684 *Sarah*, b July 11, 1833.

329. SHERLOCK.

SHERLOCK COOK, son of Merriman and Mary Cook, married Milly Thurston about 1812. They removed to Western, N. Y., and he is supposed to have died there in 1850. Only four of his children are supposed to be living—present residence unknown.

332. SAMUEL.

SAMUEL COOK, son of Philip and Thankful T. Cook, married Fanny Fuller of Sandisfield, Mass., Feb. 20, 1803. They went to Nassau, N. Y., and from thence to Ballston Spa, where he died May 15, 1815. His 2nd wife, Harriet Cook of Goshen, Ct., died April 15, 1828.

Children: 685 *James M.*, b Nov. 19, 1807. By 2d marriage: 686 *Samuel H.*, b July 18, 1823.

334. ERASTUS.

ERASTUS COOK, son of Philip and Thankful T. Cook, married Jerusha Hewins of Richmond, Mass., in 1800. He died at Ashtabula, Ohio, 1850.

Children: 686 *Althea*, b March 18, 1801; 686 1-2 *Maria T.*, b April 19, 1802; 687 *Amanda*, d young; 688 *Silas*; 689 *Joseph*.

338. AMASA.

AMASA COOK, son of Daniel and Eliza Cook, married 1st, Polly Churchill, 2nd, Sally Rowe. He was accidentally killed by a cart, while entering his barn with a load of hay, in 1817.

Child: 690 *Philip*, b in Goshen, Ct.

339. PHINEAS.

PHINEAS COOK, son of Daniel and Eliza Cook, married Irene Churchill, and removed to Michigan in 1836 or 1837.

Children: 691 *Betsey;* 692 *Daniel,* m Mary Kirby; 693 *Eliza,* m Salmon Hall; 694 *Darius,* m Jane Adams; 695 *Mary Ann;* 696 *Plumas;* 697 *Harriet.*

340. GEORGE.

GEORGE COOK, son of Moses and Lydia Cook, married Roxy Grant, of Norfolk. She died Oct. 24, 1841, æ. 47 yrs. He died in 1864.

Children: 698 *Caroline M.,* b June 10, 1818; 699 *Ralph F.,* b May 10, 1821, has resided in New London, and Goshen, Conn.

343. FREDERICK.

FREDERICK COOK, son of Moses and Roxy Cook, married Louisa McKinley of Georgia, in April, 1827, and settled at Lexington, Ga., where he died April 4, 1843.

Child: 700 *Maria Elizabeth,* b Feb. 28, 1828, m Alexander Allen.

344. MOSES.

MOSES COOK, son of Moses and Roxy Cook, married Emily M. Beecher of Goshen. He is an inn-keeper near the center of Goshen.

Children: 701 *Harriet E.,* b Oct. 17, 1832; 702 *Emily,* b May 7, 1834; 703 *Frederick A.,* b Jan. 27, 1838, 1st Lieut. 2nd Conn. Artillery; 704 *Moses,* b March 26, 1842, d 1863, Sergt. of 2nd Comp. Artillery; 705 *William R.,* b July 4, 1852; 706 *George B.,* b May 17, 1855, 1st Lieut. Comp. D, 4th Reg. Conn. volunteers.

345. ELIAS.

ELIAS COOK, son of Benjamin and Charity E Cook of Guildhall, Vt., married Maria Brookins, May 26, 1825. He had been a teacher in various parts of the country; is at this time a resident of Ware, Hocking Co., Ohio.

Children: 707 *Caroline E.,* b March 12, 1826, m Peter

Smith, May 2, 1832; 708 *Martha A.*, b May 10, 1827; 709 *Helen S.*, b May 28, 1829, m Wm. Comstock, June 16, 1849; 710 *Raphael G.*, b Jan. 17, 1832, d Sept., 1833; 711 *Raphael E.*, b June 7, 1833, U. S. Army, 1862; 712 *Cyrus B.*, b Dec. 1, 1834; 713 *Harriet E.*, b Sept. 6, 1836, m James Parden, March, 1857; 714 *Albert F.*, b Sept. 5, 1840; 715 *Emma L.*, b Dec., 1842.

347. BENJAMIN.

BENJAMIN COOK, son of Benjamin and Charity L. Cook, m Betsey ———; residence, Petersham, Mass.

Children; 716 *Harriet S.*, b April 23, 1830, has been twice married; 717 *Sandford B.*, b May 6, 1832; 718 *George O.*, b Oct. 14, 1834; 719 *Charles Elliot*, b Sept. 6, 1836; 720 *Mary Elizabeth*, b April 30, 1839, m Nathan Knowlton.

349. IRA.

IRA COOK, son of Benjamin and Charity E. Cook, married Lucy Clapp, Oct, 3, 1837, and settled at Athol Depot, Mass., as a boot and shoemaker. He married for 2d wife, Sarah Kimball, May 10, 1853. His first wife died March 12, 1852.

Children: 721 *Eliza Jane*, b Sept. 13, 1838, m Samuel Searls, May 7, 1857; 722 *Vernon Stiles*, b April 2, 1841, in U. S. Army, 1862; 723 *Lucy Ellen*, b Dec. 30, 1845, d in 1852. By 2nd marriage: 724 *Sarah Ellen*, b Oct. 18, 1855.

379. JOHN.

JOHN COOK, son of Merriman and Sally Cook of Cheshire, Ct., married Meroa, daughter of Josiah and Thankful Smith of Cheshire, March, 1804. He went to Ohio and settled at Burton in 1806, where he died March 21, 1848.

Children: 725 *Nabby*, b Aug. 16, 1805, d Oct. 23, 1806; 726 *Harriet E.*, b Aug. 20, 1807, m His Excellency Seabury Todd, Esq., of Ohio; 727 *Josiah S.*, b May 10, 1810; 728, *Sally R.*, b Feb. 25, 1815, m Geo. Boughton.

380. HIRAM.

HIRAM COOK, son of Merriman and Sally Cook, of Cheshire, married Lucinda, dau. of Ichabod and Lydia Hitchcock of Cheshire. They removed to Ohio in 1815, and settled in Burton, Ohio.

Children: 729 *Sally A.*, b July 10, 1807, m Raymond Gaylord; 730 *Lydia*, b Aug. 3, 1816, m Sherman Goodwin, M. D.; 731 *Eliza A.*, b Sept. 8, 1818, m Peter Hitchcock, Esq.; 732 *Sarilla*, b Dec. 20, 1827, m Richard Dayton, she d in 1833.

382. ELZAR.

ELZAR COOK, son of Merriman and Sally Cook, married Maria Beard of Huntington, Conn. He went to Ohio in 1807, at the age of eight years.

Child: 733 *Elizabeth*, b March 24, 1830.

384. SAMUEL.

SAMUEL COOK, son of Samuel and Sue Cook of Cheshire, m Esther Curtis, Feb. 17, 1817. He was deputy sheriff for a number of years at Cheshire, where he died Feb. 19, 1859, æ. 68 years.

Children: 734 *Samuel*, died young; 735 *Robert H.*, b Dec. 18, 1823.

386. STEPHEN.

STEPHEN J. C., son of Ephraim and Sukey Cook, married Lucinda Dudley of North Guilford, Conn., Jan. 1, 1828.

Children: 736 *Abigail*, b Dec. 23, 1829, d March 18, 1833; 737 *Samuel D.*, b April 14, 1832; 738 *Abigail*, b Aug. 18, 1836, d Sept. 12, 1842; 739 *Celestina*, b March 7, 1440; 740 *Ephraim F.*, b Feb. 21, 1843.

391. HORACE.

HORACE COOK, son of Ephraim and Sukey Cook, married Lydia E. Hickox, Dec. 15, 1842, res. in Burton, Ohio.

Children: 741 *Melissa N.*, b July 24, 1845; 742 *Sarah*, b Aug. 8, 1849; 743 *Eliza N.*, b Jan. 8, 1852.

396. ETHELBERT.

ETHELBERT COOK, son of Elam and Rebecca B. Cook of Cheshire, Conn., married Philander Sanford of Prospect; he died March 7, 1853; she died Nov. 8, 1854.

Child: 744 *Lauren E.*, b April 17, 1833, m Carrie Perkins, Nov. 12, 1860.

401. ELAM.

ELAM COOK, son of Elam and Rebecca Cook of Cheshire, Ct., m Lois, daughter of Jesse and Eliza Humiston of said town.

Children: 745 *Eliza A.*, b Feb. 6, 1842; 746 *Theodore A.*, b March 17, 1845; 747 *Amelia R.*, b Feb. 8, 1856.

404. RUSSEL.

RUSSEL COOK, son of Samuel and Mary K. Cook of Wallingford, married Miss Hall of Cheshire, where he resided for some time. From Cheshire he went, it is supposed, to Ohio, where it is supposed by his friends that he died.

406. BILLIOUS.

BILLIOUS COOK, son of Samuel and Mary R. Cook, married Sarah Munson, daughter of Elizabeth. He died July 25, 1828, ae. 45 years. She died May 4, 1855, ae. 70 years.

Children: 748 *Chauncey M.*, b Oct. 10, 1805; 749 *Mary K.*, b Jan. 1, 1807, m Edwin L. Hall; 750 *Russel*, b Oct. 21, 1809; 751 *Sarah*, b April 30, 1811, m Horace Tuttle of Hamden, Ct.; 752 *Turhand K.*, b July 11, 1817; 753 *Jane R.*, b March 6, 1819, m Ambrose Todd of Fair Haven, Ct.; 754 *Emily*, b 1824, died in infancy.

408. TURHAND.

TURHAND K. COOK, son of Samuel and Mary K. Cook, married Catharine Van Bergen of Catskill, N. Y., and resided there until his decease. He was a merchant, inn-keeper and clerk of the county of Greene, N. Y. He died December 3d, 1851, aged 64 years. He married Catharine A. Allen, for his 3d wife, in January, 1848.

Children: 755 *Ann Eliza*, b Nov. 26, 1827, was at Cincinnati in 1856; 756 *Mary Kirtland*, b August 3, 1829, married Charles J. Russ in 1847; 757 *Wm. Van Buren*, b March, 1831, d Sept 24, 1849; 758 *John Washburton*, b Dec. 7, 1839.

409. SAMUEL.

SAMUEL COOK, son of Samuel and Mary K. Cook, married Martha Culver, daughter of Benjamin. He was three years high sheriff of New Haven county, postmaster and town clerk of Wallingford. He died Dec. 18, 1843, æ. 55 years, at Cheshire. His remains were interred in Wallingford. His widow died at the house of her son Samuel A. Cook, in Waterbury, July 6, 1861, æ. 67 years.

Children: 759 *Delos Ford*, d in Wallingford of consumption; 760 *Henry A.*, m Delia Cook, dau. of Benj. T.; 761 *Harriet*, m Wm. Frisbie of Branford, she d Dec. 26, 1860; 762 *Kirtland*, b 1822, m —— Tuttle, d at Cheshire; 763 *Samuel A.*, m Lucinda Hitchcock; 764 *William*, res. at Pond Hill, Wallingford.

410. THADDEUS.

COL. THADDEUS COOK, son of Samuel and Mary K. Cook, married 1st, Julia Cook, daughter of Stephen, of Cheshire; 2d, Sylvia Hall, dau. of Andrew and Diana Hall; 3d, Thankful, and 4th, Martha Hall. The two last were daughters of Josiah Hall, of Wallingford.

Child by first marriage: 765 *Julia*, m 1st, Horace Tuttle, 2d, Wm. Francis. Child by 2d marriage: 766 *Catherine*, m David Hall of Wallingford. Children by 4th marriage: 767 *Caroline*, m Rev. Benjamin Paddock, of Detroit, Michigan; 768 *Sarah*, m O. Ives Martin, of Wallingford; 769 *Emma*, m Edwin F. Cook, son of Leander; 770 *Francelia*, b Oct. 12, 1825, d Feb. 25, 1836.

411. GEORGE.

GEORGE COOK, son of Samuel and Mary Kirtland Cook, married Lavinia, daughter of Benjamin Culver. He died at Wallingford, Feb. 18, 1844. She died Nov., 1869.

Children: 771 *Mary K.*, b May 24, 1821; 772 *Eliza*, b Feb. 20, 1823, m Frederic Bartholomew, d July 24, 1862, æ. 41 yrs.; 773 *Lavinia*, m Samuel Parmelee; 774 *Martha*; 775 infant, died at Cheshire; 776 *Fanny*, m Emery Morse, March 1, 1855.

412. FRIEND.

DR. FRIEND COOK, son of Samuel and Mary K. Cook, graduated at Union Gollege, studied medicine with Dr. N. Smith of New Haven, commenced practice at Windsor, Conn. He married Emily, dau. of Dea. Joshua Atwater, of Wallingford. Afterwards he practiced his profession there until he removed to Atwater, Ohio, where she died. He married Sarah Folger Reynolds for his second wife. He died of a cancer in the stomach, after a long and distressing illness, Feb. 8, 1857.

Children: 777 *Helen A.*, b Nov. 12, 1825, d Feb. 1, 1827, in Wallingford; 778 *Joshua A.*, b Sept. 29, 1829, d Nov. 1, 1844, in Ohio; 779 *Frances A.*, b Nov, 25, 1833, d July 20, 1834, in Wallingford; 780 *Emma G.*, b Nov. 29, 1836; 781 *Frances I.*, b May 18, 1840; 782 *William Shelton*, b July 13, 1862, d Dec. 31, 1848, in Ohio. Child by 2d marriage, 783 *Henry M.*, b March, 1848.

413. JOHN.

JOHN COOK, son of Samuel and Mary K. Cook, married Mary Munson, June 25, 1823. He died Jan. 1, 1858, æ. 57 years.

Children: 784 *Samuel M.*, m —— Bartholomew; 785 *Mary K.*, m Tilton E. Doolittle Esq.; 786 *Ellen*, m Charles Jones of Wallingford; 787 *George*, d Nov. 17, 1869.

418. RUFUS.

RUFUS Cook, son of Cornelius B. and Mary B. Cook, married Betsey Curtis. He died Aug. 12, 1826, æ. 36 years, at Cheshire, Conn.

Children: 788 *Cornelius B.*, b Dec. 15, 1810; 789 *Rufus*, b July 5, 1812: 790 *Maroa*, m Russel B. Ives. She died at Cheshire, Conn.

420. BROOKS.

BROOKS COOK, son of Cornelius B. and Mary Cook, m Sarah, dau. of Jonah Hotchkiss, of Cheshire. He died Sept. 23, 1824, æ 26. She died Sept. 11, 1843, æ. 45 years.

Children: 791 *Mary*, d in Cheshire; 792 *Louisa*, m George Pardee; 793 *Amelia*, m Leverett Goodyear, of Hamden, Conn.

427. AARON.

AARON COOK, son of Aaron and Betsey Cook, married Emily, dau. of Seth Hitchcock. He died in Cheshire.

Children: 794 *Elizabeth*, m Asahel Talmadge, of Cheshire; 795 *Julius;* 796 *Mary;* 797 *Melissa*, m Robert Lyman; 798 *Julia M.*, m Wm. F. Thompkins.

426. ALFRED.

ALFRED COOK, son of Aaron and Mary Cook of Cheshire. He went to Windham, Greene Co., N. Y., where he married his wife. He has children, and is now (1869) in Cheshire, Conn.

436. STEPHEN.

STEPHEN COOK, son of Stephen and Emma Cook, married Julia E. Smith, of North Haven; he died Oct. 21, 1840, ae. 40 yrs. His widow m Willis Smith, Esq., of Meriden.

Children: 799 *Julia E.*, b Sept. 27, 1831, m Daniel Wright; 800 *Sarah E.*, b Aug. 10, 1827, m Edward Cowell; 801 *Leander D.*, b Jan. 22, 1825, d Oct. 17, 1854, ae. 29; 802 *Stephen C.*, b March 28, 1834, m —— Baldwin of New Haven; 803 *Eunice C.*, b Aug. 21, 1836, m John Riker; 804 *Edson L.*, b April 5, 1840.

440. HUBBARD.

HUBBARD COOK, son of Samuel, m Abigail Dorman, Oct. 15, 1811. She died Jan. 2, 1853, and he married Ardelia Hinman, Sept. 15, 1853.

Children: 805 *Carlisle D.*, resides in Milwaukie, Wisconsin; 806 *Jennette*, b April 30, 1813, m Job C. Phelps, Jan. 1, 1839; 807 *Caroline M.*, b Sept. 25, 1818, m Harrison O. Smith, Oct. 1, 1842; 808 *Emily A.*, b Feb. 28, 1821; 809 *Delia*, b Dec. 16, 1824, d Aug. 4, 1842; 810 *Margaret*, b April 20, 1826; 811 *Ruth*, b Nov. 3, 1828, m Claxton Harrington, Oct. 16, 1850; 812 *Fanny D.*, b Aug. 17, 1832.

447. CHAUNCEY.

REV. CHAUNCEY COOK, son of Stephen and Sylvia M. Cook of Wallingford, married Mary Carpenter, Jan. 8, 1812; she died Dec. 15, 1814, at Adams, N. Y., ae. 23. He afterwards married Almira Cassitt, May 11, 1850; she died Dec. 21, 1842.

Child by 1st marriage: 813 *Eliza*, b Oct. 21, 1812, m Chas. Campbell, she d June 2, 1847. By 2d marriage: 814 *Burton C.*, b May 11, 1819, m Elizabeth Hunt; 815 *Mary*, b July 7, 1824; 816 *Sarah*, m West Morse, Dec. 2, 1847.

454. STEPHEN.

Rev. Stephen Cook, son of Stephen and Sylvia M. Cook, married Janet Wyse, Feb. 10, 1819, resides at Oberlin, Ohio.

Children: 817 *William W.*, b April 2, 1820; 818 *James N.*, b Sept. 7, 1821; 819 *John F.*, b May 21, 1823; 820 *Julia A.*, b Jan. 21, 1826.

458. NELSON.

Rev. Nelson Cook, son of Stephen and Sylvia M. Cook, married Mercy Eliza Heath, Jan. 1, 1831; she died Aug. 9, 1854. He married 2d, Elizabeth Arbella Leeds, Aug. 27, 1843; residence, Half Day, Lake Co., Illinois.

Children: 821 *Susan F.*, b. Jan. 16, 1845, d May 15, 1847; 822 *Gurdon L.*, b March 5, 1846, d Aug. 27, 1848; 823 *Otis N.*, b Oct. 6, 1848, d same day; 824 *Lyman M.*, b Jan. 23, 1850; 825 *Love Ann*, b May 27, 1852; 826 *Burton H.*, b Aug. 1, 1854.

HENRY.

Henry Cook, a brother of Samuel, came into Wallingford about 1674, and I suppose he married his wife Mary there, but at what date does not appear. Of his history little can be learned, except that he was a farmer, and was frequently elected to offices of trust and responsibility by his townsmen. That he was a brother of the first Samuel there is no doubt, as it is clearly shown by the records of Wallingford. He died in 1705, æ. 51 years. His widow Mary died Oct. 31, 1718.

Children: 1 *Mary*, b 1679, m Nathaniel Rexford, July 7, 1708; 2 *Jane*, b 1681, m Jehiel Preston, July 7, 1708; 3 *Henry*, b 1683; 4 *John*, b 1684; 5 *Hannah*, b 1687, m Timothy Beach, Nov. 26, 1713; 6 *Isaac*, b 1693; 7 *Elizabeth*, b 1694, m Adam Mott, Aug. 28, 1717; 8 *Jonathan*, b 1698; 9 *David*, b 1701, settled in Wallingford where he died; 10 *Jedediah*, b 1703.

3. HENRY.

HENRY COOK, son of Henry and Mary Cook, married 1st, Experience ———. She died Oct. 8, 1809. He married 2d, Mary (Wheadon) Frost, dau. of John and Mary Frost, of Branford, in 1710. From Branford he went to Waterbury in 1728, and was there admitted an inhabitant. His residence was near the line of Litchfield.

Children: 11 *Sarah*, b May 5, 1720; 12 *Ebenezer*, b March 5, 1721; 13 *Henry*, b Aug. 17, 1723; 14 *Thankful*, b June, 1725, bap. in Cheshire, June 20, 1725; 15 *Jonathan*, admitted a freeman from Northbury, in 1748.

4. JOHN.

JOHN COOK, son of Mary and Henry Cook, married Abigail, dau. of Daniel Johnson of Wallingford, Dec. 12, 1710. He died Aug. 15, 1761, ae. 77 years. She died Aug. 15, 1761, ae. 81 years.

Children: 16 *Dinah*, b 1714; 17 *Sarah*, b Jan. 7, 1717; 18 *Mary*, b Sept. 26, 1719; 19 *Tryphenia*, b 1722; 20 *Benjamin*, b April 22, 1725, m Hannah Thorp, resided in the eastern part of Wallingford, on the old Durham road; 21 *John*, b Oct. 23, 1727.

6. ISAAC.

ISAAC COOK, son of Henry and Mary of Wallingford, married Hannah ———, and removed to Branford, where he died.

Children: 22 *Isaac Jr.*, b July 19, 1716, d at Branford, 1760; 23 *Demetrius*, b April 23, 1718, d at Branford; 24 *Uzzel*, b May 9, 1722; 25 *Anna*, b June 24, 1724; 26 *Waitstill*, b Jan. 28, 1727; 27 *Jerusha*, b Nov. 19, 1736.

8. JONATHAN.

JONATHAN COOK, son of Henry and Mary Cook, of Wallingford, married Ruth, daughter of William Luddington of

North Haven, June 15, 1735. They settled at Northbury (then a Parish from Waterbury), now Plymouth.

Children: 28 *Jonathan*, b March 29, 1736; 29 *Jesse*, b Feb. 1, 1739, d 1784; 30 *Titus*, b May 2, 1741; 31 *Sarah*, b Oct. 31, 1744; 32 *Abel*, b May 18, 1747.

9. DAVID.

Capt. DAVID COOK, son of Henry and Mary Cook, of Wallingford. He married 1st, Rebecca Wilson; after her decease he married Mary Lamson, of Boston. He was a very extensive ship owner, and was largely engaged in commerce, sailing from the port of New Haven one ship and three brigs. In religion he was a zealous friend of the church of England. He generously paid one-quarter of the cost of building the old church which was erected in the old Mix Lane, just opposite the residence of the late Isaac Peck. He also presented the church an organ; this same organ was a few years since sold to the Episcopal church in North Haven, and in 1869 they sold it to Wm. P. Gardner, an organ builder in New Haven. This organ was more than one hundred years old, and perhaps the oldest in the state.

Children: 33 *David*, b 1723, res. in Woodbridge and New Haven; 34 *Rachel*, b March 19, 1724, m Samuel Munson, he d 1748; 35 *Leah*, b 1726, m Phineas Peck, she d in Wallingford; 36 *Phineas*, b April 3, 1729, settled in Middletown or Durham; 37 *Wilson*, b April 21, 1730, left Wallingford during the Revolutionary war and settled in Middletown; 38 *Jesse*, b July 8, 1732; 39 *Rebecca*, b April 7, 1734, m Rev. Ichabod Camp and went to Nova Scotia; 40 *Jedediah*, b April 4, 1735, res. in New Haven; 41 *Benjamin*, b April 3, 1739; 42 *Nathaniel*, b May 31, 1740; 43 *Ephraim*, b 1744, res., in Wallingford.

10. JEDEDIAH.

JEDEDIAH COOK, son of Henry and Mary Cook, of Wallingford, married Sarah, daughter of Arthur Rexford, Aug. 10, 1727. He was a mariner, and resided in New Haven. His dwelling house was on the south-west corner of State and

Chapel-sts., New Haven. I have ascertained the name of one child only.

Child: 44 *Mary*, b Oct. 7, 1728, in New Haven.

12. EBENEZER.

EBENEZER COOK, son of Henry and Experience Cook, of Waterbury, Conn., married Phebe, daughter of Moses Blakeslee, May 10, 1744.

Children: 45 *Huldah*, b April 26, 1744; 46 *Joel*, b Aug. 5, 1746; 47 *Justus*, b May 25, 1748, grad. at Yale College; 48 *Jonah*, b Aug. 11, 1750; 49 *Eric*, b Oct. 20, 1752; 50 *Rozell*, b May 1, 1755, grad. at Yale College; 51 *Nise*, b April 17, 1758; 52 *Arba*, b April 4, 1760; 53 *Lucinda*, b Sept. 20, 1764; 54 *Uri*; 55 *Ebenezer*, a Cong. clergyman at Montville, Conn.

13. HENRY.

HENRY COOK, son of Henry and Experience Cook, married Hannah, dau. of Nathan Benham, Nov. 7, 1745, and settled at Northbury, now Plymouth, Conn.

Children: 56 *Thankful*, b June 12, 1747; 57 *Mary*, b March 30, 1748, d June 11, 1760; 58 *Sarah*, b March 5, 1750, d June 15, 1760; 59 *Zuba*, b Dec. 24, 1751, d June 17, 1760; 60 *Lemuel*, b Dec. 7, 1754, d June 24, 1760; 61 *Selah*, b Dec. 19, 1756, he was a soldier in the Revolutionary war; 62 *Trueworthy*, b Sept. 29, 1759, settled with his brother Selah, in Onondaga Co., N. Y. in 1792.

15. JONATHAN.

JONATHAN COOK, son of Henry and Experience Cook, married Hannah, dau. of Nathan Benham, Nov. 7, 1745, and settled at Northbury, Plymouth, in 1748. No account of this family has been received.

22. ISAAC.

ISAAC COOK, son of Isaac and Hannah Cook, of Branford, married Mary Hubbard, of Guilford, Nov. 14, 1739. He died March 22, 1760, ae. 44 years.

Children: 63 *Isaac*, b Oct. 1, 1740, d 1744; 64 *Isaac*, b March 14, 1747, d Nov. 24, 1748; 65 *Rachel*, b Nov. 12, 1751.

23. DEMETRIUS.

DEMETRIUS COOK, son of Isaac and Hannah Cook, married Elizabeth Rogers, of Branford, Conn., April 26, 1739. They both died at Stony Creek, Branford, and were buried in a small grave-yard at a place called Damascus.

Children: 66 *Demetrius*, b Jan 6, 1740; 67 *Elizabeth*, b April 23, 1753; 68 *Elihu*, b Oct. 11, 1755; 69 *Jerusha*, b Jan. 19, 1760.

24. UZZEL.

UZZEL COOK, son of Isaac and Hannah Cook, married Zeruah Barns, of East Hampton, L. I., May 20, 1745, and settled in Branford, where they died.

Children: 70 *Desire*, b Dec. 29, 1745; 71 *Lydia*, b March 6, 1750; 72 *Abraham*, b June 1, 1754; 73 *Isaac*, b Oct. 9, 1757; 74 *Uzzel*, b July 21, 1761; 75 *Patience*, b May 13, 1764.

26. WAITSTILL.

WAITSTILL COOK, son of Isaac and Hannah Cook, married Elizabeth ——.

Children: 76 *Jane*, b April 10, 1751; 77 *Hannah*, b March 11, 1753; 78 *Jacob*, b July 15, 1755; 79 *Ebenezer H.*, b Sept. 6, 1759; 80 *William*, b May 9, 1762; 81 *Elizabeth*, b March 13, 1764; 82 *John*, b May 14, 1768; 83 *Huldah*, b May 14, 1768; 84 *Benjamin*, b April 6, 1771.

43. EPHRAIM.

EPHRAIM COOK was a son of Capt. David and Mary Cook. He was a magistrate for a long term of years, and was regarded as a sound, able and discriminating judge by all who had occasion to employ his services or come before him. He died Feb. 12, 1826, æ. 82 yrs. Mrs. Phebe, his wife, died Nov. 26, 1816, æ. 73 yrs. She was a daughter of John Tyler of Wallingford, and a sister of the Rev. John Tyler, late of Norwich, and an Episcopal clergyman.

Children: 85 *Phineas*, b Oct. 6, 1765, d Nov. 9, 1765; 86 *Elizabeth*, b April 24, 1766; 87 *Ephraim*, b March 1, 1768, m Sarah Lewis, dau. of Samuel; 88 *Darius*, b Aug. 8,

1769, d Dec. 28, 1791; 89 *Lyman*, b Nov. 17, 1770, d April 9, 1773; 90 *Mary*, b Oct. 24, 1772, m Charles Rogers, d Nov. 9, 1840; 91 *Sylvia*, b Dec. 8, 1774, m Charles Clock of Catskill, N. Y.; 92 *Phineas Lyman*, b June 22, 1776, d in the West Indies, May 8, 1801; 93 *Lucius*, b Oct. 15, 1777; 94 *Benjamin Tyler*, b May 30, 1778, m Diana Hull; 95 *Electa*, b April 9, 1780, d May 1, 1780; 96 *George*, b Oct. 16, 1783; 97 *Nathaniel*, b April 17, 1786, m Caroline Ward, of Middletown, Conn.

87. EPHRAIM.

EPHRAIM COOK Jr., son of Ephraim and Phebe Cook, married Sarah, daughter of Samuel Lewis. She died Dec. 10, 1849. He died at Williamsburgh, L. I., Feb., 1868, ae. 90 yrs.

Children: 98 *Dr. Purcell*, d in N. Y., Dec. 24, 1860, no family; 99 *Darius*, d at Catskill, N. Y., ae. 24 yrs; 100 *Lyman*, a wealthy retired merchant in N. Y. city; 101 *Mary*, unm. in N. Y. city; 102 *Sarah Ann*, d in 1854, at Williamsburgh, L. I.; 103 *Dr. Chauncey*, resides in Williamsburgh, N. Y.; 194 *Delia*, d at Catskill, N. Y., ae. 24 yrs.

93. LUCIUS.

LUCIUS COOK, son of Ephraim and Phebe Cook, married 1st, Ruth Churchill; after her death he married Mrs. Phebe Ward, of Middletown, and settled there. He died in 1845, ae. 79 yrs.

Child by 1st marriage: 105 *Lucius*, resides at Yellow Banks, Illinois. Children by 2d marriage: 106 *Wilson;* 107 *Benjamin*, d a young man; 108 *Lucina*, m Mr. Coe, of Middlefield, Conn.

94. BENJAMIN.

BENJAMIN TYLER COOK, son of Ephraim and Phebe Cook, married Diana, daughter of John and Lois Hull. Mr. Cook died Jan. 30, 1851, æ. 73 years. He was a large man, weighing nearly 300 pounds.

Children: 109 *William*, b March 3, 1803, m Julia Foster of Meriden, Ct.; 110 *Edward*, b Feb. 3, 1805; 111 *George*, b 1807, d in Chicago, Illinois; 112 *John Tyler*, b July 12, 1810, d May 29, 1811, in Wallingford; 113 *John Tyler;* 114 *Emeline*, m Lorenzo Williams, of Rocky Hill; 115 *Augustus;* 116 *Joel;* 117 *Delia*, m Henry A. Cook, of Wallingford; 118 *Phebe*, b 1817, d Feb. 24, 1817, æ. 2 weeks; 119 *David*, b 1823, d Jan. 25, 1826, æ. 2 yrs., 9 mos.; 120 *Julia*, b 1829, d May 6, 1829.

96. GEORGE.

GEORGE COOK, son of Ephraim and Phebe Cook, married Betsey Pierce of Catskill, N. Y., where he resided for some time, after which he removed to Newburg, N. Y., where he died Aug. 12, 1819, æ. 36 years.

Children: 121 *Sylvester*, was drowned in Hudson river; 122 *Alexander;* 123 *George Henry*, d at Burlington, N. J.; 124 *Maria*, m John Tyler Cook; 125 *Catherine*, m Lewis Germain, of N. J.

97. NATHANIEL.

NATHANIEL COOK, son of Ephraim and Phebe Cook, married Caroline Ward, of Middletown, Conn., after which he came to reside on the old homestead of his father, where he remained for several years, teaching school in the winter, and working the farm in the summer. He sold the old homestead, and removed his family to Earlville, Illinois, where he died April 24, 1855, æ. 69 years.

Children: 126 *Nelson*, b March 15, 1815; 127 *Emily*, b Sept. 5, 1817, m Elias Newton, Dec. 24, 1825; 128 *Phebe Tyler*, b Feb. 7, 1819, m Nehemiah Rice Ives, 1839, and Warren Baker, in 1852; 129 *Sylvester*, b Feb. 7, 1821; 130 *Caroline*, b Nov. 14, 1823, m Hiram Taft, Dec. 1, 1845; 131 *Lyman*, b Nov. 12, 1828; 132 *Ann M.*, b Jan. 12, 1831, m Jas. Ballard, of Earlville, July 4, 1850; 133 *David R.*, b Nov. 9, 1836.

COWLES, OR COLES FAMILY.[1]

JOSEPH.

JOSEPH COLES married Abigail Royce, July 13, 1699. She died May 24, 1714. He afterwards married Mary Wapels, May 19, 1717, and for his third wife, he married widow Ann Yale, Aug. 7, 1715. She died Feb. 27, 1715. This appears to be one of the first families of the name in Wallingford.

Children: 1 *Louis*, b April 25, 1700; 2 *Samuel*, b Dec. 10, 1701, d Feb. 18, 1704; 3 *Abigail*, b Jan. 17, 1702–3; 4 *Samuel*, b Feb. 2, 1705, d Feb. 15, 1705; 5 *Hannah*, b April 11, 1706; 6 *Eunice*, b April 28, 1708, m Moses Curtis, Nov. 9, 1726; 7 *Joseph*, b March 1, 1710; 8 *Samuel*, b March 14, 1712; 9 *Hannah Waulch*, adopted daughter, d Aug. 18, 1721; 10 *Benjamin*, b Feb. 23, 1715, by Ann, 3d wife.

WILLIAM.

WILLIAM COLES married Sarah Conger, July 27, 1688. He married 2d, Experience Gaylord, Dec. 22, 1721. This William was also among the early settlers, and doubtless a brother of the above Joseph.

Children: 11 *Samuel*, b May 7, 1688; 12 *John*, b May 28, 1691, m Mary ——; 13 *Sarah*, b Oct. 14, 1693; 14 *William*, b Feb. 15, 1696; 15 *James*, b March 7, 1707; 16 *Thomas*, b Sept. 10, 1719. By 2d marriage: 17 *Phineas*, b Jan. 20, 1724; 18 *Phebe*, b 1726: 19 *Thomas*, b Sept. 10, 1722; 20 *Experience*, b March 16, 1728; 21 *David*, b Oct. 29, 1730.

7. JOSEPH.

JOSEPH COLES married Eunice ——.

Child by Mindwell, 1st wife: 22 *Ebenezer*, b Feb. 26, 1718. By Eunice, 2d wife: 23 *Timothy*, b April 18, 1737, lived in Meriden, had a son Joel.

---

1 For collateral branches, see Andrews' Hist. of New Britain, 230, 231, 272; Doolittle's Hist. Belchertown, Mass., 270; Judd and Boltwood's Hist. and Gen. of Hadley, Mass., 471–3; Morse's Memorial of Morses, 166; Savage's Gen. Dict., I. 466.

11. SAMUEL.

SAMUEL COLES married 1st, Mercy Scranton, Aug. 5, 1725; 2d, Martha Brooks, Sept. 25, 1734; 3d, Susannah Cook, Dec. 1, 1735.

Children by 1st marriage: 24 *Moses*, b June 16, 1726; 25 *Mercy*, b Aug. 10, 1729. By 2d marriage: 26 *Samuel*, b July 30, 1735.

12. JOHN.

JOHN COLES married Mary ——, Nov. 20, 1717. He died 1761.

Children: 27 *Mary*, b Nov. 20, 1717; 28 *Comfort*, b Sept. 12, 1718; 29 *Dinah*, b March 12, 1720; 30 *Mary*, b Sept. 15, 1721; 31 *Lydia*, b Oct. 1, 1723; 32 *Timothy*, b Oct. 17, 1726, res. in Meriden; 33 *John*, b Feb. 1, 1727; 34 *Prudence*, b March 26, 1729; 35 *Thankful*, b Feb. 6, 1731; 36 *Sarah*, b March 21, 1733.

22. EBENEZER.

EBENEZER COLES.

Children: 37 *Elisha*, merchant and manufacturer; 38 *Ebenezer*, marble-cutter and stone-mason.

CULVER.[1]

JOSHUA.

JOSHUA CULVER, with Elizabeth Ford, his wife, to whom he was married Dec. 23, 1676, were among the first planters in Wallingford. He was a son of Edward Culver, Sen., of Dedham, Mass., New London, Groton and New Haven, Conn., and had three brothers in the vicinity of New London, who were heads of families at the time of his settling in Wallingford. He died April 23, 1713, ae. 70 yrs.

Children: 1 *Elizabeth*, d May 2, 1676, at New Haven, Conn.; 2 *Ann*, d Sept. 8, 1677, at New Haven, Conn.; 3–4

---

1 For collateral branches, see Caulkins' Hist. of New London, 309, 310; Howell's Hist. of Southampton, L. I., 217, 218; Savage's Gen. Dict., I. 482, 483.

Joshua and *Samuel* (twins), b Sept. 21, 1684 ; 5 *Abigail*, b Dec. 26, 1686 ; 6 *Sarah*, b Jan. 23, 1688 ; 7 *Ephraim*, b Sept. 7, 1692.

3. JOSHUA.

SERGT. JOSHUA and Catharine Culver, m April 23, 1713. He died June 14,? 1730, æ. 46 yrs.

Children : 8 *Benjamin*, b Sept. 3, 1716 ; 9 *Stephen*, b Jan. 24, 1718, d July 6, 1721 ; 10 *Samuel*, b May 10, 1720 ; 11 *Stephen*, b May 19, 1722 ; 12 *Joshua*, b May 20, 1729 ; 13 *Daniel*, b Sept. 1, 1723 ; 14 *Titus*, b April 7, 1725 ; 15 *Joshua*, b April 15, 1727, d July 16, 1729.

4. SAMUEL.

SAMUEL CULVER married 1st, Sarah, 2d, Ruth Sedgwick, Jan. 3, 1728.

Children : 16 *Elizabeth*, b Feb. 12, 1715 ; 17 *Sarah*, b Dec. 23, 1716 ; 18 *Abigail*, b Dec. 17, 1718 ; 19 *Esther*, b March 17, 1721, d May 5, 1741 ; 20 *Caleb*, b Feb. 18, 1723, m Lois ——— ; 21 *Anna*, b Oct. 3, 1732, d Nov. 21, 1733 ; 22 *Enoch*, b Jan. 30, 1725 ; 23 *Ebenezer*, b Dec. 9, 1726. By 2d marriage : 24 *Samuel*, b Sept. 25, 1728.

8. BENJAMIN.

BENJAMIN CULVER m Lydia ——.

Children : 24 *Joshua*, b Nov, 1, 1741, d ; 25 *Joshua*, b April 4, 1743.

9. STEPHEN.

STEPHEN CULVER m Eunice ———.

Children : 26 *Jesse*, b April 4, 1748 ; 27 *Esther*, b June 24, 1750 ; 28 *Eunice*, b March 19, 1753 ; 29 *Dan*, b May 12, 1756 ; 30 *Jesse*, b April 4, 1758.

13. DANIEL.

DANIEL CULVER married Patience ———.

Child : 31 *Samuel*, b May 24, 1747.

20. CALEB.

CALEB CULVER married Lois ——.

Children : 32 *Ruth*, b Jan. 10, 1746 ; 33 *Ruth*, b Nov. 25,

1751; 34 *Josiah*, b Sept. 7, 1748; 35 *Samuel*, b July 5, 1750.

22. ENOCH.

ENOCH CULVER married Lois ——.

Children: 36 *Esther*, b July 24, 1751; 37 *Lois*, b June 4, 1756.

CURTIS.[1]

WILLIAM.

WILLIAM CURTIS embarked in the ship Lion, June 22, 1632, and landed Dec. 16, 1632, at Scituate, Mass. He brought with him four children, Thomas, Mary, John, and Philip. He removed with his family to Roxbury, Mass., whence they removed to Stratford, Conn. By the records of Stratford, it appears that the father of these must have died before the removal of the family thither, and that previous to that event, a son William had been born to him, as the first of the name that appears on those records are John, William, and their mother, widow Elizabeth Curtis. It is stated that at the date of their removal to Stratford, John was about 28 years of age, and William about 18. Thomas died in Mass., "7th month, 1650;" widow Elizabeth died in 1658. Will proved, Nov. 4, 1658.

John married 1st, Elizabeth ———, who died in 1682; 2d, Margaret ———, who died in 1714. He died Dec. 6, 1707, æ. 96 years.

Children: 1 *John*, b 1642; 2 *Israel*, b 1644; 3 *Elizabeth*,

---

1 For collateral branches, see Bradbury's Hist. Kennebunkport, Me., 235, 236; Brown's Gen. W. Simsbury, Conn., Settlers, 31–4; Cothren's Hist. Woodbury, Conn., 531–9; Deane's Hist. Scituate, Mass., 251–4; Dod's Hist. E. Haven, Conn., 115; Draper's Hist. Spencer, Mass., 183; Eaton's Hist. Thomaston, Me., 197; Ellis's Hist. Roxbury, Mass., 94; Hinman's Conn. Settlers, 776–88; Kingman's N. Bridgewater, Mass., 476; Mitchell's Hist. Bridgewater, Mass., 144; N. E. Hist. and Gen. Reg., XVI. 137; Savage's Gen. Dict., I. 484–8; Winsor's Hist. Duxbury, Mass., 249; Andrews' Hist. New Britain, Conn., 247; Barry's Hist. Hanover, Mass., 272–88.

b 1647; 4 *Thomas*, b 1648; 5 *Joseph*, b 1650; 6 *Benjamin*, b 1652; 7 *Hannah*, b 1654.

4. THOMAS.

THOMAS CURTIS married Mary ———, June 9, 1674. He was born in Stratford, but removed to Wallingford.

Children; 8 *Mary*, b Oct. 13, 1675; 9 *Nathaniel*, b May 14, 1677, m Sarah Hall; 10 *Samuel*, b Feb. 3, 1678, m Elizabeth Frederick, Jan. 4, 1705; 11 *Elizabeth*, b Sept. 11, 1680, m Nathaniel Hall; 12 *Hannah*, b Dec. 3, 1682, d Oct. 12, 1703; 13 *Thomas*, b Aug. 16, 1685, m Mary ———; 14 *Sarah*, b Oct. 1, 1687, m James Parker in 1705; 15 *Abigail*, b Nov. 3, 1689, m Joseph Hall, 1709; 16 *Joseph*, b Aug. 10, 1691, d Jan. 11, 1713; 17 *Jemima*, b Jan. 15, 1694, m Nathaniel Beach; 18 *Rebecca*, b Aug. 21, 1697, m Lambert Johnson; 19 *John*, b Sept. 18, 1699, m Jemima Abernathy, 1723.

9. NATHANIEL.

NATHANIEL CURTIS, m 1st, Sarah Hall, April 6, 1697. She died Dec. 13, 1700. He married 2nd, Sarah How, July 9, 1702.

Children: 20 *Benjamin*, b April 27, 1703, m Jemima Munson, 1727; 21 *Hannah*, b Feb. 19, 1705; 22 *Moses*, b Aug. 4, 1706; 23 *Nathan*, b May 19, 1709, m Esther Merriam; 24 *Jacob*, b Aug. 23, 1710, m Abigail ——; 25 *Sarah*, b Mar. 30, 1712; 26 *Abigail*, b April 9, 1713; 27 *Lydia*, b March 20, 1714; 28 *Comfort*, b Oct. 30, 1716; 29 *Nathaniel*, b July 1, 1718, m Lois ———

10. SAMUEL.

SAMUEL CURTIS, married to Elizabeth Curtis, by Justice Hall, Jan. 3, 1704–5.

Children: 30 *Titus*, b Jan. 28, 1733, d Jan., 1733; 31 *Mary*, b Nov. 8, 1736; 32 *Comfort*, b June 25, 1744; 33 *Enos*, b Jan. 27, 1746; 34 *Lois*, b March 1, 1752.

16. JOSEPH.

JOSEPH CURTIS, son of Thomas and Mary Curtis, married Rebecca ——.

Children: 35 *Sybil*, b April 12, 1750; 36 *Jeptha*, b March 21, 1752.

19. JOHN.

JOHN CURTIS, m Jemima Abernathy, 1723.

Children: 37 *John*, b Feb. 3, 1735; 38 *Giles*, b Jan. 4, 1737; 39 *Jemima*, b March 18, 1739; 40 *Elizabeth*, b April 11, 1741; 41 *Sarah*, b June 28, 1744.

20. BENJAMIN.

BENJAMIN CURTIS, son of Nathaniel and Sarah Curtis, married Miriam ——.

Children: 42 *Esther*, b Oct. 2, 1728; 43 *Abel*, b Dec. 22, 1729; 44 *Susannah*, b Nov. 9, 1732; 45 *Lois*, b Sept. 30, 1733; 46 *Benjamin*, b Oct. 27, 1735; 47 *Mariam*, b Aug. 30, 1737; 48 *Sarah*, b May 29, 1739; 49 *Aaron*, b Nov. 8, 1744.

23. NATHAN.

NATHAN and Esther Curtis.

Children: 50 *Moses*, b May 8, 1741; 51 *Amos*, b March 24, 1743; 52 *Esther*, b March 7, 1745.

24. JACOB.

JACOB and Abigail Curtis.

Child: 53 *Jacob*, b Oct. 1, 1738.

29. NATHANIEL.

NATHANIEL CURTIS married Lois ——.

Children: 54 *Eunice*, b April 12, 1750; 55 *Nathaniel*, b June 13, 1756; 56 *Jacob*, b Sept. 14, 1758.

33. ENOS.

ENOS CURTIS, son of Samuel and Elizabeth Curtis, married Mary Yale, May 28, 1733.

Children: 57 *Titus*, b Jan. 28, 1733, d Jan., 1733; 58 *Mary*, b Nov. 8, 1736; 59 *Comfort*, b June 25, 1744; 60 *Enos*, b June 27, 1746; 61 *Lois*, b March 1, 1752.

RICHARD.

RICHARD CURTIS, who was among the first planters in Wallingford, was the father of Isaac Curtis, who married

Sarah Ford, of Branford, Aug. 13, 1682, and died July 15, 1712. Richard Curtis died in Wallingford, Sept. 17, 1681, æ. 70 years. Estate, £50.

Children: 62 *Isaac*, b Nov. 6, 1683; 63 *Sarah*, b June 11, 1685; 64 *Joseph*, b July 18, 1689, m Ann Stevens, Jan. 11, 1713; 65 *Ebenezer*, b Oct. 6, 1691, d July 20, 1717; 66 *Isaac*, b March 8, 1693–4, m Abigail Tuttle; 67 *Elizabeth*, b Aug. 10, 1701; 68 *Benjamin*, b March 2, 1702–3; 69 *Moses*, b Aug. 9, 1706; 70 *Phebe*, d Aug. 5, 1718; 71 *Joshua*, d July 20, 1719.

62. ISAAC.

ISAAC CURTIS married Abigail Tuttle; she died, and he married Mary Tuttle, Oct. 1, 1729.

Children by 1st marriage: 72 *David*, b Aug. 7, 1707; 73 *Phebe*, b April 4, 1718; 74 *Joshua*, b April 26, 1719; 75 *Ebenezer*, b Jan. 17, 1720.

64. JOSEPH.

JOSEPH CURTIS, m Ann Stephens, Jan. 11, 1713.

Children: 76 *Philip*, b July 20, 1727; 77 *Joseph*, b Sept. 31, 1719; 78 *Johanna*, b June 1, 1723; 79 *Peter*, m Christiana Parker, Nov. 22, 1732.

68. BENJAMIN.

BENJAMIN CURTIS married Joanna Munson, of New Haven.

Children: 80 *Asa*, b May 11, 1731; 81 *Elizabeth*, b Dec. 24, 1732; 82 *Asa*, b Feb. 13, 1740.

79. PETER.

PETER CURTIS, son of Joseph and Ann Curtis, married Christiana ———.

Children: 83 *Abner*, b Aug. 8, 1738; 84 *Achsah*, b Oct. 5, 1739; 85 *Mary*, b June 6, 1741; 86 *Silas*, b Jan. 21, 1744; 87 *Eunice*, b April 2, 1746; 88 *Jesse*, b April 2, 1748; 89 *Daniel*, b Feb. 21, 1750; 90 *Amos*, b April 4, 1752.

TITUS.

TITUS CURTIS, married Mary ———.

Children: 91 *Gideon*, m ——— Merriman; 92 *Thomas*; 93 *Rachel*; 94 *Margaretta*; 95 *Mary*; 96 *Phebe*.

DAVIDSON.

WILLIAM.

WILLIAM DAVIDSON was the first of the name in Wallingford, where he married Elizabeth, daughter of Zachariah How, Oct. 6, 1741. After the decease of Mr. How, he became the owner, probably through his wife, of the farm of Mr. How, which is the same that is now owned and occupied by the heirs of the late Samuel Davidson and Zachariah Davidson, west of the Falls plain, near South Meriden or Hanover.

Children: 1 *Anna*, b Dec. 21, 1742; 2 *Elizabeth*, b Dec. 23, 1744; 3 *William*, b June 6, 1747; 4 *Andrew*, b Aug. 19, 1749; 5 *John*, b Sept. 10, 1751; 6 *James*, b Oct. 6, 1753.

DOOLITTLE.[1]

ABRAHAM.

ABRAHAM DOOLITTLE, the emigrant, was the progenitor of all who bear the name of Doolittle in this country. Himself and his brother John were in Massachusetts very early. John died childless at Salem, Mass. Abraham was in New Haven before 1642, and the owner of a house. In 1644, he took the freeman's oath, and was made the chief executive officer (or sheriff) of the county. He was chosen by the people of New Haven as one of the Committee to superintend the affairs of the new settlement, then (1669) just commenced at the village. The name of the village was changed to that of Wallingford, and was incorporated May 12, 1670, by an act of the general court, then sitting at Hartford. He was one of the first who settled in the place, and was there before its incorporation, some two or three years. He was a member of the vigilance committee in the time of "King Philip's war." His dwelling was fortified during this time by

---

1 For collateral branches, see Andrews' Hist. New Britain, Conn., 324; Doolittle's Hist. Belchertown, Mass., 273–7; N. E. Hist. and Gen. Reg., VI. 293; Savage's Gen. Dict., II. 59.

a picket fort, against any attack which might be made by the Indians. He was several times chosen a deputy from New Haven, and afterwards from Wallingford, to the general court. He was several times elected townsman, or selectman, and appears to have been a very valuable and highly respected citizen. He died Aug. 11, 1690, æ. 70 years. He left an estate of £342. His 1st wife dying, he married Abigail Moss, July 2, 1663. She died Nov. 5, 1710, æ. 69 yrs.

Children by 1st marriage: 1 *Abraham*, b Feb. 12, 1649, d Nov. 10, 1732, æ. 83 years; 2 *Elizabeth*, b April 12, 1652; 3 *Mary*, b Feb. 22, 1653; 4 *John*, b June 14, 1655, m Mary Peck, Feb. 3, 1682. By 2d m: 5 *Samuel*, b July 7, 1665; 6, *Joseph*, b Feb. 12, 1666; 7 *Abigail*, b Feb. 26, 1668–9; 8 *Ebenezer*, b July 6, 1672, d Dec. 6, 1711; 9 *Mary*, b March 4, 1673, m Solomon Goff, Jan., 1713; 10 *Daniel*, b Dec. 29, 1675; 11 *Theophilus*, b July 28, 1678.

1. ABRAHAM.

ABRAHAM DOOLITTLE, Jr., married 1st, Mary, daughter of Wm. Hoult, of New Haven, Nov. 9, 1680. He died Dec. 15, 1732, æ. 83 years. He married for his 2d wife, Ruth Lothrop, of New London, Feb. 12, 1689. She died without issue. His 3d wife was Elizabeth Thorp, to whom he was married by Rev. Mr. Street, June 5, 1695. She died in 1736, æ. 60 years.

Children by 1st marriage: 12 *John*, b Aug. 13, 1681, m Mary Frederick, Feb. 28, 1705; 13 *Abraham*, b March 27, 1684, m Mary Lewis, Aug. 10, 1710; 14 *Sarah*, b Feb. 5, 1686; 15 *Susannah*, b April 15, 1688, m ——— Armstrong. By 3d marriage: 16 *Thorp*, b Feb. 15, 1696; 17 *Samuel*, b March 14, 1698; 18 *Joseph*, b March 13, 1700, m Rachel Cole, Dec. 15, 1726; 19 *Thomas*, b May 17, 1705, m Sarah Abernathy; 20 *Lydia*, b June 26, 1710, m John Joyce.

4. JOHN.

JOHN DOOLITTLE, son of Abraham and Abigail Doolittle, married Mary Peck, Feb. 13, 1682. He married 2d, Grace Blakeslee, Jan. 29, 1717.

Children: 21 *Esther*, b Jan. 24, 1683; 22 *Samuel*, b Feb. 4, 1685; 23 *Sarah*, b Feb. 15, 1686; 24 *Susannah*, b April 5, 1688; 25 *Benjamin*, b July 10, 1695, grad. at Yale, 1716; 26 *Susannah*, b Feb. 24, 1706; 27 *Eunice*, b May 30, 1707; 28 *John*, b Feb. 6, 1712.

5. SAMUEL.

SAMUEL DOOLITTLE, son of Abraham and Abigail Doolittle, married 1st, Mary ——, 2d, Eunice ——, and settled at Middletown, Conn.

Children: 30 *Jonathan*, b Aug. 21, 1689; 31 *Samuel*, b Aug. 3, 1691, m Jane Wheeler, Aug. 1, 1714; 32 *Mary*, b Nov. 24, 1693; 33 *Abraham*, b Sept. 21, 1695; 34 *Abigail*, b 1697; 35 *Martha*, b April 6, 1698; 36 *Hannah*, b Oct. 29, 1700; 37 *Thankful*, b June 3, 1702; 38 *Joseph*, b June 20, 1704, m Mary Hitchcock, May 24, 1729; 39 *Nathaniel*, b Jan. 15, 1706, d of small pox; 40 *Esther*, b July 16, 1709; 41 *Abel*, b May 15, 1724; 42 *Benjamin*, b Jan. 17, 1730.

6. JOSEPH.

CAPT. JOSEPH DOOLITTLE, son of Abraham and Abigail Doolittle, married Sarah, daughter of Samuel and Sarah Brown; she was born Aug. 8, 1672, and married by Thomas Yale, Esq., April 24, 1690. He died May 15, 1733, æ. 66 years. His 2d wife was Elizabeth Hoult, whom he married Oct. 5, 1720; she died June 3, 1768, æ. 73 years.

Children: 43 *Isaac*, b Aug. 13, 1721; 44 *Enos*, b March 2, 1727, m Mary ——, he d in 1756. By 2d marriage: 45 *Dinah*, b April 24, 1729; 46 *Elizabeth*, b Jan. 3, 1731, d April 13, 1731; 47 *Ichabod*, b Aug. 21, 1732; 48 *Sarah*, b Dec. 27, 1735.

8. EBENEZER.

EBENEZER DOOLITTLE, son of Abraham and Abigail Doolittle, married Hannah, only daughter of Samuel and Hannah Hall, April 6, 1697. She was born March 11, 1673, and died July 27, 1758. He died Dec. 6, 1711; settled in Cheshire.

Children: 49 *Hannah*, b 1699; 50 *Ebenezer*, b April 15,

1700, m Lydia Warner, June 11, 1728; 51 *Moses*, b 1702, d April 10, 1781, m Ruth Richardson; 52 *Sarah*, b 1704; 53 *Caleb*, b Feb. 3, 1706, d 1781: 54 *Joshua*, b March 2, 1708; 55 *Zadock*, b March 17, 1711.

10. DANIEL.

DANIEL DOOLITTLE, son of Abraham and Abigail Doolittle, married to Hannah Cornwall of Middletown, Conn., by Mr. Hamlin. After the birth of their first child they removed to Middletown, and after a residence of a few years in that place they returned to Wallingford, where he died, in 1755, æ. 80 yrs. She died Jan. 16, 1736.

Children: 56 *Hannah*, b Jan. 27, 1699, m Joseph Doolittle, Sept. 10, 1722; 57 *Elizabeth*, b Oct. 15, 1700; 59 *Matthew*, b April 16, 1703; 60 *Dinah*, b Oct. 4, 17—, d Sept. 14, 1719; 61 *Daniel*, b Feb. 3, 1707, d Sept., 1791, æ. 84 yrs.; 62 *Joseph*, b July 3, 1709; 63 *Stephen*, b Sept. 14, 1710; 64 *Abigail*, b May 6, 1712; 65 *Ezra*, b July 24, 1718, d Oct. 24, 1744, at Cheshire, Conn.

11. THEOPHILUS.

THEOPHILUS DOOLITTLE, son of Abraham and Abigail Doolittle, married to Thankful, dau. of David Hall, by Mr. Street, Jan. 5, 1698. She died June 2, 1715. He died March 26, 1740, æ. 62 yrs. He married Elizabeth Howe for his 2d wife.

Children: 67 *Thankful*, b May 2, 1700, m Timothy Page; 68 *Sarah*, b June 1, 1703, m Isaac Tuttle, she d 1713; 69 *Henry*, b 1704, d 1733, æ. 29 yrs.; 70 *Theophilus*, b June 20, 1709, m Sarah Dorcher (or Dorchester), Nov. 15, 1738; 71 *Solomon*, b Aug. 13, 1713, m Eunice Hall, Feb. 24, 17—; 72 *Benjamin*, b Sept. 28, 1723.

12. JOHN.

JOHN DOOLITTLE, son of Abraham Jr. and Mercy Doolittle, married Mary Frederick, of New Haven, Feb. 28, 1705; he married 2d, Mary Lewis. He died 1745.

Children: 73 *Benjamin*, b July 10, 1705; 74 *Susannah*, b Feb. 24, 1707; 75 *Eunice*, b May 30, 1709; 76 *John*, b Feb.

6, 1712, m Hannah —— ; 77 *Phebe*, b Nov. 26, 1713, m Josiah Mix; 78 *Frederick T.*, b Oct. 20, 1715, d Sept. 2, 1746; 79 *Obed*, b Oct. 2, 1717, d Nov. 4, 1746, ae. 29 yrs.; 80 *Nathan*, b July 22, 1720, d Aug. 20, 1728; 81 *Mary*, b Oct. 26, 1723, d Dec. 21, 1724; 82 *Keziah*, b Jan. 31, 1728, d Sept. 22, 1746; 83 *Patience*, b June 17, 1732.

13. ABRAHAM.

ABRAHAM DOOLITTLE, son of Abraham Jr. and Mercy Doolittle, married Mary Lewis, Aug. 10, 1710. He died May 10, 1733.

Children: 84, 85 *Ezekiah*, *Josiah*, b May 25, 1711; 86 *Dinah*, d Sept. 14, 1719; 87 *Zebulon*, b March 1, 1712, d March 1, 1714; 88 *Ambrose*, b Nov. 23, 1719, m Martha Munson; 89 *Nathan*, b July 22, 1720; 89 1-2 *Mary*, b Dec. 15, 1727; 90 *Abraham*, b Aug. 29, 1728; 81 *Deliverance*, b Nov. 9, 1730.

17. SAMUEL.

SAMUEL DOOLITTLE, son of Abraham and Elizabeth (Thorp) Doolittle, married Jane Wheeler, Aug. 1, 1714.

Children: 92 *Sarah*, b Sept. 24, 1714; 93 *Joseph*, b May 4, 1715; 94 *Samuel*, b Feb. 28, 1725, m Eunice ——— ; 95 *Mehitable*, b Sept. 23, 1726; 96 *Benjamin*, b Jan. 17, 1730.

18. JOSEPH.

JOSEPH DOOLITTLE, son of Abraham and Elizabeth Doolittle, married 1st, Rachel Cowles, March 14, 1728. He married 2nd, Martha Hitchcock, Feb. 5, 1735.

Children: 97 *Dinah*, b April 24, 1729; 98 *Ichabod*, b Aug. 31, 1731; 99 *Sarah*, b Dec. 27, 1735; 100 *Joseph*, b Jan. 25, 1738.

19. THOMAS.

THOMAS DOOLITTLE, son of Abraham and Elizabeth Doolittle, married Sarah Abernathy, May 27, 1730. He resided in Waterbury in 1764, was a Tory in the Revolution, and joined the English. He went to Nova Scotia with his brother James. He married his second wife, Hannah Fenn, March 5, 1732.

Children by 1st marriage: 101 *Thomas*, b 1729, died in Cheshire, Nov. 19, 1760; 102 *Anna*, b Dec. 20, 1730; 103 *Samuel*, b Dec. 29, 1731, d Jan. 11, 1732; 104 *Jemima*, b Dec. 31, 1732; 105 *Esther*, b Aug. 30, 1734. By 2d marriage: 106 *James*, b Feb. 7, 1734; 107 *Hannah*, b Oct. 12, 1735; 108 *Catherine*, b Jan. 10, 1738; 109 *Thomas*, b Jan. 22, 1742.

22. SAMUEL.

SAMUEL DOOLITTLE, son of John and Mary Doolittle, married Mehitable ———, and settled in Northfield, Mass., where he died in 1736.

Children: 110 *Mary*, b June 16, 1712; 111 *Ephraim;* 112 *Moses;* 113 *Mindwell*, b June 15, 1715.

25. BENJAMIN.

REV. BENJAMIN DOOLITTLE, son of John and Mary Doolittle, grad. at Yale in 1716, married Lydia Todd, Oct. 14, 1717, and settled in the ministry at Northfield, Mass., in 1718. He died suddenly Jan. 9, 1748, æ. 53 years, having been settled in the ministry about 30 years. His widow died June 16, 1790, æ. 92 years.

Children: 114 *Olive*, b Oct. 28, 1718; 115 *Lydia*, b Aug. 24, 1720; 116 *Charles*, b July 31, 1722; 117 *Eunice*, b July 31, 1734; 118 *Susannah*, b June 13, 1726; 119 *Lucius*, b May 16, 1728; 120 *Chloe*, b May 4, 1730; 121 *Lucy*, b Feb. 27, 1731; 122 *Thankful*, b Jan. 20, 1733; 123 *Amzi*, b Nov. 15, 1737; 124 *Lucy*, b July 15, 1741.

28. JOHN.

JOHN DOOLITTLE, son of John and Mary, married Hannah ———. He died in Wallingford in 1746–7, æ. 35.

Children: 125 *Philemon*, b Feb. 25, 1740, m Lydia Hall, Jan. 5, 1757; 126 *Eunice*, b Jan. 31, 1741; 127 *Margery;* 128 *Hannah*, b May 12, 1744; 129 *Titus*, b June 12, 1745, m Mary, dau. of Dr. Lewis, Nov. 20, 1764.

31. SAMUEL.

SAMUEL DOOLITTLE, son of Samuel and Mary Doolittle, married Elizabeth ——.

Children: 130 *Elizabeth*, b Jan. 2, 1755; 131 *Ephraim*, b Sept. 30, 1756; 132 *George*, b Jan. 14, 1759.

33. ABRAHAM.

ABRAHAM DOOLITTLE, son of Samuel and Mary Doolittle, married Damaris ——.

Child: 133 *Abraham*, b Nov., 1754.

38. JOSEPH.

JOSEPH DOOLITTLE, son of Samuel and Mary Doolittle, married Mary Hitchcock, May 24, 1729. She died, and he married Mary Strickland, at Middletown, Conn., May 24, 1739.

Children: 134 *Mary*, d young; 135 *Elizabeth*, d young; 136 *Joseph*, d in Middletown, Aug. 6, 1771; 137 *Seth*, b Jan. 4, 1745, m Hannah Dow, Feb. 4, 1768; 138 *Abisha*, d in Cheshire about 1837, no family; 139 *Mary;* 140 *Elizabeth;* 141 *Joseph;* 142 *Jared*, d July 13, 1769; 143 *Joel*, b July 7, 1769.

42. BENJAMIN.

BENJAMIN DOOLITTLE, son of Samuel and Mary Doolittle, married Elizabeth ——.

Children: 144 *Benjamin*, b July 15, 1753; 145 *Sarah*, b Feb. 21, 1756.

43. ISAAC.

ISAAC DOOLITTLE, son of Capt. Joseph and Sarah Doolittle, was a brass founder in New Haven, where he died, Feb. 13, 1800, ae. 99. He married Phebe Cook. He was the ancestor of Gov. English on the maternal side.

Child: *Jesse*, b Feb. 25, 1777.

44. ENOS.

ENOS DOOLITTLE, son of Capt. Joseph and Sarah Doolittle, married Mary ———. He died Oct. 27, 1756, ae. 22 years.

Children: 147 *Keziah*, b June 27, 1748; 148 *Katharine*, b Aug. 17, 1749; 149 *John*, b Dec. 31, 1754, d July 8, 1756; 150 *Patience*, b May 4, 1756.

50. EBENEZER.

EBENEZER DOOLITTLE, son of Ebenezer and Hannah, married Lydia Warner, June 11, 1728, and settled in Cheshire. He died May 20, 1774, æ. 74 years.

Children: 151 *Ruth*, b Aug. 20, 1735; 152 *Ebenezer*, b Oct. 12, 1736; 153 *Jesse*, b Aug. 12, 1738; 154 *Zopher*, b Aug. 7, 1740.

51. MOSES.

MOSES DOOLITTLE, son of Ebenezer and Hannah, married 1st, Ruth Hills; 2d, Lydia Richardson, March 23, 1720, died April 10, 1781, ae. 79 years, at Cheshire.

Children: 155 *Thomas*, b Feb. 8, 1730, d April 13, 1731; 156 *Hannah*, b Nov. 9, 1731; 157 *Eunice*, b Oct. 27, 1733; 158 *Damaris*, b May 28, 1735.

53. CALEB.

CALEB DOOLITTLE, son of Ebenezer and Hannah, married Tamar Thompson, April 24, 1734. They settled in the south-west part of Cheshire, on land now owned and occupied by Julius Brooks, Esq., and others. He died March 11, 1781, æ. 75 years.

Children: 159 *Joseph*, b April 30, 1734, was a farmer in Cheshire, near where the present Joseph Doolittle lives; 160 *Caleb*, b Jan. 5, 1735, settled in Westwoods, Hamden, left sons and daughters; 161 *Tamar*, b Aug. 12, 1736; 162 *Benjamin*, b March 5, 1738, settled in Cheshire one-half mile west of the village; 163 *Lois*, b April 8, 1746; 164 *Amos*, was a farmer in the south-west part of Cheshire; 165 *Ephraim*, b June 15, 1754.

54. JOSHUA.

JOSHUA DOOLITTLE, son of Ebenezer and Hannah, married Martha Hitchcock, Feb. 5, 1735, died Nov. 15, 1779, ae. 71 years. Having no children, he gave all his property to Joshua Doolittle Waterman, son of the Rev. Simeon Waterman, of Plymouth, Conn.

55. ZADOCK.

ZADOCK DOOLITTLE, son of Ebenezer and Hannah, married Rhoda ———.

Children: 166 *Hannah*, b July 22, 1740; 167 *Lydia*, b

March 3, 1742; 168 *Rhoda*, b June 28, 1744; 169 *Eunice*, b Sept. 5, 1746; 170 *Zachariah*, b May 13, 1749; 171 *Sarah*, b Sept. 24, 1751.

61. DANIEL.

DANIEL DOOLITTLE, son of Daniel and Hannah, married Elizabeth Dayton and settled in North Haven, two miles north of the center, on the Wallingford road. He died Sept., 1791, ae. 84.

Children: 172 *Giles*, b Nov. 6, 1734; 173 *Michael*, b April 12, 1738; 174 *Oliver*, b Oct. 14, 1742, m —— Cook; 175 *Elizabeth*, b Jan. 8, 1745; 176 *John*, b Jan. 15, 1747; 177 *Johnson*, d in Wallingford; 178 *Ezra*, b Jan. 3, 1752, d in Cheshire.

62. JOSEPH.

JOSEPH DOOLITTLE, son of Daniel and Hannah, married Mary ———.

Children: 179 *Joseph*, b Jan. 15. 1757; 180 *Walter*, b March 27, 1759; 181 *Joel*, b Jan. 7, 1761.

63. STEPHEN.

STEPHEN DOOLITTLE, son of Daniel and Hannah, married Anna ——, May 11, 1737. He died Nov. 8, 1772, ae. 64. She died Nov. 27, 1797, ae. 92 years.

Children: 182 *Anna*, b April 27, 1738; 183 *Abigail*, b Jan. 21, 1741; 184 *Ruth*, b Oct. 29, 1742; 185 *Stephen*, b Jan. 15, 1745, d Nov. 30, 1745.

65. EZRA.

EZRA DOOLITTLE, son of Daniel and Hannah, married Hannah ——. He died Oct. 24, 1844, in Cheshire.

Children: 186 *Hannah*, d in 1747; 187 *Hannah*, b May 21, 1748.

70. THEOPHILUS.

THEOPHILUS DOOLITTLE, son of Theophilus and Thankful, married Sarah Dorcher, Nov. 15, 1738.

Children: 188 *Susannah*, b Aug. 2, 1739; 189, 190 *Solomon* and *Theophilus*, b Jan. 8, 1741, d Jan. 25, 1741; 191

Theophilus, b Feb. 5, 1742; 192 *Solomon*, b March 24, 1746; 193 *Josiah*, b July 11, 1748, married Damaris ——; 194 *Sarah*, b April 10, 1750; 195 *Elizabeth*, b June 1, 1751; 196 *Stephen*, b July 12, 1752; 197 *Isaac*, b Aug. 27, 1754.

71. SOLOMON.

SOLOMON DOOLITTLE, son of Theopilus and Thankful, married, 1st, Eunice Hall; 2nd, Jerusha Tyler, Feb. 13, 1734.

Children: 198 *Daniel*, b Oct. 4, 1706; 199 *Theophilus*, b March 19, 1769; 200 *Sarah*, b Feb. 5, 1752; 201 *Lucy*, b July 18, 1778; 202 *Joel*, b Sept. 16, 1781.

84. EZEKIAH.

EZEKIAH DOOLITTLE, son of Abraham and Mary Doolittle, m Hepzibah ——.

Children: 203 *Barnabas*, b Jan. 8, 1736; 204 *Mehitable*, b Feb. 28, 1738; 205 *Hepzibah*, b Aug. 14, 1741; 206 *Hezekiah*, b May 4, 1742; 207 *Anthony*, b Jan. 31, 1744; 208 *Mary*, b Feb. 25, 1750.

85. JOSIAH.

JOSIAH DOOLITTLE, son of Abraham and Mary Doolittle, married Damaris ——.

Children: 209 *Josiah*, b July 17, 1769, d July 30, 1769; 210 *Stephen*, b March 24, 1771.

87. ZEBULON.

ZEBULON, son of Abraham and Mary Doolittle, married Mary ——.

Children: 211 *Mary*, b Jan. 1, 1741; 212 *Sarah*, b April 7, 1745; 213 *John*, b May 24, 1748.

88. AMBROSE.

AMBROSE DOOLITTLE, son of Abraham and Mary, married Martha Munson, daughter of William and Rebecca Munson, of Cheshire. He died in Cheshire, Sept. 25, 1781, æ. 74 years.

Children: 214 *Ambrose*, b Dec. 12, 1751; 215 *Amos*, b May 8, 1754; 216 *Martha*, b Aug. 30, 1756; 217 *Eunice*, b June 21, 1758; 218 *Abner*, b July 27, 1760; 219 *Lois;* 220 *Thankful;* 221, 222 *Samuel* and *Silas*, b March 28, 1763, both d same day; 223 *Reuben*, b May 1, 1766; 224 *Lowly*, b June 9, 1769; 225 *Mary Ann*, b Feb. 23, 1771; 226 *Eliakim*, b Aug. 29, 1772.

94. SAMUEL.

SAMUEL DOOLITTLE, son of Samuel and Jane, married Eunice ——.

Child: 227 *Samuel*, b April 11, 1749.

125. PHILEMON.

PHILEMON DOOLITTLE, son of John and Hannah, married Lydia Hall, Jan. 5, 1757. Supposed to have died in western New York.

Children: 229 *Phebe*, b May 25, 1759, in Wallingford; 230 *Keziah*, b April 20, 1760, in Wallingford; 231 *Lydia*, b Oct. 22, 1761; 232 *John F.*, b Feb. 11, 1767; 233 *Rice*, b Aug. 27, 1769; 234 *Jared;* 235 *Jesse;* 236 *Patience;* 237 *Hannah.*

129. TITUS.

TITUS DOOLITTLE, son of John and Hannah, married Mary Lewis, daughter of Dr. Lewis of Wallingford, Nov. 20, 1764. He died at Westfield, Mass., Nov. 23, 1818, ae. 73 years.

Children; 239 *John*, b Jan., 1765, d in early life unm.; 240 *Elizabeth*, b 1767, m Abraham Bradley of Russell, Mass., she d April 28, 1831; 241 *Titus*, was a farmer at Westfield, Mass., m Mary Tracy in 1794, and had ten children, mostly deceased; 242 *Mary*, b 1769, m Noble Fowler of Southwick, Mass., she d March 11, 1747; 243 *Joel*, b 1774, grad. at Yale College, 1799, was a lawyer; 244 *Amasa*, b 1776, m Mary Hitchcock of Cheshire; 245 *Martha*, m Solomon Gillette of Colchester, Conn.; 246 *Mark*, a lawyer in Belchertown ,Mass., grad. at Yale College in 1804, m 1st, Betsey A. Smith, and 2d, Sarah T. Reuberteau, he d in 1818, Nov. 23, leaving no sons.

152. EBENEZER.

EBENEZER DOOLITTLE, son of Ebenezer and Lydia Warner Doolittle, owned and occupied the farm late the property of Landa Bristol, of Cheshire.

Children: 247 *Elkanah*, d in Brooklyn, N. Y.; 248 *Amaryllis*, m Landa Bristol, of Cheshire.

160. CALEB.

CALEB DOOLITTLE, son of Caleb and Tamar, married in West Woods, Hamden.

Children: 249 *Caleb;* 250 *Jesse;* 251 *Tamar*, m ——— Wooden.

162. BENJAMIN.

BENJAMIN DOOLITTLE, son of Caleb and Tamar.

Child: 252 *Joseph I.*, d in Prospect.

164. AMOS.

AMOS DOOLITTLE, son of Caleb and Tamar, married and settled in the southwestern part of Cheshire, on the farm now belonging to the heirs of his grandson, Amos Doolittle, late of Cheshire, deceased. He died March 23, 1808, ae. 75 yrs. His wife, Mrs. Abigail ———, died July 28, 1827, ae. 88 yrs.

Children: 253 *Olive*, b March 30, 1761; 254 *Amos*, b 1767, d May 21, 1816, ae. 49 yrs.; Lois his wife d March 27, 1828, ae. 57 yrs.; probably Alexander and others.

165. EPHRAIM.

EPHRAIM DOOLITTLE, son of Caleb and Tamar, married Christiana Thorp, and settled on the farm now owned by Julius Brook, Esq., in the southwest district of Cheshire. He also owned the mills since known as Gaylord's mills. His widow married Thaddeus Rich, late of Cheshire, deceased.

Children: 255 *Julia;* 256 *Rispah*, b 1800, d æ. 50 yrs.

178. EZRA.

EZRA DOOLITTLE, son of Daniel and Elizabeth, married Sarah Hall, and settled on the farm now owned by his son Levi, in the north part of Cheshire. He died suddenly on the first Monday in April, 1829.

Children: 257 *Ezra*, b May 8, 1776, settled in Barkhamstead, and died there: 258 *Leonard;* 259 *Levi*, m ——— Tuttle, of Cheshire; 260 *Sarah*, m Benjamin Dowd Doolittle; 261 *Betsey;* 262 *Eunice.*

192. SOLOMON.

SOLOMON DOOLITTLE, son of Theophilus and Sarah, married Eunice Hall, Feb. 24, 1768.

Children: 263 *Theophilus*, b March 19, 1769, m Abiah Atwater; 264 *Sarah*, b Feb. 5, 1772; 265 *Lucy*, b July 18, 1778; 266 *Joel*, b Sept. 16, 1781.

214. AMBROSE.

AMBROSE DOOLITTLE, son of Ambrose and Martha, married Miss ——— Dowd of Middletown, Conn. He died in Cheshire, Conn.

Child: 267 *Benjamin Dowd*, b 1775, d May 13, 1845, æ. 70 yrs. He m Sarah Doolittle, she d July 30, 1826, æ. 44 yrs.

215. AMOS.

AMOS DOOLITTLE, son of Ambrose and Martha, married Abigail Ives of Cheshire, Conn., dau. of Joel Ives. He was a distinguished engraver and artist. His dwelling occupied a portion of the lot on the northwest corner of College and Elm Streets, New Haven, Conn.

Child: 267 *Mary Ann*.

218. ABNER.

ABNER DOOLITTLE, son of Ambrose and Martha, married. He resided in the old homestead in Cheshire, Conn., until his death; he had several daughters.

221. SAMUEL.

SAMUEL DOOLITTLE, son of Ambrose and Martha, married. He was insane, and died in Cheshire, Conn.

Children: 268 *Calvin*, m Matilda Wincher, he d in Cheshire, Conn.; 269 *Alfred*, m ——— Brown, and d in Cheshire, Conn.; 270 *Aaron*, married, has a large family in Cheshire, Conn.

222. SILAS.

SILAS DOOLITTLE, son of Ambrose and Martha. He went to Vermont, became insane and died the same hour and minute that his brother died at Cheshire.

231. AMASA.

AMASA DOOLITTLE, son of Titus and Mary, married Mary, daughter of Amasa Hitchcock, of Cheshire. He died in 1825, ae. 49 years.

Children: 232 *Amasa Lewis*, resides in Cheshire, on the old Lewis farm; 233 *Mary*, m Reuben Palmer, of Springfield, Mass.

247. ELKANAH.

ELKANAH DOOLITTLE, son of Ebenezer and ———, married 1st, —— Cook, of Cheshire. She died and he married his 2d wife in Brooklyn, N. Y., where he resided until his death. He was a graduate of Yale College.

Children: 234 *Milton*, d at Cheshire, Conn.; 235 *Edward*, d at Cheshire; 236 *Warren*; 237 *Wm. A.*, d in Brooklyn, New York.

254. AMOS.

AMOS DOOLITTLE, son of Amos and Abigail, married Lois ——. He died May 21, 1816, ae. 49 yrs. She died March 27, 1828, ae. 57 yrs.

Child: 238 *Amos*, b 1797, d at Cheshire about 1867, ae. 70.

241. TITUS.

TITUS DOOLITTLE, son of Titus and Mary Doolittle, married Mary, daughter of Rev. Stephen Tracey, of Norwich, Mass., in 1794, and had children, most of whom have died; no sons are living. His wife died in 1843. He was living at Painesville, Ohio, in 1852.

243. JOEL.

JOEL DOOLITTLE, son of Titus and Mary Doolittle, married Sarah P. Fitch, of Pawlet. He graduated at Yale in 1799, and was tutor in Middlebury college, Vermont. He studied law and settled at Middlebury in the practice of his profession, after having filled with honor many offices in the gift of the people, as Judge of the Supreme Court, etc. He died March 9, 1841, ae. 67 yrs. He left four sons and two daughters. The three sons are in Ohio.

Children: 279 *John;* 280 *Titus;* 281 *Charles Hubbard;* 282 *Joel;* 283 *Sarah;* 284 *Elizabeth.*

244. AMASA.

AMASA DOOLITTLE, son of Titus and Mary Lewis Doolittle, married Mary, daughter of Amasa Hitchcock of Cheshire. He died in 1825, ae. 49 years.

Children: 285 *Amasa Lewis*, now living in Cheshire; 286 *Mary*, resides in Springfield, Mass. She married Reuben Palmer.

246. MARK.

MARK DOOLITTLE, son of Titus and Mary Doolittle, graduated at Yale college, 1804; studied law and settled at Belchertown, Mass. He married for his first wife Betesy Matilda Smith, daughter of Daniel Smith Esq., of West Haven, Vt. She died Nov. 14, 1814, ae. 28. He married his 2nd wife, Sarah T. Reuberteau, of Newburyport.

Children: 287 *Lucy Maria*, m Dr. Horatio Thompson, of Belchertown, Mass., 1834; 288 *Betsey Matilda*, b May, 1814, m John Strong, a graduate of Yale in 1857, residence in Addison, N. Y. By second marriage, 289 *Sarah Lorena*, d July 29, 1849, ae. 18; 290 *Wm. C.*, d in childhood.

108. ENSIGN.

ENSIGN JOSEPH DOOLITTLE, son of Joseph and Rachel, married Martha Hitchcock, and was a farmer on the west side of the river in Wallingford.

Children: 291 *Joseph;* 292 *Walter;* 293 *Joel;* 294 *Reuben.*

291. JOSEPH.

JOSEPH DOOLITTLE, son of Joseph and Martha.

Children: 295 *Jared*, was a merchant in New Haven; *Nathaniel*, was the owner of the mills at Quinnipiac; 29 *Patty*, m Oliver Deming, of New Haven.

293. JOEL.

JOEL DOOLITTLE, son of Joseph and Martha.

Children: 298 *Joel*, b 1790, is living at North Haven; 299

Lucy, no further information about her appears on the records.

294. REUBEN.

REUBEN DOOLITTLE was a farmer in the south-westerly part of the town of Wallingford.

Children: 300 *Rufus;* 301 *Almon;* 302 *Rhoda*, m Augustus Hall Esq., of Wallingford.

DUDLEY.

JOHN.

JOHN and Lois Dudley, came into Wallingford about the year 1750, and settled on the west side of the river, a short distance below the present residence of Street Jones, Esq., who is the present owner of the old Dudley house. Of their history very little is now known.

JEDEDIAH.

JEDEDIAH DUDLEY, their son, was born in Wallingford, Jan. 1, 1759, married ——, and occupied the house of his father until his decease.

Children: 1 *John*, d in Branford, buried in Wallingford, 1869; 2 *Caleb*, d in Wallingford; 3 *Elias*, m Laura Preston, and died in Cheshire; 4 *Jedediah*, d unm., and was insane several years; 5 *Isaac*, d; 6 a daughter.

DUTTON.[1]

JOSEPH.

JOSEPH DUTTON, the ancestor of the family of that name in Wallingford, was of Machimoodus, or East Haddam. He purchased land in Wallingford in 1718 and 1719, which he gave to his sons, whose names are as follows:

1 *Benjamin*, b 1696, m Mary ——; 2 *David*, m Lydia Cook; 3 *Thomas*, m Abigail Merriman.

---

1 For collateral branches, see Hill's Hist. Mason, N. H., 201; Savage's Gen. Dict., II. 84, 85.

1. BENJAMIN.

BENJAMIN DUTTON, married Mary ——, had children born in Wallingford. He died in Cheshire Parish, Jan. 27, 1791, æ. 95 yrs. She died Oct. 27, 1785, æ. 80 yrs.

Children: 4 *Joseph*, b Jan. 5, 1720; 5 *Benjamin*, b March 10, 1723; 6 *Susannah*, b June 17, 1725; 7 *John*, b Jan. 23, 1730; 8 *Sarah*, b Dec. 6, 1735; 9 *Charles*, b 1736, d Sept. 19, 1829, æ. 93 yrs.; 10 *Elizabeth*, b July 25, 1737; 11 *Eunice*, b April 5, 1739; 12 *Daniel*, b Nov. 30, 1740.

2. DAVID.

DAVID DUTTON married Lydia, daughter of Samuel and Hope Cook, Sept. 14, 1722. She died Oct. 12, 1735, ae. 40. He married Sarah Doolittle, Feb. 21, 1739.

Children by 1st marriage: 13 *Mary*, b July 16, 1723, m Gideon Royce, Oct. 4, 1743; 14 *Charles*, b Oct. 30, 1727, m Eunice Jones, 1761, he d Oct. 9, 1789; 15 *Jesse*, b Dec. 24, 1729, d Feb. 4, 1745, at Cape Breton, in the old French war; 16 *Ambrose*, b March 30, 1732; 17 *Joel*, b March 20, 1734; 18 *Lydia*, b Oct. 27, 1738, d Sept. 27, 1739. By 2d marriage: 19 *David*, b June 23, 1741; 20 *Amos*, b Oct. 13, 1745, d Oct. 3, 1788, æ. 61; 21 *Jonathan*, b Jan. 25, 1743–4.

3. THOMAS.

THOMAS DUTTON married Abigail Merriman, May 6, 1729.

Children: 22 *John*, b Feb., 1730; 23 *Abigail*, b Jan. 8, 1732; 24 *Thomas*, b Jan. 31, 1735; 25 *Samuel*, b Jan. 24, 1737; 26 *Lois*, b Aug. 8, 1738; 27 *Matthew*, b Nov. 11, 1740; 28 *John*, b April 3, 1743; 29, 30 *Amasa*, and *Asahel*, b July 30, 1745; 31 *Nathaniel*, b June 18, 1747; 32 *Phebe*, b Oct. 11, 1749; 33 *Asahel*, b Feb. 2, 1753.

4. JOSEPH.

JOSEPH DUTTON, son of Benjamin and Mary, of Wallingford, married Elizabeth ———. She died Jan. 25, 1700, æ. 72. He died in Southington, Ct., Oct. 26, 1788, æ. 68 years, and was buried at Plantsville, Southington, by the side of his wife.

Child: 34 *Mindwell*, b May 18, 1746, m in Wallingford.

5. BENJAMIN.

BENJAMIN DUTTON, son of Benjamin and Mary, m Abigail Jones, March 16, 1747.

Children: 35 *Eunice*, b April 5, 1749; 36 *Abigail*, b Nov. 21, 1750.

14. CHARLES.

CHARLES DUTTON, son of Daniel and Lydia Dutton, married Eunice Jones, 1761. He died Oct. 9, 1781.

Children: 37 *Jesse*, settled in the State of Maine; 38 *Amos*, b June 3, 1767, d March 21, 1845, æ. 73 years; 39 *Charles*, d in Ohio where he resided.

FENN.[1]

EDWARD.

EDWARD FENN married Mary Thorp, Nov. 15, 1688. He died Feb. 2, 1728, ae. 84 yrs. She died July 24, 1725, and he married Abigail Williams, Jan. 26, 1726. He belonged in Wallingford.

Children: 1 *Mary*, b Sept. 27, 1689; 2 *Hannah*, b Feb. 4, 1698, d Feb. 14, 1698; 3 *Theophilus*, b Jan. 31, 1689; 4 *Elizabeth*, b April 29, 1692; 5 *Sarah*, b Nov. 24, 1694; 6 *Theophilus*, b Jan. 28, 1698, m Martha ——; 7 *John*, b March 23, 1702, m Sarah ——; 8 *Hannah*, b Dec. 13, 1704; 9 *Thomas*, b Sept. 13, 1707, m Lydia ——; 10 *Naomi*, b May 10, 1712, m Samuel Frost, March 21, 1723.

6. THEOPHILUS.

THEOPHILUS FENN, m Martha Doolittle, May 24, 1722.

Children: 10 *Elizabeth*, b Oct. 25, 1723; 11 *Edward*, b Sept. 2, 1732; 12 *Martha*, b Sept. 23, 1725; 13 *Bethiah*, b Feb, 18, 1728; 14 *Benjamin*, b Aug. 3, 1730; 15 *Phebe*, b Feb. 12, 1735; 16 *Theophilus*, b Feb. 20, 1737, d Nov. 8, 1737; 17 *Eunice*, b March 16, 1741; 18 *Susannah*, b Sept. 28, 1746.

---

1 For collateral branches, see Savage's Gen. Dict., II. 151, 152.

7. JOHN.

JOHN FENN married Sarah ——.

Children: 20 *Mary*, b Dec. 4, 1730; 21 *John*, b July 15, 1732: 22 *Lois*, b Aug. 2, 1735; 23 *Samuel*, b Sept. 10, 1739; 24 *Amos*, b May 30, 1745.

9. THOMAS.

THOMAS FENN, married Lydia Ackley, March 22, 1731. She died Dec. 4, 1741. He married, 2d, Christina ——.

Children by 1st marriage: 25 *Lydia*, b July 11, 1733; 26 *Thomas*, b Dec. 1, 1735; 27 *Samuel*, b Dec. 27, 1737; 28 *Hannah*, b March 24, 1740. By 2d marriage: 29 *Esther*, b Oct. 20, 1743; 30 *Theophilus*, b June 29, 1744.

FOOT.[1]

ROBERT.

ROBERT FOOT was first of Wethersfield, afterwards of that part of New Haven now known as Wallingford, and in 1678 and thereafter, until his death at Branford, was married to Sarah ——, 1659. After his decease, his widow married Aaron Blatchley of Branford, in 1686. Mr. Foot was a son of Nathaniel Foot, the settler. He died suddenly in 1681, æ. 52. John Foot, the sixth child of Robert and Sarah, was born at Branford, July 24, 1670. He married Mary ——, and had seven children. He died in 1713, ae. 43.

JOHN.

JOHN FOOT, fourth child of John and Mary Foot, was born in 1700, and settled in North Branford. He married 1st, Elizabeth Frisbee, Dec. 25, 1733; she died Feb. 3, 1737, æ. 22. He married 2d, Abigail Frisbee, Aug. 16, 1738. He died Jan. 26, 1777, æ. 77. His widow Abigail died May, 1779, æ. 67.

---

1 For collateral branches, see Brown's Gen. W. Simsbury, Conn., 53-56; Caulkins' Hist. New London, Conn., 308; Goodwin's Foote Family Gen.; Judd and Boltwood's Hist. and Gen. of Hadley, Mass., 494; Matthews' Hist. Cornwall, Vt., 285; Nash's Gen. of Nash Family, 42; N. E. Hist. and Gen. Reg., IX. 272; Savage's Gen. Dict., II. 179–82.

Children by 1st marriage: 1 *Jonathan*, b Jan. 23, 1737, d in North Branford, 1801. By 2d marriage: 2 *John*, b April 5, 1742, in North Branford, m Abigail, dau. of Rev. Samuel Hall, of (Cheshire) Wallingford, granddaughter of Gov. Jonathan Law, who d Nov. 19, 1788, ae. 39, m Eunice, dau. of John Hall, Esq., Apr. 28, 1761, was grad. at Yale College in 1765, studied Divinity, and succeeded Rev. Mr. Hall as pastor of the Congregational Church in Cheshire, d Aug. 31, 1813, ae. 71, his wife Eunice d Jan. 31, 1817; 3 *Abigail Sarah Hall*, b Jan. 2, 1769, d Jan 20, 1775; 4 *Mary Ann*, b Sept. 21, 1770, d Sept. 25, 1775; 5 *Lucinda*, b May 19, 1772, m Dr. Thomas T. Cornwall, and was mother to Hon. Edward A. Cornwall, of Cheshire; 6 *John Alfred*, b Jan. 2, 1774, d Aug. 25, 1794, ae. 20; 7 *Abigail M. A.*, b Sept. 16, 1776, d Aug. 9, 1778, ae. 22; 8 *Wm. Lambert*, b Oct. 10, 1778, was a physician in Cheshire; 9 *Samuel Augustus*, b Nov. 8, 1780, mem. of Congress, Senator in Congress, and Gov. of Conn.; 10 *Roderick*, b Dec. 15, 1782, d May 16, 1791, ae. 8; 11 *Matilda*, b May 6, 1785, d Oct. 9, 1787.

8. WILLIAM.

DR. WM. LAMBERT FOOT, son of Rev. John, was a prominent man in his native town, was town clerk and judge of the Probate court, and practiced his profession, until a short time before his death. He married Mary, dau. of Capt. Dan Scoville of Saybrook, March, 1801. Both died in Cheshire.

Children: 12 *William L.*, M. D., b Nov. 21, 1802, m Mary Butler of Branford in 1827; 13 *Mary A.*, b May 23, 1806; 14 *Abigail H.*, b April 28, 1808, m Edward Doolittle, he died March 4, 1837, ae. 29; 15 *Scoville D.*, b April 10, 1810, m Martha Whiting, of Milford, Conn., June, 1836, she was born 1807; 16 *Eliza S.*, b June 29, 1812; 17 *John L.*, b Sept. 14, 1817, merchant in Cheshire.

9. SAMUEL.

His Excellency SAMUEL A. FOOT, son of Rev. John and Abigail, married Eudocia Hull, daughter of General Andrew and Elizabeth Mary Ann Hull, of Cheshire. He died Sept

16, 1846, in his 66th year. She died at the residence of her son John A. Foot Esq., Cleveland, Ohio, Jan. 12, 1849, ae. 66 years. Her remains were brought to Cheshire for interment.

Children: 18 *John Alfred*, b Nov. 22, 1803, attorney at Cleveland, Ohio; 19 *Andrew Hull*, b Sept. 12, 1806, Rear Admiral U. S. N., now deceased; 20 *Roderick A.*, b Oct. 1, 1808, d Feb. 24, 1810; 21 *Augustus Edwin*, b Dec. 31, 1810, cashier at Cleveland, Ohio; 22 *Wm. Henry*, b Feb. 1, 1817, d March 6, 1827; 23 *Edward Dorr*, b Feb. 3, 1820, d Feb. 9, 1831.

BENJAMIN.

Benjamin Foot, of Wallingford, son of Daniel and Mary Foot, of Branford, who was the son of Daniel and Sarah Foot, of Northford, who was the son of Joseph and Abigail Foot, of Northford, who was the son of Robert and Sarah Foot, of New Haven, Wallingford and Branford, who was the son of Nathaniel the settler, was born at Northford, Conn., Aug. 1, 1778, and was the youngest but one of thirteen children. He married, 1st, Sally P., daughter of Joel Hall, April 24, 1803; she died, July 24, 1804, æ. 25 years; 2d, Betsey, daughter of Andrew Hall, June 2, 1805, she died Sept. 20, 1831, æ. 44 years; 3d, Mrs. Harriet, widow of Willis Humaston, and daughter of Newbury Button, of North Haven, May 3, 1832. He died in Wallingford, Nov., 1869, æ. 91 years.

Children by 1st marriage: 24 *Sally H.*, b Feb., 1804, d May 13, 1804. Children by 2d marriage: 25 *Andrew H.*, b Nov. 15, 1806, m Frances, dau. of Simon Hoadley of New Haven; 26 *Henry A.*, b July 14, 1809, d Oct. 2, 1818; 27 *James*, b Aug. 15, 1811, m Emeline Slead of Wallingford, Oct. 8, 1834; 28 *Sally H.*, b Jan. 16, 1815, m Charles B. Hall of Wallingford, Oct. 1, 1835; 29 *Benjamin*, b Oct. 18, 1817, m Sarah, dau. of Hiel Hall of Wallingford, Nov. 19, 1840; 30 *Henry Clay*, b June 19, 1820, m Catherine W., dau. of Hiel Hall, Aug. 17, 1842, she resided in Philadelphia, d in 1868.

GAYLORD.[1]

WILLIAM.

Dea. William Gaylord, a leading man of Windsor, Conn., was the father of Walter Gaylord, whose son Joseph was born May 13, 1649, and married July 14, 1670, Sarah, daughter of John Stanley of Farmington, Conn. It is not exactly clear as to whether he went from Windsor to Farmington, or Waterbury first; but it is certain that he was at Mattatuck (Waterbury), in the spring of 1678, having been previously accepted as an inhabitant, Jan. 17, 1677. He had a three acre lot on the corner of East and North Main-sts., which then bounded north on John Stanley. He sold his house and lot Feb. 2, 1703, reserving a quarter of an acre on which his son Joseph had built a house, after which he resided at a place called Breakneck, built a house there, and had twenty acres of land which he sold Feb. 26, 1705 or 1706. As no traces of him are found in Waterbury after this date, it is quite probable that he went to Durham in 1706, where several of his family had previously gone, and we find him there in the early part of 1706. He died in Durham previous to 1713. His children were,

1 *Sarah*, b July 11, 1671, m Thomas Judd, Jr.; 2 *Joseph*, b April 22, 1673 or 1674, m Feb. 28, 1699, to Mary, dau. of Joseph Hickox, deceased, of Woodbury, she was born May 25, 1678.

2. JOSEPH.

Joseph Gaylord went to Durham about the year 1705 or 1706. He built a house at Buckshill in 1703 or 1704, which he sold to Richard Welton.

Children: 3 *Elizabeth*; 4 *Joseph*, d in infancy; 5 *Thankful*, all b in Waterbury.

---

1 For collateral branches, see Judd and Boltwood's Hist. of Hadley, Mass., 497, 498; Savage's Gen. Dict., II. 238, 239; Stiles' Hist. Windsor, Conn., 623–7.

JOHN.

John Gaylord, born April 12, 1677, resided at Buckshill, adjoining his brother Joseph, on a place he bought of John Warner. He went to Durham, and subsequently to Wallingford, where he died in 1753, in what is now Cheshire. Mrs. Elizabeth Gaylord his wife, died in Cheshire, Dec. 19, 1751, æ. 73 yrs. He left an estate of £1995 in Wallingford, and of £560 in Farmington, Conn.

Children: 6 *Samuel;* 7 *Edward;* 8 *Timothy;* 9 *Nathan;* 10 *Joseph;* 11 *John*, m Thankful ——; and five daughters, one of whom, 12 *Sarah*, d April 14, 1735.

WILLIAM.

William Gaylord had a £40 propriety set out to him in Waterbury, in 1701, which he forfeited, and removed to Woodbury, where he joined the church, Jan. 13, 1706. Subsequently he went to New Milford, where he died about 1753. His will was proved Nov. 23, 1753, in which his wife Mercy and six children were named. Joanna, his first wife, joined the church in Woodbury, Dec. 7, 1712. His son Nathan, of New Milford, married Hannah, daughter of John Bronson, who was a son of Isaac Bronson.

Children: 13 *Benjamin*, resided in Durham and Wallingford, was in Wallingford in 1722; 14 *Elizabeth*, b Nov. 21, 1680, m Joseph Hickox, son of Samuel; 15 *Mary*, m Stephen Welton, she d July 18, 1719; 16 *Joanna*, m Robert Royce of Wallingford, in 1716, or before; 17 *Ruth*, m Stephen Hickox, and settled in Durham.

13. BENJAMIN.

Benjamin Gaylord, m 1st, Jerusha Frisbie of Branford, Conn., Jan. 28, 1729. She died May 11, 1734. He married 2d, Mary Ashley, Feb. 14, 1738.

Children: 18 *Levi*, b Jan. 10, 1730; 19 *Jerusha*, b July 1, 1731; 20 *Enos*, b Jan. 27, 1733, d Jan., 1734.

6. SAMUEL.

Samuel Gaylord, son of John and Elizabeth, married Thankful Munson, Aug. 19, 1729.

Children: 21 *Agnes*, b June 5, 1730; 22 *Justus*, b Mar. 12, 1732; 23 *Annie*, b April 24, 1734; 24 *Mamre*, b March 3, 1736.

7. EDWARD.

EDWARD GAYLORD, son of John and Elizabeth, m Mehitable Brooks, Aug. 16, 1733, at Cheshire, Conn.

Children: 55 *Jesse*, b Feb. 23, 1734, d; 26 *Jesse*, b Sept. 10, 1735.

8. TIMOTHY.

TIMOTHY GAYLORD, son of John and Elizabeth, m Prudence Royce, April 25, 1733.

Children: 27 *Prudence*, b Jan. 31, 1734; 28 *Timothy*, b May 3, 1735, d; 29 *Timothy*, b Aug. 1, 1736; 30 *Royce*, b July 17, 1737; 31 *Reuben*, b June 17, 1742.

9. NATHAN.

NATHAN GAYLORD, b 1724, d at Cheshire, Conn., July 2, 1802, ae. 78.

Children: 33 *John*, d in Wallingford; 34 *Nathan*, d in Cheshire; 35 *Elias*, d in Cheshire, m —— Hitchcock.

10. JOSEPH.

JOSEPH GAYLORD, son of John and Elizabeth, married Elizabeth Rich, Nov. 9, 1738.

Child: 32 *Charles*, b Sept 22, 1739, in Wallingford or Cheshire.

33. JOHN.

JOHN GAYLORD resided on Parker's farms in Wallingford, in the house now owned by Silas Y. Andrews.

Child: 36 *John*, m —— Tuttle, had a son David T. and a daughter.

34. NATHAN.

NATHAN died in Cheshire, and was the owner of the old mills in the south part of the town.

Children: 37 *Titus*, d in Cheshire; 38 *Hannah*, m Ebenezer Atwater; 39 *Jerusha*, m Rufus Plum; 40 *Nathan*, m ——

Bradley; 41 *Eveline*, m Billious Brooks; 42 *Enos*, is living in Prospect, m Celia Moss.

35. ELIAS.

ELIAS GAYLORD, married 1st, —— Hitchcock. She died and he married 2d, a widow Thorp.

Children: 43 *Horace*, m ——— Bradley; 44 *Elias*, m Amanda Bristol; 45 *Hannah*, m George Bristol.

HALL.[1]

JOHN.

JOHN HALL senior, (the emigrant), appears first, at Boston, and afterwards at New Haven. He evidently was not an original settler at New Haven, as his name does not appear in any list which I have been able to discover until after 1650. From whence he came is uncertain. The name (Hall) is a difficult one to trace, on account of the great number of original settlers of that name, 28 having come to America previous to 1660, of whom seven bore the name of John.

That John Hall of Boston, New Haven and Wallingford

---

1 For collateral branches, see Adams' Haven Genealogy, 2d part, 27, 28; Bouton's Hist. Concord, N. H., 707, 708; Brooke's Hist. Medford, Mass., 517–27; Clarke's Hist. Norton, Mass., 82, 83; Draper's Hist. Spencer, Mass., 211, 212; Eaton's Annals of Warren, Me., 396, 397; Eaton's Hist. Thomaston, Me., 247–50; Freeman's Hist. Cape Cod, Mass., II. 137, 202, 209, 214, 507, 589, 707–9, 717; Goodwin's Gen. of Foote family, 107, 108; Hill's Hist. Mason, N. H., 203; Hinman's Conn. Settlers, 1st ed., 170–8; Hudson's Hist. Lexington, Mass., 83; Jackson's Hist. Newton, Mass., 295–7; Kellogg's Memorials of Elder John White, 33; Kingman's Hist. North Bridgewater, Mass., 529, 530; Lewis and Newhall's Hist. Lynn, Mass., 120; Littell's Passaic Valley Gen., 160–4; Matthews' Hist. Cornwall, Vt., 286; Mitchell's Hist. Bridgewater, Mass., 169, 170; N. E. Hist. and Gen. Reg., VI. 259, 260; XIII. 15, 16; XV. 59, 381, 382; New Hampshire Hist. Soc. Coll., VII. 381, 382; Savage's Gen. Dict., II. 332–9; Sewell's Hist. Woburn, Mass., 616; Stiles' Hist. Windsor, Ct., 651; Thurston's Hist. Winthrop, Me., 186; Ward's Hist. Shrewsbury, Mass., 304, 305; Whitmore's Gen. of Hall family; Winsor's Hist. Duxbury, Mass., 263, 264.

was an emigrant, appears quite evident, from his having sons old enough to be married in 1666. He moved to Wallingford after the settlement had commenced, which accounts for the non-appearance of his name on the first Plantation covenant, in 1669–70. His sons John, Thomas and Samuel, were signers to that instrument. His name appears on the covenant of 1672, and it is quite certain that he had then been sometime in the place. In 1675, himself and his son John were chosen selectmen of Wallingford.

John Hall senior, was freed from training in 1665, being then in his 60th year, and was most certainly in New Haven as early as 1639, and at Wallingford about the year 1670, with the early settlers there. He died early in the year 1676, ae. 71 years. The maiden name of his wife was Jane Woolen.

Children: 1 *John*, baptized Aug. 9, 1646, d Sept. 2, 1721; 2 *Richard*, b July 11, 1645, m Hannah ———; 3 *Samuel*, b May 21, 1646, d March 5, 1725; 4 *Sarah*, baptized Aug. 9, 1646, at New Haven; 5 *Thomas*, b March 25, 1649; 6 *Jonathan*, b April 5, 1651; 7 *David*, b March 18, 1652, d July 17, 1727, æ. 75 yrs.

1. RICHARD.

RICHARD HALL, son of John and Jane Hall, married Hannah ———. He died in 1726, in New Haven.

Children: 8 *Samuel*, b Aug. 2, 1700, m Hannah Brown; 9 *Hannah*, b Jan. 31, 1702; 10 *John*, b Jan. 17, 1714, m Abiah Macomber; 11 *Jonathan*, grad. at Yale in 1737; 12 *Mary*, b March 19, 1712, d young and before her father.

2. SAMUEL.

SAMUEL HALL, son of John and Jane Hall, went to Wallingford with the first planters in 1670. He married Hannah Walker, May, 1668, and died March 5, 1725, æ. 77 years. She died Dec. 20, 1728.

Children: 13 *John*, b Dec. 23, 1670, m Mary Lyman; 14 *Hannah*, b March 11, 1673, m Ebenezer Doolittle; 15 *Sarah*, b June 20, 1677, d March 18, 1712; 16 *Samuel*, b Dec. 10,

1680, d June 15, 1770, ae. 90 yrs; 17 *Theophilus*, b Feb. 5, 1686; 18 *Elizabeth*, b March 6, 1690, m John Moss.

4. THOMAS.

THOMAS HALL, son of John and Jane Hall, married Grace ——, June 5, 1673, she died May 1, 1731; he died Sept. 17, 1731, æ. 62 years, 5 mos. and 17 days.

Children: 19 *Abigail*, b Jan. 7, 1674, m John Tyler; 20 *Thomas*, b July 17, 1676, m Abigail, dau. of John Atwater; 21 *Mary*, b Nov. 22, 1677; 22 *Jonathan*, b July 25, 1679, m Dinah Andrews, May 12, 1703; 23 *Joseph*, b July 8, 1681, m Bertha Terrel, Nov. 13, 1706; 24 *Esther*, b Feb. 23, 1682, m Benoni Atkins; 25 *Benjamin*, b April 19, 1684, m Mary Ives; 26 *Peter*, b Dec. 28, 1686, m Rebecca Bartholomew; 27 *Daniel*, b Jan. 27, 1689; 28 *Rebecca*, b Jan. 6, 1691, m Daniel Holt, who was b Oct. 6, 1689; 29 *Israel*, b Oct. 8, 1696, m Abigail Palmer.

5. JOHN.

JOHN HALL, son of John and Jane Hall, married Mary, daughter of Edward Parker, at New Haven, Dec. 6, 1666. They settled in Wallingford with the first planters, in 1670. He died Sept. 2, 1721, æ. 86 yrs. She died Sept. 22, 1725.

Children: 30 *Elizabeth*, b Aug. 11, 1670, in New Haven; 31 *Daniel*, b July 26, 1672, m Thankful Lyman, March 15, 1693; 32 *Mary*, b June 23, 1675; 33 *Nathaniel*, b Feb. 8, 1677, m Elizabeth Curtis; 34 *John*, b March 14, 1681, m Elizabeth Royce; 35 *Lydia*, b Jan. 21, 1683; 36 *Samuel*, b Dec. 24, 1686, d Nov. 1, 1689; 37 *Esther*, b Aug. 30, 1693; 38 *Caleb*, b Sept. 14, 1697.

7. DAVID.

DAVID HALL, son of John and Jane Hall, married Mary Rutherford, of New Haven, Nov. 11, 1670; 2d, Sarah Rockwell, Dec. 24, 1676. She died Nov. 3, 1732; he died July 7, 1727, ae. 76 yrs.

Children: 39 *Daniel*, b Aug. 9, 1672, d Jan. 13, 1673; 40 *Rutherford*, b April 20, 1675. By 2d marriage: 41 *John*, b May 9, 1678, m Thankful Doolittle; 42 *Thankful*, b Dec. 29,

1679; 43 *Sarah*, b Dec. 28, 1681, m Nathaniel Curtis; 44 *Ruth*, b Nov. 10, 1685; 45 *Jerusha*, b Oct. 28, 1687, m John Mattoon, Oct. 20, 1706; 46 *Mabel*, b Aug. 15, 1691; 47 *David*, b Dec. 1, 1693, m Martha Doolittle, April 20, 1721.

13. JOHN.

JOHN HALL, son of Samuel and Hannah, married Mary Lyman; she died Oct. 16, 1740; he died April 29, 1730, ae. 60 yrs. Rev. Mr. Whittelsey preached his funeral sermon.

Children: 48 *John*, b Sept. 13, 1679; 49 *Esther*, b Aug. 30, 1694; 50 *Samuel*, b Oct. 4, 1695; 51 *Caleb*, b Sept. 14, 1697, graduated at Yale; 52 *Eunice*, b March 7, 1700; 53 *Benjamin*, b Aug. 28, 1702; 54 *Benjamin*, b Dec. 17, 1704; 55 *Sarah*, b April 15, 1706; 56 *Eliakim*, b Aug. 9, 1711; 56 *Elihu*, b Feb. 17, 1714, graduated at Yale, was King's Attorney in 1770, d in London; 58 *Nancy*.

16. SAMUEL.

SAMUEL HALL, son of Samuel and Hannah Hall, married Sue, daughter of Nathaniel and Esther Royce; 2d, Bridget ——; he died June 15, 1770, ae. 90 yrs.

Children: 59 *Theophilus*, b April 1, 1707; 60 *Samuel*, b June 8, 1709; 61 *Hannah*, b July 15, 1711; 62 *Sarah*, b Dec. 6, 1713; 63 *Mehitable*, b April 25, 1716; 64 *Esther*, b Nov. 7, 1719.

20. THOMAS.

THOMAS HALL, son of Thomas and Grace Hall, married Abigail Atwater, April 26, 1710; he died Aug. 27, 1741.

Children: 65 *Thomas*, b March 10, 1712, m Lydia Curtis, April 24, 1734; 66 *Phineas*, b April 12, 1715; 67 *Abigail*, b April 12, 1719, d Jan. 12, 1737; 68 *Joshua*, b May 23, 1722.

22. JONATHAN.

JONATHAN HALL, son of Thomas and Grace Hall, married Dinah Andrews, May 12, 1703; he was born July 25, 1679, d Jan. 15, 1760, ae. 80 years and 17 days; she was born 1684, and died at the age of 79 yrs., 2 mos. and 29 days.

Children: 69 *David*, b Oct. 16, 1705, m Sept. 23, 1731, to Alice ——; 70 *Jonathan*, b Jan. 13, 1708, m Dec. 15, 1739, to Sarah, dau. of John Cook; 71 *Joseph*, b May 31, 1710, m April 19, 1736, to Hannah Scoville; 72 *Anna*, b Jan. 18, 1713; 73 *Isaac*, b July 11, 1714, m Nov. 5, 1739, d March 7, 1781, m Mary Moss; 74 *Phebe*, b Feb. 12, 1717, d May 14, 1735; 75 *Ezekiel*, b May 13, 1719, m Anna Andrews, Oct. 29, 1763; 76 *Thankful*, b Sept. 20, 1722; 77 *Benjamin*, b Oct. 20, 1725; 78 *Temperance*, b April 16, 1727.

23. JOSEPH.

JOSEPH HALL, son of Thomas and Grace Hall, married Bertha Terrel, Nov. 13, 1706; she died Dec. 28, 1753; he died Nov. 3, 1748.

Children: 79 *Temperance*, b July 15, 1714, d Dec. 7, 1716; 80 *Joseph*, b Sept. 23, 1718, d Sept. 6, 1737; 81 *Ephraim*, b April 25, 1723, m 1st, Eunice ——, she d May 9, 1763, he m 2d, Chloe Moss, Oct. 13, 1763.

25. BENJAMIN.

BENJAMIN HALL, son of Thomas and Grace Hall, married Mary Ives, Dec. 27, 1752.

Children: 82 *Benjamin*, b Sept. 25, 1753, d Oct. 8, 1755; 83 *Eliab*, b Feb. 17, 1755, d in camp during the Revolution, at N. Y.; 84 *Benjamin*, b Nov. 3, 1756.

26. PETER.

PETER HALL, son of Thomas and Grace Hall, married Rebecca Bartholomew, Oct. 19, 1732; he died Sept. 25, 1798, æ. 90 yrs. She died Oct. 31, 1798, æ. 87 yrs.

Children: 85 *Susannah*, b Feb. 26, 1733; 86 *Hiel*, b May 6, 1735; 87 *Abigail*, b May 15, 1737; 88 *Rebecca*, b July 3, 1740; 89 *Eunice*, b Nov. 8, 1742; 90 *Josiah*, b July 3, 1743; 91 *Peter*, b June 7, 1748, d as shown by date on stone, —; 92 *Andrew*, b Sept. 16, 1750, d Oct. 14, 1776; 93 *Anna*, b March 30, 1753; 94 *Keziah*, b June 16, 1755; 95 *Lois*, b Sept. 25, 1757.

27. DANIEL.

DANIEL HALL, son of Thomas and Grace Hall, married Martha Doolittle, April 20, 1721.

Children: 96 *Abraham*, b Jan. 27, 1722, m Sarah Doolittle; 97 *John*, b Jan. 29, 1724, d in Meriden, May 13, 1795, æ. 72; 98 *Hannah*, b Sept. 11, 1725, m Benjamin Tyler, of Branford; 99 *Daniel*, b June 1, 1727; 100 *Martha*, b June 14, 1729; 101 *Samuel*, b May 5, 1731; 102 *Mary*, b Sept. 7, 1733; 103 *Abigail*, b April 27, 1739.

29. ISRAEL.

ISRAEL HALL, son of Thomas and Grace Hall, m Abigail Powell, April 11, 1721.

Children: 104, 105 *Sarah*, and *Israel*, b March 14, 1722; 106 *Enos*, b March 30, 1726; 107 *Israel*, b Oct. 22, 1728; 108 *Abigail*, b Mar. 22, 1731, d Aug. 5, 1743; 109 *Jotham*, b Feb. 6, 1737; 110 *Abigail*, b July 5, 1744; 111 *Mary*, b June 23, 1749; 112 *Eunice*, b Feb. 6, 1751.

31. DANIEL.

DANIEL HALL, son of John and Mary Hall, married Thankful Lyman, March 15, 1693.

Children: 113 *Daniel*, b Jan. 4, 1693, d; 114 *Daniel*, b Feb. 19, 1695, d 1727; 115 *Samuel*, b Nov. 5, 1697; 116 *Silence*, b Oct. 6, 1699; 117 *Preserved*, b Jan. 15, 1700, was an imbecile, his brother Abraham had the care of him; 118 *Sarah*, b June 21, 1703; 119 *Benjamin*, b Dec. 17, 1704; 150 *Jacob*, b 1705; 121 *David*, b Oct. 16, 1706; 122 *Abraham*, b Feb. 5, 1709, d Sept. 16, 1761, æ. 53.

33. NATHANIEL.

NATHANIEL HALL, son of John and Mary Hall, married Elizabeth Curtis, May, 1699; he died Aug. 16, 1757. She died Sept. 30, 1735, and he married Lydia Johnson, Sept 15, 1736.

Children: 123 *Amos*, b Jan. 24, 1700, m Ruth Royce; 124 *Margaretta*, b Dec. 21, 1701, d Oct. 30, 1707; 125 *Caleb*, b Jan. 3, 1703, d May 11, 1766, ae. 62 yrs.; 126 *Moses*, b June

6, 1706, d Feb. 15, 1765, ae. 59 yrs.; 127 *Mary*, b Oct. 30, 1707; 128 *Nathaniel*, b April 17, 1711, d Dec. 18, 1727; 129 *James*, b April 23, 1713; 130 *Elizabeth*, b Sept. 22, 1715; 131 *Desire*, b June 19, 1719; 132 *Harmon*, b Oct. 17, 1720.

34. JOHN.

DEA. JOHN HALL, son of John and Mary Hall, married Elizabeth Rice, June 28, 1707. He died April 27, 1766, ae. 86. She died Sept. 2, 1755, æ. 66 years.

Children: 133, 134 *Isaac* and *Peter*, b July 22, 1709, the latter m Rebecca ——, he d Sept. 25, 1798; 135 *John*, b Dec. 28, 1712; 136 *Abel;* 137 *Asahel*, b Jan. 19, 1717; 138 *Royce*, b Dec. 26, 1718, grad. at Yale, 1737, d May 29, 1752; 139 *Abigail*, b March 7, 1723; 140 *Elizabeth*, b July 9, 1725; 141 *Benjamin*, b April 4, 1728, m Phebe Hall, d Dec. 11, 1806; 142 *Elisha*, b Sept. 15, 1730; 143 *Sarah*, b Aug. 25, 1732.

47. DANIEL.

DANIEL HALL, son of Daniel and Sarah Hall, was born Dec. 1, 1693, married Martha Doolittle, April 20, 1721.

Children: 144 *Abraham*, b Jan. 27, 1722, m Sarah Doolittle; 145 *John*, b Jan. 29, 1724, settled in Meriden; 146 *Hannah*, b Sept. 11, 1725, m Benajah Tyler; 147 *Daniel*, b June 1, 1727, settled in Meriden; 148 *Martha*, b June 14, 1729; 149 *Samuel*, b May 5, 1731; 150 *Mary*, b Sept. 7, 1733; 151 *Abigail*, b April 27, 1739.

48. JOHN.

JOHN HALL, son of John and Mary Lyman Hall, married Mary Street, March 5, 1716. She died Oct. 12, 1778, aged 81 years. He died June 18, 1773, ae. 80 years.

Children: 152 *Hannah*, b Jan. 29, 1717; 153 *John*, d April 25, 1737; 154 *Eunice*, m Dr. Dickinson of Middletown, Conn.; 155 *Lyman*, Gov., b April 12, 1724, signed the Declaration of Independence; 156 *Street*, b Nov. 12, 1721, d in Wallingford; 157 *Susannah*, b April 9, 1726, m —— Whittelsey; 158 *Giles*, b Feb. 18, 1733, d March 11, 1789, ae. 56; 159 *Rhoda*, b April 14, 1734, d Aug. 23, 1751, ae. 17; 160 *Mary*, m ——— Foote.

50. SAMUEL.

REV. SAMUEL HALL, son of John and Mary Lyman Hall, grad. at Yale in 1716, married Anna Law, Jan. 25, 1727, and was settled as a minister over the Congregational church at Cheshire in 1724. He died Feb. 26, 1776. She was born in Milford, Aug. 1, 1702, died Aug. 23, 1775.

Children: 161 *Samuel*, b July 23, 1727, d Aug. 23, 1727; 162 *Jonathan*, b July 11, 1728, d July 12, 1728; 163 *Benoni*, b Nov. 4, 1729, d Nov. 19, 1729; 164 *Lucy*, b Sept. 11, 1730, m Chas. Whittelsey; 165 *Samuel*, b Jan. 11, 1732, d May 19, 1732; 166 *Ann*, b May 10, 1733; 167 *Samuel*, b May 31, 1735, grad. at Yale; 168 *Mary*, b Nov, 5, 1736; 169 *Brenton*, b April 2, 1738, d Nov. 25, 1720, ae. 82; 170 *Elisha*, b March 10, 1740, grad. at Yale in 1764; 171 *Sarah*, b Aug. 8, 1742; 172 *Jonathan*, b July 19, 1745, settled in Cheshire, kept a tavern; 173 *Abigail*, b Dec. 7, 1748, m Rev. John Foote of Cheshire.

51. CALEB.

CALEB HALL, son of John and Mary Lyman Hall, married Damaris Atwater, May 15, 1721; he died July 27, 1749; she died July 29, 1762, æ. 64 years.

Children: 174 *Damaris*, b Nov. 25, 1722, d Feb. 22, 1740; 175 *Stephen*, b Nov. 7, 1724, m Ruth Miles in 1762, d July 27, 1749; 176 *Ruth*, b April 26, 1729; 177 *Caleb*, b Aug. 29, 1731, grad. at Yale in 1752; 178 *Jeremiah*, b Sept. 1, 1733, d Sept. 4, 1740; 179 *Lydia*, b Aug. 26, 1730; 180 *Timothy*, m Abigail Miles.

54. BENJAMIN.

BENJAMIN HALL, son of John and Mary Lyman Hall, married Abigail, daughter of Rev. Nathaniel Chauncey, of Durham, Feb. 20, 1727, and settled in Cheshire on the place now known as the Law farm.

Children: 181 *Benjamin*, b Nov. 22, 1727, d Dec. 3, 1727; 182 *Charles Chauncey*, b Dec. 12, 1728, d Dec. 20, 1776, æ. 48; 183 *Sarah*, b July 20, 1730, m Thaddeus Cook; 184 *Dorothy*, b Feb. 29, 1732, d May 13, 1737; 185 *Dorothy*, m

Charles, son of John Peck; 186 *Abigail*, b Oct. 11, 1733, d April 15, 1737; 187 *Benjamin*, b Sept. 27, 1736, grad. at Yale in 1754, d 1786, æ. 50; 188 *Abigail*, b May 1, 1737, m Moses Moss; 189 *Eunice*, b March 4, 1742, m Rev. Mr. Waterman.

56. ELIAKIM.

ELIAKIM HALL, son of John and Mary Lyman Hall, married Ruth Dickerman Oct. 17, 1734; she died Dec. 18, 1752, and he married Elizabeth ——; she died Aug. 9, 1803; he died April 19, 1794, æ. 80 years.

Children: 190 *Isaac*, b Nov. 4, 1735; 191 *Mary*, b Nov. 6, 1737; 192 *Eliakim*, b Feb. 13, 1740; 193 *Hezekiah*, b July 13, 1743; 194 *Ruth*, b May 1, 1750.

57. ELIHU.

COL. ELIHU HALL, son of John and Mary Lyman Hall, married Lois Whittelsey, Jan. 2, 1734, was King's Attorney in 1750; went to England and died in London in 1784, æ. 70; his widow died Sept. 29, 1780, ae. 66 yrs; he was a grad. of Yale College.

Children: 195 *Lois*, b May 11, 1735; 196 *Hezekiah*, b May 4, 1737; 197 *Sarah*, b July 24, 1729; 198 *John*, b Jan. 18, 1739, m Mary Jones; 199 *Damaris*, b Oct. 6, 1741; 200 *Elihu*, b Aug. 13, 1744; 201 *Elihu*, b March 15, 1745, m Sarah ——; 202 *Eunice*, b March 2, 1749; 203 *Lucy*, b Nov. 14, 1781; 204 *Eunice*, b Aug. 11, 1754.

59. THEOPHILUS.

REV. THEOPHILUS HALL, son of Samuel and Love Hall, married Hannah Avery, May 21, 1734, graduated at Yale in 1727, was ordained Oct. 29, 1729, and was the first settled minister of the Congregational church in Meriden; he died March 25, 1769, ae. 60 yrs., in the thirty-eighth year of his ministry.

Children: 205 *Hannah*, b March 11, 1735; 206 *Theophilus*, b Aug. 5, 1736, d May 9, 1739; 207 *Avery*, b Dec. 2, 1737, he was a clergyman; 208 *Samuel*, b July 16, 1739; 209, 210 *Theophilus* and *Lucy*, b Aug. 26, 1741, the former married

Elizabeth Couch, d May 17, 1804, ae. 63 yrs; 211 *Elisha*, b 1742, d Jan. 2, 1757, ae. 9 yrs; 212 *Mary*, b June 24, 1743; 213 *Elisha*, b March 3, 1745, m Ann Hopkins, Feb. 25, 1767; 214 *Mehitable*, b 1751, d Sept. 11, 1767.

60. SAMUEL.

SAMUEL HALL, son of Samuel and Love Hall, was born June 8, 1709. He married Sarah Hull, Dec. 7, 1732; he died Dec. 24, 1771.

Children: *Samuel*, b July 11, 1732, d in infancy; 215 *Hezekiah*, b Dec. 27, 1733; 216 *Louisa*, b June 30, 1736; 217 *Sarah*, b Dec. 5, 1737; 218 *Esther*, b Jan. 21, 1740; 219 *Love*, b April 30, 1742; 220 *Elizabeth*, b Jan 23, 1745; 221 *Samuel*, b Feb. 28, 1750, d Feb. 27, 1821; 222 *Damaris*, b Jan. 23, 1754.

65. THOMAS.

THOMAS HALL, son of Thomas and Abigail Hall, married Lydia Curtis. She died Sept. 24, 1777. He was born March 12, 1712.

Children: 223 *Ambrose*, b Feb. 3, 1735; 224 *Titus*, b June 28, 1737, d May 1, 1773; 225 *Abigail*, b Aug. 27, 1741; 226 *Thomas*, b Dec. 28, 1743; 227 *Amasa*, b Feb. 9, 1746; 228 *Lydia*, b Sept. 6, 1749; 229 *Rhoda*, b June 6, 1753.

66. PHINEAS.

PHINEAS HALL, son of Thomas and Abigail Hall, married Anna ———.

Children: 230 *Abigail;* 231 *Thankful;* 232 *Phineas;* 233 *Levi;* 234 *Eunice;* 235 *Barnabas;* 236 *Annis*.

68. JOSHUA.

JOSHUA HALL, son of Thomas and Abigail Hall, married Hannah ——.

Children: 237 *Susannah*, b Nov. 16, 1742; 238 *Medad*, b July 26, 1743; 239 *Abigail*, b April 25, 1745; 240, 241 *Giles*, and *Abigail*, b Feb. 24, 1747; 242 *Samuel*, b Jan. 29, 1749; 243 *Joshua*, b Sept. 9, 1767.

69. DAVID.

DAVID HALL, son of Jonathan and Dinah Andrews Hall, married Alice Hale, Sept. 23, 1730; he died about 1755.

Children: 244 *Alice*, b Sept. 8, 1731; 245 *David*, b Nov. 2, 1732, d March 21, 1795, æ. 63; 246 *Benijah*, b Feb. 12, 1734, left no family; 247 *Asaph*, b June 11, 1735; 248 *Bates*, b Dec. 5, 1736; 249 *Phebe*, b June 24, 1739; 250 *Lois*, b Feb. 2, 1741, d Nov. 11, 1760; 251 *Elkanah*, b Oct. 20, 1742, d Nov. 30, 1763; 252 *Lucy*, b July 24, 1744.

70. JONATHAN.

JONATHAN HALL, son of Jonathan and Dinah Hall, married Sarah Cook, Dec. 15, 1739; she died Aug. 12, 1740; he married 2d, Abigail ———, and she died Nov. 19, 1779; he married 3d, Jerusha Gaylord.

Child: 253 *Sarah*, b Aug. 12, 1740, d Aug. 13, 1740.

71. JOSEPH.

JOSEPH HALL, son of Jonathan and Dinah Hall, married 1st, Abigail Judd; she died July 31, 1751, æ. 39; he married 2d, Rebecca Plum, Nov. 7, 1753; she died Feb. 24, 1769, æ. 47 yrs.

Children: 254 *Phebe*, b March 26, 1738; 255, *Phebe*, 256, *Abigail*, b March 30, 1740; 257 *Esther*, b July 21, 1742; 258 *Esther*, b March 19, 1743; 259 *Joseph*, b July 9, 1746; 260 *David*, b June 20, 1758; 261 *Phebe*, b Sept. 15, 1761.

73. ISAAC.

DR. ISAAC HALL, son of Jonathan and Dinah Hall, was the first physician of Meriden. He married Mary Morse, Nov. 5, 1739; died March 7, 1781, æ. 66 years. She died Oct. 9, 1791, æ. 74 years.

Children: 262 *Mary*, b Oct. 6, 1742, m John Ives, grandfather of Rev. Dr. Levi Silliman Ives; 263 *Isaac*, b May 7, 1745, m Lois Buckley; 264 *Joel*, b April 3, 1747, d Oct. 22, 1748; 265 *Esther*, b March 18, 1751; 266 *Elizabeth*, b June 11, 1752; 267 *Jonathan*, b Dec 11, 1757, m Martha Collins, he died June 6, 1832.

75. EZEKIEL.

EZEKIEL HALL, son of Jonathan and Dinah Hall, married Annah Andrews, Oct. 20, 1743.

Children: 268 *Ezekiel*, b Oct. 24, 1744; 269 *Titus*, b Oct. 19, 1746, d Sept. 4, 1748; 270 *Eben*, b May 25, 1749; 271 *Benijah*, b 1762, m Ruth ———.

77. BENJAMIN.

BENJAMIN HALL, son of Jonathan and Dinah Hall, married Mary Ives, Dec. 27, 1752.

Children: 272 *Benjamin*, b Sept. 25, 1753; 273 *Eliab*, b Feb. 17, 1755; 274 *Benjamin*, b Nov. 3, 1756.

81. EPHRAIM.

EPHRAIM HALL, son of Joseph and Bertha Hall, married Eunice——. She died May 9, 1763, and he married Chloe Moss, Oct. 13, 1763.

Children: 275 *Temperance*, b Aug. 10, 1764. By 2nd marriage: 276 *Joseph*, b March 17, 1776; 277 *Ephraim*, b Oct. 5, 1768; 278 *Chloe*, b Nov. 13, 1770; 279 *Comfort*, b Feb. 25, 1773, settled on a farm in Middletown, Westfield society, where he died; 280 *Reuben*, b 1775; 281 *David Moss*, b Oct. 24, 1777; 282 *Content*, b March 15, 1780; 283 *Bethiah*, b March 27, 1782.

86. HIEL.

HIEL HALL, son of Peter and Rebecca Hall, married Catharine ———; she died June 4, 1788, ae. 42 yrs; he died Sept. 7, 1707, ae. 73 yrs.

Children: 284 *Josiah*, b 1774, d Dec. 15, 1821, ae. 47; 285 *Catharine*, b Jan. 2, 1776; 286 *Andrew*, b 1777, d June 25, 1812, ae. 35; 287 *Chauncey*, b Sept. 8, 1778, m Marilla Hall; 288 *Peter*, b May 31, 1780, m Delight Kirtland; 289 *Hiel*, b Feb. 7, 1782, m Sarah Kirtland; 290 *Rice*, b May 2, 1784; 291 *Justus*, d Feb. 14, 1777.

91. PETER.

PETER HALL, son of Peter and Rebecca Hall, married

Lydia Brown of Cheshire, March 17, 1774. She died May 2, 1805, æ. 52. He died Sept. 25, 1732, æ. 86 yrs.

Children: 292 *Jesse;* 293 *Wooster;* 294 *Roxy*, b 1779, d Sept. 26, 1756; 295 *Marcus;* 296 *Major Atwater*, b July 18, 1785, d March 28, 1848; 297 *Philo*, m Thankful Morse; 298 *Albert;* 299 *Peter Ufford*, d in Southington, in 1836; 300 *Sally;* 301 *Betsey.*

92. ANDREW.

ANDREW HALL, son of Peter and Rebecca Hall, married Sept. 16, 1750, Thankful ———. She died Oct. 14, 1776.

Children: 302 *John Todd;* 303 *Merritt;* 304 *Charry;* 305 *Anna*, b Feb. 3, 1773; 306 *Thankful*, b Aug. 4, 1776.

96. ABRAHAM.

ABRAHAM HALL, son of Daniel and Abigail Hall, married Sarah Doolittle, May 5, 1741; he died Sept. 16, 1761, æ. 53 yrs. She died March 14, 1781, æ. 77 yrs.

Children: 307 *Eldad*, b Feb. 4, 1742; 308 *Medad*, b July 26, 1745; 309 *Bildad*, b Sept. 3, 1747; 310 *Isaac*, b July 26, 1749; 311 *Isaac*, b Aug. 11, 1753.

107. ISRAEL.

ISRAEL HALL, son of Israel and Abigail Powell Hall, married Eunice Rice, Feb. 26, 1778.

Children: 312 *Elisha*, b Dec. 26, 1778; 313 *Eunice*, b Jan. 6, 1787.

109. JOTHAM.

JOTHAM HALL, son of Israel and Abigail Powell Hall, married Elizabeth ——.

Children: *Sarah*, b May 11, 1758; 314 *Jotham*, b March 1, 1761; 315 *Elizabeth*, b Aug. 27, 1763; 316 *George*, b April 27, 1768; 317 *Mary*, b Sept. 23, 1770; 318 *Joseph*, b July 23, 1773; 319 *Chloe*, b July 11, 1775.

120. JACOB.

JACOB HALL, son of Daniel and Thankful Hall, married Elizabeth Royce, Dec. 21, 1726.

Children: 320 *Phebe*, b Dec. 26, 1727; 321 *Mindwell*, b

May 21, 1730; 322 *Jacob*, b July 20, 1731; 323 *Giles*, b June 7, 1732; 324 *Lydia*, b April 20, 1736; 325 *Daniel*, b July 21, 1738; 326 *Daniel*, b Nov. 17, 1740, d Oct. 24, 1789; 327 *Thankful*, b July 29, 1744; 328 *Lois*, b Nov. 5, 1746.

121. DAVID.

David Hall, son of Daniel and Thankful Hall, married Alice ——; he was born Feb. 19, 1695.

Children: 329 *David*, b Nov. 2, 1732, d March 2, 1795, æ. 63, m Thankful ——; 330 *Benajah*, b Feb. 12, 1734; 331 *Asaph*, b June 15, 1735; 332 *Kate*, b Dec. 5, 1736; 333 *Phebe*, b June 24, 1737; 334 *Lucy*, b July 25, 1747, æ. 51.

123. AMOS.

Amos Hall, son of Nathaniel and Elizabeth Hall, was born Jan. 24, 1700; he married Ruth Royce, June 8, 1720. She died Feb. 2, 1775, ae. 75. He died Nov. 30, 1752, ae. 52 years.

Children: 335 *Reuben*, b Dec. 20, 1721, m Mary ——; 336 *Amos*, b Sept. 9, 1722, d Dec. 24, 1782, ae. 31 yrs.; 337 *Eunice*, b Aug. 21, 1724, m Abner Avered; 338 *Lois*, b Oct. 26, 1727, m Caleb Culver; 339 *Moses*, b Aug. 25, 1735, m Elizabeth How, Dec. 21, 1726, she d and he m Elizabeth Johnson, March 20, 1754.

125. CALEB.

Caleb Hall, son of Nathaniel and Elizabeth Hall, was born Jan. 3, 1703, m Esther Umberfield, May 11, 1726; he died May 11, 1766, ae. 62 yrs.

Children: 340 *Margaret*, b March 28, 1727, d Nov. 14, 1749; 341 *Esther*, b April 24, 1729, m Ichabod Lewis; 342 *Nathaniel*, b April 8, 1732; 343 *Caleb*, b Sept. 12, 1734; 344 *Moses*, b May 13, 1736; 345 *Lydia*, b July 9, 1738; 346 *Desire*, b June 20, 1740, m Moses Holt; 347 *Sarah*, b April 10, 1742, m Noah Todd; 348 *Margaret*, b Aug. 31, 1744; 349 *Titus*, b Aug. 16, 1746; 350 *Rhoda*, b June 15, 1748, d Oct. 10, 17—; 351 *Jonah*, b Feb. 23, 1749–50; 352 *Rhoda*, b July 4, 1753; 353 *Lucretia*, b Feb. 16, 1757.

126. MOSES.

MOSES HALL, son of Nathaniel and Elizabeth Hall, was born June 6, 1706, married Elizabeth Howe, Dec. 21, 1726. He married 2d, Phebe ———. He died Feb. 15, 1765, ae. 59. His will gave his property to Caleb and Heman his brothers, and to Amos, Moses and Miles, his cousins. No children.

129. JAMES.

JAMES HALL, son of Nathaniel and Elizabeth Curtis Hall, was born Aug. 23, 1713, married Hannah Cook, Sept. 15, 1735.

Children: 354 *Miles*, b Oct. 17, 1736; 355 *Bethia*, b April 13, 1740; 356 *Phebe*, b Nov. 16, 1741; 357 *James*, b July 22, 1743; 358 *Olive*, b May 20, 1745.

133. ISAAC.

ISAAC HALL, son of John and Elizabeth Hall, was born July 23, 1709, married Mary Moss Nov. 5, 1739. She died Oct. 9, 1721, ae. 75. He died March 7, 1781.

Children: 359 *Mary*, b Oct. 5, 1742; 360 *Isaac*, b March 7, 1745; 361 *Joel*, b April 3, 1747, d Oct. 22, 1748; 362 *Esther*, b March 18, 1751; 363 *Elizabeth*, b June 11, 1752; 364 *Jonathan*, b Nov. 8, 1755, d 1756, ae. ten mos.; 365 *Jonathan*, b Dec. 11, 1757.

135. JOHN.

JOHN HALL, son of John and Elizabeth Hall, born Dec. 28, 1712, married Abigail Russel, June 11, 1739, died May 13, 1795.

Children: 366 *Elias*, b March 10, 1740; 367 *Jared*, b July 19, 1741; 368 *Abigail*, b Oct. 16, 1743; 369 *John*, b Dec. 6, 1744; 370 *Elizabeth*, b Sept. 28, 1745; 371 *William*, b June 15, 1747; 372 *Mary*, b Jan. 23, 1749; 373 *Eunice*, b July 6, 1751; 374 *Anna C.*, b Aug. 15, 1755; 375 *Benjamin*, b July 2, 1757, m Lydia ———.

136. ABEL.

ABEL HALL, son of John and Elizabeth Hall, married Ruth Johnson, May 12, 1743.

Children: 376 *Elizabeth*, b Feb. 12, 1743-4; 377 *Abel*, b Oct. 12, 1745; 378 *Ruth*, b Oct. 19, 1748; 379 *Rice*, b May 28, 1750; 380 *John*, b Dec. 23, 1751, m Hannah Atwater; 381 *Lucy*, b Oct. 3, 1753; 382 *Esther*, b July 10, 1754; 383 *Hezekiah*, b April 20, 1757, m Susannah ——; 384 *Simon*, b Oct. 6, 1759; 385 *Daniel Johnson*, b July 4, 1761; 386 *Mary*, b July 17, 1764.

137. ASAHEL.

ASAHEL HALL, son of John and Elizabeth Hall, born June 19, 1717, m Sarah Goldsmith, July 29, 17—. She died Feb. 25, 1784. He died Nov. 11, 1795.

Children: 387 *Catharine*, b Aug. 6, 1739: 388 *Joel*, b May 21, 1741; 389 *Sarah*, b March 5, 1743; 390 *Asahel*, b March 15, 1745, d April 20, 1745; 391 *Jerusha*, b Aug. 31, 1746, d March 10, 1752; 392 *Sarah*, b June 9, 1748, d Dec. 25, 1747; 393 *Asahel*, b July 16, 1750, d March 4, 1752; 394 *Mehitable*, b March 13, 1753; 395 *Aaron*, b July 28, 1755, d Oct. 6, 1756; 396 *Charles*, b Nov. 12, 1757; 397 *Asahel*, b Jan. 14, 1759, m Ruth Johnson, Sept. 21, 1786; 398 *Aaron*, b Nov. 4, 1760; 399 *Sarah*, d Feb. 5, 1749.

141. BENJAMIN.

BENJAMIN HALL, son of John and Elizabeth Hall, born April 4, 1728, died Dec. 11, 1806, ae. 79; he married Phebe Hall, she died Dec. 12, 1779.

Children: 400 *Susannah*, b Jan. 15, 1759; 401 *Bede*, b Sept. 16, 1764; 402 *Statira*, b March 20, 1766; 403 *Benjamin*, b June 30, 1767; 404 *Samuel*, b April 19, 1771.

142. ELISHA.

SERGT. ELISHA HALL, son of John and Elizabeth Royce Hall, born Sept. 15, 1730, married Thankful Atwater, June 14, 1755. He died Jan. 19, 1800, ae. 70 yrs. She died Jan. 28, 1792, æ. 59 yrs.

Children: 405 *Phebe*, b Feb. 10, 1756, m —— Parmelee, of Durham; 406 *Sarah*, b April 5, 1758, m John Fields, of Cheshire; 407 *Joseph*, b July 25, 1759, m Mercy Cornwall,

May 31, 1799; 408 *Lydia*, b July 17, 1761, m ——— Curtis, and went to Durham; 409 *Sally*, b Dec 8, 1763; 410 *Elizabeth*, b Oct. 3, 1765, m Benjamin Hall; 411 *Hannah*, b Jan. 26, 1769; 412 *John*, b July 13, 1770, m Grace D. Hall; 413 *Eunice*, b Aug. 1, 1772, m Miles, son of Nicholas Peck.

144. ABRAHAM.

ABRAHAM HALL, son of Daniel and Martha Hall, was born June 27, 1722, married Mary Prindle, June 23, 1746. She died May 12, 1747. For his second wife he married Hannah ———. He died 1757.

Children by 1st marriage: 414 *Mary*, b May 10, 1747. By 2d marriage: 415 *Rufus*, b July 25, 1751; 416 *Sarah*; 417 *Josiah*; 418 *Abraham*.

145. JOHN.

JOHN HALL, son of Daniel and Martha Hall, born Jan. 29, 1724, settled in Meriden, married Elizabeth Prindle, May 4, 1749; he died May 13, 1795, ae. 72 yrs. She died Oct 21, 1802, ae. 71 yrs.

Children: 419 *Prindle*, b June 30, 1750, d Dec. 6, 1821; 420 *John*, b May 8, 1752, d 1764; 421 *Mary*, b Sept. 10, 1754, d March 1, 1825; 422 *Elizabeth*, b April 20, 1757, died March 30, 1847; 423 *Sarah*, b May 11, 1759, d 1760; 424 *David*, b Sept. 16, 1761, d Aug. 3, 1843; 425 *Sarah*, b Feb. 13, 1764, d 1777; 426 *Abigail*, b Feb. 24, 1766, d Oct. 28, 1828; 427 *John*, b Jan. 9, 1768, d April 21, 1851; 428 *Joseph*, b Oct. 28, 1770, d March 13, 1831, m Hannah ——; 429 *Jedutham*, April 25, 1773, d July 9, 1851; 430 *Isaac*, b May 28, 1776, d Jan. 1, 1838.

149. SAMUEL.

SAMUEL HALL, son of Daniel and Martha Hall, was born May 5. 1731, married Mamre Ives, Aug. 28, 1755.

Children: 431 *Jesse*, b Jan. 24, 1757; 432 *Sarah*, b Jan. 24, 1758; 433 *Samuel*, b July 4, 1760.

155. LYMAN.

LYMAN HALL, son of John and Mary Street Hall, was

graduated at Yale college in 1747, Representative in Congress from the state of Georgia, signer of the Declaration of Independence in 1776. He died in 1791, he left no children, was Governor of the state of Georgia in 1790.

156. STREET.

COL. STREET HALL, son of John and Mary Street Hall, was born Nov. 12, 1721. He died 1809; he married Hannah Fowler, June 30, 1748.

Children: 434 *Hannah*, b July 3, 1751; 435 *Anna*, b Feb. 28, 1753, d Dec. 24, 1755; 436 *Thaddeus*, b Feb. 28, 1757; 437 *Rebecca*, b Feb. 15, 1758; 438 *Street T.*, b Feb. 26, 1762; 439 *Mary A.*, b June 9, 1764; 440 ——.

158. GILES.

GILES HALL, son of John and Mary Street Hall, was born Feb. 18, 1733, married 1st, Martha Robinson, Nov., 1759, m 2d, Thankful Merriman, of Wallingford. He died March 17, 1789, æ. 41 yrs. Mrs. Thankful died July 14, 1796, æ. 47 years.

Children: 441 *Lucy*, b April 11, 1771; 442 *David M.*, b 1773, d April 21, 1792; 443 *Martha R.*, b Aug. 22, 1777; 444 *Mary Street*, b March 17, 1780; 445 *John*, b July 27, 1782; 446 *Hannah*, b 1783; 447 *Elizabeth*, b May 2, 1785; 447 *Giles*, b June 7, 1788; 449 *Lois*, b Feb. 82, 1789; 450 *John*, b April 20, 1793, d Feb. 26, 1835, ae. 53 yrs.

169. BRENTON.

BRENTON HALL, son of Rev. Samuel and Ann Hall, was born April 2, 1738, married Lament Collins, Feb. 18, 1762, and settled in the eastern part of Meriden, where he died Nov. 25, 1820, ae. 82 yrs. His 2d wife Abigail ——, died May 5, 1837, ae. 88 yrs.

Children: 451 *Wm Brenton*, b May 31, 1764; 452 *Collins*, b Jan. 8, 1766; 453 *Samuel*, b June 10, 1768; 454 *Lament*, b July 14, 1776; 455 *Joab*.

170. ELISHA.

ELISHA HALL, son of Rev. Samuel and Ann Hall of

Cheshire, Conn., graduated at Yale College in 1774. He married for his 2d wife, Oct. 22, 1795, Lois, widow of Jesse Street, and daughter of Col. Thaddeus Cook. She was mother of Col. Thaddeus Street, late of Cheshire.

172. JONATHAN.

JONATHAN HALL, son of Rev. Samuel and Ann Hall, married Mary ———. He was a farmer and inn-keeper in Cheshire, for many years.

Children: 456 *Millicent;* 457 *Lucy;* 458 *George;* 459 *Salmon;* 460 *Leverett;* 461 *Sylvester.*

177. CALEB.

CALEB HALL, son of Caleb and Damaris Hall. He graduated at Yale College in 1752, studied medicine and became a physician. He married Prudence Holt. She died Nov. 30, 1807, æ. 67 yrs. He died Sept. 21, 1783, æ. 67 yrs.

Children: 462 *Caleb Johnson*, b Sept. 22, 1763; 463 *Augustus*, b Aug. 16, 1765; 464 *Abigail*, b Jan. 29, 1767, m 1st, Lemuel Carrington, 2d, Nehemiah Rice; 465 *Eunice*, b Aug. 24, 1770; 466 *Benjamin*, b July 26, 1772; 467 *Horatio Gates*, b Jan. 17, 1778, d at Wallingford; 468, 469 *George* and *Damaris*, b Feb. 10, 1782.

180. TIMOTHY.

TIMOTHY HALL, son of Caleb and Damaris Hall, married Abigail Miles, and settled on Cheshire street; he was a farmer. She died Nov. 22, 1748. He married Athildred Parker, June 10, 1748–9.

Children: 470 *Jeremiah*, b April 20, 1750; 471 *Aaron*, b June 27, 1751; 472 *Timothy*, b Oct. 13, 1752; 473 *Amasa*, b Dec. 7, 1754; 473 1–2 *Abigail*, b Dec. 5, 1756; 474 *Archibald*, b May 23, 1758; 475 *Zenas*, b June 8, d Nov. 6, 1759; 476 *Zenas*, b Oct. 7, 1759; 477 *Josiah*, b Nov. 6, 1761; 478 *Aaron.*

182. CHARLES.

CHARLES CHAUNCEY HALL, son of Benjamin and Abigail Hall, married Lydia Holt, Dec. 5, 1751, and died at Cheshire.

Children: 479 *Abigail*, b July 8, 1753; 480 *Benjamin Holt*, b Oct. 6, 1754, died at Cheshire, a farmer; 481 *Lydia*, b May 26, 1755; 482 *Charles C.*, b March 9, 1762, died at Cheshire, a farmer; 483 *Rachel*, b July 4, 1764; 484 *Charlotte*, b Jan. 20, 1769; 485 *Lyman*, b Jan. 4, 1761, died at Cheshire, a farmer.

187. BENJAMIN.

BENJAMIN HALL, son of Benjamin and Abigail Hall, born at Cheshire, Sept. 27, 1736, grad. at Yale in 1754, married Mary Ives, Dec. 27, 1752. He built the house late the property of Wm. Law, Esq., and more recently of Sheldon Spencer, Esq.

Children: 486 *Eliab*, b Feb. 17, 1755; 487 *Benjamin*, d Oct. 8, 1755; 488 *Benjamin*, b Nov. 3, 1756.

190. ISAAC.

ISAAC HALL, son of Eliakim and Ruth Hall, was born Nov. 4, 1737, married Esther Mosely, Dec. 1, 1764, died Feb. 7, 1796, æ. 61. His widow Esther, died March 22, 1827, æ. 86 yrs.

Children: 489, 490 *Abner* and *Elizabeth*, b April 28, 1764, d in infancy; 491 *Esther*, b Dec. 15, 1765; 492 *Mary*, b Nov. 24, 1767; 493, 494 *Elizabeth*, and *Eliakim*, b Jan. 21, 1770; 495 *Dickerman*, b 1774, d Sept. 18, 1838, ae. 64 yrs.; 496 *Isaac*, b July 19, 1776, went to Wallingford, Vt.; 497 *Abigail*, b Nov. 22, 1778; 498 *Day*, b Aug. 20, 1781; 499 *Lyman*, b March 31, 1784.

192. ELIAKIM.

ELIAKIM HALL, Esq., son of Eliakim and Ruth Hall, was born Feb. 13, 1740, married Eunice Morse, May 29, 1769. She died July 18, 1789; he married 2d, Sarah ——, she died Sept. 27, 1806, ae. 56 yrs. He died Sept. 6, 1806, ae. 67 yrs.

Children: 500 *Eunice*, b Feb. 19, 1770; 501 *Pamelia*, b Dec. 13, 1771; 502 *Sarah*, b June 19, 1773; 503 *John Morse*, b May 25, 1775, d Dec. 11, 1837, ae. 62 yrs.; 504 *Phebe*, b Dec. 8, 1777; 505 *Sophia*, b Dec. 1, 1782; 506 *Electa*, b Oct. 27, 1785; 507 *Elizabeth*, b Jan. 29, 1788.

193. HEZEKIAH.

HEZEKIAH HALL, son of Eliakim and Ruth Hall, was born July 13, 1743, married Elizabeth Merriman, Oct. 30, 1769; he died Sept. 7, 1815, ae. 73 yrs. She died Nov. 21, 1801, ae. 50 yrs.

Children: 508 *Ruth*, b Feb. 8, 1771, m Nehemiah Rice; 509 *Elizabeth*, b March 14, 1772, m David M. Cook; 510 *Thankful*, b May 25, 1775, m Chester Cook; 511 *Hope*, b Sept. 26, 1780, m Samuel Francis; 512 *Lucy*, b Oct. 9, 1782, m Jacob Francis; 513 *Ophelia*, b March 1, 1785; 514 *Nathan*, b Nov. 6, 1788, d Aug. 18, 1741, ae. 53 yrs; 515 *Laura*, b 1792.

198. JOHN.

JOHN HALL, son of Elihu and Lois Hall, married Mary Jones, Oct. 19, 1772.

Child: 516 *Nicholas Street*, b March 27, 1773.

201. ELIHU.

ELIHU HALL, son of Elihu and Lois Hall, was born Mar. 15, 1795, m Sarah ———. This person commenced life with a large fortune, his possessions being much larger than those of most young men. For many years he owned large tracts of land in Wallingford, and the whole township of Guildhall, in the State of Vermont, besides slaves, horses, cattle, etc. His entire want of economy and tact in the management of his business cost him in a few years his whole estate, and he died a subject of the town's charge. His wife died some years before him.

Children: 517 *John*, b May 20, 1774, left Wallingford; 518 *Frederick*, b Jan. 8, 1777; 519 *Lois*, b June 18, 1779; 520 *Louisa*, m a Mr. Armour, and died in New Haven, May 1, 1850.

207. AVERY.

AVERY HALL, son of Rev. Theophilus and Hannah Hall of Meriden, was b Dec. 2, 1737. He settled in the ministry at Rochester, New Hampshire.

208. SAMUEL.

SAMUEL HALL, son of Rev. Theophilus and Hannah Hall of Meriden, married Eunice Lee, Feb. 10, 1757.

Children: 521 *Samuel*, b May 27, 1759; 522 *Eunice*, b April 16, 1765; 523 *Caleb*, b Nov. 9, 1768; 524 *Eunice*, b June 22, 1770.

209. THEOPHILUS.

THEOPHILUS HALL, son of Rev. Theophilus and Hannah Hall, m Elizabeth Couch, March 10, 1768. He died May 17, 1804, æ. 63. She died March 11, 1824, æ. 74, in Meriden.

Children: 525 *Mehitable*, b March 23, 1769, died Sept. 30, 1776; 526 *Clarissa*, b April 3, 1771; 527 *Theophilus*, b April 20, 1773, d Sept. 26, 1815, æ. 62 yrs.; 528 *Mehitable*, b Aug. 4, 1777; 529 *Avery*, b May 25, 1779; 530, 531 *Hannah* and *Elizabeth*, b Jan. 20, 1782.

213. ELISHA.

ELISHA HALL, son of Rev. Theophilus and Hannah Hall, married Ann Hopkins, June 25, 1767. He died March 13, 1759.

Children: 532 *Luther Elisha*, b Sept. 3, 1770; 533 *Ann Law*, b Dec. 20, 1772; 534 *Sylvester*, b May 13, 1778.

221. SAMUEL.

DEA. SAMUEL HALL, son of Samuel and Sarah Hall, b Feb. 28, 1750, m Elizabeth Parsons, May 10, 1774. He died Feb. 27, 1821, ae. 71. She died Sept. 27, 1823, ae. 71 yrs.

Children: 535 *Samuel*, b Dec. 2, 1776; 536 *Hezekiah*, b June 11, 1778; 537 *George*, b Aug. 13, 1780; 538 *Marilla*, b Dec. 28, 1782, married Chauncey Hall; 539 *Richard*, b Jan. 26, 1785; 540 *Jared*, b Aug. 24, 1792, d April 24, 1861.

224. TITUS.

TITUS HALL, son of Thomas and Lydia Hall, was one of the first separates in Wallingford; he married Elizabeth Mack, Aug. 23, 1762, and died in 1773, æ. 36.

Children: 541 *Thomas;* 542 *Elizabeth*, b Feb. 25, 1765; 543 *Titus*, b July 30, 1767; 544 *Elias*, b Aug. 24, 1769; 545 *Lydia*, b April 17, 1771.

227. AMASA.

AMASA HALL, son of Thomas and Lydia Hall, married Dinah Ives, Dec. 15, 1775.

Children: 546, 547 *Major* and *Phebe*, b Feb. 17, 1775; 548 *Hannah*, b Feb. 17, 1777.

232. PHINEAS.

PHINEAS HALL, son of Phineas and Annah Hall, born April 12, 1715, married Agnes Yale, Nov. 18, 1774, a widow.

Children; 549 *Mary*, b July 28, 1775; 550 *Abigail;* 551 *Thankful;* 552 *Phineas;* 553 *Levi;* 554 *Eunice;* 555 *Barnabas;* 556 *Annis.*

240. GILES.

GILES HALL, son of Joshua and Hannah Hall, was born Feb. 24, 1747, married Lois Ives.

Children: 557 *Abel*, b Dec. 10, 1778, d at Atwater, Ohio; 558 *Sarah*, b Aug. 20, 1780; 559 *Giles*, d April 21, 1791; 560 *Joshua;* 561 *Lois*, m Andrew Andrews; 562 *Lucy;* 563 *Hannah;* 564 *John.*

243. JOSHUA.

JOSHUA HALL, son of Joshua and Hannah Hall.

Children: 565 *Susannah*, b Nov. 16, 1742; 566 *Abigail*, b April 25, 1745; 567 *Giles*, b Feb. 24, 1747; 568 *Samuel*, b Jan. 29, 1749.

245. DAVID.

DAVID HALL, son of David and Alice Hall. He died 1795, æ. 63 years.

Child: 569 *Elkanah*, b Nov. 30, 1767.

247. ASAPH.

ASAPH HALL, son of David and Alice Hall.

Children: 570 *Benajah*, b 1762; 571 *Asa;* 572 daughter, m —— Hopson.

267. JONATHAN.

DR. JONATHAN HALL, son of Isaac and Mary Hall, residence Meriden, Ct., married Martha Collins, May 14, 1777. He died June 6, 1832, ae. 54. She died May, 1841, ae. 83, in the state of New York. He settled at New Hartford, N. Y., in 1787.

Children: 573 *Isaac*, b Feb. 22, 1778; 574 *Keturah*, b Nov. 17, 1780; 575 *Sylvia*, b Sept. 18, 1782; 576 *Jonathan*, b Aug. 14, 1784; 577 *Eli*, b May 14, 1786; 578 *Ira*, b July 10, 1788; 579 *Mary Moss*, b April 12, 1790; 580 *Agnes Collins*, b Aug. 6, 1793; 581 *Amos Hull*, b Feb. 13, 1796; 582 *Jedediah Sanger*, b Nov. 2, 1797; 583 *Sarah T.*, b May 6, 1799.

269. TITUS.

TITUS HALL, son of Ezekiel and Anna Hall, was born Oct. 19, 1746, married Olive Barnes, Nov. 26, 1767.

Children: 584 *Abigail*, b Sept. 21, 1768; 585 *Caleb*, b Jan. 11, 1771; 586 *Lucy*, b Dec. 14, 1775; 587 *Caleb*, b Aug. 27, 1781; 588 *Ransley*, b Feb. 7, 1784.

271. BENAJAH.

BENAJAH HALL, son of Ezekiel and Annah Hall, was born 1762, married Ruth Francis, Aug. 19, 1784.

Children: 589 *Orrin*, b June 5, 1785; 590 *Esther*, b June 13, 1787; 591 *Ruth*, b Aug. 25, 1789; 592 *Nancy*, b Nov. 9, 1792; 593 *Martha*, b July 13, 1795; 594 *Philo*, b May 13, 1798; 595 *Jacob*, b April 5, 1801; 596 *Joseph*, b Oct. 17, 1803; 597 *Joel*, b Nov. 3, 1806; 598 *Lovineas*, b July 21, 1810.

274. BENJAMIN.

BENJAMIN HALL, son of Benjamin and Mary Hall, married Phebe ———, April 28, 1757, settled at Plymouth.

Children: 599 *Benjamin*; 600 *Mary*, b Jan. 29, 1758; 601 *Andrews*, b Aug. 15, 1759; 602 *Mary*, b Aug. 6, 1761; 603 *Phebe*, b Aug. 20, 1763, m —— Hart; 604 *Linus*, b Sept. 25, 1765; 605, 606 *David*, *Jonathan*, b Nov. 17, 1761; 607 *Erastus*, b Feb. 12, 1770; 608 *Adnah*, b May 8, 1772; 609 *Salmon*, b 1774; 610 *Eliab*, b Dec. 11, 1776, settled in North Killingworth; 611 *Grace Denison*, b May 5, 1776; 612 *Asaph*, b Oct. 1, 1781.

280. REUBEN.

REUBEN HALL, son of Ephraim and Chloe Hall, b Feb., 1735, m Sally Miller, May 25, 1797.

Children: 613 *Alma*, b March 23, 1798; 614 *Horace*, b April 17, 1800; 615 *Milla*, b Jan. 8, 1802; 616 *Eli*, M. D., b Nov. 5, 1803; 617 *William*, b Feb. 21, 1806; 618 *Reighly*, b April 1, 1808.

281. DAVID.

DAVID MOSS HALL, son of Ephraim and Chloe Hall, married Mindwell ———. He left Wallingford.

Child: 619 *Orrilla*, b Nov. 5, 1800.

284. JOSIAH.

DEA. JOSIAH HALL, son of Hiel and Catherine Hall, married Martha Hall, daughter of Giles Hall, April 2, 1793.

Children: 620 *Thankful*, b May 23, 1796, m Thaddeus Cook; 621 *Catherine*, b May 18, 1798; 622 *Eliza*, b May 15, 1800, died; 623 *Eliza*, b July 25, 1801; 624 *Edward* L., b May 13, 1804, m Mary K. Cook, dau. of Billious Cook; 625 *George Chauncey*, b April 19, 1706; 626 *Martha R.*, b Oct. 19, 1808, m Thaddeus Cook; 627 *Josiah*, b June 15, 1812; 628 *Ogden*, b Sept. 13, 1815; 629 *David M.*, b May 27, 1818, m Catherine Cook; 630 *James*, b April 11, 1821.

286. ANDREW.

DR. ANDREW HALL, son of Hiel and Catherine Hall, married Lydia, daughter of Ambrose Cook, Sept. 11, 1803.

Children: 631 *Alexander W.*, b May 28, 1805; 632 *Sarah R.*, b Oct. 14, 1806, m Medad W. Munson, Esq.; 633 *Andrew C.*, b June 7, 1810, d in Phila., interred in Wall.; 635 *Franklin D.*, b Sept. 20, 1811.

287. CHAUNCEY.

CHAUNCEY HALL, son of Hiel and Catherine Hall, married Marilla, daughter of Samuel and Catherine Hall, Feb. 6, 1803.

Children: 635 *Henry C.*, b Jan. 19, 1804; 636 *Samuel R.*, b Nov. 11, 1805; 637 *Elihu*, b June 2, 1807, m Martha, dau. of Samuel Cook; 638 *Lucretia*, b Dec. 1, 1809; 639 *Louisa*, b Jan, 29, 1812; 640 *Lucy A.*, b April 18, 1814, m Ira Yale, Jr.; 641 *Sidney*, b July 12, 1816; 642 *Elizabeth;* 643 *Marietta;* 644 *Celia.*

288. PETER.

PETER HALL, son of Hiel and Catherine Hall, married Delight Kirtland, Sept. 8, 1808.

Child: 645 *Charles*, m Miss Foote.

290. RICE.

DR. RICE HALL, son of Hiel and Catherine Hall, married Esther Hall, Nov. 19, 1806.

Children: 646 *Hiel Beverly*, b Feb. 18, 1811; 647 *John M.;* 648 *Marilla*, b May 25, 1813; 649 *Ophelia*, b June 2, 1818; 650 *Henrietta E.*, b Aug. 8, 1815; 651 *Elizur Rice*, b June 25, 1821; 652 *Philander*.

293. WOOSTER.

WOOSTER HALL, son of Peter and Lydia Hall, married Chloe Cooley, July 27, 1806.

Children: 653 *Samuel B.*, b Sept. 20, 1808; 654 *Lydia*, b Nov. 16, 1810; 655 *Lydia;* 656 *Asahel*, b May 3, 1812; 657 *Dinah*, b Oct. 7, 1814; 658 *Lois*, b Feb. 14, 1817.

326. DANIEL.

DANIEL HALL, son of Jacob and Elizabeth Hall, married Sarah Atwater, Oct. 7, 1761.

Children: 659 *Mary*, b June 24, 1762; 660 *Elizabeth*, b June 21, 1764; 661 *Lemuel*, b March 20, 1766; 662 *Aaron*, b May 2, 1768; 663, 664 *Ira*, and *Asa*, b Aug. 18, 1770; 665 *Joshua*, b Aug 5, 1772; 666 *Abigail*, b Dec. 16, 1776; 667 *Lemuel*, b May 2, 1779, d in New Haven, Conn.; 668 *Sally*, b June 8, 1781; 669 *Patty*, b Sept. 3, 1783; 670 *Alma*, b Nov. 15, 1785; 671 *Phebe*, b Aug. 21, 1787.

329 DAVID.

DAVID HALL, son of David and Thankful (Morse) Hall, was born Nov. 2, 1732, died March 25, 1825. She died Sept. 24, 1826, ae. 61.

Children: 672 *Almer*, b Sept. 10, 1793, d in Wallingford; 673 *Alethea*, b Oct. 11, 1795, m Wooster Martin; 674 *Charlotte*, b July 24, 1791, m ——— Lindley; 675 *Stephen*, went west, supposed to Ohio.

335. REUBEN.

REUBEN HALL, son of Amos and Ruth Hall, married Mary ———. He was born Dec. 20, 1721.

Children: 676 *Mary*, b Oct. 17, 1742; 677 *Elizabeth*, b Feb. 12, 1743; 678 *Abel*, b Oct. 12, 1745.

AMOS.

AMOS HALL, SON of Asaph and Ruth Hall, died Dec. 24, 1782, ae. 31 years.

Children: 679 *Reuben;* 680 *Moses;* 681 *Eunice;* 682 *Louis.*

336. MOSES.

MOSES HALL, son of Amos and Ruth Hall.

Children: 683 *Moses*, b Dec. 26, 1754; 684 *Enos*, b March 8, 1756.

342. NATHANIEL.

NATHANIEL HALL, son of Caleb and Esther Hall, born April 8, 1732, married Lydia ——. She died Jan. 15, 1760.

Child: 685 *Lurena*, b Feb. 21, 1759.

343. CALEB.

CALEB HALL, son of Caleb and Esther Hall, b Sept. 12, 1734.

Child: 686 *Susannah*, b Feb. 8, 1759.

349. TITUS.

TITUS HALL, son of Caleb and Esther Hall, was born Aug. 16, 1746, married Olive Barnes, Nov. 26, 1767.

Children: 687 *Abigail*, b Sept. 21, 1768; 688 *Caleb*, b Jan. 21, 1771, d Nov. 12, 1824; 689 *Lucy*, b Dec. 14, 1775; 690 *Caleb*, b Aug. 29, 1781; 691 *Ransley*, b Feb. 7, 1784.

354. MILES.

MILES HALL, son of James and Hannah C. Hall, born Oct. 17, 1736, married Abigail Tyler, Sept. 30, 1764.

Children: 692 *Abigail*, b Dec. 3, 1767; 693 *James*, b Oct. 14, 1769; 694 *William Tyler*, b Jan. 15, 1772.

357. JAMES.

JAMES HALL, son of James and Hannah C. Hall, born July 22, 1743.

Child: 695 *Phebe*, b Nov. 16, 1741.

360. ISAAC.

ISAAC HALL, son of Isaac and Mary Moss Hall, was born March 7, 1745, married Phebe Ives, Sept. 6, 1764.

Children: 696 *Mary*, b July 21, 1766; 697 *John*, b July 3, 1768; 698 *Phebe*, b Jan. 31, 1770; 699 *Elizabeth*, b Sept. 23, 1771; 700 *Isaac*, b May 19, 1775; 701 *Jonathan*, b Sept. 15, 1776; 702 *Clarissa*, b Aug. 12, 1779; 703 *Abijah*, b 1781; 704 *Sally*, b 1784.

365. JONATHAN.

JONATHAN HALL, son of Isaac and Mary Hall, was born Dec. 11, 1757, married Martha Collins, May 14, 1777.

Children: 705 *Isaac*, b Feb. 22, 1778; 706 *Katurah*. b Nov. 17, 1780.

366. ELIAS.

ELIAS HALL, son of John and Abigail Hall, was born Mar. 10, 1740, married 1st, Mary Humiston, Dec. 15, 1763. She died Aug. 14, 1774, and he married 2d, Rubama ——.

Children by 1st marriage: 707 *Martha*, b Sept. 26, 1764; 708 *Mary*, b May 26, 1766; 709 *Ruth*, b Feb. 28, 1768; 710 *Eliakim*, b May 31, 1778; 711 *Benjamin*, b Feb. 20, 1770. By 2d marriage: 712 *Rubama*, b Jan. 16, 1776.

367. JARED.

JARED HALL, son of John and Abigail Hall, born July 19, 1741, married Lucy Hall, July 5, 1770.

Children: 713 *Lemuel*, b Aug. 16, 1771; 714 *Amos*, b May 21, 1773; 715 *Rufus*, b Jan. 9, 1775.

369. JOHN.

JOHN HALL, son of John and Abigail Hall, born Dec. 6, 1743, married Lucy ———.

Child: 716 *Millicent*, b Sept. 3, 1768.

371. WILLIAM.

WILLIAM HALL, son of John and Abigail Hall, married Rebecca ———. He was born June 15, 1747.

Children: 717 *Benj. Russel*, b Aug. 1, 1775; 718 *Abigail*, b Sept. 20, 1777; 719 *Ambrose*, b Dec. 7, 1779.

375. BENJAMIN.

BENJAMIN HALL, son of John and Abigail Hall, married Lydia ——— ; he was born July 2, 1757, died March 12, 1770.

Children: 721 *Lyman*, b March 20, 1798; 722 *Mary*, b June 12, 1799; 723 *Emeline*, b April 14, 1800; 724 *Orrin*, b March 22, 1803.

377. ABEL.

ABEL HALL, son of Abel and Ruth Hall, born Oct. 12, 1745, married Ruth Morse, Jan. 3, 1771.

Child: 725 *Esther*.

383. HEZEKIAH.

HEZEKIAH HALL, son of Abel and Ruth Hall, born April 20, 1757, married Susannah ———.

Children: 726 *Charity*, b Oct. 3, 1784; 727 *Isaac*, b Aug. 21, 1786.

388. JOEL.

JOEL HALL, son of Asahel and Sarah Goldsmith Hall, born May 21, 1741; he was a large and thrifty farmer, married Hannah Parmalee, Oct. 30, 1765.

Children: 728 *Andrew*, b March 4, 1767, m Diana Cook, Jan. 11, 1778, he d 1796; 729 *Augustus*, b May 3, 1769, m Pamelia Hall, April 12, 1786; 730 *Joel*, b July 26, 1771; 731 *Luther*, b Aug. 16, 1776, m Sarah ——, 2d, wid. Bassett; 732 *Sarah P.*, b June 3, 1779; 733 *Asahel W.*, b May 12, 1781; 734 *James*, b Oct. 12, 1783.

396. CHARLES.

CHARLES HALL, son of Asahel and Sarah Goldsmith Hall, b Nov. 12, 1757, married Sarah ———.

Children: 735 *Jerusha*, b Oct. 23, 1772; 736 *Daniel Root*, b Aug. 30, 1779; 737 *Rice*, b Jan. 26, 1782; 738 *Sylvester*, b Aug. 29, 1784; 739 *Thomas G.*, b Aug. 17, 1787; 740 *Sarah*, b Nov. 25, 1789; 741 *Susan*, b Dec. 2, 1791; 742 *Charles*; 743 *Sarah*.

397. ASAHEL

ASAHEL HALL, son of Asahel and Sarah Goldsmith Hall,

born Jan. 14, 1759, married Ruth Johnson, Sept. 21, 1786.

Children: 744 *Catherine*, b April 17, 1787; 745 *Asahel*, b April 8, 1789; 746 *John D.*, b June 22, 1790; 747 *Sarah*, b April 5, 1792.

398. AARON.

AARON HALL, son of Asahel and Sarah Hall, was born Nov. 4, 1760, married Elizabeth Cook, May 24, 1781; she died and he married 2d, Sarah, widow of Charles Hall, Dec. 11, 1820; 3d, Anna Brooks, June 18, 1827. He died Sept. 30, 1839, ae. 79 yrs.

Children: 748 *Benjamin Atwater*, b April 6, 1782; 749 *Elizabeth*, b Oct. 23, 1783; 750 *Electa*, b Sept. 9, 1785; 751 *Aaron C.*, b Nov. 11, 1787, went to Catskill, N. Y.; 752 *Mary*, b Jan. 20, 1790; 753 *Asahel*, b April 6, 1792; 754 *Salmon*, b Aug. 12, 1793; 755 *Anna*, b Jan. 6, 1796; 756 *Caroline*, b Dec. 21, 1798; 757 *B. Kirtland*, b July 4, 1805.

407. JOSEPH.

JOSEPH HALL, son of Elisha and Thankful Hall, married Mercy Cornwall, May 31, 1799.

Child: 758 *Sarah G.*, m Israel Harrison, Oct. 21, 1841.

412. JOHN.

JOHN HALL, 3d son of Elisha and Thankful Hall, married Grace Denison Hall, April 3, 1800. She died Jan. 21, 1840, æ. 69.

Children: 759 *Jeremiah Atwater*, b 1806; 760 *John*, b Oct. 8, 1808; 761 *Thankful A.*, b Sept. 6, 1801, m ——— Hopson; 762 *Lowly*, b April 21, 1804, m ——— Johnson; 763 *Phebe*, b Dec. 18, 1810; 764 *Denison D.*, b Dec. 9, 1815; 765 *Grace D.*, b July 18, 1813, m George Simpson; 766 *Elisha*, b March 15, 1818; 767 *Jennette*, b May 31, 1820; 768 *Patty*.

415. RUFUS.

RUFUS HALL, son of Abraham and Hannah Hall, b July 25, 1751, married Experience Foster, Nov. 14, 1772.

Children: 769 *Hannah*, b Nov. 20, 1776; 770 *Abraham*, b May 5, 1778; 771 *Anne*, b Aug. 13, 1779.

419. PRINDLE.

PRINDLE HALL, son of John and Elizabeth Prindle Hall, b June 19, 1750, married Anna Mix, Dec. 5, 1771.

Children: 772 *Ebenezer*, b March 26, 1773; 773 *Annah*, b March 9, 1774; 774 *Anna*, b Oct. 7, 1776; 775 *Lydia*, b Sept. 13, 1778; 776 *Sarah*, b April 25, 1780.

438. STREET.

STREET T. HALL, son of Col. Street and Hannah Hall, born Feb. 26, 1762.

Children: 777 *Sherlock*, b Nov. 3, 1792; 778, 779 *Elisha* and *Rebecca Ann*, b Feb. 17, 1795; 780 *Alfred*, b July 17, 1797; 781 *Ransom*, b April 28, 1803; 782 *Carlos*, b July 4, 1806; 783 *Wm. Street*, b March 6, 1809; 784 *Mary Ann*, b July 8, 1841.

448. GILES.

GILES HALL, son of Giles and Martha Hall, married Susan Hall, and occupies the old home of his father.

Children: 785 *Elizabeth*, b Oct. 21, 1815, m Elijah Rice; 786 *Wm. Cook*, b April 12, 1818, m Julia A. Johnson, Sept. 12, 1843; 787 *Emily*, b Aug. 16, 1820; 788 *Henry Lyman*, b Nov. 25, 1824, a school teacher and farmer.

450. JOHN.

JOHN HALL, son of Giles and Martha Hall, married 1st, Abigail ———. She died, and he married Dency Strong.

Children by 1st marriage: 789 *Stanley*, b March 20, 1805; 790 *Apollos*, b July 12, 1807; 791 *Henry Franklin*, b June 28, 1807. By second marriage: 792 *Dency*; 793 *Dwight*, b Aug. 19, 1814, hotel-keeper in the village; 794 *Elizur*, b Jan. 25, 1817, d Sept. 26, 1857; 795 *Adeline*, b June 2, 1820, d Aug. 5, 1834; 796 *Wolcott*, b Oct. 30, 1824.

452. COLLINS.

COLLINS HALL, son of Brenton and Lament Hall, was born Jan. 8, 1766, m Rebecca ———, March 17, 1795. She was born Jan. 10, 1764.

Children: 797 *Abigail*, b Nov. 25, 1796; 798 *Alma*, b Oct. 5, 1799; 799 *Elisha*, b May 1, 1803; 800 *Erastus*, b Jan. 2, 1805; 801 *Augustus*, b Oct. 30, 1806.

467. HORATIO.

HORATIO G. HALL, son of Caleb and Prudence Hall, married Polly, daughter of Benjamin Byington. She was born Aug. 25, 1777.

Children: 802 *Augustus*, b July 14, 1799, m Rhoda Doolittle; 803 *Lyman*, b May 7, 1801, m ——— Button, d at Yalesville, Conn.; 804 *Horace*, b May 25, 1804, m 1st ———, 2d, ——— Bull; 805 *Mary*, b March 16, 1807, m Leverett Allen; 806 *Josiah H.;* 807 *Abigail.*

482. CHARLES.

CHARLES C. HALL, son of Charles Chauncey and Lydia H. Hall, was born March 9, 1762.

Children: 808 *Charles C.;* 809 *Eliza*, m Jesse L. Nichols of Wolcott; 810 *Lyman*, d in New Haven; 811 *Augustus*, res. in Branford; 812 *George*, res. in Cheshire; 813 *James R.*, res. in Cheshire, m ——— Cook.

485. LYMAN.

LYMAN HALL, son of Charles C. and Lydia Hall, was born Jan. 4, 1761.

Children: 814 *William*, m Mary Horton; 815 *Charles C.*

494. ELIAKIM.

COL. ELIAKIM HALL, married Clarissa Cook, March 13, 1794; he kept an inn in the Muddy River district.

Children: 816 *Sukey*, b Jan. 15, 1797; 817 *Ogden*, b 1802, d Feb. 23, 1803, æ. 6 mos.; 818 *Jane Ann*, b Aug. 5, 1806; 819 *Margaret*, b Jan. 5, 1810.

495. DICKERMAN.

DICKERMAN HALL, son of Isaac and Esther Mosely Hall, married 1st, Lucy Hough, March 13, 1796, and 2d, Miss ——— Bishop, in 1803. He died Sept. 18, 1838.

Children: 820 *Rebecca*, b Feb. 23, 1797; 821 *Hannah*, b

March 22, 1799, m 1st, John Hull, 2d, ——— Andrews; 822 *Lucy*, b July 2, 1801; 823 *Henrietta*, b June 28, 1804; 824 *William Mosely*, b Feb. 11, 1806; 825 *Mary Ann*, b Oct. 31, 1807; 826 *Cornelia*, b Feb. 17, 1811; 827 *Frances A.*, b Oct. 9, 1813; 828 *Harriet*.

503. JOHN MORSE.

JOHN MORSE HALL, son of Eliakim and Eunice Morse Hall, was born May 25, 1775, married Lizzie Meigs, April 14, 1800; he died Dec. 11, 1837, æ. 62 yrs. His wife died Dec. 13, 1843, æ. 63 yrs.

Children: 829 *Lizzie*, b Nov. 17, 1801; 830 *Mary*, b Dec. 6, 1802; 831 *John Meigs*, d July 3, 1851, in Wallingford, m Miss —— Gilbert, a sister of Rev. E. R. Gilbert; 832 *Ellen A.*; 833 a daughter; 834 *Eliza M.*; 835 *Helen*; 836 *Mary*.

514. NATHAN.

NATHAN HALL, son of Hezekiah and Elizabeth Merriman Hall, married Polly Andrews, daughter of Nathaniel; he died, æ. 53.

Children: 837 *Ruth*, b March 16, 1815, m Sherman Austin; 838 *Hezekiah*, b June 4, 1817, m —— Coe of Meriden; 839 *Lucretia D.*, b March 18, 1821; 840 *Viney*, b Dec. 23, 1822.

529. AVERY.

AVERY HALL, son of Theophilus and Elizabeth Hall, was born Nov. 9, 1768.

Children: 841 *Selden*, b Sept. 21, 1801; 842 *Alfred*, b May 18, 1803.

537. GEORGE.

GEORGE HALL, son of Samuel and Elizabeth P. Hall, born Aug. 13, 1780, married Lucinda ———.

Children: 843 *Mary A.*, b Nov. 11, 1843; 844 *Julia E. H.*, b Sept. 14, 1815; 845 *George*, b July 28, 1818; 846 *Lament P.*, b Oct. 7, 1820; 847 *Nancy*, b Oct. 3, 1822; 848 *Julia*, b Dec. 23, 1834.

539. RICHARD.

RICHARD HALL, son of Samuel and Elizabeth P. Hall, b Jan. 26, 1785, married Nancy, daughter of Ambrose Cook.

Children: 849 *Philander*, b July 25, 1806; 850 *Susan*, b Sept. 16, 1808, m —— Phinney; 851 *Jerusha*, b Nov. 9, 1809, m Wm. Elton; 852 *Eliza*, m Wm. Lewis.

560. JOSHUA.

JOSHUA HALL, son of Giles and Lois Hall, married Sophronia Gates, March 21, 1804.

Children: 853 *Wm. Chauncey*, b May 5, 1805; 854 *Roderick*, b Dec. 21, 1806; 855 *James M.*, b March 3, 1809; 856 *Delight*, b Jan. 24, 1811; 857 *Delilah*, b March 29, 1813; 858 *Henrietta*, b June 24, 1815; 859 *Lois*, b Feb. 3, 1818; 860 *Jennette*, b Dec. 18, 1821; 861 *Alexander*, b Aug. 24, 1824, m —— Potter of Northford.

569. ELKANAH.

ELKANAH HALL, son of David and Alice Hall, was born in 1761, died March 23, 1738, æ. 71 years, married Sarah ——.

Children: 862 *Harry*, b July 28, 1797; 863 *Eliakim*, b Nov. 19, 1799; 864 *Isaac N.*, b Feb. 14, 1802; 865 *Alexander*, b Jan., 1805.

578. IRA.

IRA HALL, son of Dr. Jonathan and Martha Collins Hall, married 1st, Kate Rose, and 2d, Marcia Rounds. He died Jan. 19, 1860, in New York, ae. 71 yrs., 5 mos.

Children: 866 *Nathan Kelsey*, b March 28, 1810; 867 *Ira V.*, b Aug. 3, 1811; 868 *Ira*, b Aug. 4, 1814; 869 *Catherine*, b Dec. 3, 1816; 870 *Mary*, b Sept. 17, 1819; 871 *Eli Q.*, b June 21, 1822; 872 *Sylvester R.*, b July 3, 1826; 873 *Sarah*, b March 1, 1829; 874 *Maria*, b Sept. 29, 1831; 875 *Jane*, b April 4, 1836.

594. PHILO.

PHILO HALL, son of Benajah and Ruth Hall, was born May 13, 1798, married Thankful Morse.

Children: 876 *Lavinia*, b March 13, 1823; 877 *Bennet*, b

May 10, 1824; 878 *Philo Fayette*, b Sept. 15, 1825; 879 *Emery Osgood*, b Sept. 1, 1827; 880 *Almira C.*, b Feb. 18, 1828; 881 *Truman Gerrard*, b Jan. 24, 1832; 882 *Harriet Newell*, b Feb. 18, 1833.

601. ANDREWS.

ANDREWS HALL, son of Benjamin and Phebe Hall, born Aug. 15, 1759, married Sylvia Blakeslee, Dec. 3, 1800.

Children: 883 *William A.*, b June 8, 1803; 884 *Sylvia*, b April 18, 1805; 885 *Abigail*, b June 14, 1807; 886 *Mary*, b April 24, 1810, m ——— McKenzie.

608. ADNAH.

ADNAH HALL, son of Benjamin and Phebe Hall, married Elizabeth ———, she died 1860; he died June 17, 1838, æ. 66 yrs.

Children: 887 *Valucia*, b March 29, 1811; 888 *Wilfred*, b July 25, 1815; 889 *Temperance*, b May 24, 1817; 890 *Harvey S.*, b April 9, 1819; 891 *Ezekiel*, b Jan. 23, 1822.

612. ASAPH.

ASAPH HALL, son of Benjamin and Phebe Hall, born Oct. 1, 1781, married Thankful ———; he died Feb. 12, 1839, æ. 58 years.

Children: 899 *Merab*, b June 24, 1812, m George Peck, of Cheshire, Conn.; 900 *Benjamin H.*, b Aug. 2, 1815; 901 *Asa*, b July 6, 1821.

663. IRA.

IRA HALL, son of Daniel and Sarah Hall, married Abigail ———.

Children: 902 *Elizur*, b June 28, 1798; 903 *Cornelia*, b Nov. 20, 1800; 904 *Edward*, b Sept. 30, 1802; 905 *Abigail*, b June 27, 1807; 906 *Elizabeth*, b Oct. 2, 1816.

667. LEMUEL.

LEMUEL HALL, son of Daniel and Sarah Hall, was a merchant in New Haven. He built and was the owner of the store now owned by Austin & Gilbert, on the corner of Elm and Church-sts.

Children: 907 *Henry*, d in New Haven; 908 *Grace;* and several other children.

672. ALMER.

DEA. ALMER HALL, son of Daniel and Thankful Hall, married 2d, widow of Merrick Cook; he was a merchant and deacon of the Baptist church for several years.

Child: 909 *Almer I.*, m —— Hall.

728. ANDREW.

ANDREW HALL, son of Joel and Hannah Hall, was born Jan. 11, 1757, married Diana Cook.

Children: 910 *Betsey*, b Feb. 3, 1788; 911 *Russell*, b Oct. 18, 1789, m Polly Kirtland; 912 *Liverius*, b Aug. 13, 1790; 913 *Clarissa C.*, b Nov. 28, 1793, m Almer Hall, Esq.; 914 *Susan*, b March 18, 1795; 915 *Sylvia*, b March 13, 1797, m Thaddeus Cook; 916 *Sinai*, b June 25, 1799, m Frederick Lewis; 917 *Wm. Cook*, b Jan. 11, 1802.

AUGUSTUS.

AUGUSTUS HALL, son of Joel and Hannah Hall, married Pamelia Hall, Feb. 10, 1794; he died in Wallingford.

Children: 918 *Eunice*, b March 3, 1796; 919 *Joel*, b July 6, 1799.

731 LUTHER.

LUTHER HALL, son of Joel and Hannah Hall, married Sarah ———.

Children: 920 *Emily*, b Sept. 6, 1800; 921 *Julia A.*, b Oct. 6, 1801; 922 *William*, b Jan. 10, 1804; 923 *Sally E.*, b May 17, 1806; 924 *Abraham R.*, b Sept. 25, 1808; 925 *Betsey P.*, b May 8, 1815.

866. NATHAN.

NATHAN KELSEY HALL, son of Ira and Catharine Hall, of Skaneateles, N. Y., married Emily Payne. She was born Aug. 5, 1811, married Nov. 16, 1832. He is a lawyer at Buffalo, N. Y.

Children: 926 *Nathan R.* Jr., b Oct. 13, 1833, d at Buffalo, Oct. 22, 1835; 927, *Frederick Aug.*, b Jan. 10, 1836, d at Andover, N. Y., Jan. 7, 1852; 928 *Emily A.*, b Oct. 9, 1838, m George Gorham of Canandagua, N. Y.; 929 *Frank*, b Jan. 7, 1845, d at Washington, D. C., May 23, 1848; 930 *Grace*, b May 16, 1850.

701. JONATHAN.

JONATHAN HALL, son of Isaac and Mary Morse Hall, married 1st, Elizabeth, daughter of John G. Hoadley, 2d, Sally, daughter of William Jencks. He died Feb. 22, 1741, ae. 64 years, 5 mos., 29 days. Residence of this family was at Leyden, Lewis Co., N. Y.

Children: 931 *Jehiel*, b Nov. 16, 1803, m Louisa Wilson, Aug. 10, 1826; 932 *Daniel*, b July 30, 1805, m Mary D. Sperry, Oct. 23, 1834; 933 *Mary*, b June 23, 1812, m Silas Cary, Feb. 6, 1812; 934 *Abigail*, b Dec. 22, 1813, m Rev. David A. Barney, March 5, 1834; 935 *Jonathan*, b Aug. 22, 1815, m Ann Henry, Nov. 9, 1840; 936 *Sally*, b April 28, 1817, m Robert Harvey, Sept. 9, 1839; 937 *Isaac*, Capt., b Nov. 6, 1818, m Amanda Thayer, May 1, 1845; 938 *Julia*, b April 5, 1820; 939 *William Jencks*, b Dec. 22, 1821, m Emeline Stone; 940 *Phebe Ives*, b Feb. 18, 1824, m Amos Chamberlain, Nov. 3, 1844; 941 *Eunice*, b Feb. 18, 1827, m Franklin A. Thomas, April 26, 1866; 942 *Newton*, Maj., b Sept. 16, 1829, m Elmira Brainard, April 26, 1866; 943 *Maria K.*, b July 4, 1831, m Charles G. Dewey, Nov. 16, 1854.

911. RUSSEL.

COL. RUSSEL and Polly Hall.

Children: 944 *Caroline Diana*, b Sept. 3, 1815; 945 *Eliza Ann*, b Sept. 13, 1817; 946 *George Kirtland*, b July 7, 1819; 947 *Mary Augusta*, b May 11, 1822; 948 *Sarah Potter*, b July 26, 1824.

428. JOSEPH.

JOSEPH HALL, son of John and Elizabeth Prindle Hall, married Hannah ——.

Children: 949 *Sherman*, b April 26, 1806; 950 *John*, b June 5, 1808, d July 9, 1836; 951 *Emery*, b Sept. 29, 1809, d Dec. 6, 1869; 952 *Lucy*, b May 27, 1811, d Feb 18, 1818;

953 *Julius*, b June 7, 1813, m Laura E. Parker, May 1, 1852, 6 children; 954 *Maria*, b August 30, 1815, d May 5, 1846, ae. 30 years.

HARRIMAN.

SAMUEL.

SAMUEL HARRIMAN was in New Haven at an early date, where he had a considerable family. Among his children was John, who graduated at Harvard College in 1663. He went to Wallingford with the first planters in 1670, and was the acting minister among the people of the village for two years, though not an ordained minister. Mrs. Elizabeth Harriman, his mother, died in Wallingford, Sept. 23, 1684. His wife died Jan. 10, 1680. His house lot was that on which the houses of the late Mr. Almer Hall and Liverius Carrington now stand.

Children: 1 *John*, b Jan. 25, 1666, d Nov. 21, 1683, ae. 17 years; 2 *Samuel;* 3 *Anna*, b July 6, 1678; 4 *Mary*, b Nov. 7, 1680; 5 *Leonard*, b June 5, 1683; 6 *Richard*, b Aug. 9, 1685.

HART.[1]

HAWKINS.

HAWKINS HART of Farmington came to Wallingford at the age of 24 years, and married Sarah Royce, who was nineteen years of age. Their marriage was consummated Sept. 17, 1701. She died Jan. 31, 1733. He died May 24, 1735. They resided after their marriage a short time in Farmington, but returned to Wallingford Oct. 4, 1705, where they resided for the remainder of their lives.

1 For collateral branches, see Andrews' Hist. New Britain, Conn., 149–51, 163–4, 170–8, 188–91; Davis' Gen. Hart Family, Lewis and Newhall's Hist. Lynn, Mass., 227; Littell's Passaic Valley Gen., 179; Savage's Gen. Dict., II. 367–8; Sibley's Hist. Union, Me., 459.

Children : 1 *Nathaniel*, b June 19, 1702, in Farmington, Ct. ; 2 *Ruth*, b Aug. 13, 1704, in Farmington, Ct. ; 3 *Hawkins*, b Sept. 16, 1706, d in Wallingford, Sept. 22, 1706 ; 4 *Hawkins*, b March 1, 1708, m 1st, Mary Street, Jan. 30, 1734, 2nd, Abigail Hall, Feb. 12, 1761 ; 5 *Sarah*, b March 21, 1710 ; 6 *Esther*, b Aug. 12, 1712 ; 7 *Thomas*, b Sept. 29, 1714 ; 8 *Mary*, b June 21, 1719 ; 9 *Benjamin*, b Jan. 28, 1722. Mr. Hart married for his 2nd wife, Mary, daughter of Rev. Joseph and Mary Elliot of Guilford, 1734. She was born 1688, and had 10 *Samuel*, born July 13, 1735, who was a lieutenant in the American army, and was wounded in the battle at Saratoga during the Revolutionary war. He died at Durham, Ct., Jan. 12, 1805.

1. NATHANIEL

NATHANIEL HART m Martha Lee, Dec. 21, 1727. He died Oct. 2, 1750, ae. 48 years.

Children: 11 *Nathaniel*, b Sept. 5, 1729, m Alice Hall, Jan. 23, 1753, he went to Goshen where he d ae. 80 years, had Nathaniel, b Nov. 8, 1754 ; 12 *Timothy*, b May 24, 1731 ; 13 *Martha*, b June 21, 1733 ; 14 *Ebenezer*, b March 26, 1739 ; 15 *Josiah*, b Feb. 22, 1742 ; 16 *Phebe*, b April 22, 1746, m 1st, Stephen Yale, 2nd, Eliasaph Preston, Feb. 17, 1764.

4. HAWKINS.

LIEUT. HAWKINS HART, married to Susannah Merriman by Rev. Theophilus Hall, Nov. 20, 1730. After her decease he married Mary Street, Jan. 30, 1734. She died, and he married Abigail Hall, Feb. 12, 1761. He died April 17, 1756.

Children: 17 *Samuel;* 18 *Sarah*, b 1750, d Nov. 27, 1765 ; 19 *Susannah*, b 1747, d Oct. 26, 1757 ; 20 *Benjamin*, b 1751, d Oct. 7, 1836, m Jerusha Rich, Feb. 25, 1776, she d Aug. 26, 1832.

20. BENJAMIN.

BENJAMIN HART, son of Lieut. Hawkins Hart, married Jerusha Rich.

Children: 21 *Esther*, b Nov. 8, 1776, m Marvel Andrews

for his 4th wife; 22 *Lucy*, b Dec. 20, 1779; 23 *Susannah*, b Jan. 15, 1782; 24 *Webb*, b Feb. 21, 1786; 25 *Jerusha*, b Sept. 11, 1788, m Abel D. Clark; 26 *Samuel*, *I.*, b Nov. 22, 1792.

26. SAMUEL.

SAMUEL IVES HART, son of Benjamin and Jerusha Rich Hart, married Abigail D. Hall, Sept. 20, 1814; he is now living in the east part of Meriden.

Children: 27 *Daniel H.*, b June 19, 1815, m Harriet G. Miller; 28 *Edmund*, b Aug. 12, 1817; 29 *Edmund*, b Feb. 16, 1818; 30 *Jerusha*, b Aug. 22, 1822, m Horace Pratt of Meriden; 31 *Elizabeth*, b Aug. 22, 1822, m Edward B. Miller of Meriden.

HOW.[1]

Four persons of this name were early at New Haven, viz.: Jeremiah Sen., Ephraim, Zachariah Sen., and Nathaniel. These persons all but Ephraim, went to Wallingford, in 1670, and he followed them in 1672, as appears by the records, having been at New Haven then, about 20 years. John How, one of the sons, returned to New Haven about the year 1700.

JEREMIAH.

Children: 1 *Jeremiah*, b July 8, 1650; 2, 3 *John* and *Ebenezer*, b June 26, 1656; all born in New Haven. John married Abigail ——.

EPHRAIM.

EPHRAIM HOW is supposed to have removed from Wallingford, as no mention of marriages or deaths are found on the Wallingford records.

Children born in New Haven: 4 *Ephraim*, b April 3, 1653;

1 For collateral branches, see Bond's Hist. Watertown, Mass., 303–4; Kidder's Hist. New Ipswich, N. H., 391; Morse's Memorial of Morses, Appendix No. 67 3-4; N. E. Hist. and Gen. Reg. XVI. 314; Worcester Mag. and Hist. Jour., II. 130–1.

5 *Sarah*, b June 25, 1654; 6 *Nancy*, b Nov. 17, 1656; 7 *Samuel*, b 1658; 8 *Daniel*, b Jan. 4, 1663; 9 *Isaac*, b Aug. 26, 1666; 10 *Abigail*, b April 23, 1668; 11 *Esther*, b Nov. 28, 1671; 12 *Mary*, b Dec. 8, 1674.

NATHANIEL.

NATHANIEL and Elizabeth How were with the first planters in Wallingford; she died Dec. 29, 1713, æ. 70 yrs. He married 2d, Sarah Curtis, August 9, 1714; he died at Wallingford, Feb. 12, 1722.

Children: 13 *Elijah*, b Sept. 9, 1673, m Mary Bellamy, Jan. 25, 1703; 14 *Lydia*, b Nov. 6, 1675; 15 *Daniel*, b Mar. 8, 1677, m 1st, Margery ——, 2d, Sarah ——; 16 *Abigail*, b Aug. 7, 1680.

ZACHARIAH.

ZACHARIAH How died at Wallingford, Sept. 22, 1740; he died June, 1703.

Children born in New Haven: 17 *John*, b Jan. 16, 1666, m Abigail ———; 18 *Zachariah*, b May 30, 1669, m Elizabeth Hemingway, he d May 12, 1712; 19 *Nathaniel*, b Jan. 2, 1672, m Mary Tracey, Oct. 15, 1711; 20 *Matthew*, b Jan. 2, 1672, m Elizabeth Winston, Dec. 31, 1717, both born in Wallingford; 21 *Sarah*, b Oct. 30, 1675, d Feb. 2, 1713, æ. 36 yrs.; *Mary*, b Dec. 14, 1677.

I. JEREMIAH.

JEREMIAH How married Elizabeth ———, Oct. 29, 1674. He died at Wallingford, Sept. 22, 1740, æ. 90 yrs.; Elizabeth, his wife died Oct. 4, 1704. He married a widow, Mary Cook, April 9, 1705.

Children by 1st marriage, born at Wallingford: 22 *Jeremiah*, b Sept. 15, 1675; *Jerusha*, b Sept. 13, 1677; *Ephraim*, b Feb. 20, 1681; 25 *Martha*, b Aug. 2, 1684; 26 *Maria*, b Sept. 20, 1687; 27 *Ebenezer*, b March 3, 1690; 28 *Joshua*, b Dec. 2, 1702. Children by 2d marriage: 29 *Sarah*, b April 16, 1709; 30 *Dinah*, b Feb. 28, 1716; 31 *Ichabod*, b Sept. 11, 1717; 32 *Joshua*, b April 1, 1720.

22. JEREMIAH.

JEREMIAH HOW married Judith Cook, April 20, 1704; she died March 20, 1708. He was living June 28, 1745.

Children: 33 *Judith*, b Oct. 22, 1703, m Elihu Yale; 34 *Jeremiah*, b Feb. 17, 1705, m Elizabeth Gaylord.

31. JEREMIAH.

JEREMIAH HOW of Wallingford married Elizabeth Gaylord, March 11, 1730. He was designated as Jeremiah How 3d; he emigrated to Goshen in the summer of 1747.

Children born in Wallingford: 35 *Judith*, b Dec. 19, 1730; 36 *John*, b Oct. 1, 1732; 37 *Jeremiah*, b Dec. 24, 1734, d 1736; 38 *Jeremiah*, b Nov. 17, 1736, m Martha North; 39 *Elizabeth*, b Sept. 18, 1738, m Daniel Norton; 40 *Benjamin*, b Oct. 26, 1739, d; 41 *Benjamin*, b Jan. 22, 1740; 42 *Joel*, d Jan. 28, 1745; 43 *Esther*, b March 5, 1744, m Daniel Merrills; 44 *Joseph*, b Nov. 9, 1746, m Prudence Norton; 45 *Ruth*, b Oct. 4, 1748, m Royce Orvis, she was b in Goshen.

36. JOHN.

JOHN HOW married Mary Wadams, daughter of Noah Wadams of Goshen. She died, and he married Lydia Norton, April 15, 1766.

Children born in Goshen: 46 *Mary*, b Sept. 10, 1757, m Wait Hinman; 47 *Experience*, b Dec. 29, 1759, m Nathan Norton; 48 *Anna*, b April 10, 1762, m Israel Everett and went to Vermont; 49 *Deliverance*, b June 25, 1764. By second marriage: 50 *John*, b April 22, 1767, m Esther Walter of Cornwall, Conn.; 51 *Ichabod*, b June 5, 1769, m C. Moss Norton of Cornwall, Conn; 52 *Isaac*, b 1771, d æ. 8 yrs; 53 *Luman*, b Aug. 6, 1774, m Esther Meacham; 54 *Daniel*; 55 *Seth*, m Achsah Washburn of Penn.; 56 *Lydia*, committed suicide at the age of 14 yrs.

The above John How remained in Goshen, Conn., till Dec. 30, 1766, when he sold to Wistal Willoughby, and removed to Canaan, Conn.

41. JOSEPH.

JOSEPH HOW married Prudence Norton, Oct. 24, 1768, daughter and youngest child of Joseph, who was from Durham, Conn.; he died at Goshen, April 17, 1807, æ. 61 yrs. She died Jan. 15, 1825.

Children: 57 *Prudence*, b Oct. 15, 1769, m Amasa Robinson of Litchfield, Conn.; 58 *Melzar*, b Oct. 19, 1772, m ——— Willoughby; 59 *Philo*, m Roxy Tuttle; 60 *Clara*, m Allen Dean.

HITCHCOCK.[1]

JOHN.

JOHN and Abigail Hitchcock were the first of the name who came into the town of Wallingford, which was about 1675.

Children: 1 *Mary*, b Dec. 10, 1676; 2 *Nathaniel*, b April 18, 1679, d May 12, 1710, ae. 31; 3 *Margery*, b Sept. 9, 1681; 4 *Elizabeth*, b April 8, 1684; 5 *John*, b Oct. 18, 1685, m Marlow Munson, Nov. 21, 1712; 6 *Matthias*, b May 26, 1688, m Thankful Andrews; 7 *Hannah*, b Jan. 9, 1690; 8 *Damaris*, b June 11, 1693; 9 *Benjamin*, b March 24, 1696, m Elizabeth Ives.

2. NATHANIEL.

NATHANIEL HITCHCOCK m Sarah Lewis Jennings, April 3, 1704. He died May 12, 1714.

Children: 10 *Sarah*, b March 13, 1705; 11 *Elizabeth*, b Jan. 26, 1707; 12 *Hannah*, b June 11, 1709.

5. JOHN.

JOHN HITCHCOCK, m Marlow Munson, Nov. 21, 1712. She died July 1, 1739.

Children: 13 *Peter*, b Oct. 14, 1713; 14 *Martha*, b April 1,

---

1 For collateral branches, see Dodd's Hist. E. Haven, Conn., 126, 127; Kellogg's Memorials of Elder John White, 121; Savage's Gen. Dict., II. 428, 429; Wilbraham, Mass., Centennial Celebration, 1863, 298, 299.

1715; 15 *John*, b May 11, 1717; 16 *Eliakim*, b Sept. 7, 1719, d April 5, 1723; 17 *Jotham*, b Feb. 4, 1722, m Mary ——; 18 *Dan*, b March 14, 1724, m Esther ——; 19 *Eliakim*, b June 13, 1726; 20 *Titus*, b Jan. 31, 1729, m Hannah Munson July 30, 1759; 21 *Catherine*, b July 10, 1731.

6. MATTHIAS.

MATTHIAS HITCHCOCK m Thankful Andrews, Dec. 27, 1710.

Children: 22 *Oliver*, b Nov. 14, 1716; 23 *Jason*, b Aug. 16, 1718; 24 *William*, b Oct. 16, 1720; 25 *Matthias*, b June 19, 1711, d April 7, 1726; 26 *Nathaniel*, b Oct. 15, 1712; 27 *Valentine*, b Feb. 14, 1715; 28 *Nathaniel*, b May 7, 1733; 29 *Thankful*, b March 29, 1725; 30 *Matthias*, b Feb. 11, 1727, m Sarah ——; 31 *Ebenezer*, b Sept. 14, 1728; 32 *Tabitha*, b Feb. 26, 1730; 33 *Enos*, b April 27, 1735; 34 *Hannah*, b April 27, 1735.

9. BENJAMIN.

CAPT. BENJAMIN HITCHCOCK was married to Elizabeth Ives by Capt. Yale, Oct. 1, 1718. He died Feb. 12, 1767. She died Aug. 8, 1762.

Children: 35 *Bela*, b Oct. 27, 1719; 36 *Hannah*, b Sept. 12, 1721; 37 *Benjamin*, b Feb. 23, 1724; 38 *Joseph*, b July 12, 1737; 39 *Abigail*, b May 10, 1728; 40 *David*, b June 29, 1742; 41 *Samuel*, b April 1, 1730; 42 *Damaris*, b Sept. 3, 1745; 43 *Nathaniel*, b June 20, 1732; 44 *Nathaniel*, b Sept. 20, 1739; 45 *Damaris*, b Nov. 25, 1756.

15. JOHN.

JOHN and Elizabeth Chatterton Hitchcock, married Nov. 29, 1739.

Children: 46 *Amos*, b Dec. 28, 1740; 47, 48 *Elizabeth* and *Elisha*, b Oct. 24, 1743; 49 *David*, b Sept. 27, 1742.

17. JOTHAM.

JOTHAM and Mary Hitchcock.

Children: 50 *Sarah*, b Sept. 11, 1747; 51 *Lyman*, b March 15, 1749; 52 *Mary*, b Dec. 4, 1750; 53 *Marlow*, b Dec. 26, 1752; 54 *Jotham*, b Nov. 6, 1754.

13. PETER.

PETER HITCHCOCK married Hannah Smith, June 18, 1737.

Children: 55 *Reuben*, b May 11, 1738; 56 *Amasa*, b Oct. 3, 1739; 57 *Valentine*, b April 18, 1741; 58 *Peter*, b May 17, 1743, d May 16, 1744; 59 *Peter*, b Feb. 6, 1743; 60 *David*, b Nov. 10, 1754.

18. DAN.

DAN HITCHCOCK married Esther Miles, of Cheshire, Aug. 17, 1743.

Children: 61 *Asahel*, b Dec. 24, 1743; 62 *Martha*, b April 10, 1748; 63 *Susannah;* 64 *Eunice*, b Nov. 28, 1754; 65 *Seth;* 66 *Lydia;* 67 *Benajah;* 68 *Eliakim*, b Aug. 8, 1746; 69 *Esther*, b May 23, 1750; 70 *Dan*, b Oct. 19, 1752; 71 *Sarah*, b Sept. 6, 1757; 72 *Miriam;* 73 *George.*

19. ELIAKIM.

ELIAKIM HITCHCOCK married Esther ——; he died June 19, 1788, æ. 62 yrs.

Children: 74 *Abigail*, b Dec. 6, 1756; 75 *Rufus*, b April 1, 1760, was a Judge of Probate, Town Clerk, etc.; 76 *Jared*, b July 30, 1758.

20. TITUS.

TITUS HITCHCOCK married Hannah Munson, July 30, 1759.

Child: 77 *Obedienee*, b Oct. 8, 1761.

22. OLIVER.

OLIVER HITCHCOCK married Thankful Parker, Oct. 19, 1744.

Children: 78 *Mary*, b July 8, 1745; 79 *Thankful*, b May 13, 1747; 80 *Rebecca*, b Jan. 18, 1749; 81 *Hannah*, b Oct. 11, 1750, d Nov. 5, 1752; 82 *Oliver*, b Feb. 24, 1755; 83 *Sarah*, b March 19, 1757; 84 *Damaris*, b Nov. 6, 1758; 85 *Dinah*, b Nov. 23, 1760.

23. JASON.

JASON HITCHCOCK, married Lydia Cook, Sept. 20, 1743; she died Dec. 30, 1753.

Children: 86 *William*, b June 26, 1744; 87 *Thomas*, b

Dec. 20, 1746; 88 *Lemuel*, b Dec. 20, 1749; 89 *Jason*, b July 12, 1752; 90 *Jason*, b Oct. 10, 1755; 91 *Ichabod*, b Dec. 18, 1756; 92 *Thankful*, b March 20, 1761.

30. MATTHIAS.

MATTHIAS HITCHCOCK married Sarah ———.

Children: 93 *Oliver;* 94 *Jason;* 95 *Thankful;* 96 *Matthias;* 97 *Ebenezer;* 98 *Tabitha;* 99 *Nathaniel;* 100 *Hannah.*

35. BELA.

BELA HITCHCOCK married Sarah Atwater, Dec. 25, 1744; she died Oct. 23, 1746; he married Hannah Cook, and she died June 28, 1805, æ. 83; he died Oct. 12, 1796, æ. 77 yrs., in Cheshire.

Child by 1st marriage: 101 *Isaac*, b Jan. 23, 1746, d Jan. 28, 1746. Children by 2nd marriage: 102 *Isaac*, b Oct. 26, 1748, d May 27, 1749; 103 *Bela*, b Sept. 21, 1750; 104 *Hannah*, b Dec. 31, 1752; 105 *Asa*, b Feb. 11, 1755; 106 *Sarah*, b Aug. 1, 1757; 107 *Aaron*, b Dec. 6, 1759.

37. BENJAMIN.

BENJAMIN HITCHCOCK married Rhoda Cook, Feb. 27, 1745. Children: 108 *Thaddeus*, b Dec. 13, 1745; 109 *Hannah*, b March 9, 1748; 110, 111 *Benjamin* and *Rhoda*, b Nov 24, 1752; 112 *Lucy*, b March 24, 1755; 113 *Damaris*, b Dec. 5, 1756; 114 *Thaddeus*, b Dec. 10, 1760.

56. AMASA.

Children: 115 *Amasa;* 116 *Silas;* 117 *James;* 118 *David;* several daughters.

57. VALENTINE.

Children: 119 Hon. *Peter;* 120 Rev. *Roger;* 121 *Polly.*

60. DAVID.

Children; 122 *Marcus;* 123 *David;* 124 *Gaius.*

68. ELIAKIM.

ELIAKIM HITCHCOCK, son of Dan and Esther Hitchcock, married Betty Hill, July 23, 1734, she died Nov. 21, 1754.

Child: 125 *Betty Hill*, b March 2, 1754.

61. ASAHEL.

ASAHEL HITCHCOCK lived in the village of Cheshire.

Child: 126 *Miles*, went to New York, where he died.

70. DAN.

DAN HITCHCOCK was a blacksmith, and resided, when living, in a house then standing a little east of the late residence of Titus and Almon Preston.

Children: 127 *Samuel;* 128 *Clarissa*, m —— Perkins; 129 *Chauncey;* 130 *Esther;* 131 *Lyman;* 132 *Rebecca*, m A. Perkins; 133 *Dan;* 134 *Annah*, m John Reed; 135 *Matilda;* 136 *Betsey*, m Amos Bristol.

73. RUFUS.

RUFUS HITCHCOCK was twice married; he died in 1832, was a Judge of Probate, Town Clerk, etc.

Children: 137 *Wm. Rufus*, m Mary Hall, d in Waterbury; 138 *Lucretia*, m Rev. P. G. Clark.

91. ICHABOD.

ICHABOD HITCHCOCK, son of Jason and ——— Hitchcock, died in Cheshire.

Children: 139 *Pliny*, m —— Bradley; 140 *Sarilla*, m Geo. Stevens; 141 *Jason;* 142 *Hannah*, m T. L. Gaylord; 143 *Lucinda*, m Richard Beach. By 2d marriage: 144 *Abigail*, m and went to Kentucky.

65. SETH.

SETH HITCHCOCK, son of Dan and Esther Miles Hitchcock, died in Cheshire.

Children; 145 *Alfred;* 146 *Emily*, m Aaron Cook, late of Cheshire.

HOLT.[1]

William Holt died in Wallingford, Sept. 1, 1683, aged 83; consequently was born in 1600, in the old country. He was buried in the cemetery at Wallingford, where his tomb-stone

---

1 For collateral branches, see Abbot's Hist. Andover, Mass., 22;

still remains to mark his grave. Benjamin Holt also died in Wallingford, Aug. 2, 1693, aged 32 years.

JOSEPH.

JOSEPH HOLT was an early settler in Wallingford, though not an original subscriber. He was married to Elizabeth French or Tench, by Major Nash, Nov. 20, 1684. He died Dec. 19, 1697, ae. 42 years.

Children: 1 *Joseph*, b Sept. 10, 1685, m Abigail Curtis, June 8, 1709; 2 *Daniel*, b Oct. 6, 1687, m Rebecca ———; 3 *Benjamin*, b Sept. 3, 1690, m Abigail Curtis; 4 *Mary*, b Jan. 29, 1691; 5 *Elizabeth*, b March 23, 1696; 6 *John*.

1. JOSEPH.

JOSEPH HOLT married Abigail Curtis, June 8, 1709. She died Jan. 12, 1730.

Children: 7 *Tamar*, b Oct. 31, 1711; 8 *Susannah*, b Feb. 12, 1716; 9 *Mary*, b Feb. 9, 1714; 10 *Samuel*, b May 14, 1718; 11 *Lucy*, b Dec. 12, 1722; 12 *Lydia*, b April 24, 1725; 13 *Abigail*, b July 20, 1727; 14 *Prudence*, b Dec. 29, 1728; 15 *Mehitable*, b Dec. 26, 1729; 16 *Mabel*, d Dec. 28, 1727.

2. DANIEL.

DANIEL and Rebecca Holt.

Children: 17 *Phebe*, b Dec. 24, 1716; 18 *Hannah*, b April 28, 1719; 19 *Mary*, b May 21, 1718; 20 *Thomas*, b Jan. 22, 1721; 21 *Eunice*, b Nov. 26, 1724; 22 *Uriah*, b Jan. 22, 1721; 23 *Joseph*, b Feb. 25, 1726; 24 *Lois*, b Oct. 30, 1726; 25, 26 *Rebecca* and *Abigail*, b May 11, 1738; 27 *Daniel*, b May 27, 1729.

3. BENJAMIN.

BENJAMIN and Abigail Holt.

Children: 28 *Elizabeth*, b Dec. 25, 1729; 29 *Prudence*, d May 23, 1737; 30 *Lydia*, b August 15, 1732; 31 *Benjamin*, b

---

Caulkins' Hist. New London, Ct., 314, 315; Dodd's Hist. East Haven, Ct., 127, 128; Durrie's Gen. of Holt Family; Savage's Gen. Dict., II. 454, 455.

June 14, 1734, d May 2, 1735; 32 *Benjamin*, b August 22, 1737.

HOTCHKISS.[1]

SAMUEL.

SAMUEL HOTCHKISS came from Essex, England, and is supposed to have been a brother of John Hotchkiss, who settled at Guilford, Conn. This name is spelled in some instances, Hodghe, Hodgkins, and Hotchkins. He was at New Haven as early as 1641. In Aug., 1642, he married Elizabeth Cleverly; he died Dec. 28, 1663.

Children: 1 *John*, b 1643, m Elizabeth Peck, Dec. 4, 1672, and remained in New Haven; 2 *Samuel*, b 1645, m Sarah Talmadge in 1678, settled at East Haven, Conn.; 3 *James*, b 1647; 4 *Joshua*, b Sept. 16, 1651, m two or three wives, resided in New Haven; 5 *Thomas*, b 1654, m Sarah Wilmot; 6 *David*, b 1657, m Esther Sperry.

1. JOHN.

JOHN HOTCHKISS married Elizabeth Peck, daughter of Henry Peck of New Haven, Dec. 4, 1672. They had John, born 1673; he married Mary Chatterton in 1694, and settled on the west side of Wallingford, now Cheshire.

Child: 7 *John*, b 1694, m Miriam Wood, March 10, 1717, he d in Cheshire, April 30, 1732, she d Jan 10, 1765, æ. 65 yrs.

7. JOHN.

Children: 8 *Robbins*, b May 12, 1709; 9 *Mary*, b Feb. 20, 1712, d Aug., 1718; 10 *Henry*, b April 1, 1715; 11 *Benjamin*, b May 10, 1718; 12 *Jason*, b May 12, 1719, m Abigail ——, she d Feb. 22, 1773, ae. 40 yrs.; 13 *Sarah*, b July 13, 1721; 14 *Dorothy*, b Dec. 28, 1723; 15 *Hannah*, b July 30, 1726; 16 *Naomi*, b Feb. 23, 1731; 17 *John*, b Sept. 16, 1733.

---

1 For collateral branches, see Andrews' Hist. New Britain, Conn., 155, 156, 171, 172, 224, 295; Bronson's Hist. Waterbury, Conn., 505–8; Cothren's Hist. Woodbury, Conn., 579, 580; Dodd's Hist. East Haven, Conn., 512–19.

12. JASON.

JASON HOTCHKISS married Abigail ———; he died in Cheshire, May 19, 1776, ae. 58 years. She died Feb. 22, 1773, ae. 40 yrs.

Children: 18 *Abigail*, b July 12, 1746; 19 *David*, b March 8, 1752; 20 *Jonathan*, b May 7, 1754; 21 *Abigail*, b Sept 19, 1756; 22 *Sarah*, b May 1, 1776, m William Law Esq. of Cheshire, and was the mother of Samuel Law Esq. of Meredith, N. Y., and of William and Jonathan Law of Cheshire, and John of Whitehall, N. Y., all deceased.

2. SAMUEL.

SAMUEL HOTCHKISS married Sarah Talmadge in 1678.

Children, born in East Haven: 23 *Mary*; 24 *Sarah*; 25 *Samuel*; 26 *James*, b 1747, m Tamar ——; 27 *Abigail*; 28 *Eben*; 29 *Enos*.

4. JOSHUA.

ENS. JOSHUA HOTCHKISS was twice or more times married. The name of his last wife was Mary Hotchkiss. She died Nov. 15, 1787, ae. 88 yrs. He died 1788, ae. 88 yrs.; he resided in New Haven, and was a leading man there.

Children: 30 *Mary*, b April 30, 1679; 31 *Stephen*, b Aug. 12, 1681, settled in Wallingford, parish of Cheshire; 32 *Martha*, b Dec. 14, 1680, m Thomas Brooks of New Haven, in 1702, and settled in Cheshire (then Wallingford); 33 *Priscilla*, b 1688; 34 *Abraham*, settled in Bethany, Conn., d 1702; 35 *Desire*, d 1702; 36 *Isaac*, b June, 1701. Among the children were Abraham, Isaac and Jacob, all residents of Bethany, as was their father. 37 *Jacob*, b Feb. 7, 1704, remained on the old homestead in New Haven for some time, and subsequently removed to Hamden, one of his sons went to Derby, Conn.; 38 *John*, b Feb. 27, 1733; 39 *Elizabeth*, b March 23, 1735; 40 *Mary*, b Aug. 11, 1737, d; 41 *Mary*, b June 17, 1738.

5. THOMAS.

THOMAS HOTCHKISS married Sarah Wilmot, Nov. 28, 1697. He died in 1711. Children: 42 *Samuel*; 43 *Anna*; 44 *Sarah*.

6. DAVID.

DAVID HOTCHKISS married 1st, Esther Sperry, June 20, 1683. He married 2nd, Eunice ——. He died in 1712.

Children: 45 *Eliza;* 46 *Daniel*, m Mamre ——; 47 *Obadiah*, m Eunice Beach, Jan., 1716, they had Lewis, b Jan. 16, 1717; 48 *Thankful*, b Feb. 15, 1753; 49 *Eunice*, b Jan. 8, 1755; 50 *Rebecca;* 51 *Isaac*, b March 4, 1757; 52 *Hannah*, b June 5, 1761; 53 *Rebecca.*

10. HENRY.

CAPT. HENRY HOTCHKISS married Sarah ——, and settled at Wallingford, in the parish of Cheshire, where he was married Nov. 23, 1736. He died June 9, 1799, ae. 84. She died Nov. 19, 1751, ae. 34 years.

Children: 54 *Henry*, b Sept. 2, 1737; 55 *Joseph*, b Dec. 18, 1738; 56 *Henry*, b 1723, d Sept. 29, 1742; 57 *Jonah*, d July 26, 1741; 58 *Sarah*, b Feb. 5, 1742; 59 *Mary*, b Feb. 1, 1745; 60 *Jonah*, b Oct. 28, 1748.

31. STEPHEN.

DEA. STEPHEN HOTCHKISS, b 1681, son of Joshua, m Elizabeth, daughter of John Sperry of New Haven, Dec. 12, 1704. He purchased land in Cheshire in 1706, and settled upon it in 1707. He died March 5, 1755, ae. 74 years. He was deacon of the church at Cheshire for 31 years.

Children: 61 *Joshua*, b Aug. 26, 1705; *Elizabeth*, b 1706, d 1788; 62 *Mary*, b July 1, 1708, m Nathan Burns M. D.; 63 *Hannah*, b Jan. 10, 1710, m Stephen Atwater; 64 *Esther*, b Feb. 8, 1712; 65 *Elizabeth*, b Aug. 15, 1715; 66 *Gideon*, b Dec. 5, 1715, first Dea. of the Congregational Church in Salem; 67 *Stephen*, b Dec. 1, 1717; 68 *Silas*, b Nov. 20, 1719, m widow Alcott; 69, 70 *Hannah* and *Stephen*, b Feb. 23, 1722; 71 *Bashua*, b Sept. 7, 1726; 72 *Benjamin*, b Feb. 1, 1728, m Elizabeth Roberts; 73 *Noah*, b Nov. 24, 1731, d Jan. 13, 1760.

26. JAMES.

JAMES HOTCHKISS, son of Samuel and Sarah, married Tamar ——.

Children: 74 *Asa*, b Nov. 24, 1731; 75 *Robert*, b June 17, 1733; 76 *Eunice*, b March 28, 1734; 77 *Tamar*, b Aug. 24, 1736; 78 *Reuben*, b Feb. 5, 1743; 79 *Lydia*, b Aug. 11, 1745.

JOSIAH.

JOSIAH HOTCHKISS married Abigail ———. He died of small pox in May, 1732, at Cheshire; she died of the same disease near the same time.

Children: 80 *Josiah*, b Oct. 13, 1716; 81 *Josiah*, b April 3, 1720; 82 *Elizabeth*, b Jan. 25, 1723; 83 *Ludwick*, b Jan. 15, 1720; 84 *Tyrrel*, b 1718; 85 *Lent*, b June 2, 1726.

66. GIDEON.

DEA. GIDEON HOTCHKISS, m Anna Brockett, Jan. 18, 1737. She died, and afterwards he married Mabel, daughter of Isaac Stiles, of Southbury. He located on a farm in the southeasterly part of Waterbury in 1736, and was chosen a Deacon of the Congregational Church at Salem now (Naugatuck), at its organization. He was one of the principal men who founded the Congregational Church at Prospect (then Columbia), and was a leading man there. He served in the French and Revolutionary wars, and died full of years, Sept. 3, 1807, æ. 91 years, leaving 105 grandchildren, 155 great grandchildren, and four of the fifth generation.

Children: 86 *Isaac*, b 1738; 87 *David*, b 1743; 88 *Gideon*, b Dec., 1744; 89 *Huldah*, b June 27, 1747, m Josiah Paine; 90 *Anna*, b Oct. 22, 1749, m Reuben Williams; 91 *Amos*, b Nov. 24, 1751; 92 *Submit*. b June 2, 1753, m David Paine; 93 *Titus*, b June 26, 1755, m Rachel Guernsey; 94 *Eben*, b Dec. 13, 1757, m Mary, dau. of Gideon Sanford, Feb. 15, 1781; 95 *Asahel*, born Feb. 16, 1760; 96 *Benoni*, born ———; 97 *Mabel*, born May 23, 1764, m Chauncey Judd, May 5, 1797; 98 *Phebe*, b Aug. 3, 1765, m Reuben Williams; he died in 1780; 99 *Stiles*, b Jan. 1, 1768, m Polly Horton, and had five children; 100 *Olive*, b Nov. 21, 1769, m William Jones; 101 *Millicent*, b May 2, 1771, m David Sanford; 102 *Amzi*, b July 3, 1774, resided in Meriden.[1]

1 See Bronson's Hist. of Waterbury, 505–8, for descendants of above.

HOUGH.[1]

SAMUEL.

SAMUEL HOUGH married Susannah, daughter of Simeon Wrotham, of Farmington, Conn. His father, William Hough, was a son of Edward Hough, of Westchester, Cheshire Co., England. Samuel was born in New London, Conn., and was by trade a mill-wright. He came to Wallingford to assist in the construction of the first mill in the township. Mrs. Hough died in Wallingford, Sept. 5, 1684. He married 2d, Mary, daughter of James Bates, of Haddam, Aug. 18, 1685 ; he died March 14, 1714.

Children: 1 *William*, b Aug. 22, 1680, m Mehitable —— ; 2 *Samuel*, b Feb. 15, 1681, d Nov. 30, 1702, ae. 21 yrs. ; 3 *Susannah*, b Nov. 27, 1683, m —— Andrews, of Farmington, Conn. By 2d marriage: 4 *James*, b Dec. 15, 1688, m Sarah Newhall, July 29, 1718 ; 5 *Hannah*, b Nov. 8, 1691.

1. WILLIAM.

WILLIAM HOUGH, son of Samuel and Susannah Hough, married Mehitable ——— ; she died Feb. 5, 1726. He married 2d, Elizabeth ——— ; she died June 3, 1740.

Children: 6 *Mary*, b Sept. 10, 1710 ; 7 *Samuel*, b July 5, 1712, d Oct. 8, 1713 ; 8, 9 *William*, and *Mehitable*, b Aug. 14, 1714 ; 10 *Deborah*, b Dec. 17, 1716 ; 11 *Anna*, b Dec. 28, 1718 ; 12 *Abiah*, b May 15, 1721. By 2d marriage : 13 *Nathaniel*, b Dec. 28, 1727 ; 14 *Simeon*, b Jan. 11, 1734.

4. JAMES.

JAMES HOUGH, son of Samuel and Susannah, married Sarah Newhall, July 19, 1718.

Children: 15 *Ephraim*, b April 9, 1719 ; 16 *Daniel*, b March 6, 1721, d July 25, 1768, ae. 49 yrs ; 17 *Ebenezer*, b Jan. 22, 1726, m Lydia ———, d July 20, 1737, she d July

---

1 For collateral branches, see Andrews' Hist. of New Britain, Conn., 352 ; Babson's Hist. Gloucester, Mass., 105 ; Caulkins' Hist. New London, Conn., 302, 303 ; Caulkins' Hist. Norwich, Conn., Ed. 1867, 233 ; Savage's Gen. Dict., II. 468–9 ; Wadsworth's Hyde Gen., II. 1100–11, 1152–9.

19, 1757; 18 *David*, b Feb. 8, 1728, d Oct. 18, 1729; 19 *Sarah*, b Oct. 18, 1730, d Nov. 10, 1741; 20 *David*, b Jan. 28, 1733, d June 27, 1752, ae. 19 yrs.; 21 *James*, b March 24, 1735, m Lucy ———, she d Oct. 5, 1775, æ. 51; 22 *Barnabas*, b Sept. 5, 1736; 23 *Mary*, b Nov. 25, 1739.

8. WILLIAM.

WILLIAM HOUGH, son of William and Mehitable Hough, married Mary Hall, Dec. 20, 1752.

Children: 24 *Susannah*, b May 24, 1754, d Nov. 24, 1756; 25 *Mary*, b June 22, 1756.

15. EPHRAIM.

EPHRAIM HOUGH, son of James and Sarah Newell Hough, married Hannah ——.

Children: 26 *Abigail*, b Nov. 29, 1740, d Aug. 16, 1743; 27 *Sarah*, b Jan. 26, 1742; 28 *Abigail*, b Aug. 10, 1743, d Aug. 16, 1743; 29 *Abigail*, b Feb. 21, 1744; 30 *Ephraim*, b Jan. 6, 1746; 31 *Andrew*, b Dec. 27, 1747; 32 *Andrew*, b Dec. 17, 1749; 33 *Hannah*, b Jan. 17, 1751; 34 *Thankful*, b May 29, 1753, d Aug. 18, 1780; 35 *Ambrose*, b Sept. 2, 1754; 36 *Lois*, b June 3, 1756.

16. DANIEL.

DANIEL HOUGH, son of James and Sarah (Newell), married 1st, Mindwell ——. She died March 21, 1741–2. He married for 2d wife, Violet Benton, Nov. 29, 1743. He settled in Meriden where he died.

Children: 37 *Mindwell*, b May 5, 1745; 38 *Ensign*, M. D., b Sept. 1, 1746; 39 *Elijah*, b Jan. 23, 1747; 40 *Samuel*, b March 12, 1750–1; 41 *Eunice*, b March 30, 1755; 42 *Dolly*, b Jan. 30, 1756; 43 *Caleb*, b Feb. 13, 1757; 44 *Hannah*, b Feb. 4, 1762.

17. EBENEZER.

EBENEZER HOUGH, son of James and Sarah, married Lydia ——. She died July 20, 1757.

Children: 45 *Buel*, b June, 1743; 46 *Lydia*, b Aug. 28, 1749, d July 19, 1759; 47 *Lucy*, b April 23, 1756.

SAMUEL.

SAMUEL HOUGH married Hannah ——. Supposed son of Samuel and Hannah was in W., about 1700.

Children: 48 *Samuel*, b July 12, 1712, m Mehitable ——; 40 *Phineas*, b April 11, 1714, d Sept. 1, 1797, ae. 83 years.

ENSIGN.

DR. ENSIGN HOUGH, son of Daniel and Violet Hough, of Meriden, died in 1813. He kept a hotel and practiced his profession as a physician.

Children: 50 *Dr. Isaac I.*, b 1781, d in Meriden, unmarried, Feb. 26, 1825; 51 *Ensign*, d in Meriden; he had other children.

49. PHINEAS.

PHINEAS HOUGH, son of Samuel and Hannah Hough, married Hannah ——.

Children: 52 *Rachel*, b May 27, 1740; 53 *James*, b July 31, 1743; 54 *Phineas*, b Sept 16, 1745; 55 *Mary*, b Aug. 14, 1747; 56 *Rachel*, b April 22, 1750; 57 *Anna*, b April 18, 1752.

JOSEPH.

JOSEPH HOUGH married Catherine, daughter of Capt. Theophilus and Sarah Street Yale, June 27, 1745. He was born 1717, and died Jan. 5, 1809, ae. 92 years. Catherine, his wife, died Oct. 5, 1767, ae. 46 years.

Children: 58 *Joseph*, b Sept. 12, 1745; 59 *Mary*, b July 15, 1746; 60 *Lois*, b June 24, 1747, d Nov. 12, 1748; 61 *Lent*, b April 4, 1751; 62 *Lois*, b Dec. 5, 1752; 63 *David*, b Nov. 2, 1754; 64 *Joel*, b Jan. 27, 1757, d Sept. 9, 1843, in Hamden, Ct.; 65 *James*, d Dec. 3, 1762; 66 *James*, d in Wallingford; 67 *Catherine*, m Edmund Smith; 68 *Sarah*, m ——— Rice, and settled at Homer, N. Y.

58. JOSEPH.

CAPT. JOSEPH HOUGH, son of Joseph and Catherine Yale Hough, settled on the farm of his father at Clapboard Hill. He built the house now occupied by his grandson Joseph Hough. He died Sept. 11, 1811.

Children: 69 *Chauncey*, m Lura, daughter of James Rice, of Wallingford, and had Mary, Elizabeth, Joseph and Chauncey; 70 *Betsey*, m Salmon Carter of W. and had Salmon, Betsey and William; 71 *Horace*, went to New Haven, Ohio, and died there, leaving several sons.

61. LENT.

LENT HOUGH, son of Joseph and Catherine Yale Hough, married 1st, Rebecca Tuttle. She died Aug. 22, 1798, ae. 44. He married Mary Andrews, who was Mary Pierrepont of North Haven before her 1st marriage. She died June 27, 1832, ae. 75. He died Oct. 8, 1837, ae. 87 yrs.

Children by 1st marriage: 72 *Lucy;* 73 *Hannah;* 74 *Serrajah*, b March 26, 1780, m Elizabeth S. Avery in 1801. By 2d marriage: 75 *Almira*, b Nov. 6, 1797, m Eveline Dutton, Nov. 6, 1821, d in Canada, May 15, 1841, æ. 42 yrs.

64. JOEL.

JOEL HOUGH, son of Joseph and Catherine Hough, settled in Hamden, Mt. Carmel society, where he died; he was a shoemaker and farmer.

Children: 76 *Ira*, settled in Wolcott, Conn., and d there; 77 *Joseph*, settled in Cheshire, Conn., m —— Moss, dau. of Bowers Moss, of that place; 78 ———, went to western New York; 79 *Amos*, m Nancy, dau. of Nehemiah Rice, of Wallingford, d at Hamden in 1869; 80 *Joel*, went to the state of N. Y.

66. JAMES.

JAMES HOUGH, son of Joseph and Catherine Yale Hough, married and settled in the North Farms district, Wallingford, where he died. He was a farmer.

Children: 81 *James*, m Mary, dau. of Nehemiah Rice, they had Elijah, and daughters; 82, daughters; 83 *Joel*, m, is now on the farm of his father in Wallingford.

74. SERRAJAH.

SERRAJAH HOUGH, only son of Lent and Rebecca Hough, m Elizabeth S., daughter of Abner Avery, of Wallingford, Feb.

18, 1801. She was born Sept. 27, 1782. Mr. Hough died at Meriden, Aug. 3, 1853, æ. 73 years.

Children: 84 *Lyman Worcester*, b March 7, 1802, d Aug. 1834, in Meriden; 85 *Lent Serrajah*, b Jan. 20, 1804, m Hannah Smith, of Wallingford, July 12, 1831, settled in Wolcott, Conn.; 86 *Nancy Avery*, b Feb. 1, 1806, d March 11, 1823, ae. 17 years; 87 *Rebecca Tuttle*, b Jan. 3, 1808, m Rev. Sam'l. F. Curtis, she died March 25, 1842; 88 *Alonzo Bennett*, b Mar. 25, 1810, resided in Vineland, N. J.; 89 *George Sherman*, b Oct. 7, 1812, now at Pittsburg, Pa., 1867; 90 *John Meers*, b Oct. 12, 1815, resides in Tyrrell Co., N. C.; 91 *Wm. Augustus*, b Aug. 14, 1818, d at Ravenna, Ohio, Dec. 25, 1837; 92 *Julius Ogden*, b July 21, 1822, d at Wallingford Jan. 1, 1823, ae. 6 months.

HULL.[1]

This name was early in Connecticut, and came from Derbyshire, England. George Hull was at Windsor, Conn., in 1636, and was a surveyor at Wethersfield the same year, and a member of the General Court 1637-8-9. He married Elizabeth Loomis in 1641.

Richard and Andrew Hull were both at New Haven in 1639, and had families.

JOHN.

Dr. John Hulls, as he wrote his name, was at Stratford in 1661, when he was admitted a planter. It is not quite certain whether he came from England, or was a son of Richard Hull of New Haven. Dr. John was at Derby in 1668, and at Wallingford in 1687. He died Dec. 6, 1711, at the latter place. He was probably somewhat advanced in life when he came to Wallingford. He married Mary Jones, Oct. 19, 1672, probably his second wife; she dying, he married

1 For collateral branches, see Am. Antiq. Soc. Coll., III. 269; Andrews' Hist. New Britain, Conn., 367; Cothren's Hist. Woodbury, Conn., 577-9; Rhode Island Hist. Soc. Coll., III. 292, 293; Savage's Gen. Dict., II. 492-5; Stiles' Hist. Windsor, Conn., 672, 673.

Rebecca Turner, Sept. 20, 1699. He exchanged his house and land at Stratford, with Benjamin Lewis, for his house and land at Wallingford, in 1687. The town of Wallingford set out to Dr. Hull a tract of land which they supposed contained 700 acres, lying between the north side of Broad Swamp and the Quinnipiac river, the east and west boundaries not being so clearly defined. This grant was more than a mile square, and was known as Dr. Hull's large farm.

Children: 1 *John*, b March 14, 1661, m Mary ———; 2 *Samuel*, b Feb. 4, 1663; 3 *Mary*, b Oct. 31, 1666; 4 *Joseph*, b 1668, m Mary Nichols of Derby; 5 *Benjamin*, M. D., b Oct. 7, 1672, m Elizabeth Andrews, Dec. 14, 1695; 6 *Ebenezer*, b 1673, m Lydia Mix, Mar. 4, 1706, he died in 1709; 7 *Richard*, b 1674; 8 *Jeremiah*, M. D., b 1679, at Derby, m Hannah Cook, of Wallingford; 9 *Archer*.

1. JOHN.

JOHN HULL, son of Dr. John Hull, was born in Stratford, March 14, 1661–2, married Mary ——, and settled in Derby.

Children: 10 *Deborah*, b 1691, at Derby; 11 *John*, b 1693; 12 *Daniel*, m May 2, 1732; 13 *Miles*, b 1700, m Mary Tuttle, Dec. 4, 1729; 14 *Ebenezer*, m Hannah Bates, Sept. 1, 1734; 15 *Mary*; 16 *Martha*; 17 *Priscilla*, b 1702.

4. JOSEPH.

CAPT. JOSEPH HULL, of Derby, was a son of Dr. John Hull of Wallingford. He married Mary Nichols of Derby, where they lived and died. The name of his second wife was Hannah ———, whom he left a widow.

Children: 18 *Samuel*, b 1692, had a family in Derby; 19 *Joseph*, b 1694, left 3 children, Sarah, b 1726, Joseph, b 1737, Elizabeth, b 1738; 20 *Caleb*, b Feb 4, 1695, settled in Cheshire by request of his grandfather; 21 *Abijah*, b 1697; 22 *Archer*, b 1698; 23 *Sarah*, m ——— Beach of Stamford; 24 *Mary*, m ——— Russel of Derby, Conn.

5. BENJAMIN.

DOCT. BENJAMIN HULL, son of Dr. John Hull, came to Wallingford with his father in 1687, married Elizabeth Andrews, Dec. 14, 1693. She died April 27, 1732. He died March 30, 1741.

Children: 25 *Andrew*, b Aug. 17, 1694, d Dec. 10, 1717; 26 *Mary*, b Aug. 31, 1696, m Ebenezer Bronson; 27 *Elizabeth*, b April 8, 1698, m Nathaniel Merriman, Nov. 12, 1725; 28 *Damaris*, b Feb. 4, 1700, m Elnathan Street; 29 *John*, M. D., b Oct. 6, 1702, m Mary Andrews; 30 *Abigail*, b Feb. 14, 1704, m Ens. Merriman; 31 Capt. *Samuel*, b Sept. 1, 1706, m Sarah Hall, Feb. 21, 1733; 32 *Sarah*, b March 30, 1710, m Samuel Hall, Dec. 27, 1733; 33 *Benjamin*, M. D., b July 6, 1712, m Hannah Parmalee, Dec. 17, 1735.

6. EBENEZER.

EBENEZER HULL, son of Dr. John Hull, married Lydia Mix, May 7, 1706; he died Nov. 9, 1709, æ. 36 years. His widow Lydia administered on the estate.

Child: 34 *Hannah*, b March 23, 1708.

8. JEREMIAH.

DR. JEREMIAH HULL, son of Dr. Benjamin Hull of Wallingford, married Hannah, daughter of Samuel and Hope Cook, May 24, 1711, at Wallingford; she died Dec. 11, 1741; he died May 14, 1736, in Wallingford.

Children: 35 *John*, b Nov. 13, 1712, m Mary Andrews, Oct. 26, 1735; 36 *Moses*, b Dec. 26, 1714, d June 3, 1736, æ. 22 yrs.; 37 *Tabitha*, b March 3, 1717; 38 *Hannah*, b March 18, 1720; 39 *Anna;* 40 *Jeremiah*, b Jan. 5, 1729, m Mary Merriman in 1753; 41 *Joseph*, b March 24, 1733, m Hannah Corbitt in 1754; 42 *Patience*, b Oct. 20, 1735; 43 *Keturah.*

11. JOHN.

JOHN HULL, son of John and Mary Jacobs Hull, of Derby, was born Jan. 1, 1695.

Children: 44 *John*, b Oct. 22, 1703; 45 *Tamar*, b Nov. 27, 1705; 46 *Mary*, b Feb. 17, 1708; 47 *Ebenezer*, b Oct. 18, 1715; 48 *Susannah*, b Sept. 29, 1726.

12. DANIEL.

DANIEL HULL, son of John of Derby, who was son of

Dr. John Hulls of Wallingford, married Elizabeth Lane of Derby, in 1731 or 1732.

Children: 49 *Daniel*, b 1734; 50 *Samuel*, b 1735; 51 *Elizabeth*, b 1738; 52 *Ebenezer*, b 1741; 53 *John*, b 1744.

13. MILES.

MILES HULL, son of John of Derby, who was son of Dr. John Hulls ot Wallingford, married Mary Tuttle of Wallingford, and settled in that place.

Children: 54 *Martha*, b Nov. 29, 1730, d in infancy; 55 *Martha*, b Nov. 23, 1732; 56 *Esther*, b Sept. 15, 1733; 57 *Elizabeth*, b 1735; 58 *Elijah*, b March 10, 1736, d May 19, 1736; 59 *Eunice*, b March 29, 1738; 60 *Mary*, b July 15, 1740; 61 *Miles*, b March 24, 1743, m Eunice Hulls, Dec. 4, 1761; 62 *Abigail*, b June 11, 1745, m Elam Cook, Jan. 8, 1761; 63 *Abijah*, b June 10, 1747.

14. EBENEZER.

EBENEZER HULL, son of John and Mary Hull of Derby, married Hannah Bates, Sept. 1, 1731; he died in Wallingford in 1774.

Children: 64 *Joseph*, b Sept., 1731, d March 13, 1732; 65 *Daniel*, b Feb. 29, 1732; 66 *Lydia*, b April 14, 1734, m Nicholas Andrews of Wallingford; 67 *Eunice*, b 1736, m Miles Hull of Cheshire; 68 *Esther*, b 1737; 69 *Anna*, b Oct. 13, 1738, m Elijah Gaylord of Wallingford; 70 *Mary*, m ——— Tuttle of Wallingford; 71 *Joseph*, b 1740; 72 *Rena*; 73 *Joseph*, b March 1, 1742; 74 *Sarah*, m Benjamin Sperry of Wallingford; 75 *Ebenezer*, b 1750, m Patience ———; 76 *Esther*, b March 27, 1756, survived her father.

18. SAMUEL.

SAMUEL HULL, son of Capt. Joseph Hull of Derby, who was a son of Dr. John Hull of Wallingford.

Children: 77 Infant, b 1725; 78 *Hannah*, b 1726; 79 *Eunice*, b 1727.

19. JOSEPH.

JOSEPH HULL, son of Capt. Joseph Hull of Derby, who

was son of Dr. John Hull of Wallingford, was twice married: 1st, to Bertha ——, 2d, to Sarah —— ; he died June 12, 1778, æ. 85 yrs. Mrs. Sarah died at the age of 92 yrs.

Child by 1st marriage: 80 *Temperance*, b 1714. By 2d marriage: 81 *Sarah*, b 1726, m Rev. Dr. Mansfield of Derby, Conn.; 82 *Joseph*, b 1727, m Elizabeth Masters, she d Feb. 11, 1825, æ. 94 yrs.; 83 *Elizabeth*, b 1728, d in 1738, ae. 10 yrs.

20. CALEB.

CALEB HULL, son of Capt. Joseph and Mary Hull, and grandson of Dr. John Hull, of Wallingford, married Mercy Benham, of Wallingford, May 1, 1724; he was then 28 years old. The chimney-place of his residence in 1751 is now visible, at Broad swamp, so called, near the north-eastern part of Cheshire, east nearly a mile from the Jared Bishop place, late the residence of Capt. Munson Cook, and now of his son Joel Cook. She died April 19, 1766. He died Sept., 1788. In 1710, he, Caleb, then fourteen years old, received from his grandfather, Dr. John Hull, 100 acres of land, deeded to Joseph from Caleb, conditioned that Caleb should come and live with him till 21 years old, or until his decease. Dr. Hull died Dec. 6, 1711. Doubtless Caleb went. The 100 acres is on record.

Children: 84 *Sarah*, b April 25, 1725, m Reuben Atwater of Cheshire; 85 *Andrew*, b Aug. 23, 1726, d Sept. 21, 1774, ae. 49 yrs., m Lowly Cook; 86 *Mary*, b Apr. 27, 1728, m Jonathan Hitchcock, Oct. 3, 1745; 87 *Samuel*, b Mar. 22, 1730, m Eunice Cook in 1753; 88 *Joseph*, b Aug. 29, 1732; 89 *Abijah*, b Oct. 11, 1733, d Dec. 14, 1733; 90 *Joseph*, b June 10, 1734, d Dec. 4, 1735; 91 *Caleb*, b May 21, 1735, d Aug. 8, 1735; 92 *Submit*, b Dec. 12, 1736, d Feb. 13, 1737; 93 *Patience*, b Oct. 15, 1740, d Sept., 1764, ae. 25; 94 *Joseph*, b April 18, 1741; 95 *Caleb*, b Dec. 16, 1742, d June 4, 1767, ae. 25, m Mary Street.

21. ABIJAH.

ABIJAH HULL, son of Capt. Joseph and Mary Hull, and

grandson of Dr. John and Mary Hull of Wallingford, m Abigail Harger, of Derby, Nov. 20, 1727.

Children: 96 *Esther*, b 1728; 97, daughter.

29. JOHN.

DR. JOHN HULL, son of Dr. Benjamin and Elizabeth Hull, married Sarah Ives, June 21, 1727. She died Nov. 29, 1760. He married for his 2d wife, Damaris Frost, Oct. 20, 1761. He died May 22, 1762–3.

Children: 98 *Zephaniah*, b Aug. 15, 1728, m Hannah Doolittle, March 28, 1749; 99 *John*, d May 27, 1739; 100 *Elizabeth*, b Feb. 14, 1733, m Ephraim Cook, Jan. 1, 1752, in Cheshire; 101 *Sarah*, b 1737, d Jan. 23, 1740; 102 *John*, b Apr. 17, 1739; 103 *Desire*, b June 6, 1740; 104 *Sarah*, b Sept. 17, 1741; 105 *John*, b Feb. 15, 1744; 106 *Amos*, b May 27, 1745, m 1st, Martha Hitchcock, 1764, 2d, —— Norton.

31. SAMUEL.

CAPT. SAMUEL HULL, son of Dr. Benjamin and Elizabeth Hull, married Sarah Hall, Feb. 21, 1733, and settled in Cheshire, where he died Jan. 17, 1789, ae. 82 years. She died June 11, 1763, ae. 50 years. He was born in 1707.

Children: 107 *Sarah*, b Jan. 26, 1734, d May 3, 1734; 108 *Samuel*, b April 6, 1735, d May 22, 1735; 109 *Samuel*, b Aug. 12, 1737, m Sarah Humiston, Jan. 22, 1761, she died Sept. 4, 1775, ae. 31; 110, 111 *Sarah* and *Love*, b Aug. 27, 1738, the latter m Thomas Atwater, Dec. 8, 1757; 112 *Jesse*, b Jan. 27, 1745, m Ruth Preston, he settled on a farm at Broad Swamp, Cheshire; 113 *Benjamin*, b about 1775, m Mary Andrews; 114 *Levi*, d Oct. 30, 1751. The last two were by 2d marriage.

33. BENJAMIN.

DR. BENJAMIN HULL, son of Dr. Benjamin, son of Dr. John Hull, of Wallingford, married Hannah Parmalee, Dec. 17, 1735.

Children: 115 *Patience*, b 1736; 116 *Phebe*, b May 2, 1737; 117 *Hannah*, b May 3, 1739; 118 *Dr. Benjamin*, b Oct. 20, 1741, m Esther ——, in 1763; 119, 120 *Eliakim*, and

Charles, b May 1, 1744, the latter settled in Wallingford, m Sarah Atwater, he died May 4, 1819; 121 *Sybil*, b Aug. 15, 1746, d June 2, 1758; 122 *Joel*, b Aug. 6, 1749, settled in Yalesville, m Sarah ——, she d Aug. 23, 1816; 123 *Beda*, b April 11, 1753; 124 *Lois*, b Jan. 1, 1757; 125 *Asahel*, b Aug. 4, 1759, settled in Wallingford; 126 *Ephraim*, b 1767.

35. JOHN.

DR. JOHN HULL, son of Dr. Jeremiah and Hannah Cook Hull, married Mary Andrews, Oct. 26, 1735; he died Aug. 15, 1755; m 2d, Damaris Frost, Oct. 20, 1761.

Children: 127 *Sarah*, b Jan. 12, 1736; 128 *Molly*, b March 12, 1738, m Thomas Shephard, May 5, 1732; 129 *Sarah*, b Sept. 17, 1741, m Col. Asa, father of Hoadly Brothers, late of East Haven; 130 *Moses*, m Mary Ives, April 28, 1757; 131 *John*, b March 7, 1741–2, m Lois Beadles, March, 1759; 132 *Nathaniel*, b March 17, 1743, m Mehitable Beadles, April 13, 1763; 133 *Aaron*, b July 17, 1745; 134 *Abigail*, b Dec. 1, 1747; 135 *Hannah*, b July 6, 1750.

40. JEREMIAH.

JEREMIAH HULL, son of Dr. Jeremiah and Hannah Cook Hull, and grandson of Dr. John Hull, married Mary Merriman, Jan. 18, 1753. She died Aug. 22, 1774, ae. 41 years. He died Aug. 24, 1790, ae. 60. He was twice married.

Children: 136 *Caleb*, b Dec. 1, 1753, m —— Tyler; 137 *Jeremiah*, m 1st, Sarah ——, 2nd, Phebe Hart; 138, *Samuel*, m Lois Peck of Wallingford; 139 *Ann*, m Jacob Rice. By 2nd marriage: 140 *Benjamin;* 141 *Levi*, m and settled near his brother Jeremiah in Wallingford; 142 *Hannah*, m —— Heath in Wallingford; 143 *Eunice*, m —— Pratt of Essex, Ct.

41. JOSEPH.

JOSEPH HULL, son of Dr. Jeremiah and Hannah Cook Hull, married Hannah Corbitt in 1754. I have been unable to ascertain when they died. They may have removed from Wallingford in early life.

Children: 144 *Mary*, b Sept. 20, 1755; 145 *Caldwell*, b Jan. 2, 1759.

61. MILES.

Capt. Miles Hull, son of Miles and Mary Hull, married Eunice, daughter of Ebenezer and Hannah Hull of Wallingford, Dec. 4, 1761. He died at Cheshire. When living he owned the farms of the late Jared Bishop, and Capt. Munson Cook.

Children: 146 *Amzi*, went to Canada; 147 *Luther;* 148 *Miles;* 149 *Polly*, m Levi Douglas of Meriden; 150 Daughter, m —— Sizer, of Meriden.

75. EBENEZER.

Ebenezer Hull, son of Ebenezer and Hannah Bates Hull, m Patience ——. He was a farmer at what is now Yalesville, where he died June 10, 1807, ae. 57 years. She died a few years later.

Children: 151 *Joseph*, m Rebecca, daughter of Josiah Mix; 152 *Ira*, d unmarried in 1812, at Broadswamp, Cheshire; 153 *Sarah*, m Amos Austin of Meriden; 154 *Amy*, m Lyman Hitchcock, son of Dan ——.

85. ANDREW.

Andrew Hull, son of Caleb, son of Capt. Joseph, son of Dr. John Hull of Wallingford, married Lowly Cook, daughter of Capt. Samuel and Hannah Cook of Wallingford, Oct. 17, 1730. He died Sept. 21, 1774, æ. 49. He owned the large farm which Elias Gaylord's heirs and George Bristol now own, near Cheshire street, bounded north by the river. Mrs. Lowly Hull died about 1785.

Children: 155 *Damaris*, b Sept. 29, 1749; 156 *Lowly*, b July 16, 1753; 157 *Hannah*, b Dec. 16, 1754; 158 *Damaris*, b Sept. 18, 1755; 159 *Andrew*, b Oct. 6, 1758, m Elizabeth Mary Ann Atwater; 160 *Sarah;* 161 *Ursula*, b Nov. 10, 1760; 162 *Mary;* 163 *Esther;* 164 *Susan;* 165 *Lovisa*, m Dr. Hall, went to Vermont.

87. SAMUEL.

SAMUEL HULL, son of Caleb, son of Capt. Joseph, the son of Dr. John Hulls of Wallingford, married Eunice Cook, daughter of Capt. Samuel and Hannah Cook of Wallingford, Dec. 26, 1753. He died April 27, 1791, ae. 62. She died May 9, 1803, ae. 68 years.

Children: 166 Infant son, b Jan. 1, 1755; 167 *Jedediah*, b Feb. 26, 1756; 168 Infant son, b Feb 2, 1758, d same day; 169 *Samuel*, b May 27, 1759, d Feb. 20, 1840, ae. 80 years; 170 *Zephaniah*, b May 1, 1761, settled in Wallingford, Vt., and d Feb. 20, 1840; 171 *Epaphras*, b April 9, 1763, d April 13, 1827, in Wallingford, Vt.; 172 *Eunice*, b April 16, 1765, d Dec. 18, 1820, m Sheriff Whipple, Cazenovia, N. Y.; 173 *Lois*, b Feb. 1, 1769, d Oct. 20, 1777; 174 *Caleb*, b Nov. 9, 1768, d Aug. 9, 1816, at Wallingford, Vt.; 175 *Elizabeth*, b Oct. 28, 1770, d Oct. 13, 1777; 176 *Josephus*, b Aug. 24, 1772, d March 18, 1813, at Wallingford, Vt.; 177 *Hannah*, b Oct. 11, 1775, m A. Meacham, Wallingford, Vt., d 1850.

95. CALEB.

CALEB HULL, son of Caleb, son of Capt. Joseph, son of Dr. John Hulls, of Wallingford, married Mary Street; he died June 4, 1767, æ. 25.

Children: 178 *Ambrose;* 179 *Abraham;* 180 *Mary*, m —— Hudson, he was drowned.

98. ZEPHANIAH.

DR. ZEPHANIAH HULL, son of Dr. John, son of Dr. Benjamin and Elizabeth Hull, married Hannah Cook, March 28, 1749, and settled in Bethlem, Conn., probably through the inducement of Rev. Dr. Bellamy, with whom a close intimacy and warm friendship existed until death separated them. He died Nov. 10, 1760. She died the same day, both suddenly.

Children: 181 *Lydia*, b Dec. 22, 1749, d Feb. 21, 1750; 182 *Titus, M. D.*, b March 25, 1751, he went to Danbury in 1805, then to State of N. Y.; 183 *Lydia*, b July 23, 1753, m Ja. Judson, March 21, 1769, by whom she had four children, married 2d, Amasa Clark, of Cheshire; 184 *Andrew*, b Dec. 8, 1754, settled at Cheshire; 185 *Hannah*, b Jan. 28, 1757, d Nov. 16, 1760; 186 *Sarah*, b May 17, 1759, d Nov. 16, 1760.

105. JOHN.

JOHN HULL, son of Dr. John and Sarah Ives Hull, married Hannah Hitchcock, Dec. 13, 1764.

Child: 187 *John*, b Oct. 8, 1765.

106. AMOS.

DR. AMOS HULL, son of Dr. John and Sarah Hull, married Martha Hitchcock, March 2, 1764.

Child: 188 Dr. *Amos G.*, m Lydia Cook, dau. of Aaron of Wallingford, for his last wife.

109. SAMUEL.

SAMUEL HULL, son of Capt. Samuel and Sarah Hull of Cheshire, married Sarah Humiston, Jan. 22, 1761. She died Sept. 4, 1775, ae. 31 years. He married Hannah —— for 2d wife, and she died April 4, 1811, ae. 62 years.

Child: 189 *Samuel*, b 1777, m Alma, dau. of Jesse and Lois Humiston, of Cheshire, he was a saddler and harness-maker of Cheshire, he died May 5, 1831, ae. 54, leaving one daughter, Alma, wife of Wm. Kelsey, Esq.

112. JESSE.

JESSE HULL, son of Capt. Samuel and Sarah Hull, was six years in the war of the Revolution, married Ruth Preston, and settled in Cheshire, where they died.

Children: 190 *Samuel*, b 1769, d in Cheshire, æ. 90; 191 *Thelus*, went to Ohio, and has descendants there; 192 eight daughters, most of whom went to western New York.

113. BENJAMIN.

BENJAMIN HULL, son of Capt. Samuel and Hannah Hull, married Mary ———; he was a large landholder in Broad Swamp, Cheshire. He died May 3, 1835, æ. 63 years. She died Nov. 3, 1838, æ. 63 years.

Children: 193 *Rice Andrew*, went to Canada; 194 *Lucy*, m

Samuel U. Beach, of Cheshire; 195 *Chauncey*, b 1794, d Aug. 2, 1830, æ. 36 yrs.; 196 *Darius*, m Martha ——; 197 *Amasa*, b 1806, d in Cheshire; 198 *Benjamin*, b 1806, d April 6, 1812, æ. 6 yrs.; 199 *Abiathar*, b 1814, d Oct. 10, 1839, æ. 25 yrs.; 200 *Samuel Lee*, b 1818, d Jan. 8, 1838, æ. 20 yrs.

118. BENJAMIN.

DR. BENJAMIN HULL, son of Dr. Benjamin and Hannah Hull, married Esther ——, 1763.

Child: 201 *Benjamin*, b Dec. 11, 1763.

120. CHARLES.

CHARLES HULL, son of Dr. Benjamin and Hannah Hull, married Sarah Atwater, and when living, owned what is now known as the Ruggles farm at Yalesville in Wallingford; he died May 4, 1819, æ. 75. His widow married Aaron Hall of Wallingford.

Children: 202 *Lucinda*, b 1760, d April 11, 1833, æ. 73 yrs., m Thomas Ruggles; 203 *Lucia*, b 1778, d Sept. 8, 1848, æ. 70 yrs, m Barney McCarthy.

122. JOEL.

JOEL HULL, son of Dr. Benjamin and Hannah Hull, m Sarah ——. She died Aug 23, 1816, ae. 59, in Wallingford. He sold his farm, which is the one now owned by the heirs of Ransom Jeralds at Yalesville, and removed to Ohio, where he died.

Child: 204 *Anson*, an only son, d in Ohio.

130. MOSES.

MOSES HULL, son of Dr. John and Mary Hull, married Mary Ives, April 28, 1757. He lived, and I suppose, built the house where Thomas Berry lived in his old age, and where he died. The grandson of Mr. Berry now (1870) occupies the old house.

131. JOHN.

JOHN HULL, son of Dr. John and Mary Hull, married 1st, Lois Beadles, March 20, 1759. She died Sept. 6, 1802, ae.

59 yrs. He married Phebe —— for his second wife. She died Sept. 3, 1834, ae. 93. He died Oct. 6, 1828, ae. 88 yrs. He was a large and enterprising farmer, and owned and occupied the house and land now belonging to Mr. Durand, near Yalesville.

Children: 205 *Nathaniel*, b Sept. 7, 1759, d in infancy; 206 *Mary*, b Aug. 30, 1762, m —— Beach; 207 *Sarah*, m Samuel Wolcott; 208 *Sally*, m Reuben Ives; 209 *Eunice*, m Ephraim A. Humiston; 210 *Melinda*, m Samuel J. Simpson; 211 *Diana*, m Benjamin T. Cook.

132. NATHANIEL.

NATHANIEL HULL, son of Dr. John and Mary Hull, married Mehitable Beadles, April 13, 1760.

Children: 212 Daughter, m Jonsey Curtis; 213 *Wyllis*, b 1760, m Mehitable Mix, sister of John Mix, he d May 8, 1830, ae. 70; 214 *Mary*; 215 *George*.

133. AARON.

AARON HULL, son of Dr. John and Mary Hull, settled in Meriden, was a farmer and a peddler of tin ware.

Children: 216 *Joel*, m Hannah Hall, of Wallingford, daughter of Dickerman Hall; 217 *Cornelius*.

137. JEREMIAH.

JEREMIAH HULL, son of Jeremiah and Mary Hull, m 1st, Sarah ———, 2d, Phebe, daughter of Nathaniel Hart of Wallingford. He was a noted peddler and farmer. Mrs. Sarah died at the age of 27 years. Mrs. Phebe died Nov. 9, 1855, ae. 84. He died Oct. 10, 1843, ae. 81 yrs.

Children by 1st marriage: 218 *Alma*, m Ira Morse of Wallingford; 219 *Julia*, m Ira Andrews of Wallingford. By 2d marriage: 220 *Philo*, m Betsey Cook of Wallingford; 221 *Hiram*, m Caroline Ives of Wallingford; 222 *Mary*, res. Wallingford, old homestead; 223 *Lucy*, m Senator Blakeslee, of Wallingford; 224 *Orrin*, m Ann Dowd; 225 *Jeremiah*, m Sophronia Dudley.

138. SAMUEL.

SAMUEL HULL, son of Jeremiah and Mary Hull, married Lois Peck, and settled on the old homestead of his father; he was an enterprising farmer in the north part of Wallingford.

Children: 226 *William*, m Alma, dau. of Reuben Hall; 227 *Sylvester*, m Delilah, dau. of Benijah Morse; 228 *Lois*, m Miles, son of Ichabod Ives.

151. JOSEPH.

JOSEPH HULL, son of Ebenezer and Patience Hull, married Rebecca, daughter of Josiah Mix; he died of a wound in his knee joint, produced by an axe in his own hands while pruning apple trees for the late Chester Cook, March, 1818.

Children: 229 *James Mix*; 230 *Maria*, m Jonathan Ives, of Meriden; 231 *Nancy*; 232 *Rebecca*.

152. IRA.

IRA HULL, son of Ebenezer and Patience Hull, died unmarried at Cheshire in 1812, and by his will gave his real estate to his sister Amy, she paying the legacies named therein.

159. ANDREW.

GEN. ANDREW HULL, son of Andrew and Lowly Hull, of Cheshire, married Elizabeth Mary Ann, daughter of Reuben Atwater, of Cheshire. He was a highly respectable gentleman, merchant and farmer; he died in Cheshire.

Children: 233 *Eudocia*, m Gov. Samuel A. Foot, of Cheshire; 234 infant son, d in infancy; 235 *Merab*, m Henry Whittelsey, of Cheshire; 236 *Elizabeth*, m Rev. Dr. A. Todd, of Stamford; 237 *Mary A.*, m Wm. R. Hitchcock, of Cheshire; 238 *Sarah*, m Rev. Mr. Cloud; 239 *Adeline*, m Rev. Mr. Mason.

169. SAMUEL.

SAMUEL HULL, son of Samuel and Eunice Hull, married Abigail Doolittle; she was born May 26, 1766. He was a farmer in the northern part of Cheshire, where he died, Oct. 27, 1828, ae. 70 yrs. Mrs. Abigail died Oct. 10, 1835, ae. 69.

Children: 240 *Stella*, b March 27, 1786, m Jonathan Law, Esq., she d Dec. 13, 1841, ae. 56 yrs.; 241 *Jedediah*, b 1788, was insane; 242 *Ann*, b 1793, d Aug. 27, 1818, ae. 25 yrs.; 243 *Abigail Ann*, b Jan. 13, 1794; 244 *Linda*, b Feb. 6, 1796, m David Brooks of Cheshire, she d ae. 69 yrs.; 245 *Eunice*, b Nov. 12, 1798, m Birdsey Booth, late of Cuyahoga Falls, Ohio; 246 *Charlotte L.*, b Sept. 9, 1800, m John Olmstead, late of Hartford, Conn.; 247 *Samuel Cook*, b Aug. 4, 1802, d Aug. 26, 1804; 248 *Samuel*, b Feb. 4, 1805, d at Morris, Grundy Co., Illinois; 249 *Julius*, b July 1, 1807, m Lucy Ives, and went to Ohio; 250 *Andrew Franklin*, b Jan. 13, 1811, m Adeline Munson, he d Jan. 1, 1845, ae. 34 yrs.

182. TITUS.

DR. TITUS HULL, son of Dr. Zephaniah and Hannah Hull, studied medicine with Dr. Seth Bird, of Litchfield, and settled in Bethlem; went in 1805 to Danbury, Ct. In the autumn of 1807, he went to the state of New York. He married Lucy Parmelee, daughter of Jonathan of Chatham, by whom he had two children, both of whom died in infancy. Mrs. Lucy died in Nov., 1776. In 1778 he married Olive Parmelee, widow of Abram of Goshen, her mother being a descendant of the Strong family of Northampton, Mass. He died Sept. 3, 1852.

Children: 251 *Lawrence*, M. D., b June 6, 1779, m Dorcas Ambler of Bethlem, in 1803, and had 6 sons and 3 daus.; 252 *Althea*, b Aug. 18, 1780, has six sons and a daughter; 253 *Charles*, b Jan. 4, 1782, was a physician, and practiced in Oneida Co., N. Y., and d in 1833, leaving a son and 3 daus., all married; 254 *Betsey M.*, b Sept. 17, 1783; 255 *Elias*, b April 3, 1786, has 2 chil. and lived in Alabama; 256 *Lucy*, b Aug. 23, 1788, m Ezra Starr, Oct. 17, 1807; 257 *Olive E.*, b May 13, 1790, m Col. Elijah Morse of Eaton; 258 *Andrew C.*, b Oct. 28, 1792, m Betsey Morse, in 1818, at Eaton; 259 *Leverett*, b Dec. 3, 1796, m Julia Scoville of Salisbury, Ct., in 1829; 260 *Rufus Lewis*, died in childhood.

184. ANDREW.

ANDREW HULL, son of Dr. Zephaniah and Hannah Hull, after the decease of his father, went to live with his great-grandfather on his mother's side, at Cheshire, from whom he received an estate on which he continued to reside until his death. He married Naomi ——. She died Oct. 28, 1824, æ. 70 yrs. He died March 31, 1824, æ. 70 yrs., much lamented.

Child: 261 *Naomi H.*, m Mr. Wm. Brown, of New Haven, who was lost at sea. She was the mother of Wm. A. Brown, of Cheshire, and also of Mrs. Alfred Doolittle.

187. JOHN.

JOHN HULL, son of Dr. John and Sarah Hull, married Hannah Hitchcock, Dec. 13, 1764. I find no further account of them.

Child: 262 *John*, b Oct. 8, 1765.

188. AMOS.

DR. AMOS GOULD HULL, son of Dr. Amos Hull, who married a daughter of Dr. Norton of Cheshire, and was the inventor of the celebrated Hull truss, married Lydia Cook, daughter of Aaron and Elizabeth Cook of Wallingford.

Child by Lydia, 2d or 3d wife: 263 *Aaron Cook*, was a physician at Brooklyn, N. Y., is deceased.

190. SAMUEL.

SAMUEL HULL, son of Jesse and Ruth Preston Hull, married —— Manwaring, of Essex, and settled at the old home of his father, where he died Dec. 8, 1857, ae. 90 years. He was a farmer, and during his long life maintained the character of an honest man.

Children: 264 *Caleb E.*, resides near Wallingford line, Cheshire; 265 *Josiah M.*, resides in Cheshire, a farmer; 266 *Samuel T.*, resides in Cheshire, a farmer; 267 *Richard S.*, grad. at Yale College, is a lawyer in New Haven.

195. CHAUNCEY.

CHAUNCEY HULL, son of Benjamin and Mary Hull, married Hannah, daughter of Jonah Hotchkiss, of Cheshire; he died Aug. 2, 1830, leaving several children, most of whose names are to me unknown.

Child: 268 *Chauncey*, d Jan. 1, 1821, æ. 4 yrs.

196. DARIUS.

DARIUS HULL, son of Benjamin and Mary Hull, married Martha ———. She died March 16, 1858, æ. 53 yrs. He has a considerable family of children, names unknown to me. He still lives at Cheshire.

HUMISTON.

HENRY.

HENRY HUMISTON was at New Haven as early as 1650; he married Joanna Walker, Aug. 28, 1651. He died Jan. 16, 1663.

Children: 1 *Samuel*, b Aug. 7, 1650; 2 *Nathaniel*, b Jan. 13, 1654; 3 *Thomas*, b Oct. 19, 1656; 4 *Abigail*, b May 17, 1661.

Two of the name were at Wallingford about the commencement of the last century, viz., James and John, both from New Haven. John Humiston married Hannah Royce, of Wallingford, June 28, 1711, but it does not appear that he settled in Wallingford. James Humiston married Sarah Atwater, Jan. 7, 1719, and remained in Wallingford. He died Aug. 17, 1747.

Children: 5 *Daniel*, b Nov. 16, 1721, m Lydia ———; 6 *Stephen*, b Nov. 9, 1723; 7 *Noah*, b March 1, 1729, d Sept. 3, 1729; 8 *James*, b Oct. 28, 1734, m Abiah Ives, Feb. 4, 1755–6, 2d Hannah ———; 9 *Noah*, d June 13, 1745.

5. DANIEL.

DANIEL HUMISTON, son of James and Sarah Humiston, married Lydia ———, and settled in Cheshire, where he died July 27, 1767, ae. 46 yrs. She died Jan. 1, 1809, ae. 83 yrs.

Children: 10 *Sarah*., b Dec. 14, 1744; 11 *Hannah*, b March 2, 1745; 12 *Stephen*, b July 17, 1751; 13 *Lydia*, b

March 17, 1754; 14 *Patience*, b Nov. 28, 1756; 15 *Daniel*, b April 10, 1759; 16 *Daniel*, b 1760, d Nov. 7, 1783; 17 *John*, b June 30, 1761; 18 *Jesse*, b March 12, 1764, m Lois, dau. of Amos Doolittle, of Cheshire.

8. JAMES.

JAMES HUMISTON, son of James and Sarah Humiston, married Abiah or Abigail ———, and settled on a farm at Gitteau's Corner, now known as the Humiston farm. He died in Wallingford, Feb. 18, 1812, ae. 77 yrs. She died Dec. 19, 1761.

Children: 19 *James*, owner of Humiston's Mills, Wallingford; 20 *Linus*, went to Ohio.

18. JESSE.

JESSE HUMISTON, son of Daniel and Lydia Humiston of Wallingford, married Lois, daughter of Amos Doolittle of Cheshire, and settled on a farm about a mile west of the railroad depot, in Cheshire. His decease occurred March 12, 1832, at the age of 68; Mrs Lois Humiston died Feb. 8, 1847, ae. 87 years.

Children: 21 *Daniel*, m Juliana Ives, daughter of Jared; 22 *Jesse A.*, m Lois Preston, dau. of Reuben; 23 *Alma*, m Samuel Hull of Cheshire; 24 *John*, m Rhoda Nichols, of Wolcott, Conn.

19. JAMES.

JAMES HUMISTON was the proprietor of the mills about a mile west of the village of Wallingford, and was extensively engaged in wool-carding and cloth-dressing, as well as milling.

Children: 25 *Chauncey*; 26 *Nancy*, m Almon Preston; 27 *Betsey*, m Harmon Morse; 28 *Maria*, m Samuel Allen; *Lyman*, m Jennie Johnson; *Charles*, m Lucy Bronson.

20. LINUS.

LINUS HUMISTON went to Ohio many years ago, with his family. When in Wallingford, he resided on the old Humiston place, Gitteau's Corner.

Children: 29 *Miles*; 30 *Samuel*; 31 *Philo*; 32 *Mary*: 33 *Hannah*.

21. DANIEL.

DANIEL HUMISTON, son of Jesse and Lois Humiston, married Juliana, daughter of Jared Ives, of Cheshire. He died in 1866.

Children: 34 *Chauncey A.;* 35 *John D.*, m Emily Barns, of Cheshire; 36 *Julia Ann*, b 1822.

22. JESSE.

JESSE A. HUMISTON, son of Jesse and Lois Humiston, married Lois Preston.

Children: 37 *Lauren A.*, m Hannah Moss; 38 *Lois*, m Elam Cook.

24. JOHN.

JOHN HUMISTON, son of Jesse and Lois Humiston, married Rhoda Nichols, daughter of the late Samuel Nichols, of Wolcott. He died in Cheshire.

Children: 39 *Jesse*, removed to the state of New York; 40 *John Latimer*, res. in Cheshire.

EPHRAIM.

EPHRAIM A. HUMISTON came from North Haven, and married a daughter of John Hull, and settled on the old Henry and Russel farm, and died there.

Children: 41 *Sherlock;* 42 *Hiram;* 43 *Diana;* 44 *Willis*, has become wealthy, and res. in Troy, N. Y.

IVES.[1]

JOHN.

JOHN IVES was the first of the name that settled at Wallingford. He was a farmer in Meriden. I have been unable to determine his previous residence or place of nativity.

Children: 1 *John*, b Nov. 16, 1669, d 1738 æ. 69 yrs; 2 *Hannah*, m Joseph Benham, Aug. 17, 1682; 3 *Joseph*, b Oct. 14, 1674, m Esther Benedict, May 11, 1697; 4 *Gideon*, m Mary Royce, Feb 20, 1706; 5 *Nathaniel*, b May 31, 1677, m

1 See Savage's Gen. Dict., II. 525.

Mary Cook, April 5, 1699; 6 *Ebenezer*, m Elizabeth ——; 7 *Samuel*, b June 5, 1696; 8 *Benjamin*, b Nov. 22, 1699.

1. JOHN.

JOHN Ives, son of John and Mary Ives, married Mary Gillette, Dec. 6, 1693. He died in Meriden, 1738, ae. 69 yrs.

Children: 9 *John*, b Sept. 28, 1694, m Hannah Royce, he d Aug. 4, 1745; 10 *Samuel*, b Jan. 5, 1696, m Phebe Royce, Jan. 28, 1720; 11 *Benjamin*, b Nov. 22, 1699, m 1st, Rebecca Merriman, 2d, Hannah Moss; 12 *Abijah*, b March 14, 1700, m Abigail Mix, May, 1730; 13 *Mary*, b March 10, 1702; 14 *Lazarus*, b Feb. 5, 1703, m Mabel Jerome, Jan. 5, 1730; 15 *Daniel*, b Feb. 19, 1706, m Abigail ——; 16 *Hannah*, b Feb. 10, 1708; 17 *Abraham*, b Sept. 2, 1709, m Elizabeth Stanley, he d Aug. 4, 1735; 18 *Bezaleel*, b July 4, 1712, d Oct. 28, 1714; 19 *Bezaleel*, b 1726, m Hannah Merriman.

3. JOSEPH.

DEA. JOSEPH IVES, son of John, married Esther Benedict, May 11, 1697, in the south-west part of Wallingford. He married Mamre Munson for his second wife, June 13, 1733; he died March 18, 1755, ae. 81 yrs.

Children: 20 *Thomas*, b May 30, 1698; 21 *Elizabeth*, b Feb. 6, 1700; 22 *Hannah*, b Oct. 13, 1701; 23 *Abigail*, b Aug. 27, 1704; 24 *Esther*, b Jan. 17, 1706; 25 *Joseph*, b Dec. 10, 1709, m Maria ——; 26 *Phineas*, b April 8, 1711; 27 *Nathaniel*, b Jan. 15, 1714; 28 *Ephraim*, b Jan. 4, 1717; 29 *Dinah*, b April 4, 1721.

4. GIDEON.

GIDEON IVES, son of John, m Mary Royce, Feb. 20, 1706; he was at Wallingford before 1700. She died Oct. 15, 1742, ae. 56 yrs.

Children: 30 *Sarah*, b Sept. 8, 1708; 31 *Jotham*, b Sept. 20, 1710, d Sept. 2, 1753; 32 *Amasa*, b Aug. 24, 1712; 33 *Rhoda*, b Dec. 12, 1714; 34 *Martha*, b Aug. 10, 1716; 35 *Amasa*, b Nov. 15, 1718; 36 *Gideon*, b Sept. 24, 1720; 37 *Joel*, b Jan. 13, 1723; 38 *Mary*, b Dec. 16, 1724; 39 *Susannah*, b May 26, 1727; 40 *Esther*, b Oct. 14, 1729.

5. NATHANIEL.

NATHANIEL IVES, son of John, married Mary Cook, April 5, 1699, and settled in the south-west part of the town; he died Nov. 6, 1711.

Children: 41 *Caleb*, b Feb. 3, 1700, d Nov. 6, 1710; 42 *Caleb*; 43 *Stephen*, b March 24, 1704, m Sarah Hart, Oct. 25, 1730; 44 *Thankful*, b Aug. 4, 1708; 45 *Abel*, b May 6, 1711, m Sarah Reed, March 25, 1736.

9. JOHN.

JOHN IVES, son of John and Mary Ives, married Hannah Royce, Dec. 18, 1719. He died Aug. 4, 1795. She died Nov. 5, 1770, ae. 70 yrs., at Meriden; was daughter of Samuel and Hannah Royce.

Children: 46 *Eunice*, b April 20, 1721, d Sept. 11, 1727; 47 *Anna*, b April 20, 1725; 48 *Eunice*, b Sept. 11, 1727, d Sept. 13, 1727; 49 *John*, b July 4, 1729; 50 *Titus*, b Feb. 17, 1732; 51 *Levi*, b Jan. 19, 1733; 52, 53 *Joseph* and *John*, b April 2, 1735: 54 *Levi*, b July 30, 1736, d Dec. 20, 1739; 55 *Jesse*, b April 2, 1738; 56 *Joseph*, b June, 1745; 57 *Jesse*.

10. SAMUEL.

SAMUEL IVES, son of John and Mary Ives, married Phebe Royce, Jan. 28, 1720. He died Aug. 29, 1734.

Children: 58 *Mehitable*, b March 29, 1724; 59 *Bezaleel*, b Dec. 14, 1726; 60 *Samuel*, b Jan. 28, 1733.

11. BENJAMIN.

BENJAMIN, son of John and Hannah Royce, married 1st, Hannah Moss, May 6, 1728.

Children: 61 *Rebecca*, b March 29, 1723, d Dec. 9, 1724; 62 *Rebecca*, b Nov. 18, 1725; 63 *Benjamin*, b April 15, 1727, d June 19, 1727; 65 *Benjamin*, b Jan. 26, 1729; 66 *Hannah*, b Dec. 18, 1732; 67 *Lois*, b March 10, 1734; 68 *David*, b July 9, 1736, d Feb 20 1737; 69 *Ruth*, b Jan. 31, 1738; 70 *David*, b Jan. 15, 1740; 71 *Levi*, b July 23, 1743; 72 *Thankful*, b Jan. 1, 1746; 73 *Levi*, b Sept. 18, 1748.

12. ABIJAH.

ABIJAH IVES, son of John and Hannah Ives, married ———. She died May 6, 1753. He died July 17, 1762.

Children: 74 *Moses*, b March 6, 1731; 75 *Mary*, b Sept. 22, 1732; 76 *Abijah*, b March 24, 1734, d Aug. 16, 1741; 77 *Aaron*, b May 26, 1736, d Nov. 24, 1742; 78 *Abigail*, b Feb. 14, 1738; 79 *Phebe*, b March 23, 1740; 80 *Martha*, b May 17, 1742; 81 *Prudence*, b June 19, 1744; 82 *Aaron*, b April 6, 1746; 83 *Anna*, b Feb. 21, 1749, d June 25, 1751.

14. LAZARUS.

LAZARUS IVES, son of John and Mary, married Mabel Jerome, Jan. 5, 1731. His 2d wife was Isabella ———.

Children by 1st marriage: 84 *Timothy*, b Oct. 16, 1731; 85 *Mary*, b Sept. 10, 1733; 86 *Lazarus*, b Nov. 2, 1734. By 2d marriage: 87 *Ambrose*, b May 22, 1736; 88 *Isabella*, b April 19, 1738; 89 *Joshua*, b March 16, 1740; 90 *Amasa*, bap. March 13, 1743; 91 *John*, bap. May 17, 1747; 92 *Phebe*, bap. Nov. 26, 1752.

15. DANIEL.

DANIEL IVES, son of John and Mary Ives, married Abigail Parker, Oct. 28, 1738.

Children: 93 *Abigail*, b July 30, 1736; 94 *Lydia*, b June 11, 1738; 95 *Martha*, b Feb. 29, 1740; 96 *Olive*, b Nov. 29, 1741: 97 *Daniel*, b Jan. 31, 1743; 98 *Samuel*, b March 9, 1745; 99 *John*, b Feb. 19, 1747; 100 *Levi*, b March 29, 1750.

17. ABRAHAM.

ABRAHAM IVES, son of John and Mary Gillette Ives, married Elizabeth Stanley. She died Aug. 4, 1735, and he married Barbara Johnson, May 11, 1736.

Children: 101 *Elizabeth*, b July 22, 1735; 102 *Sarah*, b Dec. 23, 1736; 103 *Reuben*, b Dec. 11, 1738; 104 *Barbara*, b Oct. 9, 1739; 105 *Abraham*, b June 8, 1743; 106 *Abraham*, b March 8, 1746; 107 *Barbara*, b Oct. 5, 1747; 108 *Ambrose*, b June 30, 1748, m Lucy ———; 109 *Sarah*, b Oct. 8, 1749.

19. BEZALEEL.

CAPT. BEZALEEL IVES, son of John and Mary Gillette Ives, married Hannah Merriman, Feb. 14, 1753. He died Nov. 24, 1798, ae. 72 yrs. She died March 21, 1815, ae. 84 yrs.

Child: 110 *Capt. Samuel*, b Jan. 5, 1752, m Lucretia, dau. of John Ives, d in Meriden, Oct. 18, 1803.

20. THOMAS.

THOMAS IVES, son of Dea. Joseph and Esther Ives, married Abigail How, Sept. 2, 1702; he married 2d, Rebecca Hotchkiss, Nov. 15, 1720.

Children: 111 *Isaac*, b Nov. 8, 1721; 112 *Andrew*, b July 2, 1724; 113 *Lent*, b May 17, 1726, d July 11, 1726; 114 *Enos*, b May 14, 1727.

25. JOSEPH.

JOSEPH IVES, son of Dea. Joseph and Esther Ives, married Maria ———.

Children: 115 *Mary*, b March 26, 1734; 116 *Lent*, b Sept. 12, 1735; 117 *Joseph*, b Jan. 17, 1737.

26. PHINEAS.

PHINEAS IVES, son of Dea. Joseph and Esther Ives, married Margery Munson, Jan. 26, 1738.

Child: 118 *Phineas*, b Oct. 31, 1746.

27. NATHANIEL.

NATHANIEL IVES, son of Dea. Joseph and Esther Ives, married Zeruah ———.

Children: 119 *Mary*, b Sept. 6, 1746; 120 *Abigail*, b Oct. 17, 1748; 121 *Joseph*, b June 15, 1749; 122 *Nathaniel*, b April 23, 1741; 123 *Zeruah*, b Dec. 15, 1753; 124 *Samuel*, b May 1, 1756.

28. EPHRAIM.

EPHRAIM IVES, son of Dea. Joseph and Esther Ives, married Elizabeth Atwater, March 12, 1741.

Children: 125 *Sarah*, b Nov. 19, 1741; 126 *Ephraim*, b Jan. 7, 1744; 127 *Phineas*, b June 12, 1746; 128 *Elnathan*, b Dec. 21, 1748; 129 *Elizabeth*, b Nov. 6, 1751; 130 *Eunice*, b Feb. 19, 1755.

42. CALEB.

CALEB IVES, son of Nathaniel and Mary Ives, married 1st, Mary ———, 2d, Sarah ———, 3d, Elizabeth Plant, Feb. 27, 1733. He died April 13, 1752.

Children: 131 *Nathaniel*, b Jan. 12, 1722; 132 *Sarah*, b Aug. 6, 1725, d Feb. 15, 1735. By 3d marriage: 133 *Charles*, b Sept. 5, 1734; 134 *Eunice*, b Sept. 13, 1736; 135 *Elizabeth*, b Dec. 25, 1738; 136 *Olive*, b May 10, 1742; 137 *Caleb*, b May 19, 1745; 138 *Caleb*, b Feb. 9, 1748; 139 *Amos*, b May 1, 1750.

43. STEPHEN.

STEPHEN IVES, son of Nathaniel and Mary Ives, married Sarah Hart, Oct. 25, 1730.

Children: 140 *Sarah*, b May 29, 1733; 141 *Mary*, b April 16, 1735; 142 *Lois*, b Jan. 9, 1737.

45. ABEL.

ABEL IVES, son of Nathaniel and Mary Ives, married Sarah Read, March 25, 1736. She died Jan. 1, 1787, æ. 85 years. He died Jan. 31, 1781, æ. 80 years.

Children: 143 *Elizabeth*, b Aug. 30, 1730; 144 *Abel*, b Dec. 9, 1736; 145 *Anna*, b Dec. 20, 1739; 146 *Anna*, b Aug. 1st, 1740; 147 *Sarah*, b June 24, 1743; 148 *Elizabeth*, b Aug. 30, 1746; 149 *Esther*, b June 4, 1751; 150 *Lois*, b Mar. 27, 1754.

53. JOHN.

JOHN IVES, son of John and Hannah, married Sarah ——.
Child: 151 *Sarah*, b Jan. 12, 1737.

56. JOSEPH.

JOSEPH IVES, son of John and Hannah, married Mary ——.
Child: 152 *Anna*, b Dec. 7, 1750.

36. GIDEON.

GIDEON, son of Gideon and Mary Royce Ives, married and settled in Wallingford in a house still in existence, and standing a little north and in the rear of the residence of the late Benajah Morse.

Children: 153 *Amos*, bap. Jan. 5, 1752; 154 *Enos*, bap. Dec. 2, 1753; 155 *Gideon*, bap. May 15, 1757; 156 *Jerusha*, bap. Oct. 12, 1755.

ELNATHAN.

Children: 157 *Elnathan*, bap. March 21, 1731, m Ann Yale, March 9, 1758; 158 *Abigail*, bap. Feb. 11, 1732; 159 *Jerusha*, bap. Feb. 28, 1735; 160 *Josiah*, bap. March 18, 1738; 161 *Reuben*, bap. March 13, 1744; 162 *Huldah*, bap. Jan. 17, 1748.

31. JOTHAM.

JOTHAM IVES, son of Gideon and Mary Royce Ives, married Abigail Burroughs, Feb. 28, 1736. He died Sept. 2, 1753, ae. 43.

Child: 163 *Zachariah*, b Jan. 31, 1737, settled near the Honey Pot brook in Cheshire, d March 9, 1815, ae. 78, and with his wife Lois was buried in the Episcopal churchyard, Cheshire. Children of Zacharias: 164 Rev. *Reuben*, b in 1761, graduated at Yale in 1785, ordained by Bishop Seabury in 1786, Rector of St. Peter's Church, Cheshire, about thirty years, d Oct. 14, 1836, ae. 75 yrs.; 165 *Chauncey*, b in 1762, d Nov. 17, 1778, in his 16th year; 166 *Lowly*, m Seth De Wolf; 167 *Jared*, a farmer, d in Cheshire; 168 *Amos H.*, m Lois Cook, d in Cheshire; 169 *Jesse*, settled on a farm in Meriden.

49. JOHN.

JOHN, son of John and Hannah Royce Ives, b July 4, 1729, m 1st, Mary, daughter of Dr. Isaac Hall. She d Feb., 1788. He married 2nd, Sarah ———, who d Nov. 24, 1804. He d Feb., 1816.

Children: 170 *Lucretia*, m Capt. Samuel Ives; 171 *John*, m Martha Merriman; 172 *Isaac*, m 1st, ——— Benedict, m 2d, —— White of Danbury; 173 *Levi*, m Fanny Silliman, June 18, 1789, he was father of Bishop Ives; 174 *Joseph*, m Lucy, daughter of Benjamin Hall; 175 *Joel*, m —— Hart; 176 *Othniel*, b Aug. 17, 1779, married 1st, Sarah, daughter of

Nathaniel Yale, Oct 28, 1800, m 2d, Rosetta Yale, Oct. 26, 1815; 177 *Titus*, m Ximena Yale; 178 *Eli*, d unmarried; 179 *Anna*, m Noah Foster; 180 *Polly*, m John Hooker; 181 *Meriel*, m —— Clark, and moved to Canada.

177. OTHNIEL.

OTHNIEL, son of John and Mary Hall Ives, lived in the east part of Meriden in the house now occupied by Othniel jr.

Children: 182, *Eliza*, b Jan. 17, 1804, m Edwin R. Yale, March 14, 1824, she died March 9, 1846; 183 *Elias*, b Jan. 7, 1806, m Cornelius Pomeroy, Aug. 22, 1827; 184 *Eli*, b Jan. 7, 1809, m Gelina Ann Pomeroy; 185 *Othniel*, b Nov. 26, 1812, m 1st, Julia Cook, 2d, Mary Howard; 186 *Isaac I.*, b Jan. 21, 1817, m Eloise White of Danbury, 1847, d Oct. 14, 1850; 187 *Sarah Rosetta*, b Nov. 23, 1818, m Harvey Miller; 188 *Juliette*, b May 13, 1822, m Eli Butler, Nov. 10, 1842, d March 1. 1855; 189 *John*, b Dec. 26, 1825, m 1st, Alina Birdsey, Oct. 12, 1847, 2d Wealthy Merwin; 190 *Frederick W.*, b Jan. 27, 1828, m Frances Jones; 191 *Russell Jennings*, b July 17, 1830, m 1st, Flora Ann White, Sept. 15, 1853, 2d, Eliza, daughter of Deacon John Yale.

JOHNSON.[1]

Fitz James came from Normandy with William the Conqueror about the 11th century, and settled in the north of England. It was customary before the Conquest to change a name by adding *son*, as we find *Grimkelson*, *Gamelson*, &c.,

---

1 For collateral branches, see Abbot's Hist. Andover, Mass., 35, 36; Barry's Hist. Framingham, Mass., 303, 304; Bond's Hist. Watertown, Mass., 539–42; Brown's Gen. W. Simsbury Settlers, 88, 89; Chase's Hist. Haverhill, Mass., 276, 634–37; Cope's Record of Cope family of Penn. 52, 115, 116; Cothren's Hist. Woodbury, Ct., 600–2; Deane's Hist. Scituate, Mass., 296, 297; Eaton's Hist. Thomaston, Me., 284, 285; Ellis's Hist. Roxbury, Mass., 122; Fox's Hist. Dunstable, Mass., 246; Gage's Hist. Rowley, Mass., 446; Heraldic Journal, III. (867,) 43–5, 182, 183; Hudson's Hist. Lexington, Mass., 111, 112; Hudson's Hist. Marlborough, Mass., 403–6; Kellogg's Memorial of John White, 37; Leland's Gen. of

in the time of Edward the Confessor, if not earlier. The Norman *Fitz*, a corruption of *fils*, was used the same way, and among the conquered Saxons was sometimes adopted instead. Thus, Fitz Harding became *Hardingson;* Fitz Clark, *Clarkson;* Fitz James, *Jameson;* and Fitz John, *Johnson.*[1] The Fitz James mentioned above, changed his name to *Johnson*, and had a numerous family. One branch of it went to Scotland, where the name became quite numerous. Some of these added a *t* to the name, and thereby made it read *Johnston.*[2] In the reign of Queen Elizabeth one branch went to Ireland, and became quite numerous. Sir William Johnston was of this branch of the family. In later ages the family were settled in Kingston-on-Hull. At the time of Dr. Johnson's visit, as agent from Connecticut, to England, he found the family almost extinct, there being but one, a maiden lady of thirty years, left in the place. On visiting the church-yard, he found a large number of tomb-stones and monuments with the name of Johnson inscribed upon them. Three brothers had gone from Kingston to North America, one of whom, a clergyman, settled near Boston, and was killed by the Indians. He left a considerable family, from whom have descended most of the name in Massachusetts and Rhode Island. One settled in the western part of Connecticut. Most of his descendants went to New Jersey, and were

---

Leland Family, 249, 250; Littell's Passaic Valley Gen., 192–5; Mitchell's Hist. Bridgewater, Mass., 204–6; Morse's Gen. Reg. Sherborn and Holliston, Mass., 155, 156; N. E. Hist. and Gen. Reg., VIII. 232, 358–62; Pierce's Hist. Gorham, Me., 180; Poor's Hist. and Gen. Researches, 107; Savage's Gen. Dict., II. 549–59; Sewall's Hist. Woburn, Mass., 73–6, 165–8, 617, 618; Ward's Hist. Shrewsbury., Mass., 334–6; Washburn's Hist. Leicester, Mass., 379, 380.

1 The use of the prefix Fitz. has, with propriety, been revived in modern times. The eldest son of Harris, Earl of Malmsbury, is, by title of courtesy, Viscount FitzHarris.

2 Most of the persons bearing the name of Johnston in Scotland, derive the name from the village of Johnston in Renfrewshire. The family are descended from Hugo de Johnstone, in the time of Alexander II.

numerous. Robert, the 3d brother, settled in New Haven, Conn., and was one of its first founders.

Children: 1 *John;* 2 *Robert;* 3 *Thomas;* 4 *William*, and possibly others.

Edward Johnson originated from Kent, in England, in a parish within which county, called in his will Heron Hill, i. e. Herne Hill, or Herne, and at a place in that parish called Waterham. He probably came to this country in the fleet with Winthrop, in 1630. He died April 23, 1672. He left five sons: Edward, George, William, Matthew and John, and two daughters, Susan and Martha. They have many descendants in Massachusetts.

4. WILLIAM.

WILLIAM JOHNSON, son of Robert, the emigrant, appeared early in New Haven. He was one of the original subscribers to the compact for the settlement of Wallingford, in 1670, and had assigned him a lot, bounded as follows: "20 rods wide north and south, 19 rods and 4 ft. east and west, and bounded east by ye street, and north by Jeremiah How, and west by Nathan Andrews." This piece of land he sold, with consent of his wife Sarah ——, to Isaac Curtis, in 1694. Mr. Johnson does not appear to have ever had a residence in Wallingford, but was simply a subscriber for the benefit of his heirs who might settle in the place.

JACOB.

JACOB JOHNSON, son of William, married Abigail Hitchcock, Dec. 14, 1693. He built his house on the north side of the road that leads past the residence of the late Col. Thaddeus Cook, and nearly opposite the barn built within the last few years by Chauncey M. Cook. He was a tailor by trade; he died July 26, 1749, æ. 80 yrs. Mrs. Abigail d Jan. 9, 1726. He married 2d, Parkis Lindley, 1726.

Children: 5 *Reuben*, b Aug. 27, 1694, m Mary ——; 6 *Isaac*, b Feb. 25, 1696–7, m Sarah Osborne, he d April 23, 1779, ae. 84; 7 *Enos*, b 1698, d Jan. 31, 1786, ae. 88; 8 *Abigail*, b 1699; 9 *Israel;* 10 *Abner*, b Aug. 2, 1702, m

Charity Dayton, Dec. 14, 1726; 11 *Caleb*, b 1733-4, d Oct. 13, 1777, ae. 73 yrs., m Rachel Brockett, Jan. 28, 1731, was a merchant in Wallingford; 12 *Daniel*, b 1709, d Oct. 14, 1780, ae. 72 yrs.; 13 *Sarah*, b 1710, m Matthew Bellamy, March 31, 1721; 14 *Jacob*, b April, 1713, grad. of Yale, was Cong. min., settled at Groton, Conn.; 15 *Lydia*, d June 3, 1729.

5. REUBEN.

REUBEN JOHNSON married Mary Dayton, March 11, 1718, and settled on the place now owned by Almon Doolittle, and built a house there.

Children: 16 *Justus*, b April 6, 1720, d May 12, 1720; 17 *Justus*, b March 26, 1721; 18 *Ephraim;* 19 *Rebecca*, b July 14, 1723; 20 *Zaccheus;* and probably others. Ephraim occupied the old house where his father lived; he took it down and built the one now owned by Mr. Rufus Doolittle. Zaccheus lived in the house that stood opposite the Caleb Dudley house.

6. ISAAC.

DEA. ISAAC JOHNSON married Sarah Osborne, March 26, 1723. She died Nov. 16, 1766, æ. 65. He built and occupied the Caleb Dudley house, and lived there; he died April 29, 1779, æ. 84 yrs.

Children: 21 *Isaac;* 22 *Abigail*, b Feb. 11, 1722; 23 *Joseph*. b Jan. 21, 1725; 24 *Sarah*, b Feb. 10, 1729; 25 *Isaac*, b June 23, 1731, m Elizabeth ——; 26 *Esther*, b Nov. 31, 1735; 27 *Lois*, b Feb. 15, 1738; 28 *Rachel*, b March 6, 1740.

7. ENOS.

ENOS JOHNSON lived in the house of his father Jacob.

Child: 29 *Enos*.

9. ISRAEL.

ISRAEL JOHNSON married Sarah Miles, Jan. 26, 1732. His house was built by Caleb Johnson, and stood on the lot just east of the present residence of Turhand Cook. He also lived on the place now owned by the heirs of the late Liverius Carrington, in the village. He was a smith of some kind, and a worker of brass, &c., &c. He died 1747, leaving an Estate of £2226 12*s*.

Children: 30 *Eunice*, b Jan. 13, 1734; 31 *Prudence*, b Jan. 11, 1738; 32 *Caleb*, b Sept. 17, 1739; 33 *Anna*, b Apr. 12, 1736; 34 *Miles*, b Oct. 31, 1741; 35 *Rebecca*, b Aug 4, 1744; 36 *Warren*, b Apr. 17, 1747; 37 *Silas*, b Jan. 21, 1749; 38 *Jacob*, b July 21, 1742.

10. ABNER.

CAPT. ABNER JOHNSON married Charity Dayton, Dec. 14, 1726, and lived on the place where afterward his son Hezekiah lived. He died Dec. 28, 1757.

Children: 39 *Dayton*, b Feb. 8, 1728, m Hannah ——; 40 *Hezekiah*, b March 12, 1732; 41 *Abner*, b Aug. 26, 1738, graduated at Yale College and settled in Waterbury; 42 *Anna*, b Apr. 18, 1736; 43 *Charles*, b May 19, 1736; 44 *Jacob*, b July 21, 1742; 45 *Lydia*, m E. Fitch Esq.; 46 *Charity*, b May 19, 1736.

15. DANIEL.

DANIEL JOHNSON married Joanna Preston, Dec. 24, 1734, and first occupied a house that stood a little east of where his father Jacob lived. He afterwards removed to the Sam'l Parker place. He died Oct. 14, 1780, ae. 72. She died Jan. 18, 1781.

Children: 47 *Charles*, b Nov. 13, 1735, d at sea, brought to New Haven and buried; 48 *Solomon*, b May 4, 1740, built the John B. Johnson house; 49 *Dan*, b Mar. 24, 1746; 50 *Israel*, b July 8, 1748, settled in Meriden near Hanging Hills; 51 *Justin*, b Mar. 4, 1752; 52 *Mindwell*, b May 19, 1738, m —— Merrow; 53 *Joanna*, b Apr. 4, 1743, m —— Lee; 54 *Abigail*, b Dec. 23, 1753; 55 *Joshua*, b July 26, 1757, m —— Brockett; 56 *Rebecca*, b March 29, 1759, d March 31, 1759; 57 *Rebecca*.

JOHN.

JOHN JOHNSON, the son of John, the son of Robert, married 1st, Mary Chatterton of New Haven, came to Wallingford before 1710; the date of this marriage is Dec. 12, 1710. She died within that year, and he married Sarah Hitchcock, July 12, 1711. His house occupied the same piece of ground as that now occupied by the dwelling-house of Russell Cook, and formerly known as the Pond house or place. He died July 24, 1748, ae. 64 years. Born 1687.

Children: 58 *Esther*, b May 4, 1712, m Merriman Munson; 59 *Barbara*, b Feb. 5, 1714, m Abraham Ives; 60 *Damaris*, b June 31, 1716; 61 *Daniel*, b Dec. 14, 1717, m Ruth ——, he d in 1761; 62 *Phebe*, b April 28, 1720, m Dydimus Parker; 63 *Jennings*, b Jan. 7, 1722, m Sarah ——, 1745, owned the Pond place; 64 *Ruth*, b Oct. 10, 1723; 65 *Amos*, b March 4, 1726, d during the Revolutionary war near White Plains, N. Y.; 66 *Patience*, b July 28, 1728.

18. EPHRAIM.

EPHRAIM JOHNSON, son of Reuben and Mary Dayton, married Hannah ——.

Children: 67 *Content*, b July 14, 1755; 68 *Luther*, b June 25, 1759.

20. ZACCHEUS.

ZACCHEUS JOHNSON, son of Reuben and Mary Dayton, married Phebe ——.

Children: 69 *Justus*, b Dec. 6, 1756; 70 *Sybil*, b Jan. 27, 1769.

39. DAYTON.

DAYTON JOHNSON, son of Abner and Charity Dayton Johnson, married Hannah ———. She died Jan. 6, 1723, æ. 46 yrs. He died Feb. 19, 1798, ae. 70 yrs.

Children: 71 *Mamre*, b Aug. 15, 1752; 72 *Eliakim*, b Dec. 31, 1753; 73 *Hannah*, b April 28, 1756.

40. HEZEKIAH.

HEZEKIAH JOHNSON, son of Abner and Charity Dayton Johnson, married Ruth ———.

Children: 74 *Caleb*, b July 11, 1759; 75 *George*, b March 11, 1760; 76 *Charles*, b Nov. 21, 1761.

48. SOLOMON.

SOLOMON JOHNSON, son of Daniel and Joanna Preston Johnson, married Mary, daughter of John Barker. She died Sept. 7, 1825. He died April 4, 1779, ae. 59.

Child: 77 *John Barker*, married —— Munson, he d in Wallingford.

49. DAN.

DAN JOHNSON, son of Daniel and Joanna P. Johnson, married 1st, Rebecca Hitchcock. She died July 25, 1813, ae. 65. His 2d wife, Lucy Dudley, died Jan. 22, 1825, ae. 69. He died Sept. 2, 1830, ae. 85.

Children: 78 *Cephas*, m —— Frost; 79 *Dan*, b on the old Humiston place, m —— Dudley; 80 *Willard;* 81 *Augustus*, m —— Frost; 82 *Ransom;* 83 *Laura*, m Amos Curtis of Meriden.

50. ISRAEL.

ISRAEL JOHNSON, son of Daniel and Joanna Preston Johnson, settled near the Hanging Hills in the parish of Meriden. Some of the family are still on that farm.

Children: 84 *Andrew;* 85 *Peter;* 86 *William*, still living on the farm, a bachelor; 87 *Huldah*.

63. JENNINGS.

JENNINGS JOHNSON, son of John and Sarah H. Johnson, married Sarah Johnson. He cut the stone cider mill trough that was afterwards Samuel Cook's.

Children: 88 *Sarah*, b June 4, 1749; 89 *Damaris*, b June 26, 1753; 90 *Stephen*, b March 18, 1754; 91 *Esther*, b March 27, 1756; 92 *Rachel*, b Oct. 29, 1759.

65. AMOS.

AMOS JOHNSON, son of John and Sarah H. Johnson, married Abigail ———.

Children: 93 *Lucy*, b Sept. 11, 1747; 94 *Esther*, b Nov. 16, 1749; 95 *Sybil*, b Sept. 16, 1751.

JONES.

THEOPHILUS.

THEOPHILUS and Hannah Jones are the first recorded of that name in Wallingford; he married Hannah Mix, Dec.

26, 1711. She died Nov. 26, 1754. He married 2d, Sarah Moss, Sept. 22, 1755.

Children: 1 *Nathaniel*, b March 30, 1717, m Sarah Merriman; 2 *Theophilus*, b Nov. 1, 1723, m Anna Street; 3 *Caleb*, b Nov. 4, 1712, m Mary How, Oct. 6, 1741; 4 *Lydia*, b Nov. 9, 1714, m Joseph Moss, Feb. 4, 1735; 5 *Hannah*, b Oct. 4, 1720, m Jehiel Merriman, Aug. 5, 1740; 6 *Abigail*, b Dec. 28, 1726, m Benjamin Dutton, March 16, 1747; 7 *Daniel*, b Oct. 28, 1731, d May 1, 1737; 8 *Nicholas*, b Dec. 17, 1729, m 1st, Mary ———, 2d, Eunice ———.

1. NATHANIEL.

NATHANIEL JONES, son of Theophilus and Hannah, married Sarah Merriman, June 8, 1743, in Wallingford.

Children: 9 *Abigail*, b Sept. 26, 1744; 10 *Daniel*, b Oct. 17, 1748; 11 *Sarah*, b Aug. 16, 1750; 12 *Eunice*, b Jan. 27, 1752; 13 *Benjamin*, b Feb. 5, 1757; 14 *Amos*, b Aug. 3, 1758; 15 *Reuben*, b Oct. 11, 1759, m Sarah ———, he d Oct. 6, 1840; 16 *Hannah*, b Feb. 25, 1761.

2. THEOPHILUS.

THEOPHILUS JONES, son of Theophilus and Hannah, married Anna Street, May 24, 1757; she died Aug. 10, 1811, ae. 76 yrs. He died Oct. 8, 1815, ae. 91 yrs.

Children: 17 *Sarah*, b March 30, 1758, m Elisha Whittelsey; 18 *Nicholas*, b Nov. 25, 1760, d Aug. 25, 1848, ae. 88; 19 *Anna*, b 1772, d Oct. 1, 1776.

3. CALEB.

CALEB JONES, son of Theophilus and Hannah, married Mary How, dau. of Zachariah.

Children: 20 *Anna*, b August 19, 1742; 21 *Zachariah H.*, b Sept. 3, 1744; 22 *Hannah*, b Jan. 8, 1746; 23 *Caleb*, b Sept. 3, 1748; 24 *Samuel*, b May 15, 1754.

8. NICHOLAS.

NICHOLAS JONES, son of Theophilus and Hannah, married 1st, Mary ———, 2d, Eunice ———. He died April 24, 1760.

Children by 1st marriage: 25 *Charles*, b May 19, 1752;

26 *Patience*, b March 27, 1754. By 2d marriage: 27 *Mary*, b April 30, 1756, d May 6, 1760; 28 *Eunice*, b Feb. 26, 1758, d March 31, 1758; 29 *Mary*, b Feb. 26, 1760.

15. REUBEN.

REUBEN, son of Nathaniel and Sarah Jones, married Sarah ——. He lived about a mile east of Wallingford village, where his descendants are still living, 1869. He died Oct. 6, 1843, æ. 84 years. Mrs. Sarah his wife d March 12, 1833, æ. 72 years.

18. NICHOLAS.

NICHOLAS JONES, son of Theophilus and Anna Jones, married Elizabeth ——, and remained on the old farm of his fathers, on the west side of the river, where his son Street Jones Esq. now resides. He was a very enterprising and prosperous farmer, and died Aug. 25, 1848, ae 88 yrs., and his wife died Feb. 8, 1845, ae. 81 yrs.

Children: 30 *Betsey*, m Rufus Bradley, Cheshire; 31 *Anna*, b 1785, d Nov. 19, 1861, ae. 76, m Jared Doolittle of North Haven; 32 *Street*, m 1st, —— Eastman, 2d —— Parsons; 33 *Sarah*, m Dea. Ezra Dickerman of Hamden.

SAMUEL.

SAMUEL JONES was, with his wife Sarah, born in Wallingford, previous to 1721; she died Nov. 9, 1760. He was possibly a brother of Theophilus Jones. He married Esther Pratt, April 12, 1762.

Children: 34 *Mary*, b Dec. 5, 1721; 35 *William*, b May 31, 1722; 36 *Diadate*, b March 15, 1724; 37 *Hester*, b March 9, 1727, m Dennis Covert, March 10, 1758; 38 *Eaton*, b Aug. 26, 1730; 39 *John*, b May 25, 1747; 40 *Daniel*, b March 18, 1745–6.

KIRTLAND.[1]

The name of Kirtland is of Scotch descent; and among the first 36 settlers of Saybrook in 1635, was John Kirtland,

1 For collateral branches, see Chapman's Gen. of Chapman family, 71

who came from Silver-street, London. He had a son John, who was the father of Daniel, who was the father of the noted missionary, Rev. Samuel Kirkland, who was born in 1701, graduated at Yale in 1720, under the name of Kirtland.

JOHN.

JOHN KIRTLAND was married to his first wife in Saybrook, March 3, 1703; 2d, Lydia Baldwin.

Children: 1 *Hester*, b March 10, 1704; 2 *John*, b July 5, 1708, d March, 1787; 3 *Temperance*, b Nov. 10, 1710. By 2d marriage: 4 *Elisha*, b July 21, 1718; 5 *Elisha*, b Aug. 17, 1719, killed at Fort Edward, March 16, 1756; 6 *Lydia*, b Oct. 29, 1721, d June 30, 1770, at Horton, Nova Scotia; 7 *Parmel*, b Jan. 29, 1724; 8 *Constant*, b Jan. 24, 1726, d young; 9 *Constant*, b Dec. 24, 1727, d at Wallingford; 10 *Ezra*, b Oct. 11, 1730, d at Saybrook, Aug., 1801; 11 *Elizabeth*, b Oct. 13, 1732; 12 *Dorothy*, b Sept. 21, 1735.

8. CONSTANT.

CONSTANT KIRTLAND, son of John and Lury Kirtland, of Saybrook, married Rachel, daughter of Isaac and —— Brockett, of Wallingford, April 19, 1753. She was born May 23, 1732, died at Northford, Feb. 17, 1812.

Children: 13 *Isaac*, b March 9, 1754, d Sept, 30, 1807, in Wallingford; 14 *Turhand*, b Nov. 16, 1755, d Aug. 16, 1854, at Poland, Ohio; 15 *Mary*, b Dec. 23, 1757, m Samuel Cook, d March 3, 1839; 16 *John*, b Dec. 20, 1759, d at Granville, N. Y., May 19, 1843; 17 *Billious*, b June 9, 1762, d Oct. 25, 1805, at Wallingford; 18 *Rachel*, b July 9, 1764, m Col. Edward Barker, d June 13, 1823, at Wallingford; 19 *Jared*, b Aug. 8, 1766, d April 16, 1831, at Poland, Ohio; 20 *George*, b July 2, 1769, d April 10, 1793, at Wallingford; 21 *Lydia*, b Feb. 27, 1772, m Jonathan Fowler, of Guilford, d Aug. 16, 1850, at Poland, Ohio; 22 *Sarah*, b March 19, 1778, m Capt.

72, 96, 133; Lewis and Newhall's Hist. Lynn, Mass., 154; N. E. Hist. and Gen. Reg., XIV. 241–5; Savage's Gen. Dict., III. 31, 32.

Wm. Douglass, and had John, Sarah, Benjamin and William, d Sept. 28, 1842, at Northford.

13. ISAAC.

ISAAC KIRTLAND, son of Constant and Rachel Kirtland, married Sarah Ives.

Children: 23 *Delight*, m Peter Hall, of Wallingford; 24 *Sarah*, m Jehiel Hall, of Wallingford; 25 *Constant*, m Caroline Carrington, he died in N. Y.; 26 *Clarissa*.

14. TURHAND.

TURHAND KIRTLAND, son of Constant and Rachel Kirtland, married Mary, daughter of Moses Beach, of Wallingford; she died Nov. 24, 1792. Married 2d, Polly, daughter of Dr. Jared Potter, Jan. 19, 1793; she was born in New Haven, Feb. 10, 1772, and died at Poland, Ohio, March 21, 1850.

Children: 27 *Jared Potter, M. D.*, b Nov. 10, 1793, m Caroline, dau. of Joshua Atwater, May, 1814; 28 *Henry Turhand*, b Nov. 16, 1795, m 1st, Thalia Fitch; 29 *Mary Beach*, b Sept. 12, 1798, m Richard Hall, d in Poland, Ohio; 30 *Nancy*, b Jan. 1, 1801, m Elkanah Morse; 31 *Billious*, b Aug. 29, 1807, m Ruthan A. Frame, resides in Poland, Ohio; 32 *George*, m Helen, dau. of Randall Cook, of Wallingford.

16. JOHN.

JOHN KIRTLAND, son of Constant and Rachel Kirtland, married 1st, Lucy A. Burbank, April 10, 1788; she was born Jan. 10, 1771, d Aug. 17, 1728. Married 2d, widow Mary Tyler Benham, dau. of Moses Tyler, and widow of Silas Benham, formerly of Meriden, June 7, 1829. She died April 4, 1836, æ. 57 years.

Children: 33 *Henrietta*, b Jan. 23, 1789, m Wm. Sweetland, of Plattsburg, Nov. 19, 1811; 34 *Wm. Henry*, b Jan. 11, 1791, d April 6, 1821; 35 *Lucy Fitch*, b April 3, 1793, m Peter J. H. Myers, of Whitehall, Jan. 29, 1815; 36 *George Washington*, b April 11, 1795, m Frances Davis, Oct. 6, 1828, he is a lawyer; 37 *Ann Burbank*, b April 5, 1797, d May 11,

1797; 38 *Ann Burbank*, b April 27, 1798, m Wm. Haile, April 15, 1822, d Nov. 26, 1859; 39 *Eliza Cornelia*, b Sept. 17, 1800, m John B. Shaw, Oct. 13, 1825, d July 22, 1842; 40 *Lydia Maria*, b March 25, 1802, m S. Myers, Oct. 23, 1827, d Nov. 9, 1864; 41 *Rachel Brockett*, b Feb. 11, 1804, m Thos. A. Tomlison, May 16, 1833; 42 *John*, b Oct. 13, 1805, m Catherine Campbell, Sept. 13, 1836; 43 *Isaac Billious*, b Oct. 14, 1807, m Lucy Sperry, Dec. 8, 1835; 44 *Edward*, b July 23, 1810, m Maria Foot, Jan. 24, 1837; 45 *Jared Turhand*, b Nov. 3, 1816, m Ann T. Palmer, Sept. 6, 1849, d May 19, 1861.

17. BILLIOUS.

Dr. Billious Kirtland, son of Constant and Rachel Kirtland, married Sarah, daughter of Dr. Jared Potter.

Children: 46 *Eliza*, m Liverius Carrington; 47 *Polly*, m Col. Russell Hall; 48 *George*, d 1869; 49 *Sarah*, m Liverius Carrington.

19. JARED.

Jared Kirtland, son of Constant and Rachel Kirtland, married 1st, Lois, daughter of Elisha and Lucretia Stanley Yale, of Wallingford. He removed to Poland, Ohio, in 1802, where he died, April 16, 1831. She died Oct. 3, 1814, ae. 38 yrs., at Cookstown, Penn. He left a widow, 2d wife.

Children by 1st marriage: 50 *Lucretia*, b Nov. 2, 1796, m Dr. —— Manning; 51 *Rachel*, b Dec. 9, 1798, m Col. Caleb Wicks; 52 *Eliza*, b Aug. 2, 1803, m Philo Cook, of Wallingford; 53 *Sarah*, b Oct. 8, 1805, m Geo. G. Hills; 54 *Lois Yale*, b Sept. 21, 1813, m Eli Mygatt, M. D., of Poland, Ohio.

LEWIS.[1]

BENJAMIN.

Benjamin Lewis was the first of the name in Wallingford. He came from Stratford in 1670, and had assigned him lot ———, which he sold to Dr. John Hull, who had come

1 For collateral branches, see Alden's Coll. of Am. Epitaphs, v. 68–70;

from Derby to settle in the place as a physician. Mr Lewis soon after left Wallingford, and returned to his old home in Stratford.

Children: *Mary*, b Nov. 1, 1671, d in Wallingford; *John*, b Sept. 20, 1672; *Mary*, b Nov. 9, 1674; *Edmund*, b 1679, m Hannah Beach, May 21, 1702. He d in 1757, æ. 78 yrs.

EBENEZER.

EBENEZER LEWIS, blacksmith, married Elizabeth Merriman, Dec. 2, 1685, and settled in the eastern part of the town in 1684. He was a son of William Lewis, of Farmington. He died in 1709.

Children: 1 *Hezekiah*, b Oct. 12, 1686, d 1711, m Abigail ———; 2 *Caleb*, b Oct. 15, 1691, m Sarah Cook, Nov. 25, 1713; 3 *Selekey*, b Oct. 25, 1693; 4 *Elizabeth*, b Oct. 15, 1695; 5 *Barnabas*, b Nov. 4, 1697, m Elizabeth ———; 6 *Hannah*, b Oct. 10, 1699, m Samuel Cook Esq.; 7 Dr. *Benjamin*, b Sept. 21, 1701, m Esther Matthews, Nov. 3, 1724; 8 *Malachi*, b Oct. 4, 1703, settled in Middletown; 9 *Agape*, b Jan. 10, 1705.

2. CALEB.

CALEB LEWIS, son of Ebenezer and Elizabeth, married Sarah, dau. of Samuel and Hope Cook, Nov. 28, 1713.

Children: 10 *Ichabod*, b April 13, 1714, d March 1, 1718; 11 *Caleb*, b Feb. 28, 1717, m Eunice Welton, Jan. 10, 1736; 12 *Ichabod*, b 1716, m Sarah ———, 1777; 13 *Ebenezer*, b

---

Andrews' Hist. New Britain, Ct., 160, 161, 167, 277, 306, 307, 332, 354; Bradbury's Hist. Kennebunkport, Me., 257; Bronson's Hist. Waterbury, Ct., 518, 519; Caulkins' Hist. New London, Ct., 295, 296; Deane's Hist. Scituate, Mass., 303, 304; Fields' Hist. Haddam, Ct., 46; Freeman's Hist. Cape Cod, Mass., I. 614, II. 285, 404, 465, 471, 480, 481, 507, 661, 676; Howe's Hist. Col. Virginia, 181–3; Hudson's Hist. Lexington, Mass., 281; Judd & Boltwood's Hist. Hadley, Mass., 530, 531; Lewis & Newhall's Hist. Lynn, Mass., 180–2; Meade's Old Churches and Families of Virginia, II. 231–3, 325, 326; N. E. Hist. and Gen., Reg., XVII. 162–6; Pierce's Hist. Gorham, Me., 181–3; Savage's Gen. Dict., III. 84–90; Sheppard's Account of Lewis Family; Smith's Hist. Delaware Co., Penn., 478–80; Virginia Hist. Reg., V. 24, 25.

April 14, 1715, m Sarah Avered, June 12, 1735; 14 *Hezekiah*, b Oct. 14, 1720, m Abigail Chamberlain, April 25, 1744.

5. BARNABAS.

BARNABAS LEWIS, son of Ebenezer and Elizabeth, married Elizabeth ———; he died Oct. 1, 1729.

Children: 15 *Lucy*, b March 23, 1724; 16 *Lois*, b May 26, 1728.

7. BENJAMIN.

DR. BENJAMIN LEWIS, son of Ebenezer and Elizabeth, married Esther Matthews, Nov. 3, 1724.

Children: 17 *Bela*, b Sept. 28, 1724; 18 *Bela*, b Jan. 10, 1725; 19 *Elizabeth*, b March 6, 1727, m Cornelius Johnson, Dec. 9, 1746; 20 *Benjamin*, b Jan. 11, 1728, m Mary Maltbie, April 3, 1773; 21 *Barnabas*, b Aug. 17, 1733, m Rachel Curtis, Feb. 24, 1762; 22 *Jesse*, b Jan. 29, 1734; 23 *Caleb*, b May 22, 1736, m Lucy Holt, March 13, 1748–9; 24 *Samuel*, b March 8, 1741; 25 *Esther*, b Oct. 23, 1738, m Nathaniel Douglass, Feb. 1, 1759; 26 *Mary*, b Oct. 10, 1743; 27 *Mary*, b June 11, 1747; 28 *Levi*, b Oct. 19, 1750; 29 *Levi*, b Oct. 19, 1751; 30 *Lucy*, b March 23, 1754, m Zebulon Frisbie.

11. CALEB.

CALEB LEWIS, son of Caleb and Sarah, married Eunice Welton, Jan. 10, 1736.

Children: 31 *Jacob*, b Sept. 7, 1736; 32 *Eunice*, b April 6, 1738; 33 *Amy*, b Jan. 31, 1745; 34 *Caleb*, b April 15, 1752.

12. ICHABOD.

ICHABOD LEWIS, son of Caleb and Sarah, married 1st, Sarah ——, 2d, Esther ——; she was burned to death in 1812.

Children: 35 *Samuel*, b Oct. 9, 1748, m Esther ——, he d Feb. 8, 1824, ae. 76; 36 *Elihu*, b June 10, 1752, settled in Albany, N. Y.; 37 *Esther*, b July 11, 1756, m John Mansfield; 38 *Jared*, b May 10, 1761, m Rhoda Munson.

13. EBENEZER.

EBENEZER LEWIS, son of Caleb and Sarah Cook Lewis, married Sarah Avered, June 12, 1735.

Children: 39 *Hannah*, b Oct. 9, 1736; 40 *Malachi*.

14. HEZEKIAH.

HEZEKIAH, son of Caleb and Sarah Cook Lewis, m Abigail Chamberlain, April 28, 1744.

Children: 41 *John*, b May 22, 1745; 42 *Ebenezer*, b Oct. 14, 1746; 43, 44 *Mary* and *Hezekiah*, b April 27, 1755; 45 *Benjamin*, b Nov. 18, 1757; 46 *Abel*, b Dec. 25, 1760.

18. BELA.

BELA LEWIS, son of Benjamin and Esther Lewis, married Abigail ——.

Child: 47 *Joseph*, b May 6, 1743–4.

21. BARNABAS.

BARNABAS LEWIS, son of Dr. Benjamin and Esther Lewis, married Rachel Curtis, Feb. 24, 1762.

Children: 48 *Rachel*, b March 20, 1768; 49 *Levi*, b March 5, 1775; 50 *Merriam*, b Feb. 14, 1777.

35. SAMUEL.

SAMUEL LEWIS, son of Ichabod and Sarah Lewis, died Feb. 8, 1824, ae. 76 yrs. He married Esther ——.

Children: 51 *Sarah*, b Sept. 8, 1773; 52 *Esther*, b July 15, 1776, m Ephraim Cook, of Wall.; 53 *Elihu*, b March 12, 1777.

38. JARED.

JARED LEWIS, son of Ichabod and Sarah Lewis, married Rhoda Munson. He died in Wallingford.

Children: 54 *Isaac*, m Esther Beaumont, kept a hotel and store in Meriden; 55 *Frederick*, m Sinai Hall, of Wallingford.

JACOB.

JACOB LEWIS married Mary Martin, June 22, 1773.

Children: 56 *Jacob*, b March 10, 1776; 57 *Ezekiel*, b July 6, 1777.

ISAAC.

Dr. Isaac Lewis married Keziah ———. He lived on the west side of the river.

Children: 58 *Charles*, b May 8, 1772; 59 *Isaac*, died May 9, 1772, ae. 25 yrs.; 60 *Keziah*, d May 29, 1772, ae. 19 yrs.

Joseph Lewis of Windsor and Simsbury, had sons, Joseph and John, who had a numerous posterity, who settled in Waterbury.

Joshua Lewis, a Baptist Clergyman, came from Wales about 1780, and settled in Connecticut. His son Joshua, likewise a Baptist Clergyman, resided in Conn. and R. I., where he had a son Joshua, who removed to Saratoga, N. Y., and married a Miss Grinelle, and had a son John, who moved to the neighborhood of Auburn, N. Y., where he married Delecta Barbour, and became a farmer. They had five children, one of whom is Dr. Dio Lewis, of Lexington, Mass., born in 1825.

The name of Lewis is derived from the Welsh *Lluaws*, signifying a multitude. The name of Lewes is derived from the same source, as is also the ancient town of Lewes in Sussex, England.

MARTIN.[1]

The Martins of Plymouth, Devonshire, were originally from Kent. Capt. John Martin, of this family, went round the world with Drake, in 1577.

The name of Martin was adopted as a surname at a very early date; and few names have had a greater number to bear them. The earliest record containing it which I have found, is the "roll of Battle Abbey," on which appears the name of Le Sire de S. Martin. Battle Abbey was dedicated to St.

---

1 For collateral branches, see Babson's Hist. Gloucester, Mass., 115; Cothren's Hist. Woodbury, Conn., 620–31; Eaton's Hist. Thomaston, Me., 324; Hough's Hist. Lewis Co., N. Y., 172–4; Littell's Passaic Valley Gen., 278; Savage's Gen. Dict., III. 161–4.

Martin, and the date of its roll is 1066. The name was not only numerous on the other side of the water, but has been the same in this country from its first settlement. There was a William Martin at London, England, who assisted the Puritans in preparing for their voyage to Plymouth Rock; but it does not appear that he came with them. John Martyn, afterwards Capt. John Martyn or Martin of Plymouth, and son of —— Martin of Bridgetown, near Totness, who had male issue living at that place in 1620, sailed round the globe with Sir Francis Drake, leaving Plymouth Nov. 15, 1577, and returning to the same port Sept. 26, 1580.

Christopher Martin with his wife and son Christopher, and one whose name is not given, came over in the Mayflower in 1620; but they all died during the first winter. Others of the name however, came in almost every ship that brought over a company, for some years. They settled in various parts of Massachusetts, Connecticut, Virginia and other colonies. Anthony died at Middletown, Conn., 1693; William of Stratford at Woodbury, Conn. It is proposed in this to trace only the Wallingford families. As early as 1684, John and Elizabeth Martin made their appearance in Wallingford, and were married by Mr. Moss, Jan. 15, 1684; how long they continued in the place does not now appear. In 1735, Robert Martin and his wife Abigail appear to have been in Wallingford.

Children: 1 *James*, b March 3, 1735, m Agnes Crawford, March 8, 1718; 2 *Lydia*, b Oct. 27, 1740; 3 *Elizabeth*, b Sept. 23, 1742; 4 *Samuel*, b May 1, 1744; 5 *Abigail*, b Dec. 9, 1745; 6 *Isaac*, b April 25, 1748; 7 *Mary*, b Aug. 30, 1750; 8 *John*, b Sept. 27, 1754.

WOOSTER.

WOOSTER MARTIN came into Wallingford early in the present century, and settled on the North Farms as a wagon-maker, and by industry and perseverance accumulated a very handsome estate. He was twice married; 1st, to Althea

Hall, 2d, Delilah Morse, widow of the late Sylvester Hull. He died in Wallingford, May 4, 1862, ae. 72.

Children by 1st marriage: 9 *Othniel Ives*, m ——, daughter of Augustus Hall, 2d, —— Cook, daughter of Colonel T. Cook; 10 ————; 11 *Henry*, m —— Hall, daughter of Joel Hall. By 2d marriage, 12 ————.

1. JAMES.

James Martin, son of Robert and Abigail, m Agnes Crawford, March 8, 1758.

Children: 13 *Mary*, b Dec. 28, 1758, in Wallingford; 14 *James*, b Nov. 10, 1761, in Wallingford.

MANSFIELD.

Capt. John Mansfield married Esther Lewis, and owned and occupied the house and lot now owned and occupied by Mr. Harrison, and formerly by John Hiddleson, Esq. Mr. Mansfield was in the service of his country during the Revolution, and received for that service a pension from the government. He died highly respected.

Children: 1 *Ira*, he settled at Atwater, Ohio; 2 *Sybil*, m John Hiddleson of Georgetown, S. C.; both d in Wallingford.

MATTOON.[1]

Philip, son of Philip and Mary Mattoon, was doubtless the first of the name in Wallingford. He settled in the northeast part of the town.

JOHN.

John Mattoon, son of Philip and Mary, who also settled in Wallingford, was born in 1682, and married Jerusha Hall, Oct. 20, 1706. He died Feb. 19, 1754; she died Sept. 28, 1760, ae. 71 yrs.

Children: 1 *Eleazer*, b Dec. 13, 1727, no knowledge of

---

1 For collateral branches, see Judd & Boltman's Hist. and Gen. Hadley, Mass., 535, 536; Savage's Gen. Dict., III. 177, 178.

him or family; 2 *Gershom*, b Aug. 18, 1730; 3 *Ebenezer*, b April 4, 1735, m Martha ——, she d Nov. 10, 1802, he d May 27, 1814; 4 *David;* 5 *Isaac;* 6 *Nathaniel;* 7 *Sarah;* 8 *Mary*, m ——— Brooks; 9 *John*, d Jan. 6, 1808, ae. 51.

4. DAVID.

DAVID MATTOON m Phebe Curtis, Oct., 5, 1742.

Children: 10 *Charles*, b Dec 12, 1744; 11 *Phebe*, b Jan. 15, 1748; 12 *Eunice*, b March 19, 1751.

6. NATHANIEL.

NATHANIEL MATTOON married Mary Curtis, Feb. 17, 1745.

Children: 13 *Joel*, b Jan. 24, 1749; 14 *Seth*, b March 21, 1753.

MERRIMAN.

This name is often spelled on the old records Merriam and Merriman, both names referring to the same person. Joseph Merriam took the freeman's oath in Lexington, Mass., March 14, 1638. He died Jan. 1, 1641, and some of his descendants assumed the name of, or were recorded as Merriman.

NATHANIEL.

CAPT. NATHANIEL MERRIMAN was one of the original settlers in Wallingford in 1670. Lots Nos. 1 and 2 were set him on the north, west and east corners of the south cross street, also No. 2 adjoining the west lot. These corner lots are now owned by Peter Whittelsey, Esq., and Rev. Edgar J. Doolittle. These extra lots were set to him in consideration of some out land which the committee had given out to other parties to his damage. Capt. Merriman built his house on the lot where Mr. Whittelsey's house now stands, but a short distance to the west of it. A large elm tree stands nearly in front of the old site. He died Feb. 13, 1693. ae. 80 years.

Children: 1 *John*, d Sept. 26, 1651; 2 *Hannah*, b May 16, 1651; 3 *Abigail*, b April 18, 1654; 4 *Mamre*, b July 12, 1657, m Samuel Munson; 5 *John*, b Feb. 28, 1659, m 1st, Hannah

Lines, 2d, Mary Doolittle ; 6 *Samuel*, b Sept. 29, 1662, m 1st, Anna ——, 2d, Elizabeth Peck ; 7 *Caleb*, b May, 1665, m Mary Preston ; 8 *Moses*, b 1667 ; 9 *Elizabeth*, b Sept. 14, 1669, m Ebenezer Lewis, Dec. 2, 1685.

5. JOHN.

JOHN MERRIMAN married 1st, Hannah Lines of New Haven, March 28, 1682. He married 2d, Mary Doolittle, and after her decease married Elizabeth Peck, March 20, 1690.

Children: 10 *Esther*, b Jan. 24, 1683 ; 11 *Abigail*, b Feb. 1, 1685 ; 12 *George*, b July 14, 1688, m Susanna Abernathy. By 3d marriage: 13 *John*, b Oct. 16, 1691 ; 14 *Israel*, b June 23, 1693, m Comfort Benham, June 23, 1715 ; 15 *Sarah*, b Feb. 17, 1702 ; 16, 17 *Elizabeth* and *Susanna*, b July 20, 1703 ; 18 *Mary*, b March 15, 1705 ; 19 *Caleb*, b April 25, 1707, m Ruth ——.

6. SAMUEL.

SAMUEL MERRIMAN married 1st, Anna ——, 2d, Elizabeth Peck.

Children: 20 *Nathaniel*, b May 22, 1687 ; 21 *Nathaniel*, b March 16, 1690 ; 22 *Theophilus*, b April 28, 1692, m Mary ——, May 9, 1714 ; 23 *Samuel*, b Dec. 19, 1694, m Sarah ——.

7. CALEB.

CALEB MERRIMAN married Mary ———. He died July 9, 1703. Estate £439.

Children: 24 *Moses*, b Oct. 31, 1691 ; 25 *Elizabeth*, b May 4, 1691 ; 26 *Eliasaph*, b May 21, 1695, m Abigail Hall, Dec. 10, 1719 ; 27 *Phebe*, b June 17, 1697 ; 28 *Hannah*, b Sept. 10, 1698 ; 29 *Phebe*, b Sept. 16, 1699, m Waitstill Munson, Dec. 10, 1719 ; 30 *Lydia*, b Dec. 3, 1701 ; 31 *Lydia*, b Nov. 12, 1702.

8. MOSES.

MOSES MERRIMAN m Martha ——.

Children: 32 *Jehiel*, b Oct. 28, 1713 ; 33 *Esther*, b Nov. 11, 1716, d April 3d, 1734 ; 34 *Phebe*, b March 27, 1720 ; 35

Benjamin, b Jan. 21, 1722; 36 *Martha*, b Dec. 30, 1723; 37 *Mary*, b Feb. 26, 1726; 38 *Lent*, b May 25, 1731.

12. GEORGE.

George Merriman married 1st, Susannah Abernathy, June 28, 1713; 2d, Ruth ——.

Children: 39 *Nathan*, b Nov. 30, 1713; 40 *Nathan*, b July 16, 1717; 41 *Lois*, b Nov. 10, 1720; 42 *Susannah*, b Sept. 13, 1723; 43 *Daniel*, b Feb. 22, 1727; 44 *Molly*, b July 6, 1730; 45 *Sarah*, b May 25, 1733.

14. ISRAEL.

Israel Merriman m Comfort Benham, June 23, 1715.

Children: 46 *Joseph*, b Aug. 20, 1716; 47 *Comfort*, b Oct. 3, 1720; 48 *Jelin*, b Feb 16, 1724; 49 *Israel*, b Nov. 30, 1732; 50 *Elizabeth*, b March 11, 1734.

19. CALEB.

Caleb Merriman married Ruth ——, Aug. 31, 1732. She died before him. He died of small pox, June 2, 1770.

Children: 51 *Sarah*, b May 25, 1733; 52 *George*, b 1736, d Sept. 24, 1787; 53 *Elizabeth*, b Nov. 24, 1739; 54 *Ruth*, b Nov. 1, 1741; 55 *Anna*, d July 4, 1751; 56 *Jerusha*, d July 5, 1751; 57 *Abigail*, d Oct. 3, 1761; 58 *Caleb*, b Feb. 26, 1751, d Oct. 9, 1751.

21. NATHANIEL.

Nathaniel Merriman married Mehitable ——.

Children: 59 *Samuel*, b May 3, 1712; 60 *David*, b Feb. 11, 1715; 61 *Thankful*, b May 31, 1717; 62 *Nathaniel*, b May 31, 1720, m Prudence Austin, Dec. 19, 1743.

22. THEOPHILUS.

Theophilus Merriman married Mary ——.

Children: 63 *Anna*, b Sept. 1, 1715; 64 *Theophilus*, b Aug. 20, 1717.

23. SAMUEL.

Samuel Merriman married Sarah Wilcher.

Children: 65 *Samuel*, b Aug. 24, 1728; 66 *Samuel*, b Oct. 14, 1734; 67 *Catherine*, b Dec. 28, 1736; 68 *Nicholas*, b Feb.

17, 1737; 69 *Anna*, b March 10, 1737; 70 *Samuel*, b Feb. 28, 1739; 71 *Sarah*, b Jan. 28, 1742; 72 *Stephen*, b March 25, 1743; 73 *Miles*, b June 11, 1744; 74 *Hannah*, b Dec. 1, 1750; 75 *Eunice*, b Aug. 21, 1753.

26. ELIASAPH.

ELIASAPH MERRIMAN married Abigail Hall; she with her daughter Abigail were killed by lightning, Aug. 4, 1758. He died Aug. 14, 1758, ten days after.

Children: 76 *Eunice*, b Oct. 7, 1720, d; 77 *Eunice*, b Jan. 12, 1722, d; 78 *Eunice* b Nov. 24, 1722; 79 *Sarah*, b Nov. 18, 1723; 80 *Titus*, b Aug. 28, 1727; 81 *Caleb*, b Sept. 3, 1729; 82 *Amasa*, b about 1730; 83 *Elizabeth*, b July 27, 1732; 84 *Esther*, b Dec. 2, 1734; 85 *Abigail*, killed by lightning, Aug. 4, 1758; 86 *Elizabeth*.

38. LENT.

LENT MERRIMAN married Catherine ——.

Children: 87 *Luce*, b Feb. 14, 1755; 88 *Joel*, b Sept. 11, 1756; 89 *Mamre*, b June 30, 1758; 90 *Katherine*, b May 23, 1760; 91 *Moses*, b Oct. 30, 1761.

46. JOSEPH.

JOSEPH MERRIMAN married Deborah ——.

Children: 92 *Joseph*, b Dec. 20, 1732; 93 *Susannah*, b Sept. 9, 1745.

AMASA.

AMASA and Sarah Merriman, of Wallingford.

Children: 94 *Charles*, b Aug. 20, 1762. He enlisted into the army of the Revolution as a drummer, in 1776, became drum-major, and served through the war. He married Anna Punderson, of New Haven, May 16, 1784, and settled in Watertown, where he commenced the business of tailor, which he was compelled to relinquish in consequence of ill health. After having "ridden post" from New Haven to Suffield, Conn., four years, and made a voyage to the West Indies, he commenced the mercantile business in Watertown, in which he continued until 1829. He died Aug. 26, 1829, leaving ten children.

MILES.[1]

John Miles was in New England in 1630, and was made free in 1732.

THOMAS.

MAJ. THOMAS MILES of New Haven, married Abigail Mix, daughter of Thomas Mix, Sept. 7, 1709. His father, Richard Miles, died in New Haven in 1663, and his mother, Mrs. Katherine Miles, died in Wallingford, Jan. 27, 1683, æ. 95 yrs. Anna, the wife of Rev. Mr. Samuel Street, was their daughter. The tomb-stone of Mrs. Catherine Miles is still in the cemetery at Wallingford. Maj. Thomas Miles died Oct. 5, 1741.

Children: 1 *John*, b Jan. 14, 1711, m Sarah ——; 2 *James*, b Dec. 18, 1713, m Phebe Thompson, Jan. 10, 1733; 3 *Elizabeth*, b Sept. 18, 1718, m Daniel Clark, she d April 17, 1755; 4 *Mary*, b Nov. 19, 1719, m Josiah Stanley, March 14, 1739; 5 *Martha*, b Nov. 5, 1723; 6 *Eunice*, b Dec. 6, 1726, m Stephen Culver, Feb. 12, 1745-6; 7 *Abigail*, b April 2, 1727.

1. JOHN.

JOHN and Sarah Miles. He died Nov. 18, 1760. She died Nov. 25, 1760.

Children: 8 *Samuel*, b Dec. 18, 1714; 9 *Sarah*, b Aug. 28, 1717; 10 *John*, b Oct. 4, 1723; 11 *Esther*, b Aug. 26, 1726; 12 *Mehitable*, May 2, 1741, she died May 2, 1757.

2. JAMES.

CAPT. JAMES and Phebe Miles of Wallingford. He was Town Clerk of his native place for a great number of years. She died Oct. 23, 1756.

Children: 13 *Thomas*, b Oct. 14, 1733; 14, 15 *Samuel*, and *Anna*, b Mar. 24, 1735; 16 *Joseph*, b March 7, 1737; 17

1 For collateral branches, see Allen's Hist. Worcester, Mass. Association, 165, 166; Hill's Hist. Mason, N. H., 205; Miles' Gen. of Miles Family; Savage's Gen. Dict., III. 206-8; Smith's Hist. Delaware Co., Penn., 485; Ward's Hist. Shrewsbury, Mass., 368-70; Westminster, Mass. Centennial Celebration, 30.

John, b Nov. 24, 1739; 18 *Catherine*, b Nov. 23, 1741; 19 *James*, b Feb. 19, 1743–4; 20 *Abigail*, b Nov. 9, 1746; 21 *Sarah*, b May 20, 1749; 22 *George*, b April 22, 1752.

8. SAMUEL.

SAMUEL MILES m Phebe Tuttle, Nov. 29, 1736, and resided in Wallingford.

Children: 21 *Joseph*, b March 7, 1737; 22 *Amos*, b Feb. 6, 1738; 23 *Ruth*, b May 24, 1739, m Stephen Hall, April 21, 1762; 24 *Mabel*, b Oct. 1, 1741, m John McCleave; 25 *Martha*, b June 28, 1743; 26 *Joel*, b Nov. 18, 1749; 27 *Isaac*, b Aug, 25, 1752; 28 *Samuel*, b Aug. 12, 1757.

10. JOHN.

JOHN MILES m Martha Curtis, Nov. 14, 1743, and resided in Wallingford.

Children: 29 *John*, b Aug. 31, 1745; 30 *Simeon*, b April 4, 1746; 31 *Sarah*, b Sept. 30, 1749.

DANIEL.

DANIEL MILES married Anna ———, of Wallingford. He died Dec. 12, 1756.

Children: 32 *Samuel*, b Oct. 9, 1746; 33 *Charles*, b Feb. 8, 1748; 34 *Susannah*, b Sept. 6, 1750; 35 *Molly*, b Oct. 19, 1753; 36 *Anna*, b April 4, 1756.

22. GEORGE.

GEORGE MILES son of Capt. James Miles, came to Wallingford some thirty-five or forty years since, and remained there, until his decease, a single man, greatly advanced in life. He died Feb. 13, 1838, ae. 86 years. He was the last of the male members of the Miles family in Wallingford.

MIX.[1]

JOHN.

JOHN MIX was the first of the name who was in Wallingford. He had assigned to him in 1670, lot No. 12, the same

1 For collateral branches, see Savage's Gen. Dict., III. 222, 223.

on which now (1870) stand the houses of Joel Peck, deceased, and the heirs of the late Hon. Edgar Atwater. He was the eldest son of Thomas Mix Sen., of New Haven. Daniel, his brother, also settled in Wallingford, married Ruth ———, May 2, 1678.

Children: 1 *Thomas*, b March 25, 1678–9, m Deborah Royce, March 2, 1705; 2 *Lydia*, b July 31, 1682, m Ebenezer Hall; 3 *Daniel*, b June 1, 1685, m Lydia Erwin, May 24, 1732.

1. THOMAS.

THOMAS MIX, son of Daniel and Ruth, married Deborah Royce, daughter of Samuel and Hannah Royce; she died Dec. 15, 1738.

Children: 4 *Abigail*, b Jan. 29, 1706; 5 *Josiah*, b Nov. 20, 1707; 6 *Thomas*, b Nov. 27, 1709; 7 *Daniel*, b April 27, 1712; 8 *Deborah*, b March 17, 1744; 9, 10 *Hannah* and *Sarah*, b Jan. 30, 1716; 11 *Stephen*, b May 8, 1718, m Rebecca ——; 12 *Enos*, b May 29, 1720; 13 *Sarah*, b April 1, 1723, m Christopher Robinson, April 14, 1757; 14 *Martha*, b July 18, 1725; 15 *Timothy*, b Dec. 28, 1727; 16 *Enos*, b May 29, 1730, d Dec. 20, 1737.

3. DANIEL.

DANIEL MIX married Lydia Erwin, May 28, 1712. He was a son of Daniel and Ruth Mix.

Children: 17 *Benjamin*, b Aug. 13, 1713; 18 *Lydia*, b Sept. 21, 1716; 19 *Ruth*, b Oct. 5, 1718; 20 *Benjamin*, b Dec. 11, 1720; 21 *Isaac*, b June 7, 1723, d; 22 *Isaac*, b Nov. 5, 1727; 23 *Daniel*, b Nov. 31, 1730; 24 *Jeremiah*, b Nov. 12, 1737.

5. JOSIAH.

JOSIAH MIX, son of Thomas and Deborah Mix, married 1st, Sybil Holt; she d Aug. 5, 1731. He married 2d, Abigail Porter, Dec. 20, 1742.

Children: 25 *Jesse*, b Oct. 22, 1731, m Deborah Parker; 26 *Eldad*, b Oct. 4, 1733; 27 *Titus*, b Dec. 4, 1735, d; 28 *Sybil*, b April 5, 1738. By 2d marriage: 29 *Titus*, b Dec. 4, 1745.

6. THOMAS.

THOMAS MIX, son of Thomas and Deborah Mix, married Ruth ——.

Children: 30 *Samuel*, b Feb. 3, 1740; 31 *Thomas*, b Aug. 12, 1745; 32 *Enos*, b Feb. 2, 1747; 33 *John*, b Aug. 23, 1750, d in Wallingford; 34 *Amos*, b Dec. 2, 1753.

11. STEPHEN.

STEPHEN MIX married Rebecca ——.

Children: 35 *Rebecca*, b May 13, 1747; 36 *Stephen*, b Nov. 2, 1748; 37 *Sarah*, b Dec. 31, 1749.

25. JESSE.

JESSE MIX married Deborah Parker, Nov. 22, 1753.

Children: 38 *Ruth*, b Sept. 15, 1754; 39 *Josiah*, b Aug. 22, 1755, m 1st, Mindwell Royce, 2d, Keziah Royce.

THEOPHILUS.

THEOPHILUS and Damaris Mix were married Jan. 17, 1729. He died in Meriden July 3, 1750, ae. 53 years.

Children: 40 *Moses*, b Jan. 3, 1730, died Feb 14, 1730; 41 *Mary*, b April 3, 1731; 42 *Sarah*, b Aug. 26, 1732; 43 *Mary*, b Aug. 4, 1734, d; 44 *Mary*, b Aug., 1735, d Sept. 3, 1735; 45 *Eber*.

39. JOSIAH.

JOSIAH MIX was twice married, 1st to Mindwell Royce, Aug. 17, 1777. She died in 1802. He married her sister Keziah Royce, Jan. 2, 1803. He formerly owned and occupied the house, late the residence of Harley Morse, at Yalesville. In 1816, he, with his family, removed to Ohio and settled at Atwater. He died at Rootstown, Ohio, in his 91st year. His wife Keziah died at Atwater, Ohio, ae. 82 yrs.

Children: 46 *James*, b June 7, 1778, m Miss Curtis; 47 *Josiah*, b Sept. 15, 1779, m Sarah Mattoon, d Feb. 4, 1867; 48 *Sarah*, b June 7, 1782, m Joseph Rice, d in 1818; 49 *Mindwell*, b June 1, 1784; 50 *Rebecca*, b May 1, 1787, m 1st, Joseph Hull, 2d, Joseph Parker, d in Wallingford; 51 *Stephen*, b Feb. 14, 1790, m Polly Owens, d Jan. 10, 1832; 52

Amanda, b April 13, 1792, m Earl Hawkins, Oct. 24, 1823; 53 *Julia*, d June 10, 1801; 54 *Phebe*, b Feb. 7, 1799, m James Webber, March 1, 1827, is living in Atwater, Ohio. By 2d marriage: 55 *Julia*, b Feb. 4, 1804, m Chauncey Andrews; 56 *Emeline*, b March 14, 1805, m John B. Whittelsey, Oct. 15, 1827, d Sept. 19, 1863; 57 *Samuel*, b Feb. 23, 1807, m Jane Case, is living at Rootstown, Ohio; 58 *Lucy*, b Feb. 8, 1809, m Dr. L. W. Trask.

JOHN.

JOHN MIX married Elizabeth ———, and settled on the North Farms in Wallingford, as a blacksmith. He raised a large family of sons who learned their trades of him. He died Oct. 3, 1821, ae. 75 years. Mrs. Elizabeth died Sept. 7, 1845, ae. 81 years.

Children: 59 *John*, b 1784, m Olive Ives; 60 *Titus*, b 1787, d Aug. 31, 1833, ae. 46; 61 *Eli*, b 1802, d Dec. 16, 1848, ae. 46; 62 *Elias*, d in Prospect; 63 *William*, died at Cheshire, was a miller at Hough's Mills; 64 *Thomas*, m a daughter of Abel Sanford.

59. JOHN.

JOHN MIX married Olive Ives of Wallingford. He was a blacksmith at Yalesville or Tyler's Mills, for several years. He died April 5, 1849, ae. 65 years.

Children: 65 *Joel;* 66 *John*, m —— Barnes, residence Cheshire; 67 *Butler*, d unmarried at Prospect; 68 *Garry I.*, is a manufacturer at Yalesville, Conn.; 69 *William*, resides in New Haven; 70 *Erwin*, resides in Cheshire; 71 *Olive;* 72 *Sylvia*, m William Haywood, and resides at Brooklyn, N. Y.

60. TITUS.

TITUS MIX, son of John and Elizabeth, was a blacksmith in the southeastern part of Meriden, and was at one time celebrated as a plough-maker.

Child: 73 *Titus Mix*, lives in Cheshire.

DANIEL.

DANIEL and Ruth Mix were in Wallingford as early as 1667. The name of his 2d wife was Deborah ——.

Children by 1st marriage: 74 *Thomas*, b March 25, 1678; 75 *Lydia*, b July 22, 1682; 76 *Daniel*, b July 1, 1684, m Lydia ——, May 28, 1712. By 2d marriage: 77 *Daniel*, b April 2, 1702; 78 *Abigail*, b Jan. 29, 1706; 79 *Josiah*, b Nov. 20, 1707; 80 *Thomas*, b Nov. 27, 1709.

76. DANIEL.

DANIEL MIX m Lydia ——.

Children: 81 *Deborah*, b March 17, 1714; 82 *Hannah*, b Jan. 20, 1716; 83 *Enos*, b March 29, 1720, d Dec. 20, 1737; 84 *Sarah*, b April 21, 1723; 85 *Isaac*, b Nov. 5, 1724; 86 *Martha*, b July 18, 1725; 87 *Joanna*, b March 13, 1726; 88 *Timothy*, b Dec. 28, 1727; 89 *Daniel*, b March 31, 1730.

THEOPHILUS.

THEOPHILUS MIX married Damaris ——.

Children: 90 *Moses*, b Jan. 3, 1730; 91 *Mary*, b Aug. 4, 1733; 92 *Eben*, b Sept. 3, 1735.

MOSS.[1]

JOHN.

JOHN MOSS, the ancestor of all who bear the name in these parts, was in New Haven as early as 1645, and perhaps before that date. He was a prominent man there, frequently representing the people in the General Court. As early as 1667, we find him in what is now Wallingford, perambulating the country in that region for the purpose of settling a village there. In 1670, at the age of 67 years, we find him exerting himself before the General Court at Hartford, to procure an act of incorporation, changing the name of the village to that of Wallingford, which was carried into effect the 12th day of May, 1670. At this time he was a member of the General Court from New Haven. Afterwards he was frequently a member of said Court, as a representative from Wallingford. He was a very active member of the company,

1 For collateral branches, see Savage's Gen. Dict., III. 246, 247.

and a leader among the settlers, who were constantly filling up the place.

He was at first located on a lot at the south end of the village, a short distance below the present residence of Constant Webb, and adjoining his friends, John Brockett and Samuel Brown, to whom was assigned the lot on which the Beach house now stands. Failing to settle on it within the time limited, his title was forfeited, and the committee to whom such matters were referred, gave it to John Moss Jr., and the same remained in the possession of his heirs and descendants, until the death of the late Ebenezer Morse.

John Moss sen. died in 1707, at the advanced age of 103 years.

His sons, 1 *Mercy*, and 2 *John*, were among the early settlers of Wallingford.

MERCY.

MERCY MOSS, son of John the emigrant, married and settled in New Haven; was for a time in Wallingford.

Child: 3 *John*, b Jan. 7, 1677.

2. JOHN.

JOHN MOSS Jr., son of John the emigrant, m Martha Lathrop, 1677. She died Sept. 21, 1719, and he died March 31, 1717. He settled on the Moses Y. Beach lot, and built a house upon it, in which I suppose he died.

Children: 4 *Mary*, b Jan. 7, 1677; 5 *Esther*, b Jan. 5, 1678; 6 Dea. *Samuel*, b Nov. 18, 1680, m Susannah Hall, Dec. 15, 1703; 7 *John*, b Nov. 10, 1682, m Elizabeth Hall, Feb. 25, 1708; 8 *Martha*, b Dec. 22, 1684; 9 *Solomon*, b July 9, 1690, m Ruth Peck, Jan. 28, 1714; 10 *Isaac*, b July 6, 1692, m Hannah Royce, May 2, 1717; 11 *Mary*, b July 23, 1694, m Solomon Munson, June 28, 1714; 12 *Israel*, b Dec. 31, 1696, m Lydia ——; 13 *Benjamin*, b Feb. 10, 1702, m Abigail ——.

6. SAMUEL.

DEA. SAMUEL MOSS, son of John and Martha Lathrop Moss, married Susannah Hall, Dec. 15, 1703. He died July

29, 1765, ae. 85 yrs.; she died March 4, 1766, ae. 83 yrs.

Children: 14 *Theophilus*, b Oct. 24, 1704, m Ruth Bunny; 15 *Martha*, b June 7, 1706; 16 *Susannah*, b Dec. 5, 1708; 17 *Samuel*, b April 4, 1711, m Hannah ———; 18 *Esther*, b July 30, 1713; 19 *Isaac*, b Dec. 5, 1715, m Hannah ———, 2d, Keziah Bowers; 20 *Sarah*, b Feb. 10, 1718; 21 *Isaiah*, b Oct. 16, 1720; 22 *Bethiah*, b March 2, 1723.

7. JOHN.

JOHN MOSS, son of John and Martha Moss, married Elizabeth ———. She died Jan. 27, 1754; he died May 14, 1755.

Children: 23 *Hannah*, b Nov. 11, 1709; 24 *Elizabeth*, b Oct. 6, 1710; 25 *Samuel*, b April 4, 1711, m Mary ———; 26 *Joseph*, b Feb. 9, 1714, m Lydia Jones, Feb. 4, 1735; 27 *Mary*, b April 22, 1716; 28 *John*, b Nov. 14, 1720; 29 *Levi*, b Sept. 30, 1722; 30 *Eunice*, b Feb. 6, 1728; 31 *Thankful*, b April 26, 1729.

9. SOLOMON.

SOLOMON MOSS, son of John and Martha Moss, married Ruth Peck. She died March 29, 1728. He married Sarah ———.

Children by 1st marriage: 32 *Martha*, b June 7, 1706; 33 *Susannah*, b Dec. 5, 1708; 34 *Daniel*, b May 15, 1716; 35 *Daniel*, b Oct. 28, 1717, m Mary Watts, Oct. 3, 1737; 36 *Abigail*, b March 7, 1718; 37 *Solomon*, b Oct. 31, 1719, m Sarah ———; 38 *Ruth*, b Aug. 5, 1721; 39 *Martha*, b Sept. 30, 1723; 40 *Abigail*, b July 9, 1729. Children by 2d marriage: 41 *Lois*, b Jan. 7, 1730; 42 *Jonathan*, b Feb. 8, 1731; 43 *Sarah*, b Nov. 28, 1734.

10. ISAAC.

ISAAC MOSS, son of John and Martha Moss, married Hannah Royce, May 2, 1717.

Children: 44 *Heman*, b July 21, 1718, d May 9, 1721; 45 *Hannah*, b March 7, 1722; 46 *Orzel;* 47 *Jesse*, b March 10, 1729; 48 *Elihu*, b May 25, 1731; 49 *Mehitable*, b May 9, 1735.

12. ISRAEL.

ISRAEL MOSS, son of John and Martha, married Lydia ——.

Children: 50 *Nathaniel*, b Dec. 19, 1722; 51 *Isaiah*, b Apr. 10, 1725; *Lydia*, b March, 1727; 53 *Isaiah*, b Dec. 15, 1731; 54 *Keziah*, b Dec. 9, 1734, d Jan. 20, 1737; 55 *Asahel*, b Feb. 22, 1737; 56 *Keziah*, b July 27, 1739.

13. BENJAMIN.

BENJAMIN MOSS, son of John and Martha, married Abigail ——.

Children: 57 *Abigail*, b Dec. 28, 1728; 58 *Benjamin*, b Nov. 27, 1729; 59 *Barnabas*, b Dec. 27, 1733; 60 *Timothy*, b March 17, 1736; 61 *Abigail*, b Sept. 30, 1740; 62 *Joseph*, b Dec. 17, 1742; 63 *Martha*, b Jan. 27, 1744–5; 64 *Eunice*, b Aug. 12, 1747.

17. SAMUEL.

SAMUEL MOSS, son of Samuel and Susannah Moss, married 1st, Mary Judd, May 28, 1734; she died, and he married 2d, Hannah ——, Jan. 28, 1748.

Children: 65 *Susannah*, b Oct. 20, 1735, d Feb. 1, 1747; 66 *Samuel*, b March 31, 1739; 67 *Joshua*, b Jan. 18, 1742; 68 *Sarah*, b April 30, 1745; 69 *Thomas*, b Jan. 21, 1747; 70 *Thomas*, b July 27, 1751; 71 *Mary*, b April 9, 1753; 72 *Martha*, b May 10, 1755; 73 *Bethia*, b May 21, 1757.

19. ISAAC.

ISAAC MOSS, son of Samuel and Susannah, married Hannah ——. She died March 31, 1731, ae. 40. He married 2d, Keziah Bowers, Oct. 4, 1736.

Children: 74 *Ebenezer*, b June 15, 1723; 75 *Heman*, b Jan. 2, 1727; 76 Capt. *Jesse*, b Dec. 16, 1729, d at Cheshire, March 20, 1793, ae. 64 years; 77 *Mehitable*, d May 9, 1735; 78 *Isaac*, b Nov. 5, 1734. By 2d marriage: 79 *Keziah*, b March 18, 1746.

26. JOSEPH.

JOSEPH MOSS, son of John and Elizabeth, married Lydia Jones, Feb. 4, 1735. He died at Cheshire, July 10, 1775, ae. 62 yrs.

Children: 80 *Rhoda*, b Jan. 9, 1736; 81 *Moses*, b March 18, 1738; 82 *Eliada*, b Aug. 18, 1740; 83 *Eunice*, b May 5, 1742; 84 *Hannah*, b April 9, 1745; 85 *Joseph*, b March 21, 1747; 86 *Elizabeth*, b May 31, 1750; 87 *Isaac*, b March 29, 1754; 88 *Sarah*, b March 22, 1757; 89 *Amos*, b Oct. 2, 1760.

28. JOHN.

JOHN MOSS, son of John and Elizabeth, married Lydia ——. She died and he married for second wife, Sarah ——.

Children by 1st marriage: 90 *Amasa*, b April 22, 1746; 91 *John*, b Sept. 3, 1747; 92 *Joel*, d Jan. 12, 1726; 93 *Eunice*, b Oct. 30, 1750; 94 *John*, b April 7, 1753. By 2d marriage: 95 *Sarah*; 96 *Phebe*, b May 6, 1760.

29. LEVI.

LEVI MOSS, son of John and Elizabeth, married Martha ——.

Children: 97 *Amos*, b Nov. 17, 1744; 98 *Levi*, b Nov. 16, 1746; 99 *Elizabeth*, b Dec. 3, 1748; 100 *Eunice*, b Oct. 30, 1750; 101 *John*, b Feb. 14, 1751; 102 *Martha*, b Aug. 18, 1753; 103 *Martha*, b Nov. 28, 1755; 104 *Stephen*, b Feb. 6, 1758; 105 *Hannah*, b July 24, 1760.

35. DANIEL.

DANIEL MOSS, son of Solomon and Ruth, married Mindwell ——.

Children: 106 *Chloe*, b Dec. 6, 1739; 107 *Simeon*, b Oct. 16, 1740; 108 *David*, b Sept. 30, 1742.

47. JESSE.

JESSE MOSS, son of Isaac and Hannah Moss, married Mary ——.

Children: 109 *Hannah*, b June 16, 1754; 110 *Joel*, b Dec. 17, 1755, d Nov. 22, 1756; 111 *Jesse*, b Sept. 10, 1757; 112 *Reuben*, b June 11, 1759; 113 *Job*, b April 25, 1761; 114 *Job*, b April 25, 1762.

50. NATHANIEL.

NATHANIEL MOSS, son of Israel and Lydia Moss, married Mary ———.

Children: 115 *Stephen*, b Oct. 6, 1752; 116 *Nathaniel*, b April 15, 1754; 117 *Keziah*, b May 13, 1756; 118 *Mary*, b July 19, 1758; 119 *Lydia*, b Aug. 26, 1760.

53. ISAIAH.

ISAIAH MOSS, son of Israel and Lydia Moss, married Phebe Doolittle, April 11, 1738; she died May 10, 1758.

Children: 120 *Phebe*, b June 3, 1739; 121 *Hezekiah*, b Jan. 20, 1741, d July 10, 1742; 122 *Mehitable*, b Nov. 15, 1743; 123 *Hezekiah*, b Nov. 3, 1746; 124 *Phebe*, b Aug. 18, 1752; 125 *Linus*, b March 2, 1761.

MUNSON.[1]

SAMUEL.

SAMUEL MUNSON, the first of the name in Wallingford, married Martha Bradley of New Haven, Oct. 26, 1665. She died Jan. 9, 1707. He married for his 2d wife, Mary Merriman, March 10, 1708. He was a shoemaker and tanner of leather, and owned the lot on which now stands the house of Almer I. Hall, Esq. He died in Wallingford, Nov. 24, 1741, ae. 74 years.

Children by 1st marriage: 1 *Martha*, b May 6, 1667, in New Haven; 2 *Samuel*, b Feb. 28, 1669; 3 *Thomas*, b March 12, 1670, in New Haven, d in Cheshire, Sept. 28, 1746, ae. 76; 4 *John*, b Jan. 28, 1672; 5 *Theophilus*, b Sept. 1, 1675; 6 *Joseph*, b Nov. 1, 1677; 7 *Stephen*, b Dec. 5, 1679; 8 *Caleb*, b Nov. 19, 1682, m Elizabeth ——; 9 *Joshua*, b Feb. 7, 1684. d Dec. 9, 1711; 10 *Israel*, b March 6, 1686; 11 *Solomon*, b Feb. 18, 1689, m Mary Cooley; 12 *Samuel*, b Aug. 25, 1691, m Rachel Cook; 13 *Marlo*, b Feb. 15, 1693; 14 *William*, b Oct. 13, 1695, m Rebecca ——, in 1750; 15 *Waitstill*, b Dec. 12, 1697; 16 *Eunice*, b Sept. 13, 1700; 17 *Obedience*, b Oct. 13, 1792; 18 *Katherine*, b June 3, 1704, m John Mitchell, Oct. 12, 1702. By 2d marriage: 19 *Tamar*, b Dec. 5, 1709.

---

1 Machias Centennial Celebration, 171; Savage's Gen. Dict., III. 257; Temple's Eccles. Hist. Whately, Mass., 36.

5. THEOPHILUS.

THEOPHILUS MUNSON, son of Samuel and Martha, married to Mary Moss, by Mr. Hall, June 28, 1714.

Child: 20, *Eliasaph*, b Nov. 17, 1719.

6. JOSEPH.

JOSEPH MUNSON, son of Samuel and Martha Munson, married Margery Hitchcock, March 10, 1699.

Children: 21 *Abel*, b Jan. 10, 1701, m Sarah Peck; 22 *Abigail*, b April 3, 1704, m Ichabod Merriman, Oct. 17, 1725; 23 *Joseph*, b Dec. 21, 1705; 24 *Desire*, b Feb. 7, 1707; 25 *Thankful*, b Jan. 8, 1708; 26 *Ephraim*, b Nov. 15, 1714; 27 *Margery*, b Oct. 10, 1717; 28 *Jemima*, b March 27, 1720; 29 *Auger*, b April 7, 1725, d Dec. 17, 1726.

8. CALEB.

CALEB MUNSON, son of Samuel and Martha Munson, married Elizabeth Brewer, March 26, 1706.

Children: 30 *Keziah*, b Jan. 13, 1706; 31 *Caleb*, b Aug. 19, 1709, m Abigail Brockett, April 23, 1735; 32 *Elizabeth*, b March 31, 1717; 33 *Merriam*, b April 12, 1720.

9. JOSHUA.

JOSHUA MUNSON, son of Samuel and Martha Munson, married Katharine, daughter of Rev. Samuel Street, Dec. 20, 1710. He died Dec. 9, 1711.

Children: 34 *Joshua*, b Aug. 2, 1710; 35 *Mary*, b March 2, 1712.

11. SOLOMON.

SOLOMON MUNSON, son of Samuel and Martha Munson, married Mary Moss, June 28, 1714; m Sarah Peck, June 14, 1753.

Children: 36 *Martha*, b Sept. 14, 1715; 37 *Samuel*, b Sept. 15, 1717; 38 *Elizabeth*, b Nov. 17, 1719. By 2d marriage: 39 *Jonathan*, b June 30, 1756; 40 *Eunice*, b Nov. 19, 1754; 41 *Sarah*, b Dec. 11, 1760.

12. SAMUEL.

SAMUEL MUNSON, son of Samuel and Martha, married

Mary Merriman, March 10, 1708. She died Nov. 28, 1755. He died Nov. 23, 1741.

Children: 42 *Samuel*, b Feb. 5, 1709; 43 *Merriman*, b Nov. 30, 1710; 44 *Mamre*, b Dec. 16, 1712; 45 *Lent*, b Mar. 6, 1714.

14. WILLIAM.

William Munson, son of Samuel and Martha, married Rebecca ——, in 1750.

Children: 46 *Martha*, b April 2, 1729, m Ambrose Doolittle; 47 *William*, b July 5, 1731; 48 *Eunice*, b Aug. 15, 1733; 49 *Peter*, b Nov. 22, 1735, d at Cheshire in 1833, ae. 98 yrs.; 50 *Hannah*, b Sept 6, 1737; 51 *George*, b Oct. 7, 1739; 52 *Samuel;* 53 *Amasa*, b Jan. 27, 1741.

15. WAITSTILL.

Waitstill Munson, son of Daniel and Martha, married Phebe Merriman, Dec. 10, 1719.

Children: 54 *Reuben*, b May 9, 1721; 55 *Hannah*, b Feb. 20, 1723; 56 *Samuel*, b Dec. 7, 1724; 57 *Phebe*, b Jan. 14, 1726; 58 *Solomon*, b March 19, 1728, m Sarah Peck, June 14, 1753; 59 *Waitstill*, b Nov. 24, 1729; 60 *Mamre*, b Jan. 20, 1734, m Timothy Carrington, Sept. 26, 1751; 61 *Martha*, b June 11, 1738.

21. ABEL.

Abel Munson, son of Joseph and Margery, married Sarah Peck, Nov. 7, 1728.

Children: 62 *Mary*, b May 2, 1732, m Joseph Doolittle, March 11, 1756; 63 *Titus*, b July 5, 1734; 64 *Lud*, b May 5, 1736; 65 *Levi*, b Aug. 29, 1738; 66 *Sarah*, b Sept. 6, 1740; 67 *Nathaniel*, b Oct. 20, 1742; 68 *Abigail*, b Sept. 2, 1744; 69 *Margery*, b Nov. 3, 1746; 70 *Lydia*, b Oct., 1748; 71 *Abel*, b Jan 3, 1749; 72 *Joseph*, b Nov. 16, 1751.

30. CALEB.

Caleb Munson, son of Caleb and Elizabeth Munson, married Abigail Brockett, April 3, 1735. He died July 25, 1747.

Children: 73 *Mabel*, b June 2, 1730; 74 *Abner*, b March 2, 1736; 75 *Harmon*, b Oct. 28, 1738; 76 *Caleb*, b March 13, 1741; 77 *Cornelius*, b April 16, 1742; 78 *Benjamin*, b Aug. 23, 1744.

33. JOSHUA.

JOSHUA MUNSON, son of Joshua and Katherine Munson, married Anna ———.

Children: 79 *Joshua*, b Feb. 4, 1750; 80 *Elizabeth*, b Feb. 29, 1752; 81 *Joshua*, b Aug. 2, 1754; 82 *Lucy*, b Feb. 3, 1757; 83 *Anna*, b June 28, 1760.

42. MERRIMAN.

DEA. MERRIMAN MUNSON, son of Samuel and Mary Munson, married 1st, Esther ———. She died April 6, 1757; he m 2d, Thankful Peck, June 23, 1758.

Children: 84 *Sarah*, b Dec. 16, 1734; 85 *Esther*, b March 25, 1740; 86 *Samuel*, b Dec. 8, 1741; 87 *Mamre*, b Aug. 12, 1745, d Sept. 17, 1745. By 2d marriage: 88 *Sarah*, b Oct. 7, 1758.

44. LENT.

LENT MUNSON, son of Samuel and Mary Munson, married Mary ———.

Children: 89 *Mamre*, b Dec. 9, 1749, d Aug. 31, 1751; 90 *John*, b Aug. 25, 1754; 91 *Luce*, b Feb. 14, 1755; 92 *Mary*, b Sept. 29, 1756.

46. WILLIAM.

WILLIAM MUNSON, son of William and Rebecca, married Phebe ———.

Children: 93 *Medad*, b Aug. 31, 1731; 94 *Martha*, b Jan. 16, 1740.

48. PETER.

PETER MUNSON, son of William and Rebecca, married and settled in Cheshire, where he died ae. 92 years.

Children: 95 *Waitstill*, d in New York a Methodist minister, left numerous descendants; 96 *Reuben*, d in N. York; 97 *Levi*, d in Cheshire, Conn.

53. REUBEN.

REUBEN MUNSON, son of Waitstill and Phebe, married Mary Chittenden, Dec. 21, 1741.

Children: 98 *Stephen*, b Sept. 23, 1742; 99 *Moses*, b Sept. 24, 1744; 100 *Reuben*, b Dec. 22, 1746.

57. SOLOMON.

SOLOMON MUNSON, son of Waitstill and Phebe, married Sarah ——.

Children: 101 *Eunice*, b Nov. 19, 1754; 102 *Jonathan*, b June 3, 1756.

58. WAITSTILL.

WAITSTILL MUNSON, son of Waitstill and Phebe, married ——.

Children: 103 *Martha*, b June 11, 1738; 104 *Zerah*, was a shoemaker; 105 *Hunn*.

62. TITUS.

TITUS MUNSON, son of Abel and Sarah, married Lydia Lindsley, Sept. 22, 1759.

Child: 106 *Irene*, b March 9, 1758.

92. REUBEN.

REUBEN MUNSON, son of Peter and Rebecca Munson, married and settled in the city of New York, and became a wealthy manufacturer of combs. He had a large family of children, among whom were William and others whose names I have not learned.

96. LEVI.

LEVI MUNSON, son of Peter and ——, married Tenny Brooks of Cheshire, and settled on the old homestead of his father, about a mile and a half north of the village of Cheshire, where he died.

Children: 107 *Levi*; 108 *Abbey*, m Rier Bristol of Cheshire; 109 ——; 110 *Benjamin F.*, m 1st, Abigail Atkins, 2d, Anna Cook; 111 *Truman*, m W. Hitchcock.

98. MOSES.

MOSES MUNSON, son of Reuben and Mary, married Phebe ——.

Children: 112 *John*, b Aug. 2, 1740; 113 *Thomas E.*, b April 5, 1742; 114 *Margaretta*, b April 14, 1744; 115 *Caleb*, b May 22, 1746; 116 *Hannah*, b May 17, 1748; 117 *Moses*, b Aug. 13, 1750.

EBENEZER.

EBENEZER and Abigail Munson.

Children: 118 *Thomas*, b Oct. 24, 1741; 119 *Lydia*, b Jan. 30, 1745; 120 *Elizabeth*, b Jan. 13, 1746; 121 *Patience*, b Aug. 31, 1749; 122 *Jesse*, b July 5, 1751; 123 *John*, b Dec. 3, 1752.

OBADIAH.

OBADIAH MUNSON married 1st, Rachel Tyler, Feb. 28, 1753, 2d, Mary Williams, Oct. 15, 1755.

Children: 124 *Barnabas*, b Sept. 24, 1754; 125 *Wilmot*, b July 23, 1755; 126 *Lydia*, b Aug. 11, 1756; 127 *Hannah*, b Jan. 12, 1757; 128 *Stephen*, b Sept. 10, 1759; 129 *Daniel*, b March 23, 1761.

129. DAVID.

DAVID and Sarah Munson.

Children: 130 *David*, b Jan. 23, 1741; 131 *Amos*, b Oct. 13, 1745.

WALTER.

WALTER MUNSON married Phebe ——.

Child: 132 *Martha*, d Jan. 26, 1740.

ELIASAPH.

ELIASAPH MUNSON married Rebecca ——, and settled on a farm on the west side of the river in Wallingford. He died Jan. 1, 1826, ae. 75. Mrs. Rebecca died Aug. 9, 1849, ae. 90 years.

Children: 132 *Chauncey*; 133 *Rachel*, m John B. Johnson; 134 *Sarah*, m Billious Cook.

NOYES.[1]

JAMES.

REV. JAMES NOYES came from England in 1634, and is the ancestor of the Noyes family in Connecticut. He was born in 1608, in Choulderton, Wiltshire, England. His father was a minister of that place, and was a very learned man. He came to this country because he could not comply with the ceremonies of the Church of England. He was married to Miss Sarah Brown of Southampton, not long before he came to this country, which was in 1634. He was first called to preach in Mystic, and continued there nearly a year. Afterward he settled in Newbury, Mass., and was pastor of the church in that place for more than twenty years. He died Oct. 22, 1656, in the 48th year of his age. He had six sons and two daughters, all of whom lived to be married, and had children. Three of his sons graduated at Harvard College, and settled in the ministry.

James was pastor of a church in Stonington, Conn. Moses settled in Lyme, Conn., and died 1729, in his 86th year, after having resided with his people 60 years. Nicholas, brother of Rev. James, settled in Salem, Mass.

JAMES.

REV. JAMES NOYES of Stonington, married Dorothy Stanton, Sept. 11, 1674. He was one of the founders and first trustees of Yale College; was pastor of the church in Stonington 50 years. He died Dec. 30, 1719–20, æ. 80 yrs.

Children: 1 *James*, born in England, his sons were John, b 1619, d in Roxbury, Mass., 1682, and Robert, who settled

---

1 For collateral branches, see Coffin's Hist. Newbury, Mass., 312; Hobart's Hist. Abingdon, Mass., 423–6; Journals of Smith and Dean of Portland, Me., 158; Kingman's Hist. North Bridgewater, Mass., 582–4; Noyes' Gen. of Noyes Family; Poor's Hist. and Gen. Researches, 119, 120, 136–40, 168, 169; Savage's Gen. Dict., III. 296–299; Ward's Hist. Shrewsbury, Mass., 388–90; Wyman's Hunt Family Gen., 119, 120; also p. 291 of this history.

in Roxbury, m Sarah Lynde; 2 *Thomas;* 3 *John;* 4 *Joseph,* m Abigail Pierrepont; 5 *Moses;* 6 *Dolly.*

3. JOHN.

JOHN NOYES, son of Rev. James of Stonington, married Mary Fish, at Stonington, Nov. 16, 1758.

Children: 8 *Rebecca,* b Nov. 22, 1759, d at Stonington, May 14, 1760; 9 *Joseph,* b Feb. 14, 1761, m —— Burr; 10 *John,* b Aug. 27, 1762, m —— Skidmore; 11 *James,* b Aug. 14, 1764, m Anna Holbrook; 12 *Mary,* b June 21, 1766, d Aug., 1770; 13 *Anna.*

Mary, the wid. of John Noyes, married 2d, Gen. Gold S. Silliman of Fairfield, Conn., in 1775, and had two children by her second marriage: Gold S. Silliman, Esq., lawyer, of Brooklyn, N. Y., and the late Prof. Benjamin Silliman of Yale College.

4. JOSEPH.

REV. JOSEPH NOYES, son of Rev. James of Stonington, was born in 1688, graduated in Yale College in 1709. After receiving his first degree, being then about 22 years of age, he became tutor in Yale College, and served four years in that office. He was ordained and installed over the church in New Haven, July, 1716. He married Nov. 6, 1716, Miss Abigail Pierrepont, dau. of his predecessor, Rev. James Pierrepont. None of their children lived to be married except one son and two daughters, viz.: John, Abigail, who married Thomas Darling, Esq., of New Haven, and Sarah, who married Col. Chester, of Wethersfield, Conn. He died June 16, 1761, æ. 73 yrs.

7. JOHN.

REV. JOHN NOYES, son of Rev. Joseph, graduated at Yale College in 1756, and was licensed to preach, May 31, 1757. He died Nov. 5, 1767, æ. 32 yrs.

10. JOHN.

REV. JOHN NOYES, son of Rev. John Noyes, was born Aug. 27, 1760, graduated at Yale College, Sept., 1779, and was licensed to preach, in Oct., 1783, by the Western Association of Fairfield Co., Conn. He was ordained and installed at Northfield parish, town of Weston, Fairfield Co., Conn., May 30, 1786. He married Eunice Sherwood, March 8, 1786.

Children: 14 *Samuel Sherwood*, b May 20, 1787; 15 *Mary*, b Nov. 3, 1788; 16 *John*, b May 11, 1788; 17 *William*, b May 23, 1792; 18 *Ebenezer*, b March 27, 1794; 19 *Benjamin*, b Feb. 5, 1796, d April 21, 1815; 20 *Charles*, b June 23, 1798, d July 9, 1821; 21 *Eunice*, b Aug. 21, 1800, d Feb. 13, 1804; 22 *Burr*, b Aug. 31, 1803, d July 3, 1830.

Mrs. Eunice, wife of Rev. John Noyes, died March 25, 1824, æ. 64 yrs. Rev. John Noyes married 2d, Fanny Swann of Stonington, Conn., Oct. 16, 1827; she was born July 9, 1776. He died in Northfield, May 15, 1846, æ. nearly 84 yrs. He had written the discourse for the 60th anniversary of his ministry, and it was to have been delivered by him two weeks from the Sabbath on which he was interred.

14. SAMUEL.

SAMUEL SHERWOOD, son of Rev. John Noyes, born May 20, 1787, married Esther Chapman, who was born June 5, 1790, on Nov. 3, 1812.

Children: 23 *Samuel*, b March 12, 1815; 24 *Benjamin*, b Nov. 10, 1816; 25 *William*, b Dec. 10, 1818; 26 *Julia Chapman*, b July 25, 1820; 27 *Charles*, b Aug. 7, 1822, d March 12, 1857; 28 *Josiah Chapman*, b Jan. 22, 1824, d May 22, 1849; 29 *John*, b April 11, 1826, d Oct. 22, 1853; 30 *Elizabeth*, b May 14, 1828; 31 *James Burr*, b Sept. 17, 1830, d Dec. 4, 1851.

Dr. Samuel S. Noyes studied medicine and was licensed to practice in 1810. He settled in New Canaan, Fairfield Co., in 1811.

22. BURR.

REV. BURR NOYES, son of Rev. John Noyes, graduated at Yale College, Sept., 1824. He settled at Chester, Saybrook, Conn., was very successful in his profession, and won the confidence and esteem of the people. He died July 2, 1830.

9. JOSEPH.

JOSEPH NOYES ESQ., son of Rev. John Noyes, was born Feb. 14, 1761, died in 1817, ae. 56 yrs. He was married to Amelia Burr, Dec. 11, 1783. She was born Dec. 7, 1764, and died May 7, 1802; he married Lucy Norton, May 24, 1804; she died July 12, 1850, ae. 79 yrs.

Children: 32 *Joseph Fish*, b Oct. 9, 1784; 33 *John Noyes*, b Aug. 7, 1786; 34 *James*, b Oct. 21, 1788; 35 *Samuel*, b Sept. 15, 1791; 36 *Rebecca*, b March 3, 1794. By 2d marriage: 37 *Benjamin Silliman*, b May 5, 1805; 38 *Joseph Chester*, b Aug. 5, 1808; 39 *Thomas Norton*, b Oct. 3, 1799; 40 *Harriet Norton*, b Oct. 5, 1796; 41 *Mary Ann*, b Sept. 7, 1813.

11. JAMES.

REV. JAMES NOYES, son of Rev. John Noyes, was born Aug. 4, 1764, and died in Wallingford, Feb. 18, 1844, in the 80th year of his age, being the oldest minister in the county of New Haven. He married Anna Holbrook, of Derby, Conn., Jan. 22, 1769. She died Jan. 1, 1838, ae. 69 yrs.

Children: 42 *Catharine*, b Feb. 1, 1789, d March 19, 1811; 43 *Anna*, b Feb. 1, 1790; 44 *James*, b May 23, 1792, d Oct. 26, 1794; 45 *Mary*, b May 13, 1794, d April 23, 1844; 46 *Sally*, b Feb. 11, 1796, d Jan. 12, 1834; 47 *James*, b Jan. 27, 1708, d 1869, in East Haddam; 48 *Cornelia*, b March 23, 1800, d Jan. 16, 1835; 49 *Esther*, b March 21, 1802, d Oct. 16, 1839; 50 *Abigail*, b May 13, 1804, d April 24, 1844; 51 *Eunice*, b March 12, 1806, d Oct 3, 1824; 52 *Joseph Fish*, b July 3, 1808; 53 *John*, b July 15, 1810, d Oct. 11, 1810; 54 *Catharine*, b May 27, 1812, d Jan. 27, 1833; 55 *Harriet*, b Aug. 11, 1814.

PARKER.[1]

Parker has always been a common name in New England. We find Abraham, Amariah, Edmund, George, Jacob, James,

---

1 For collateral branches, see Abbott's Hist. Andover, Mass., 20; Bar-

Joseph, Matthew, Nicholas, Robert, Thomas, two or more Williams, and as many Johns, appearing in nearly as many of the different settlements in Massachusetts and Connecticut, at an early day. Abraham Parker was the first of the family in this country. It is supposed that he came from Wiltshire, England. He first settled in Woburn, Mass., where he married Rose Whitlock, Nov. 18, 1644.

1. WILLIAM.

WILLIAM PARKER was early in Hartford and Saybrook, and had three children: 2 *William;* 3 *Ralph*, died in 1690; 4 *John*, who removed to New Haven; he had 5 *John*, b Oct. 8, 1648, m Nov. 8, 1670, Hannah, dau. of Wm. Bassett; 6 *Mary*, b April 27, 1649, m John Hall, 1666; 7 *Hope*, b May 26, 1650, m Samuel Cook, May 2, 1677; 8 *Lydia*, b May 26, 1652–3, m John Thomas, Jan. 12, 1671; 9 *Joseph*, m Hannah Gilbert, 1673.

5. JOHN.

JOHN PARKER and HANNAH his wife were among the early planters in Wallingford, and settled at Parker's farms, about two miles west of the village, which first gave the name to that locality. He was an active business man, and did much in advancing the interests of the settlement. He died in 1711. Hannah his wife died June 7, 1726.

---

ry's Hist. Framingham, Mass., 349–51; Bouton's Hist. Concord, N. H., 682; Bridgman's Granary Burial Ground, 136–44; Butler's Hist., Groton, Mass., 421, 476,494; Caulkins' Hist. of New London, Conn., 306; Deane's Hist. Scituate, Mass., 320; Freeman's Hist. Cape Cod, Mass., II. 438, 466, 472, 642; Hill's Hist. Mason, N. H., 205; Howell's Hist. Southampton, L. I., 260; Hudson's Hist. Lexington, Mass., 169–76; Jackson's Hist. Newton, Mass., 375–81; Kidder's Hist. New Ipswich, N. H., 417–19; Littell's Passaic Valley Gen., 311; Morse's Gen. Reg. of Sherborn and Holliston, Mass., 185; Morse's Memorial of Morses, Appendix, No. 54; N. E. Hist. & Gen. Reg., IV. 139, VI. 375, 376, XVI. 41, 91–4; Poor's Hist. & Gen. Researches, 113–15, 124–8; Savage's Gen. Dict., III. 349–58; Sewall's Hist. Woburn, Mass., 628; Shattuck's Memorial, 375–7; Smith's Hist. Delaware Co., Penn., 490; Stoddard's Gen. of Stoddard Family, ed. 1865, 14, 38, 39, 63–8; Temple's Eccles. Hist. Whately, Mass., 29; Ward's Hist. Shrewsbury, Mass., 400–4.

Children: 10 *Hannah*, b Aug. 20, 1671, m Wm. Andrews, Jan. 12, 1692; 11 *Elizabeth*, m Josiah Royce, March 24, 1693; 12 *John*, b March 26, 1675, m Mary Kibbe of Springfield, Nov. 1, 1699; 13 *Rachel*, b June 16, 1680, m Thomas Relzea of New Haven, 1700; 14 *Joseph*, m Sarah Curtis, June 7, 1705; 15 *Eliphalet*, m Hannah Beach, Aug. 5, 1708; 16 *Samuel*, m Sarah Goodsell of Middletown, July 16, 1713; 17 *Edward*, b 1692, m Jerusha ——, he d Oct. 21, 1776, she d Dec. 27, 1745; 18 *Mary*, m Joseph Clark, Nov. 27, 1707; 19 *Abigail*, b March 3, 1710, m Joseph Bradley Dec. 8, 1765.

12. JOHN.

JOHN, son of John and Hannah Parker, married 1st, Mary Kibbe, 2d Sarah ——.

Children by 1st marriage: 20 *Rachel*, b Jan. 6, 1701–2; 21 *John*, b Oct., 1703, m Deborah, dau. of Thomas Matthews, Oct. 17, 1727; 22 *Aaron*, b July 8, 1704, d Jan. 12, 1727; 23 *Mary*, b Feb. 8, 1736; 24 *Elisha*, b Oct. 25, 1708, m Susanna Tuttle, Feb. 28, 1728; 25 *Abigail*, b March 3, 1710, m Robert Martin, July 15, 1734; 26 *Elizabeth*, b June 3, 1716; 27 *Lois*, b July 20, 1718, m Thomas, son of Timothy Beach, Nov. 5, 1740; 28 *Isaac*, b 1720, m Hannah, dau. of Timothy Beach, Aug. 11, 1742; 29 ——, d April 27, 1773, m Lois Royce. By 2d marriage: 30 *Sarah*, b July 22, 1739.

14. JOSEPH.

JOSEPH, son of John and Hannah Parker, married Sarah Curtis.

Children: 31 *Joseph*, b Aug. 6, 1706, d July 25, 1712; 32 *Joseph*, b July 25, 1707; 33 *Andrew*, m Susanna Blakeslee; 34 *Thomas*, b June 7, 1709, m Abigail Dutton and settled in Waterbury, Conn., in 1756; 35 *Hannah*, b Aug. 30, 1700; 36 *Ebenezer*, b March 5, 1713, m Lydia Barnes, April 1, 1735; 37 *Joseph*, b April 3, 1716, m 1st, Lucy Parmalee, Feb. 23, 1742, 2d, Mary Andrews, March 30, 1758; 38 *Ralph*, b Jan. 9, 1718, went to Vermont; 39 *Waitstill*, b July 24, 1721, m Jemima, dau. of Joseph Munson, Oct, 27, 1742; 40 *Sarah*, b

Oct. 18, 1725, m Asaph, son of Samuel Cook, Jan. 15, 1744–5.

15. ELIPHALET.

ELIPHALET, son of John and Hannah Parker, married Hannah Beach ; he died in 1757, ae. 76 yrs.

Children: 41 *Eliada*, b April 2, 1710, d March 24, 1712 ; 42 *Eliada*, b April 22, 1712, m Sarah Curtis Dec. 21, 1732 ; 43 *Chestina*, b April 18, 1714, m Peter Curtis Nov. 22, 1732 ; 44 *Aaron*, b Feb. 17, 1716, m Sarah Martin, March 11, 1756 ; 45 *Gamaliel*, b June 6, 1718, d Dec. 3, 1799, he m Elizabeth —— ; 46 *Didymus*, b Jan. 14, 1721, m Phebe, daughter of John Johnson, Dec. 22, 1742 ; 47 *Eliphalet*, b Jan. 19, 1721, m Thankful Hitchcock, May 21, 1745 ; 48 *Joanna*, b July 8, 1723, m Amos Bristol of Cheshire, June, 1740 ; 49 *Bethuel*, b April 2, 1727, m Tabitha, daughter of Matthias Hitchcock, July 19, 1749, he d March 13, 1778 ; 50 *Benjamin*, b Feb. 12, 1729, m Mary Atwater and removed to Simsbury, Conn. ; 51 *Thankful*, m Oliver Hitchcock.

16. SAMUEL.

SAMUEL, son of John and Hannah Parker, m 1st, Lydia —— ; 2d, Sarah Goodsell, July 16, 1713 ; 3d, Mary Chamberlain, Jan. 9, 1744.

Children by 1st marriage: 52 *Thomas*, b June 7, 1709 ; 53 *Sarah*, b May 17, 1714 ; 54 *Abiah*, b Aug. 2, 1716, m Daniel, son of John Ives, Oct. 28, 1735 ; 55 *Joseph*, b Aug. 2, 1716, m Lucy Parmalee, Feb. 23, 1742–3. By 2d marriage: 56 *Abraham*, b March 24, 1720, m Damaris, daughter of William Abernathy, Sept, 9, 1747, d July 26, 1775 ; 57 *Jacob*, b April 24, 1722, m Elizabeth, daughter of John Beecher, April 26, 1749, d Sept. 24, 1767 ; 58 *Titus*, b Feb. 23, 1728. By 3d marriage: 59 *Thankful*, b Oct. 8, 1745 ; 60 *Martha*, b Sept. 10, 1749 ; 61 *Lent*, b July 8, 1752.

17. EDWARD.

EDWARD, son of John and Hannah Parker, married Jerusha ———. They settled in Cheshire parish, on what is now called Cheshire street, where she died Dec. 27, 1745.

He married 2d, Rebecca Ives, Dec. 1, 1748; she died May 23, 1762, ae. 65. He married 3d, Ruth Merriman Merwin, Sept. 30, 1762.

Children: 62 *Ralph*, b Jan. 9, 1718, m Martha, daughter of Gideon Ives, Dec. 25, 1740; 63 *Athildred*, b July 1, 1719, m Timothy Hall, Jan. 10, 1748; 63 1-2 *Edward*, b March 11, 1721, m Sarah Burroughs, Aug. 21, 1744; 64 *Joel*, b Feb. 24, 1723, m Susannah Hotchkiss, Dec. 25, 1746; 65 *Ephraim*, b Aug. 23, 1725, m Bathsheba Parsons, Nov. 11, 1747; 66 *Amos*, b Nov. 26, 1726, d Aug. 20, 1748; 67 *William*, b 1728, d May 2, 1752; 68 *Eldad*, b Sept. 14, 1731, m Thankful, daughter of Matthew Bellamy, April 24, 1755, d July 6, 1779; 69 *Joseph Merriam*, b Feb. 2, 1734, d March 21, 1734; 70 *Joseph*, b Oct. 9, 1735, m Mary Andrews, May 30, 1758.

21. JOHN.

JOHN, son of John and Mary Parker, married Deborah Matthews. He died March 28, 1749.

Children: 71 *Abiah*, d Aug. 14, 1728; 72 *John*, b Dec. 25, 1730, m Eunice Beach, June 16, 1752, and had John, b Dec. 8, 1755; 73 *Deborah*, b May 4, 1834, m Jesse, son of Josiah Mix, Nov. 26, 1753; 74 *Jesse*, b March 16, 1736, m Dorothy Spenser, Feb. 16, 1758; 75 *Reuben*, b March 12, 1738, m Hannah Chapman of Waterbury, Dec. 10, 1764; 76 *Gideon*, b July 5, 1740, m Elizabeth ——, b Nov. 11, 1743; 77 *Isaiah*, b June 14, 1746, m Susanna or Damaris Yale, Feb. 14, 1771.

24. ELISHA.

ELISHA PARKER, son of John and Mary, married Susanna Tuttle.

Children: 78 *Ruth*, b Feb. 28, 1728; 79 *Aaron*, b April 9, 1730, m Sarah, dau. of Robert Martin, March 11, 1756; 80 *Elisha*, b July 25, 1735, m Esther Spencer, Aug. 10, 1759; 81 *John*, b Sept. 17, 1739; 82 *Dan;* 83 *Damaris*, b July 16, 1743, m Enos Parker, Dec. 2, 1761; 84 *Susanna*, b Dec. 7, 1745.

28. ISAAC.

ISAAC PARKER, son of John and Mary, m. Hannah Beach.

Children: 85 *Keziah*, b Feb. 12, 1743; 86 *Lois*, b April 30, 1746; 87 *Ruth*, b July 11, 1750, m Gershom Mattoon, Dec. 5, 1776; 88 *Isaac*, b Sept. 4, 1754, m Annie Parker, March 19, 1778; 89 *Mary*, b Aug. 14, 1755, m Amos Austin, Aug. 17, 1777; 90 *Timothy*, b Aug. 14, 1757; 91 *John*, b Feb. 21, 1762; 92 *Phineas*, b July 14, 1765.

34. THOMAS.

THOMAS PARKER, son of Joseph and Sarah Curtis Parker, married Abigail Dutton, Aug. 30, 1748, and settled in Waterbury. He died in 1788.

Children: 93 *Thomas*, b April 3, 1749; 94 *Amasa*, b Feb. 28, 1751, graduate of Yale, m Thankful Andrews, Aug. 28, 1771; 95 *Peter*, b March 11, 1753, removed to the State of N. Y.; 96 *Abigail*, b Aug. 28, 1755; 97 *Abner*, removed to the State of N. Y.; 98 *Joseph*, was a physician in Litchfield Co.; 99 *Daniel*, m Miriam Curtis, Nov. 18, 1762.

36. EBENEZER.

EBENEZER PARKER, son of Joseph and Sarah Curtis Parker, married Lydia Barnes.

Children: 100 *Desire*, b June 7, 1735, m Aaron Bellamy, Dec. 20, 1753; 101 *Ebenezer*, b July 6, 1737, m Anna ——, d Dec. 11, 1762; 102 *Caleb*, b March 30, 1739; 103 *Joshua*, b April 17, 1741, m Mary, dau. of Oliver Hitchcock, Oct. 30, 1765; 104 *Jared*, b Nov. 16, 1743; 105 *Lydia*, b March 8, 1745, m Abel Parker, April 23, 1762; 106 *Stephen*, b Oct. 27, 1747; 107 *Eliakim*, b July 10, 1751, m Phebe Carrington, Feb. 20, 1775, and had Eliakim, b March 13, 1777, m 2d, wid. Lois Ives, Nov. 11, 1777, and had three children; 108 *Caleb*, b Nov. 2, 1759, m Dolly Peck, Nov. 3, 1783.

39. WAITSTILL.

WAITSTILL PARKER, son of Joseph and Sarah Curtis Parker, married 1st, Jemima Munson, 2d, Jemima Beach.

Children: 109 *Margery*, b March 20, 1743-4, d Oct. 1, 1744; 110 *Justus*, b Jan. 1, 1747-8; 111 *Margery*, b Feb. 25, 1749, m Eliada Parker, Jr. By 2d marriage: 112 *Jemima*, b

June 2, 1753; 113 *Rhoda*, b March 25, 1755. By 3d marriage: 114 *Charles*, b Aug. 21, 1760, m Charity Dibble, Oct. 21, 1784; 115 *Eunice*, b Aug. 9, 1762; 116 *Justus*, b May 23, 1764; 117 *Martha*, b April 17, 1766; 118 *Abigail*, b June 10, 1768; 119 *Sarah*, b April 2, 1771.

33. ANDREW.

ANDREW, son of Joseph and Sarah Curtis Yale Parker, married Susannah Blakeslee.

Children: 120 *Ambrose*, b March 6, 1738, m Comfort Parker, March 22, 1758; 121 *Grace*, b Dec. 10, 1739, d Dec. 11, 1739; 122 *Patience*, b Dec. 10, 1739, d Dec. 13, 1739; 123 *Zeruiah*, b Nov. 28, 1741, m David Miller, Jan. 3, 1765; 124 *Oliver*, b Nov. 20, 1743, m Lucy Parker, Dec. 3, 1764, and had Thaddeus, b Jan. 26, 1766; 125 *Ezra*, b Dec. 2, 1745; 126 *Susannah*, b Dec. 2, 1747; 127 *Rachel*, b Dec. 28, 1749; 128 *Sybil*, b Feb. 9, 1753; 129 *Jason*, b Aug. 17, 1764.

42. ELIADA.

ELIADA, son of Eliphalet and Hannah Beach Parker, married Sarah Curtis.

Children: 130 *Martha*, b July 8, 1734; 131 *Lettis*, b Sept. 18, 1736; 132 *Comfort*, b Sept. 16, 1738, m Ambrose Parker, March 22, 1758; 133 *Eliada*, b Nov. 24, 1740, d March 23, 1742; 134 *Sarah*, b Jan. 23, 1743–4; 135 *Hannah*, b Sept. 23, 1746; 136 *Patience*, b Aug. 18, 1748, m Joseph Parker, June 29, 1769; 137 *Eliada*, m Margery Parker, May 10, 1770, d Sept. 12, 1776; 138 *Phebe*, b Oct. 31, 1752; 139 *Levi*, b June 8, 1757, m Lydia Bradley, July 22, 1779.

45. GAMALIEL.

GAMALIEL, son of Eliphalet and Hannah Beach Parker, married Elizabeth ——.

Children: 140 *Abel*, b Jan. 4, 1741, m Lydia Parker, Aug. 23, 1762; 141 *Elizabeth*, b Jan. 7, 1742–3; 142 *Eunice*, b Jan. 6, 1744–5; 143 *Gamaliel*, b Dec. 9, 1745, d Oct. 29, 1765; 144 *Amos*, b Jan. 20, 1748–9; 145 *Miriam*, b Jan. 28, 1753; 146 *Gamaliel*, b Oct. 22, 1755, d Nov. 8, 1755; 147 *Gamaliel*, b

Nov. 2, 1756, m Martha Parker, May 2, 1782 ; 148 *Anna*, b Feb. 8, 1759 ; 149 *Amos*, b Dec. 11, 1761, m Mary Curtis, Dec. 5, 1785.

46. DIDYMUS.

LIEUT. DIDYMUS, son of Eliphalet and Hannah Beach Parker, married Phebe Johnson.

Children : 150 *Enos*, b March 12, 1744, m Damaris Parker, Dec. 2, 1761 ; 151 *Ichabod*, b Jan. 2, 1748–9, married Susannah Cook, Dec. 3, 1766.

47. ELIPHALET.

ELIPHALET, son of Eliphalet and Hannah Beach Parker, married Thankful Hitchcock.

Children: 152 *Valentine*, b March 5, 1745–6, d Dec. 14, 1760 ; 153 *Matthias*, b Sept. 24, 1747 ; 154 *Eliphalet*, b Jan. 22, 1754 ; 155 *Thankful*, b April 3, 1756, d Nov. 28, 1763 ; 156 *Michael*, b Oct. 15, 1758.

49. BETHUEL.

BETHUEL, son of Eliphalet and Hannah Beach Parker, married Tabitha Hitchcock.

Children : 157 *Jerusha*, b April 6, 1750, m William Smith, July 10, 1777 ; 158 *David*, b March 9, 1752, d Sept. 6, 1753 ; 159 *Olive*, b March 9, 1754, m Joseph Distance, Feb. 27, 1777 ; 160 *David*, b March 18, 1756, d Oct. 9, 1776 ; 161 *Martha*, b Dec. 12, 1757, m Gamaliel Parker, May 2, 1782 ; 162 *Joanna*, b June 18, 1760 ; 163 *Tabitha*, b Nov. 16, 1762 ; 164 *Bethuel*, b Feb. 21, 1765 ; 165 *Simon*, b April 15, 1767, d Sept. 13, 1773 ; 166 *Thankful*, b June 15, 1769 ; 167 *Asa*, b Dec. 4, 1771 ; 168 *Mary*, b Sept. 29, 1776, d Dec. 15, 1777.

55. JOSEPH.

JOSEPH, son of Samuel and Lydia Parker, married Lucy Parmalee.

Children: 169 *Esther*, b Jan. 11, 1742–3, d Feb. 8, 1744–5 ; 170 *Joseph*, b Nov. 5, 1746, m Patience Parker, June 29, 1769 ; 171 *Lucy*, b March 13, 1748–9 ; 172 *Esther*, b March 27, 1754 ; 173 *Charles*, b Feb. 26, 1756.

56. ABRAHAM.

ABRAHAM, son of Samuel and Sarah Goodsell Parker, m Damaris Abernathy.

Children: 174 *Sarah*, b July 16, 1748; 175 *Abraham*, b July 20, 1753, d May 1, 1754; 176 *Benjamin*, b May 27, 1755, m Lucinda Curtis, and had two daus., June 25, 1778; 177 *Abraham*, b Aug. 23, 1757; 178 *William*, b Dec. 19, 1759; 179 *Mehitable*, b June 30, 1762.

57. JACOB.

JACOB, son of Samuel and Sarah Goodsell Parker, married Elizabeth Beecher.

Children: 180 *Samuel*, b Jan. 10, 1749, and had Jared, b April 22, 1777; 181 *Solitary*, b Jan. 7, 1752, d Aug. 31, 1754; 182 *Elizabeth*, b May 18, 1754; 183 *Jacob*, b Jan. 13, 1756, d Sept. 17, 1756; 184 *Jacob*, b July 1, 1757; 185 *Rebecca*, b Feb. 27, 1759; 186 *James*, b March 3, 1760; 187 *Solomon*, b April 12, 1762; 188 *Adah*, b Feb. 23, 1765; 189 *Abiah*, b March 8, 1767.

62. RALPH.

RALPH, son of Edward and Jerusha Parker, m Martha Ives.

Children: 190 *Jerusha*, b Nov. 1, 1741, m Robert Roys, May 27, 1762; 191 *Ralph*, b Feb. 8, 1743-4; 192 *Medad*, b March 29, 1746; 193 *Martha*, b April 18, 1749.

63 1-2. EDWARD.

EDWARD, son of Edward and Jerusha Parker, married Sarah Burroughs.

Children: 194 *Sarah*, b in Cheshire, Aug. 28, 1745; 195 *Elizabeth*, b June 7, 1748, m Enos Clark, of Southington; 196 *William*, b June 18, 1752, m Desire Bunnel, Feb. 25, 1779; 197 *Abigail*, b July 7, 1755, m Dr. Benjamin Yale, Dec. 17, 1777; 198 *Edward*, b April 21, 1760, m Rebecca Hendrick, removed to Cazenovia, N. Y.

64. JOEL.

JOEL, son of Edward and Jerusha Parker, married Susanna Hotchkiss.

Children b in Cheshire: 199 *Alhildred*, b Sept. 17, 1747, m Asa Bronson, Feb. 5, 1772; 200 *Amos*, b Oct. 22, 1749, m Hannah Hough; 201 *Susanna*, b March 8, 1752, m Allen Bronson; 202 *Joel*, b Jan. 17, 1754; 203 *Stephen*, b Aug. 5, 1759, m 1st, Sally, dau. of Joseph Twiss, May 27, 1787, m 2d, widow Rebecca Stone, dau. of Joshua Ray, b Jan. 6, 1805, d July 1, 1846.

68. ELDAD.

ELDAD, son of Edward and Jerusha Parker, m Thankful Bellamy.

Children b in Cheshire: 204 *Phebe*, b July 23, 1756; 205 *Thankful*, b Oct. 6, 1757; 206 *Anne*, b Jan. 1, 1760, m Wm. Starke, Chenango Co., N. Y.; 207 *Thankful*, b March 8, 1762, 208 *Eldad*, b Sept. 27, 1763; 209 *Levi*, b Sept. 28, 1765; 210 *Levi*, b March 19, 1767, m Phebe Scovill; 211 *Oliver*, b March 19, 1771; *Thankful*, b May 12, 1769; *Rebecca*, b March 16, 1773, m Abisha Cowles.

70. JOSEPH.

JOSEPH, son of Edward and Jerusha Parker, married Mary Andrews.

Children, born in Cheshire: 212 *Beckey*, b March 29, 1760; 213 *Joseph Merriam*, b Oct. 10, 1762; 214 *Eldad;* 215 *Zephaniah*, b Feb. 26, 1769; 216 *Mary*, b Jan. 24, 1767.

74. JESSE.

JESSE, son of John and Deborah Matthews Parker, married Dorothy Spencer.

Children: 217 *Jesse*, b May 30, 1759; 218 *Lucy*, b Sept. 17, 1761; 219 *Jared*, b Jan. 31, 1764; 220 *Jotham*, b Feb. 2, 1767; 221 *Dorothy*, b Aug. 5, 1770.

79. AARON.

AARON, son of Elisha and Susanna Tuttle Parker, married Sarah Martin.

Children: 222 *Mamre*, b Feb. 14, 1757; 223 *Robert*, b Feb. 12, 1759; 224 *Susanna*, b Feb. 20, 1762; 225 *Abigail*, b April 1, 1764; 226 *Sally*, b March 20, 1766; 227 *Lyman*, b

April 17, 1768; 228 *Eunice*, b Jan. 11, 1771; 229 *Ruth*, b Feb. 1, 1774; 230 *Lyman*, b Feb. 30, 1776.

80. ELISHA.

ELISHA, son of Elisha and Susannah Tuttle Parker, married Esther Spencer.

Children: 231 *Elisha*, b April 28, 1761; 232 *Katherine*, b March 30, 1763; 233 *Chloe*, b Dec. 28, 1765; 234 *Asahel*, b April 2, 1768; 235 *Polly*, b March 20, 1773; 236 *Shaler*, b Aug. 28, 1775; 237 *Polly*, b Sept. 13, 1778.

101. EBENEZER.

EBENEZER, son of Ebenezer and Lydia Barnes Parker, married Anne ——.

Children: 238 *Ebenezer*, b June 4, 1762; 239 *Jabez*, b July 18, 1763; 240 *Jemima Doolittle*, b Nov. 16, 1764; 241 *Thomas*, b May 1, 1767; 242 *Ebenezer*, b May 7, 1771.

103. JOSHUA.

JOSHUA, son of Ebenezer and Lydia Barnes Parker, married Mary Hitchcock.

Children: 243 *Stephen*, b April 1, 1766; 244 *Lydia*, b May 23, 1769; 245 *Hannah*, b April 21, 1773; 246 *Chestina*, b June 20, 1777; 247 *Eber*, b March 28, 1779; 248 *Jared*, b March 22, 1781; 249, 250 *Mary* and *Miriam*, b Nov. 1, 1782.

114. CHARLES.

CHARLES, son of Waitstill and Jemima Beach Parker, married Charity Dibble.

Children: 251 *Charles Pierce*, b Dec. 1, 1785, d Feb. 25, 1788; 252 *Pierce*, b March 20, 1788; 253 *Ruth*, b Feb. 17, 1790, m Sydney Smith, Dec. 16, 1807; 254 *Nancy*, b Dec. 13, 1791; 255 *Charles*, b Jan. 27, 1797.

120. AMBROSE.

AMBROSE, son of Andrew and Susanna Blakeslee Parker, married Comfort Parker.

Children: 256 *Ambrose*, b Jan. 15, 1759; 257 *Giles*, b Sept. 15, 1760; 258 *Lydia*, b May 26, 1763; 259 *Comfort*, b May 23, 1766.

137. ELIADA.

ELIADA PARKER, son of Eliada and Sarah Curtis Parker, married Margery Parker.

Children: 260 *Munson*, b Feb. 18, 1771; 261 *Chester*, b Oct. 20, 1773; 262 *Linus*, d Feb. 9, 1776.

108. CALEB.

CALEB PARKER, son of Ebenezer and Lydia Barnes Parker, married Dolly Peck.

Children: 263 *Augustus*, b Sept. 10, 1784; 264 *Caleb*, b Jan. 30, 1787; 265 *Paulina*, b Dec. 30, 1789; 266 *Nancy*, b July 5, 1792; 267 *Juliana*, b Nov. 21, 1794.

139. LEVI.

LEVI PARKER, son of Eliada and Sarah Curtis Parker, married Lydia Bradley.

Children: 268 *Sybil*, b April 28, 1780, m Amos Peck, Sept. 22, 1799; 269 *Polly*, b Sept. 25, 1782; 270 *Eliada*, b May 31, 1784, m Elizabeth Oswald, Feb. 15, 1807; 271 *Ammi Bradley*, b July 11, 1787; 272 *Lyman*, b April 3, 1790, m Malinda Harrison, March 24, 1818; 273 *Alfred*, b Oct. 19, 1792, m Fanny ——; 274 *Belinda*, b Sept. 18, 1795; *Philo* and *Orrin*, b April 18, 1798, d April 18, 1800.

44. DANIEL.

DANIEL, son of Arnon and Sarah Martin, married Miriam, daughter of Benjamin Curtis, Nov. 18, 1762.

Children: 275 *Ruth*, b Feb. 3, 1764; 276 *Denison*, b Sept. 28, 1766; 277 *Leman*, b Dec. 21, 1768; 278 *Lucinda*, b July 24, 1771; 279 *Ruth*, b Dec. 10, 1774; 280 *Daniel*, b May 24, 1775; 281 *Ruth*, b Dec. 27, 1777; 282 *Betsey*, b July 16, 1780.

147. GAMALIEL.

GAMALIEL, son of Gamaliel and Elizabeth Parker, married Martha Parker.

Children: 283 *Joel*, b April 17, 1783; 284 *Chester*, b Aug. 19, 1784; 285 *Martha Hall*, b Aug. 20, 1786; 286 *Gamaliel*, b Sept. 13, 1788; 287 *Luroxa*, b Nov. 18, 1790; 288 *Zera*, b

July 13, 1792; 289 *Laura*, b Sept. 4, 1796; 290 *Eunice*, b Dec. 28, 1798.

150. ENOS.

ENOS, son of Didymus and Phebe Johnson Parker, married Damaris Parker.

Children: 291 *Dorcas*, b Dec. 17, 1761; 292 *Dan*, b March 18, 1764.

164. BETHUEL.

BETHUEL, son of Bethuel and Tabitha Hitchcock Parker, married Eunice ——.

Children: 293 *Bethuel Virgil*, b Oct. 1, 1796, m 1st, Polly Beach, Sept. 7, 1825, 2d, Lowly Thomas, March 30, 1835; 294 *Jason*, b Feb. 14, 1798; 295 *Rhoda*, b Sept. 29, 1800.

167. ASA.

ASA, son of Bethuel and Tabitha Hitchcock Parker, married Keziah ——.

Children: 296 *Laura*, b Feb. 13, 1796; 297 *Liverius*, b March 25, 1798; 298 *James*, b May 16, 1800; 299 *Lemuel*, b April 11, 1804; 300 *Asa*, b May 14, 1806.

170. JOSEPH.

JOSEPH, son of Joseph and Lucy Parmalee Parker, married Patience Parker.

Children: 301 *Jehiel*, b Sept. 26, 1770; 302 *Lena*, b Feb. 23, 1773; 303 *Lucy*, b Nov. 20, 1775; 304 *Sarah*; 305 *Amy*, b Oct. 16, 1780.

196. WILLIAM.

WILLIAM, son of Edward and Sarah Burroughs Parker, married Desire Bunnel.

Children: 306 *Sarah*, b Nov. 7, 1779, m Chas. T. Hill; 307 *William*, m wid. Rebecca Hull; 308 *Nancy*, m Divan Lusk; 309 *Anson*; 310 *Abigail*, m Elnathan Beach; 311 *Fanny*, m 1st, Simeon Perkins, 2d, Simeon Hersey; 312 *Marcus*, m Mehitable Mathews.

198. EDWARD.

EDWARD, son of Edward and Sarah Burroughs Parker, married Rebecca Hendrick of Cazenovia, N. Y.

Children: 313 *Chauncey*, b Oct. 9, 1786, m Lydia Atwater; 314 *Elizabeth*, b Jan. 25, 1788, d June 7, 1794; 315 *Oren*, b March 9, 1790, d Aug. 4, 1790; 316 *Oren*, b July 11, 1791, d 1812; 317 *Edward*, b Sept. 2, 1793, d June 8, 1794; 318 *Edward*, b March 15, 1795, m Philomela Hitchcock, rem. to Elyria, Ohio; 319 *Don Carlos*, b April 27, 1797, m Julia Strake; 320 *Louisa*, b June 18, 1799; 321 *Wm. Hendrick*, b Aug. 9, 1801; 322 *Abigail;* 323 *Harriet A.*, m Eliakim Hall.

203. STEPHEN.

STEPHEN, son of Joel and Susanna Hotchkiss Parker, m 1st, Sally Twiss, 2d, wid. Rebecca Stone.

Children by 1st marriage: 324 *Clarissa*, b June 10, 1788, d May 27, 1789; 325 *Zeri*, b Aug. 1, 1790; 326 *Stephen*, b July 17, 1792, d Jan. 15, 1794; 327 *Stephen*, b Nov. 3, 1794, d May, 1826; 328 *Sarah*, b March 11, 1797; 329 *Clarissa*, b March 10, 1800; 330 *Joel*, b March 11, 1801; 331 *Isabella*, b Nov. 25, 1803. By 2d marriage: 332 *John*, b Aug. 30, 1805, m 1st, March, 1832, Emily Ward, she d June 1, 1867, and he m 2d, Jan. 22, 1868, Grace A. Belden; 333 *Betsey*, b May 1, 1807; 334 *Charles*, b Jan. 2, 1809, m Abi, daughter of Thomas Eddy, Oct. 6, 1831; 335 *Edmund*, b Feb. 9, 1811, m Jennette Bradley of Branford, Conn., and had seven children, four of whom are living, he d April 19, 1866.

PARMALEE.

LEANDER.

LEANDER PARMALEE came into Wallingford a carpenter and joiner, and continued to prosecute that business until elected sheriff of the county of New Haven, which office he successively held for twelve years, to the great satisfaction of his constituents, and all who came in contact with him as an officer. He married —— Blakeslee, daughter of the late Joseph Blakeslee of Wallingford. They both died in Wallingford.

Children: 1 *Samuel B.*, m Lavinia, dau. of George Cook; 2 ——, m Lorenzo Lewis, Esq.; 3 *Leander;* 4 dau.

PRESTON.[1]

The name of Preston is of great antiquity in North Britain, and was assumed by the family from their territorial possessions in Mid-Lothian, in the time of Malcolm, King of the Scots. The first of this family upon record is Leolphus De Preston, living in the time of William the Lion, about 1040, whose grandson, Sir Wm. De Preston, was one of the Scotch nobles summoned to Berwick by Edward the First, in competition for the Crown of Scotland between Bruce and Baliol, it having been submitted to Edward for decision. After the death of King Alexander III., 1291, Sir William was succeeded by his son Sir Nicol De Preston, one of the Scottish barons who swore fealty to King Edward I. He died in the beginning of the reign of David II. of Scotland, son of Robert Bruce, and was succeeded by his son, Sir Lawrence De Preston, who was succeeded by Richard De Preston, who was seated at Preston Richard in Westmoreland, in time of Henry II. Sir Richard De Preston, the fifth in descent from the above Richard, of Preston Richard, represented the county of Westmoreland in Parliament, in seventeen Edward III. His son, Sir Richard De Preston, had likewise the honor of being Knight of the shire for Westmoreland in the same reign (twenty-seven Edward III.), and in the same year (1368) obtained a license to impark five hundred acres. His successor, Sir John De Preston of Preston Richard and Preston Patrick, was a member of Parliament for Westmoreland, in the thirty-sixth, thirty-ninth and forty-sixth years of Edward III.

Children: 1 *Richard*, who left a family of daughters only; 2 *John*, who was a Judge of the Court of Common Pleas, in the reign of Henry IV. and VI., and retired from the bench

---

1 For collateral branches, see Abbot's Hist. Andover, Mass., 36; Adams' Haven Gen., 2d part, 32; Brown's Gen. of Brown Family; Cothrens' Hist. of Woodbury, Conn.; Hudson's Hist. Lexington, Mass., 187, 188; Kidder's Hist. New Ipswich, N. H., 421–3; N. E. Hist. and Gen. Reg., XIV. 26; Savage's Gen. Dict., III. 482.

in consequence of his great age, in 1427. He left John, a clergyman ; Richard, his heir ; and a daughter.

In 1593 there was a William Robert Preston, who was a relative of Sir Edward Coke.

WILLIAM.

WILLIAM PRESTON, son of John, son of George of Valley Field, England, was created Baronet of Nova Scotia in 1637. He came to America in the ship Truelove in 1635, at the age of 44 years, from Yorkshire, England, with his wife Mary, ae. 34 years. They had on their arrival in Massachusetts four children, as follows:

Children: 1 *Elijah*, b 1624, ae. 11 yrs.; 2 *Sarah*, b 1627, ae. 8 yrs.; 3 *Mary*, b 1629, ae. 6 yrs.; 4 *John*, b 1632, ae. 3 yrs. Children born in New Haven, Conn.: 5 *Jehiel*, b 1640, removed to Stratford where he had land let to him, Sept. 21, 1668; 6 *Hackaliah*, b 1643, settled at Woodbury, Conn., in 1681; 7 *Eliasaph*, b 1643, lived at Stratford and Wallingford; 8 *Joseph*, b Jan. 24, 1647.

7. ELIASAPH.

DEA. ELIASAPH PRESTON married 1st, Mary Wilcoxen, widow of Thomas Kimberly, of Stratford, July 9, 1673. She died April 16, 1674. He m 2d, Elizabeth, dau. of John Beach, of Stratford. He went to Wallingford in 1674. He was their first Town Clerk and schoolmaster, and was an energetic and very valuable member of the colony, both for the church of which he was deacon, and the township at large. He died in 1705, ae. 70 years.

Children by 1st marriage: 9 *Mary*, b April 25, 1674, m Caleb Merriman, July 9, 1690. By 2d marriage: 10 *Elizabeth*, b Jan. 29, 1776; 11 *Hannah*, b July 12, 1678, m Wm. Andrews, May 12, 1692; 12 *Eliasaph*, b Jan. 26, 1679, m Deborah Merriman, Jan. 2, 1717; 13 *Joseph*, b March 10, 1681, m Jane Cook, July 7, 1708; 14 *Esther*, b Feb. 28, 1683; 15 *Lydia*, b May 5, 1686; 16 *Jehiel*, b Aug. 25, 1688, d Nov. 24, 1689.

12. ELIASAPH.

ELIASAPH PRESTON married Rebecca Wilcoxen; she died Sept. 2, 1716. He married 2d, Deborah Merriman, Jan. 2, 1717. He married 3d, Hannah Mott, Nov. 26, 1726.

Children by 1st marriage: 17 *Ephraim*, b Sept. 8, 1703, m Patience ———; 18 *Elizabeth*, b Aug. 8, 1711, d 1715; 19 *Joanna*, b March 18, 1714. By 2d marriage: 20 *Jehiel*, b Sept. 11, 1719, m Thankful Sedgwick, Oct. 21, 1741; 21 *Rebecca*, b Sept. 25, 1721; 22 *Elizabeth*, b Dec. 28, 1727, m Abner Bunnel, Feb. 19, 1745. By 3d marriage: 23 *Isaac*, b Oct. 1, 1729; 24 *Moses*, b and d April 8, 1733; 25 *Moses*, b Oct. 30, 1734; 26 *Lois*, b Feb. 3, 1737–8.

13. JOSEPH.

JOSEPH PRESTON married Jane Cook, July 7, 1708. He married Sarah How, Jan. 30, 1734.

Children by 1st marriage: 27 *Eliasaph*, b May 9, 1709; 28 *Eliasaph*, b May 1, 1710; 29 *Joseph*, b April 7, 1711; 30 *Jonathan*, b Jan., 1713, m Sarah Williams July 28, 1740; 31 *Samuel*, b Aug. 27, 1715; 32 *John*, b June 22, 1715; 33 *Ebenezer*, b Sept. 17, 1725. By 2d marriage: 34 *Dinah*, b Nov. 19, 1734; 35 *Samuel*, b Sept. 30, 1737.

17. EPHRAIM.

LIEUT. EPHRAIM PRESTON married Rebecca ———, 2d, Patience ———. She died May 4, 1753; he died April 8, 1772, æ. 69 yrs.

Children by 1st marriage: 36 *Mary*, b Jan. 8, 1731; 37 *Phebe*, b March 6, 1732; 38 *Ephraim*, b Aug. 6, 1734, m Eunice Doolittle, March 25, 1754. Children by 2d marriage: 39 *Reuben*, b May 27, 1736; 40 *Phebe*, b Oct. 3, 1737; 41 *Patience*, b March 30, 1738, d April 18, 1738; 42 *Lent*, b March 5, 1739; 43 *Eliasaph*, b Nov. 28, 1740, m Phebe Hart, Feb. 27, 1764, d April 11, 1717, ae. 37; 44 *Titus*, b Jan. 29, 1743; 45 *Benjamin*, b Dec. 27, 1745; 46 *Elizabeth*, b Dec. 7, 1750.

20. JEHIEL.

SERGT. JEHIEL PRESTON m Thankful Sedgwick, Oct. 21, 1741. He died Nov. 22, 1758.

Children: 47 *Sarah*, b Aug. 23, 1742; 48 *Esther*, b April 1, 1744; 49 *Samuel*, b April 24, 1746; 50 *Caleb*, b April 24, 1746; 51 *Rebecca*, b Sept. 11, 1750; 52 *Thankful*, b Dec. 10, 1752; 53 *Ruth*, b Jan. 28, 1757.

28. ELIASAPH.

ELIASAPH PRESTON married Hannah ———.

Children: 54 *Isaac*, b Oct. 1, 1727; 55 *Moses*, b April 8, 1733; 56 *Lois*, b Feb. 3, 1737–8.

29. JOSEPH.

JOSEPH PRESTON married Sarah ———.

Children: 57 *Dinah*, b Nov. 19, 1734; 58 *Samuel*, b Sept. 30, 1737.

38. EPHRAIM.

EPHRAIM PRESTON married 1st, Eunice Doolittle, March 25, 1754; 2d, Esther ——. He died April 8, 1772, ae. 69.

Children: 59, 60 *Joel* and *Ebenezer*, twins, d Dec. 11, 1763.

39. REUBEN.

REUBEN PRESTON married Elizabeth ——.

Children: 61 *Charles*, d May, 1758; 62 *Mary*, b Jan., 1757.

43. ELIASAPH.

ELIASAPH PRESTON married Phebe Hart, Feb. 17, 1764. He died April 12, 1777, ae. 37 years. She m 2d, Stephen Ives.

Children: 63 *Titus*, d in Wallingford; 62 *Reuben*, d in Cheshire; 65 *Elizabeth*, d in Prospect.

REYNOLDS.[1]

HEZEKIAH.

HEZEKIAH REYNOLDS was born in Watertown, Conn., July 4, 1756. From there he went to Roxbury, Conn., and from

1 For collateral branches, see Caulkins' Hist. Norwich, Conn., ed. 1867,

thence to North Branford. He married Martha Davenport Wolcott, a daughter of Doct. Jeremiah Wolcott. She was born at Branford, Aug. 18, 1762, and died Aug, 19, 1839, ae. 77 years, at Wallingford. He died June 30, 1833, ae. 77 years. He came to Wallingford about the close of the last century, and resided for sometime in the west part of the town in what was the old Beadles house at Popple Hill. From this place he removed into the village, bought the house formerly the residence of Rev. Samuel Andrews, who was an Episcopal Clergyman before the Revolution.

Children: *Hezekiah*, b Dec., 1773, in Roxbury, Conn.; 2 *Wolcott*, b June 18, 1779; 3 *James*, b April 12, 1783, d Mar. 31, 1807, ae. 47; 4 *John D.*, b Apr. 27, 1785; 5 *Luanna*, b Apr. 23, 1784, m Nehemiah Carrington of New Haven, Dec. 23, 1825; 6 *Martha*, b Feb. 13, 1794, m Col. Thaddeus Street of Cheshire, 1823; 7 *Sarah*, b Jan. 12, 1796, m Alexander Harrison, 1819; 8 *Thomas G.*, b March 16, 1798, d Sept. 26, 1826, ae. 28; 9 *William A.*, b April 1, 1800, m Jane Lynde, of New Haven; 10 *Beverly*, b Nov. 15, 1806, d Nov. 5, 1807.

1. HEZEKIAH.

HEZEKIAH REYNOLDS, son of Hezekiah and Martha Wolcott Reynolds, married Anna Wilson, at Savannah, Georgia, in 1806.

Child: 12 *Martha Ann*, b 1807, m Henry Belden, Esq., of Hartford, Conn., in 1828.

2. WOLCOTT.

CAPT. WOLCOTT REYNOLDS, son of Hezekiah and Martha W. Reynolds, married Serephina Beaumont, in 1804. He died Sept. 28, 1842, ae. 44 years.

Child: 13 *Serephina*, b Jan. 16, 1805, d ae. 28 years.

3. JOHN.

HON. JOHN DAVENPORT REYNOLDS, son of Hezekiah and

197, 198; Chapman's Gen. of Chapman Family, 110; Kingman's Hist. N. Bridgwater, Mass., 629–35; Mitchell's Hist. Bridgwater, Mass., 282, 283; Rogers' Hist. & Gen. Researches, 116; Savage's Gen. Dict., III. 525, 526.

Martha D. Reynolds, married Lydia, daughter of John Scarritt, in 1822. He was a man eminently fitted by nature to fill almost any place of a public character in the gift of the people. He was often a Representative in the Legislature of the State from Wallingford, and a Senator from the sixth Senatorial district, and Judge of the Probate Court for the district of Wallingford, for a number of years. The duties of those, and all other public offices, he discharged with marked ability. He died Oct. 18, 1853, ae. 68 years. Mrs. Lydia, his wife, died July 28, 1862, ae. 65 years.

Children: 14 *Martha*, b March 27, 1826; 15 *John D.*, b April 20, 1828; 16 *Serephina*, b March 15, 1833, m S. N. Edmonds, Oct. 4, 1852.

10. WILLIAM.

WILLIAM A. REYNOLDS, ESQ., son of Hezekiah and Martha W. Reynolds, was born in Wallingford, married Jane Lynde, of New Haven, was a merchant and for several years a member of the firm of Harrison & Reynolds, in State-st., and for the last thirty years has been a respectable broker in New Haven.

Children: two daughters and two sons, living in 1870.

ROYCE.[1]

Among the first planters in Wallingford was 1 *Isaac*, and 2d *Nehemiah* Royce, who made their appearance in the place in 1671; 3 *Nathaniel*, 4 *Samuel*, 5 *Joseph*, and 6 *Robert* Royce, were also there soon after, all of whom had families, and are believed to be sons of Robert Royce who was at Stratford in 1644.

1. ISAAC.

ISAAC and Elizabeth Royce were in Wallingford early in 1671. He died in the autumn of 1682, leaving an estate of

---

1 For collateral branches, see Andrews' Hist. New Britain, Conn., 190; Caulkins' Hist. New London, Conn., 293–4; Caulkins' Hist. Norwich, Conn., ed. 1867, 199; Savage's Gen. Dict., III. 569–70.

£161. His widow married Ebenezer Clark for her second husband in 1696.

Children: 7 *Isaac*, b Oct. 28, 1673, d Dec. 8, 1673; 8 *Robert*, b Sept. 4, 1674; 9 *Sarah*, b March 10, 1677; 10 *Martha*, b June 1, 1679.

2. NEHEMIAH.

Nehemiah Royce (shoemaker) was in Wallingford with his wife Hannah, among the first settlers. She died June 19, 1677, and he married Esther ——, who died Sept. 12, 1706. He died Nov. 7, 1706, ae. 72 years. He was the original owner of the James Rice place at the head of Main-st., in Wallingford.

Children: 11 *Mary*, b Aug. 12, 1673, d Aug. 12, 1675; 12 *Mercy*, b Feb. 4, 1675, d Feb. 24, 1675; 14 *Esther*, b Oct. 15, 1678; 15 *Lydia*, b May 28, 1680, m Daniel Messenger; 16 *Nehemiah*, b May 18, 1682–3, m Keziah Hall, Feb. 9, 1700; 17 *Margery*, d Sept. 12, 1683.

3. NATHANIEL.

Nathaniel Royce married Esther ——, Oct. 27, 1673. She died June 19, 1677. He was married to Sarah Lathrop by Mr. Moss, April 21, 1681. She died Nov. 11, 1706. He then married Hannah Farnham, Aug. 24, 1707. She died Feb. 6, 1708, and he married Abigail Hoyt, Aug. 25, 1708. She died and he married Phebe Clark, Dec. 27, 1720. He died Feb. 8, 1736; was by trade, a carpenter and joiner and blacksmith in 1687.

Children by 1st marriage: 18 *John*, b April 11, 1675; 19 *Benjamin*, b May 6, 1677, m Rebecca Wilcoxen, d Oct. 20, 1703. By 2d marriage; 20 *Sarah*, b April 3, 1683; 21 *Hester*, b Sept. 10, 1685, d Oct. 14, 1703, ae. 18 yrs.; 22 *Lois*, b July 29, 1687, m Samuel Hall; 23 *Elizabeth*, b Dec. 28, 1689. By 4th marriage: 24 *Daniel*, b Sept. 29, 1726; 25 *Lois*, b March 27, 1728; 26 *Robert*, b Nov. 16, 1729; 27 *Elisha*, b Oct. 27, 1731; 28 *Nathaniel*, b July 1, 1733.

4. SAMUEL.

SAMUEL ROYCE married 1st, Sarah Baldwin, June 5, 1690, 2d, Hannah Benedict, Dec. 12, 1695. He died in Meriden, May 14, 1757, ae. 85 years. Mrs. Hannah died in Meriden, Jan. 12, 1761, ae. 90 yrs.

Children by 1st marriage: 29 *Abigail*, b Nov. 24, 1677, m Joseph Cole; 30 *Prudence*, b July 26, 1680; 31 *Deborah*, b Sept. 8, 1683, m Thomas Mix; 32 *Isaac*, b March 10, 1688; 33 *Ebenezer*, b Sept. 25, 1691; 34 *Nathaniel*, b Oct. 21, 1692; 35 *John*, b April 25, 1693; 36 *Mary*, b Feb. 17, 1695; 37 *Jacob*, b April 11, 1697, m Thankful Beach, dau. of Moses; By 2d marriage: 38 *Hannah*, b Feb. 19, 1697–8, m John Ives; 39 *Ezekiel*, b Feb. 10, 1699, m Anna Merwin, Apr. 26, 1723; 40 *Samuel*, b Oct. 5, 1702, settled in Cheshire, m Martha Moss, 1728; 41 *Abel*, b Jan. 10, 1700; 42 *Benjamin*, b May 23, 1705, m Mindwell Royce, April 11, 1729, was clerk of the mines, d Jan. 30, 1758; 43 *Mehitable*, b July 30, 1709; 44 *Ebenezer*, b Aug. 21, 1713, d Oct. 18, 1752, in Meriden, aged 39.

5. JOSEPH.

JOSEPH ROYCE, married to Mary Porter, by the Hon. J. Wadsworth, Oct. 1, 1684. He died March 19, 1704, or 1707, æ. 44 yrs.

Children: 45 *Mary*, b Jan. 12, 1686; 46 *Joseph*, b May 1, 1689, d June 27, 1689; 47 *Joseph*, b May 2, 1690, m Anna Andrews, March, 1710; 48 *Thomas*, b Aug. 13, 1692, m Mary —— ; 49 *Nathaniel*, b Oct. 21, 1693; 50 *James*, b July 31, 1695, d Dec. 22, 1695; 51 *Hannah*, b Nov. 6, 1696, d; 52 *Sarah*, b Feb. 24, 1699, d Dec. 6, 1711; 53 *Hannah*, b March 18, 1701; 54 *Reuben*, b Dec. 18, 1713, d Sept. 10, 1790, æ. 77 yrs.

8. ROBERT.

ROBERT ROYCE married 1st, Mary ——, June 2, 1692; 2d, Abigail Benedict, March 14, 1709. He died in 1759, ae. 94 yrs.

Children: 55 *Nathaniel*, b Oct. 23, 1694, m Phebe Clark, Dec. 20, 1720; 56 *Dinah*, b Feb. 24, 1696; 57 *Josiah*, b July 10, 1698; 58 *Ruth*, b Sept., 1701; 59 *Sarah*, b April 4, 1703, d Aug. 5, 1723; 60 *Timothy*, b June 2, 1705, m Mindwell Wassles, May 16, 1727; 61 *Mary*, b July, 1707; 62 *Elizabeth*, b Aug., 1709; 63 *Gideon*, b May 4, 1711, m Rebecca ——; 64 *Prudence*, b April 11, 1714; 65 *Moses*, b Sept. 24, 1716, m Thankful ——; 66 *Martha*, m Edmund Scott, March 16, 1730; 67 *Lydia*, b Nov. 20, 1719.

19. BENJAMIN.

BENJAMIN ROYCE, son of Nehemiah and Hannah, married Rebecca Wilcoxen of Stratford, Conn.; he d Oct. 20, 1701.

Child: 68 *Mindwell*, b Oct. 12, 1703, m Benjamin Royce, April 11, 1729.

16. NEHEMIAH.

NEHEMIAH ROYCE, son of Nehemiah and Hannah, married Keziah Hall. His farm was at the head of Falls Plain.

Children: 69 Capt. *James*, b June 30, 1711, d Jan. 20, 1796, ae. 85 yrs.; 70 *Hannah*, b Nov., 1713, d Dec. 14, 1713; 71 *Phineas*, b June 16, 1715; 72 *Ephraim*, b Feb. 9, 1717; 73 *Hannah*, b May 15, 1720, m Eunice ——; 74 *Keziah*, b March 16, 1726.

32. ISAAC.

ISAAC ROYCE, son of Samuel and Sarah, m Hannah ——.

Children: 75 *Richard*, b March 16, 1759; 76 *Hannah*, b May 20, 1761.

33. EBENEZER.

EBENEZER ROYCE, son of Samuel and Sarah, married Abigail Root, March 4, 1741. He died in Meriden, Oct. 18, 1752, ae. 39 years.

Children: 77 *Hannah*, b Jan. 5, 1743; 78 *Huldah*, b Jan. 16, 1745; 79 *Oliver*, b March 1, 1747, d at Meriden Dec. 6, 1755, ae. 7 years; 80 *Samuel*, b Oct. 25, 1751.

34. NATHANIEL.

NATHANIEL ROYCE, son of Samuel and Sarah, married Phebe Clark Dec. 27, 1720.

Children: 81 *John*, b Feb. 14, 1723; 82 *Dinah*, b Nov. 6, 1724; 83 *David*, b Sept. 29, 1726; 84 *Lois*, b March 27, 1728; 85 *Robert*, b Nov. 16, 1729; 86 *Nathaniel*. b July 1, 1733; 87 *Phebe*, b May 15, 1735; 88 *John*, b March 22, 1737; 89 *Josiah*, b March 2, 1738; 90 *Elisha*, b Oct. 27, 1739; 91 *Clark*, b Oct. 4, 1740.

37. JACOB.

JACOB ROYCE, son of Samuel and Sarah Royce, was married to Thankful Beach by Capt. Hall, Sept. 28, 1724. He died Nov. 13, 1727.

Children: 92 *Amos*, b Nov. 1, 1725, m Sarah ——; 93 *Experience*, b Dec. 1, 1727.

39. EZEKIEL.

EZEKIEL, son of Samuel and Hannah Royce, married 1st, Anna Merwin, April 25, 1723. She died Dec. 20, 1725; He married 2d, Abigail Alling, Nov. 30, 1726. He died in Meriden, Sept. 4, 1765, ae. 66 years.

Children by 1st marriage: 94 *Samuel*, b Jan. 29, 1724; 95 *Barnabas*, b Dec. 12, 1725. By 2d marriage: 96 *Anna*, b July 3, 1727; 97 *Rachel*, b Oct. 4, 1728; 98 *Ezra*, b June 7, 1730, m Anna ——; 99 *Lucy*, b March 4, 1732; 100 *Deborah*, b Aug. 17, 1734; 101 *Ezekiel*, b July 23, 1736; 102 *Ezekiel*, b Oct. 15, 1739, m Lydia ——, d Sept., 1808, ae. 69 years; 103 *Abigail*, b July 14, 1751.

40. SAMUEL.

SAMUEL ROYCE, son of Samuel and Hannah, married Martha Moss, Dec. 25, 1728.

Children: 104 *Samuel*, b May 9, 1732, m Sarah ——; 105 *Nathaniel*, b May 20, 1734, m Sybil ——; 106 *Sarah*, b Nov. 27, 1737; 107 *Ebenezer*, b April 13, 1740; 108 *Levi*, b Oct. 29, 1744; 109 *Reuben*, b June 22, 1750.

41. ABEL.

ABEL ROYCE, son of Samuel and Hannah Royce, was married to Joanna Beach, Oct. 23, 1723, by Thomas Yale.

Children: 110, *Rhoda*, b Dec. 13, 1725; 111 *Hester*, b

Dec. 21, 1727; 112, 113 *Abel* and *Joanna*, b March 30, 1730; 114 *Benedict*, b Feb. 19, 1735; 115 *Mehitable*, b April 1, 1737; 116 *Hezekiah*, b Dec. 16, 1739; 117 *Huldah*, b Nov. 6, 1742.

42. BENJAMIN.

BENJAMIN ROYCE, son of Samuel and Hannah Royce, married Mindwell ——, April 11, 1729.

Children: 118 *Benjamin*, b April 1, 1730, m Phebe ——, she d June 13, 1776, æ. 46, he d in Meriden, Feb., 1777; 119 *Solomon*, b Jan. 31, 1741.

44. EBENEZER.

EBENEZER ROYCE, son of Samuel and Hannah Royce, married Abigail Root, March 4, 1741.

Children: 120 *Hannah*, b Jan. 5, 1743; 121 *Huldah*, b Jan. 16, 1745; 122 *Olive*, b March 1, 1747; 123 *Samuel*, b Oct. 28, 1751.

48. THOMAS.

THOMAS ROYCE, son of Joseph and Mary Royce, married Mary Holt, Dec. 23, 1714, residence in Meriden. He married Anna Child, July 21, 1730.

Children: 124 *Sarah*, b June 23, 1716; 125 *Joseph*, b July 16, 1719, m Eunice ———; 126 *Mary*, b Feb. 12, 1723; 127 *Benjamin*, b June 26, 1724, m Anna Chamberlain, May 29, 1750; 128 *Thomas*, b June 29, 1727; 129 *Enos;* 130 *Anna*, b Sept. 15, 1731; 131 *Samuel*, b Nov. 20, 1733; 132 *Phebe*, b Dec. 30, 1742.

54. REUBEN.

REUBEN ROYCE, son of Joseph and Mary Royce, married Keziah Moss, Nov. 18, 1736. She died Oct. 3, 1770, ae. 53. He died Sept. 10, 1790, ae. 77 years.

Children: 133 *Anna*, b Aug. 5, 1737; 134 *Rachel*, b Nov. 26, 1753.

57. JOSIAH.

JOSIAH ROYCE, son of Robert and Abigail, married Elizabeth Parker, March 24, 1693. Married 2d, Abigail Clark, May 1, 1722.

Children: 135 *Ebenezer*, b Jan. 22, 1713. By 2d marriage: 136 *Sarah*, b June 5, 1723; 137 *Justus*, b 1725; 138 *Thankful*, b 1727; 139 *Charles*, b 1731; 140 *Stephen*, b 1733; 141 *Caleb*, b 1734.

60. TIMOTHY.

TIMOTHY ROYCE, son of Robert and Abigail, married Mindwell Wassles, May 16, 1727.

Children: 142 *Hannah*, b Dec. 29, 1727; 143 *Lydia*, b Feb. 11, 1730; 144 *Timothy*, b June 25, 1732, m Abigail ——; 145 *Ruth*, b Aug. 31, 1735.

63. GIDEON.

GIDEON ROYCE, son of Robert and Abigail, m 1st, Mary ———, 2d, Rebecca ———.

Children: 146 *Mary*, b May 10, 1743; 147 *Titus*, b Feb. 4, 1745; 148 *Wait*, b July 11, 1748; 149 *Gideon*, b Dec. 26, 1751; 150 *Mary*, b Oct. 30, 1753; 151 *Justice*, b Dec. 8, 1756, m Lois Perkins, of Meriden; 152 *Rebecca*, b April 16, 1758; 153 *Jonathan*, b March 18, 1760.

65. MOSES.

MOSES ROYCE, son of Robert and Abigail, married Thankful Austin, Jan. 6, 1740.

Children: 154 *Thankful*, b July 5, 1747; 155 *Amasa*, b March 21, 1751, d Dec. 12, 1797, ae. 47 yrs.; 156 *Abner*, b Jan. 4, 1753; 157 *Joel*, b Feb. 16, 1754; 158 *Amos*, b March 19, 1757.

69. JAMES.

CAPT. JAMES ROYCE, son of Nehemiah and Keziah, married Miriam ———. She died Aug. 20, 1757, ae. 37 years. He died Jan. 20, 1796, ae. 85 years.

Children: 159 *Elizabeth*, b Jan. 6, 1744; 160 *Keziah*, b July 27, 1746, m Janet Tyler, of Wallingford; 161 *James*, b Dec. 18, 1748, m Mary Tyler; 162 *Joel*, b Jan. 10, 1751, d July 27, 1756, ae. 6 yrs.

72. EPHRAIM.

EPHRAIM ROYCE, son of Nehemiah and Keziah, married Eunice ———.

Children: 163 *Mindwell*, b Aug. 12, 1740; 164 *Keziah*, b May 12, 1742; 165 *Margery*, b March 17, 1742; 166 *Ephraim*, b June 30, 1744; 167 *Stephen*, b Sept. 2, 1752; 168 *Mary*, b Dec. 31, 1754.

85. ROBERT.

ROBERT ROYCE, son of Nathaniel and Phebe, married Hannah Bennet, Nov. 5, 1752.

Children: 169 *Bennet*, b Nov. 11, 1752; 170 *Hannah*, b Jan. 27, 1755; 171 *Chauncey*, b April 20, 1757; 172 *David*, b Feb. 24, 1760.

86. NATHANIEL.

NATHANIEL ROYCE, son of Nathaniel and Phebe, married Sybil ———.

Children: 173 *Martha*, b Jan. 3, 1756; 174 *Sybil*, b April 11, 1760.

88. JOHN.

JOHN ROYCE, son of Nathaniel and Phebe, married Hannah ———.

Children: 175 *Mary*, b May 8, 1751; 176 *Hannah*, b Jan. 18, 1753, d; 177 *Matthew*, b Oct. 13, 1759; 178 *Hannah*, b June 2, 1761.

92. AMOS.

AMOS ROYCE, son of Jacob and Thankful, m Sarah ——.

Children: 179 *Sarah*, b Sept. 3, 1754; 180 *Jacob*, b Dec. 9, 1756, m —— Hull; 181 *John*, b Nov. 15, 1758; 182 *Hannah*, b May 22, 1761.

94. SAMUEL.

SAMUEL, son of Ezekiel and Anna Royce, married Deborah ——.

Children: 183 *Stephen*, b Oct. 21, 1756; 184 *Hannah*, b April 28, 1758; 185 *Ebenezer*, b March 24, 1760.

98. EZRA.

EZRA, son of Ezekiel and Anna Royce, married Anna Royce, Nov. 25, 1746; res. in Meriden before 1793.

Children: 186 *Jesse*, b Oct. 3, 1746; *Rachel*, b Oct. 20, 1747; 187 *Joseph*, b April 14, 1756; *Mehitable*, b April 3,

1750; 188 *Sarah*, b Nov. 9, 1751; *Seth*, b June 6, 1752; 189 *Esther*, b Aug. 2, 1754; *Asa*, b Sept. 1, 1754; 190 *Deborah*, b Sept. 6, 1757; *Lucy*, b Oct. 26, 1757; 191 *Thomas*, b Sept. 26, 1749; 192 *Ezra*, b Oct. 30, 1759, res. in Meriden.

102. EZEKIEL.

EZEKIEL, son of Ezekiel and Anna Royce, married Lydia ——. She died Oct. 28, 1813, ae. 73 yrs. He died Sept. 3, 1808, ae. 69, in Meriden.

Child: 193 *Oliver*, b July 26, 1760, d in Meriden, April 28, 1794, ae. 34 yrs.

104. SAMUEL.

SAMUEL, son of Samuel and Martha Royce, married Sarah ——.

Children: 194 *Mindwell*, b Nov. 8, 1756, m Josiah Mix in 1777; 195 *Phebe*, b Nov. 10, 1758; 196 *Lucy*, b May 1, 1761; 197 *Keziah*, b March 25, 1768, m Josiah Mix, he d in Ohio, May 13, 1845, ae. 91.

116. HEZEKIAH.

HEZEKIAH, son of Abel and Joanna Royce, died in Meriden at a very advanced age.

Children: 198 *Benajah*, d near South Meriden; 199 *Porter*, d in Wallingford.

123. SAMUEL.

SAMUEL, son of Ebenezer and Abigail Royce, married Deborah ——.

Children: 200 *Stephen*, b Oct. 21, 1756; 201 *Hannah*, b April 28, 1758; 202 *Ebenezer*, b March 24, 1760.

125. JOSEPH.

JOSEPH, son of Thomas and Mary Royce, married Eunice ——.

Child: 203 Capt. *Joseph*, b 1748, d Sept. 10, 1790, ae. 77.

144. TIMOTHY.

TIMOTHY, son of Gideon and Rebecca Royce, married Abigail ——.

Children: 204 *Mindwell*, b April 27, 1754; 205 *Timothy*, b

May 12, 1755; 206 *Elijah*, b July 26, 1756; 207 *Chauncey*, b Sept. 7, 1757; 208 *Joanna*, b Sept. 27, 1758; 209 *Katherine*, b Oct. 4, 1760.

151. JUSTICE.

JUSTICE ROYCE, son of Gideon and Rebecca Royce, married Lois Perkins of Meriden. She died in Wallingford and was buried there.

Children: 210 *Roswell*, d in Wallingford; 211 *Jotham*, went west; 212 *Ann*, m Moses Taylor; 213 *Mary*, d in Meriden; 214 *Titus*, resides in Wallingford now, 1870.

EVAN.

EVAN ROYCE married Rachel Parker, May 20, 1724. He does not appear to be of the same family of any of the preceding, yet it is quite possible that he was.

Children: 215 *John*, b May 25, 1725; 216 *Anna*, b June 23, 1724; 217 *Evan*, b June 18, 1729; 218 *Charles*, b March 28, 1731; 219 *Mary*, b Feb. 5, 1733; 220 *James*, b Jan. 1, 1735; 221 *Lois*, b Nov. 4, 1740; 222 *Rachel*, b June 30, 1743; 223 *Hannah*, b March 25, 1759; 224 *James*, b Feb. 1, 1757.

161. JAMES.

JAS. ROYCE, son of Capt. Jas. and Miriam Royce, when living, owned and occupied the house and lot at the head of Main-Street, in the village of Wallingford. The old house and lot had been owned by the family from 1670 down to 1868. Mr. James Rice died Feb. 17, 1827, ae. 79 years. His wife died Aug. 6, 1834, ae. 83 years. The maiden name of his wife was Mary, daughter of William Tyler, and sister of Samuel and Jared Tyler, late of Wallingford.

Children: 225 *Nehemiah*, b 1774, m 1st, Ruth Hall, 2d, Abigail, daughter of Caleb Hall, Esq., he d April 8, 1831, ae. 57 years; 226 *Ambrose*, b 1777, d Aug. 21, 1810, ae. 33 years; 227 *Miriam*, m Isaac Peck of Wallingford; 228 *Sedgwick*, d in western N. Y., a Baptist minister; 226 *Lura*, m Chauncey Hough of Wallingford; 230 *Joel*, b 1786, m Lucretia Yale, d Dec. 21, 1828; 231 *James*, resides in western N. Y.; 232 *Mary*, b 1782, d Aug., 1859, ae. 77; 233 *Henrietta*, b 1791, d of measles, Feb. 18, 1818, ae. 27 years; 234 *Sylvester*, b 1793, d April 1, 1820, ae. 27 years.

218. CHARLES.

CHARLES, son of Evan and Rachel Royce, married Lois ——.

Child; 235 *Thaddeus*, b Nov. 3, 1757, res. near Gitteau's corner.

STANLEY.[1]

The ancestor of the Wallingford Stanleys was John Stanley, who died on his passage over from England, leaving a son John, and a daughter Ruth, both of whom were married (the same day), Dec. 5, 1645. John the son was nephew of Timothy Stanley, of Cambridge and Hartford.

John Stanley, the grandfather of the Wallingford branch, was born in 1625, came to New England in 1634, settled early in Windsor and Farmington, joined the church in Farmington July 12, 1753, was a deputy from Farmington, four sessions to the General Court, was a Captain in King Philip's War, and a leading man in Farmington. He married Sarah, daughter of Thomas Scott, Dec. 5, 1645. He married 2d, Sarah, daughter of John Fletcher, of Milford, June 26, 1661. He died Dec. 19, 1706, and his 2d wife and widow died May 15, 1713.

Children: 1 *John*, b in Hartford, Nov. 3, 1647; 2 *Thomas*, b in Farmington, Nov. 1, 1649, m in 1690, Anne, daughter of Rev. Jeremiah Peck, she d May 23, 1718; 3 *Sarah*, b Feb., 1651–2, m Joseph Gaylord; 4 *Timothy*, b March 17, 1653–4, m Mary, dau. of John Strong, in 1676, and d childless; 5

---

1 For collateral branches, see Andrews' Hist. New Britain, Conn.; Dagget's Hist. Attleborough, Mass., 94, 95; Judd and Boltwood's Hist. Hadley, Mass., 582; Leonard's Hist. Dublin, N. H., 396–7; Morse's Memorial of Morses, App. No. 55; Savage's Gen. Dict., IV. 163–6; Thurston's Hist. Winthrop, Me., 196–7.

Elizabeth, b April 1, 1657, d ; 6 *Abigail*, b July 25, 1669, m John Hooker, Nov., 1687 ; 7 *Elizabeth*, b Nov. 28, 1672, m John Wadsworth, she d Oct. 5, 1713 ; 8 *Isaac*, b Sept. 22, 1660, was an imbecile.

1. JOHN.

JOHN STANLEY appears to have been a prominent man in Waterbury. He was the first recorder of the town and proprietors. He was appointed first by the committee, and afterward, Dec. 26, 1682, by the town, which offices he filled until his removal to Farmington. He was a good penman and well qualified for the office, as the records fully demonstrate. He married Esther, daughter of Thomas Newell of Farmington, and d May 16, 1729 ; she d in 1740.

Children: 9 *Esther*, b Dec. 2, 1672, in Farmington, d 1676, ae. 4 years ; 10 *John*, b April 9, 1675, in Farmington, m Dec. 14, 1714, d Sept. 8, 1748 ; 11 *Samuel*, b 1677, m Elizabeth, daughter of Abraham Bronson of Lyme, July 15, 1702 ; 12 *Nathaniel*, b 1679, m Sarah Smith and settled in Goshen, d 1770 ; 13 *Thomas*, b May 25, 1684, in Farmington ; 14 *Sarah*, b July 4, 1686 ; 15 *Timothy*, b June 6, 1689, m Martha Smith of Farmington, settled in Goshen after 1735.

11. SAMUEL.

SAMUEL STANLEY married Elizabeth, daughter of Abraham Bronson of Lyme. He died in 1737 ; he was a mill-wright and carpenter, and lived in Wallingford, Farmington and Durham.

Children: 16 *Samuel*, b in Waterbury ; 17 *Abraham*, b April 13, 1705, m Prudence, dau. of Isaac Pinney, of Windsor, Conn. ; 18 *John;* 19 *Esther;* 20 *Ebenezer;* 21 *Anna*, b March 8, 1713, all b in Wallingford ; 22, *Elizabeth*, b 1715 ; 23 *Asa*, b 1717 ; 24 *Ruth;* 25 *Josiah;* all b in Farmington.

17. ABRAHAM.

ABRAHAM STANLEY married Prudence Pinney of Windsor. He settled on a farm a little west of Yalesville. He died Feb. 17, 1788, ae. 85 yrs.

Children: 26 *Abraham*, b Dec. 7, 1731; 27 *Prudence*, b May 13, 1734, m Laban Andrews, April 5, 1758; 28 *Oliver*, b Oct. 10, 1743, grad. at Yale, 1768, was a lawyer; 29 *Lucretia*, b Aug. 7, 1748, m Elihu Yale.

18. JOHN.

JOHN STANLEY married Hannah Ives, May, 29, 1735. She died in Wallingford, July 13, 1750.

Children: 30 *Hannah*, b June 6, 1736, d June 28, 1750, ae. 14 yrs.; 31 *John*, b Dec. 26, 1737; 32 *Mary*, b June 11, 1740; 33 *Thomas*, b July 1, 1743; 34 *Sarah*, b July 2, 1745.

25. JOSIAH.

JOSIAH STANLEY married Mary Miles, of Wallingford, March 14, 1739. He died Oct. 31, 1756.

Children, 35 *Abigail*, b June 9, 1742; 36 *Mary*, b Aug. 9, 1744; 37 *Benjamin*, b June 3, 1748.

28. OLIVER.

OLIVER STANLEY ESQ. married ——. He was graduated at Yale College in 1768, and became a lawyer of considerable note in his native village. He owned the house and lot where Mrs. Edgar Atwater now lives (1869), and died there.

Children: 38 *George Washington*, graduated at Yale; 39 *Sarah*, m Medad Baker.

38. GEORGE.

GEORGE WASHINGTON STANLEY ESQ. married ———. He practiced his profession as a lawyer in his native place for several years, with great success; and was Town Clerk and Judge of the Probate Court. In 18— he went to Middletown, where he was made Attorney for the State. He remained there several years, and subsequently went to Cleveland, Ohio, where he soon became distinguished as a learned, discreet and faithful counselor. He died at an advanced age, leaving one son to perpetuate his name, and who is reported to be a successful business man at Cleveland.

SCARRITT.

James Scarritt was from Branford, Conn. In 1758 he was in the old French war with Miles Yale, Col. Isaac Cook, Samuel Parsons, and old Samuel Barnes. These men used to meet often and relate their experiences in that war, to the great gratification of any who might be present. Mr. Scarritt was a weaver and schoolmaster. He taught school before the Revolution, and until within the memory of the writer. He was the honored father of John Scarritt, who was also a schoolmaster, and also the highly respected Town Clerk of New Haven, for many consecutive years. He died in New Haven.

Children: 1 *Amanda*, m W. Lyon, she d in 1869; 2 *Lydia*, m John D. Reynolds; 3 *Marcus;* 4 *Louisa;* 5 *James*, m ——— Johnson, and removed to Waterbury.

STREET.[1]

NICHOLAS.

Rev. Nicholas Street came from England and settled at Farmington, Mass. In 1649 he went to New Haven where he died April 22, 1674.

Children: *Samuel*, b 1735, grad. at Harvard, 1664; *Susannah; Sarah; Abiah; Hannah.*

I. SAMUEL.

Rev. Samuel Street married Anna, daughter of Samuel Miles, Nov. 3, 1664. He was one of the original subscribers to the settlement of Wallingford in 1670, and was the first settled clergyman in the place. Four years after the settlement commenced, he was called to settle there, and continued in the work of ministry there until his decease, Jan. 17, 1717, a period of nearly 45 years. Mrs. Anna Street died July 19, 1730.

Children: 1 *Anna*, b 1665, in New Haven; 2 *Samuel*, b

---

1 For collateral branches, see Dodd's Hist. East Haven, Conn., 153; Savage's Gen. Dict., IV. 222–3.

1667, in New Haven; 3 *Mary*, b 1670, m John Hall of Wallingford; 4 *Susanna*, b June 15, 1675, in Wallingford; 5 *Nicholas*, b July 14, 1677, settled in Groton, Conn.; 6 *Katharine*, b Nov. 19, 1679; 7 *Sarah*, b Jan. 15, 1681, m Theophilus Yale.

2. SAMUEL.

SAMUEL STREET JR. married Madeline Daniels, Nov. 1, 1684. She died and he married Hannah Glover, July 14, 1690. She died July 3, 1715, and he married for his third wife, Elizabeth ——, Dec. 20, 1716.

Children by 1st marriage: 8 *Samuel*, b Nov. 3, 1685; 9 *James*, b Dec. 28, 1686, m Rebecca Scoville, Sept. 6, 1731; 10 *Anna*, b Aug. 26, 1688. By 2d marriage: 11 *Eleanor*, b Dec. 3, 1690; 12 *Nathaniel*, b Jan. 19, 1692; 13 *Elnathan*, b Sept. 2, 1695, m Damaris Hull, Feb. 6, 1722; 14 *Mehitable*, b Feb. 15, 1699; 15 *John*, b Oct. 25, 1703, m Hannah Hall, June 9, 1734; 16 *Samuel*, b May 10, 1707, d Oct. 15, 1752.

5. NICHOLAS.

NICHOLAS STREET married Jerusha Morgan, April 22, 1707.

Children: 17 *James*, b Feb. 10, 1708; 18 *Elizabeth*, b Apr. 24, 1709.

9. JAMES.

JAMES STREET m Rebecca Scoville.

Children: 19 *Samuel*, b Sept. 6, 1731; 20 *James*, b Sept. 14, 1733.

13. ELNATHAN.

ELNATHAN STREET married Damaris Hall, Feb. 6, 1722.

Children: 21 *Benjamin*, b May 18, 1723; 22 *Samuel*, b Jan. 10, 1725, d Jan. 18, 1725; 23 *Samuel*, b Dec. 8, 1728; 24 *Nicholas*, b Feb. 21, 1730, graduated at Yale, 1751, ordained Oct. 8, 1755, d at East Haven, Oct. 3, 1706; 25 *Elnathan*, b Feb, 20, 1732; 26 *Anna*, b Feb. 16, 1736; 27 *Mary*, b June 28, 1738; 28 *Jesse*, b April 24, 1741, m Lois Cook.

15. JOHN.

JOHN STREET married Hannah Hall, June 5, 1734.

Children; 29 *Thaddeus*, b March 15, 1735, d March 16, 1735; 30 *Hannah*, b June 7, 1736; 31 *Sarah*, b July 8, 1738; 32 *Mary*, b May 4, 1740; 33 *Elisha*, b Dec. 17, 1745.

16. SAMUEL.

SAMUEL STREET married 1st, Keziah Munson, Nov. 12, 1734; 2d, Sarah ———. She died Oct. 1, 1795, ae. 68 years; he died in Wallingford, 1792, ae. 85 years.

Child by 1st marriage: 34 *Glover*, b May 28, 1735. Children by 2d marriage: 35 *Titus*, b June 4, 1750, m ——— Atwater, of Cheshire; 36 *Caleb*, b Oct. 23, 1753.

THOMPSON.[1]

There are few names more common among the early settlers of New England than that of Thompson, most of whom came from London and Hertfordshire, and were probably related to each other. Of these, the principal individuals connected with the New England settlements were David Thompson, who emigrated to Portsmouth, N. H., in 1622, where he established fisheries, and in 1623, removed to an island in Boston Harbor, which still bears his name; James Thompson, who was one of the first settlers of Woburn, Mass., in 1634; Major Robert Thompson, who resided in Boston in 1639, and was a man of wealth and respectability; Maurice Thompson, a merchant of London, Governor of the East India Co., who established fisheries at Cape Ann, in 1639; Rev. William Thompson, who came to York, Maine, in 1637, and Anthony Thompson, of New Haven, Conn.

1 For collateral branches, see Andrews' Hist. New Britain, Conn., 163, 232; Barry's Hist. Hanover, Mass., 409, 410; Bradbury's Hist. Kennebunkport, Me., 297–80; Cothren's Hist. Woodbury, Conn., 727–37; Dodd's Hist. East Haven, Conn., 154–6; Eaton's Hist. Thomaston, Me., 427–9; Hooker's Memorials of James and Augustus Thompson; Journals of Smith and Dean of Portland, Me., 68; Kingman's Hist. N. Bridgwater, 314, 315; N. E. Hist. and Gen. Reg., IV. 180, XIII. 112–16, 318–20; Savage's Gen. Dict., IV. 283–90; Sewall's Hist. Woburn, Mass., 390–402, 643–5; Stiles's Hist. Windsor, Ct., 815; Thompson's Gen. of Thompson Family; Thompson's Hist. Long Island, N. Y., II. 425–31.

JOSEPH.

JOSEPH THOMPSON and his wife Elizabeth were in Wallingford among the first planters, though not an original subscriber. He was collector of taxes in 1681.

Children: 1 *Joseph*, m Hannah Clark, Feb. 1, 1700; 2 *John*, b Feb. 1, 1685, m Sarah Culver, June 23, 1710; 3 *Hannah*, b April 16, 1687.

1. JOSEPH.

JOSEPH THOMPSON, son of Joseph and Elizabeth Thompson, married Hannah Clark. He died ae. 67 years.

Children: 4 *Elizabeth*, b Oct. 23, 1710; 5 *Samuel*, b Nov. 10, 1713; 6 *Tamar*, b Sept. 18, 1715; 7 *Phebe*, b April 12, 1720; 8 *Hannah*, b Sept. 10, 1725; 9 *Keziah*, b Jan. 15, 1728.

2. JOHN.

JOHN THOMPSON, son of Joseph and Elizabeth Thompson, married Sarah Culver, June 23. 1710.

Children: 10 *Abel*, b and d Jan. 14, 1715; 11 *Abel*, b 1717, d 1798; 12 *Anna*, b Jan. 28, 1719, m Benjamin Sedgwick; 13 *Mabel*, b Nov. 11, 1721; 14 *Sarah*, b Oct. 5, 1724, m John Moss; 15 *John*, b Jan. 26, 1726.

5. SAMUEL.

SAMUEL THOMPSON, son of Joseph and Hannah Thompson, married Rachel ———.

Children: 16 *John*, b Feb. 24, 1747; 17 *Samuel*, b June 11, 1751; 18 *Phebe*, b Feb. 20, 1753; 19 *Rachel*, b April 20, 1755; 20 *Samuel*, b Oct. 5, 1757.

11. ABEL.

ABEL THOMPSON, son of John and Sarah Culver Thompson, married ———. He was the father of Abel, who was the father of Capt. Caleb Thompson, late of Wallingford, deceased.

Children: 21 *Edward*, d in Wallingford; 22 *Stiles H.*, d 1863; 23 *Lodema*, m E. S. Ives, Esq.; 24 daughter.

JOSEPH.

JOSEPH and Abigail Thompson had the following family in Wallingford.

Children: 25 *Elihu*, b Oct. 9, 1745; 26 *John*, b July 22, 1757.

THORP.[1]

SAMUEL.

SERGT. SAMUEL THORP was an early settler in the eastern part ot Wallingford, near Muddy river. His house stood on the east side of said river, on an old highway which is closed, and which ran south from the east side of the late Col. Russel Hall's barn. Lot No. 14 on the east side of the main street, in the village, was assigned him for a house lot. He died at the age of 84, Feb. 2, 1728. Mary Thorp, his wife, died March 1, 1718.

Children: 1 *Elizabeth*, b Feb. 15, 1668; 2 *Samuel*, b Mar. 8, 1670; 3 *Hannah*, b Sept. 9, 1678; 4 *Naomi*, b Jan. 31, 1681, m John Boulcott, Oct. 18, 1708; 5 *John*, b July 6, 1686; 6 *Samuel*, b Apr. 11, 1687; 7 *Hannah*.

6. SAMUEL.

SAMUEL THORP married 1st, Hannah ——, 2d, Elizabeth How. He died March 14, 1764. She died Oct. 19, 1751.

Children by 1st marriage: 8 *Samuel*, b Mar. 24, 1707; 9 *Joseph*, b Dec. 8, 1708; 10 *Elizabeth*, b Oct. 3, 1710; 11 *Daniel*, b Jan. 4, 1711; 12 *Hannah*, b Nov. 18, 1712; 13 *Samuel*, b Apr. 10, 1713; 14 *Lydia*, b Oct. 31, 1714; 15 *Hannah*, b Nov. 1, 1716; 16 *Thomas;* 17 *Benjamin*, b Sept. 13, 1715; 18 *John*, b Aug. 2, 1718; 19 *Olive*, b Mar. 14, 1720. By 2d marriage: 20 *Hannah*, b Feb. 11, 1722; 21 *Mabel*, b Jan. 12, 1724; 22 *Mary*, d Oct. 19, 1767; 23 *Abner*, b Oct. 14, 1720; 24 *Asher*, b Oct. 14, 1727; 25 *Phebe*, b April 1, 1728; 26,

---

1 For collateral branches, see Savage's Gen. Dict., IV. 243.

Elnathan, b Aug. 13, 1729; 27 *Sarah*, b Dec. 10, 1734; 28 *Tamar*, b Sept. 18, 1735.

9. JOSEPH.

JOSEPH THORP, married Abigail ——. He died Sept. 13, 1755.

Children: 29 *Sarah*, b July 7, 1741; 30 *Jared*, b Oct. 27, 1744; 31 *Joseph*, b May 1, 1750; 32 *Titus*, b Mar. 1, 1751; 33 *Abigail*, b Apr. 22, 1753.

11. DANIEL.

DANIEL THORP married Elizabeth ——. She died Oct. 16, 1751.

Child: 34 *Mary*, d Oct. 16, 1751.

13. SAMUEL.

SAMUEL THORP, son of Samuel and Hannah.

Children: 35 *Thomas*; 36 *Lois*, b Feb. 26, 1736; 37 *Sarah*, b Apr. 16, 1737; 38 *Lydia*, b Oct. 9, 1741; 39 *Lynes*, b Oct. 12, 1743.

TUTTLE.[1]

WILLIAM.

WILLIAM TUTTLE, his wife and three children, and a brother John came from Devonshire, England, in the ship Planter, as passengers, and were registered April, 1635. John was born in 1596, and settled at Ipswich, Mass.; he left numerous descendants. William's age was put at twenty-six years, his wife Elizabeth's at 23 yrs., John, their eldest child, at 3 1-2 yrs., Ann, 2 1-2 yrs., and Thomas at three months. Mrs. Elizabeth united with the church in Boston, July 24, 1636, and brought to be baptized a son, Jonathan, July 2, 1637, and another, David, April 7, 1639. Soon after, the family re-

---

1 For collateral branches, see Cothren's Hist. Woodbnry, Conn., 723–7; Dodd's Hist. East Haven, Conn., 156–8; Hall's Hist. Rec. Norwalk, Ct., 203–241, 267–269, 281–290, 297; Hudson's Hist. Lexington, Mass., 248, 249; N. E. Hist. and Gen. Reg., VIII. 132–42; Otis's Gen. Otis Family; Savage's Gen. Dict., IV. 350–2; Wyman's Hunt Family Hist., 529.

moved to New Haven; there he became a man of consequence, and was much employed in public affairs. He resided in that part of the town now called North Haven, and was there in 1659, on land that belonged to the estate of Gov. Eaton. He died in 1673, at the age of 64 years. Mrs. Elizabeth died Dec. 30, 1684, æ. 81 yrs. He was a subscriber to the compact for the settlement of East Haven. Estate, £440.

Children: 1 *John*, b 1631, in England, m Catharine Lane; 2 *Anna*, b 1633, in England; 3 *Thomas*, b 1635, m Hannah Powell, May 21, 1760; 4 *Jonathan*, b July 2, 1637, in Boston, m Rebecca, dau. of Francis Ball; 5 *David*, b April 7, 1639, in Boston, d in 1693; 6 *Joseph*, b Nov. 22, 1640, in New Haven, m Hannah Munson; 7 *Sarah*, b April, 1642, m John Hanson, Nov. 11, 1663; 8 *Elizabeth*, b Nov., 1645, m Timothy Edwards of Windsor, 1667; 9 *Simon*, b March 28, 1647, settled at Wallingford in 1670; 10 *Benjamin*, b Oct. 29, 1648; 11 *Mercy*, b April 27, 1650, m Samuel Brown of New Haven; 12 *Nathaniel*, b Feb. 29, 1652, m Sarah, dau. of Ephraim How, and settled at Woodbury, Conn., where he d Aug. 20, 1721. Cothren, in Hist. of Woodbury, gives his descendants.

1. JOHN.

JOHN TUTTLE, eldest son of William and Elizabeth Tuttle, was born in England in 1628, came to America with his parents in 1635, in the ship Planter, married Catherine Lane, Nov. 8, 1653, and died in 1683. Estate, £79.

Children: 13 *Hannah*, b Nov. 3, 1655, m Samuel Clark, Nov. 7, 1672; 14 *John*, b Sept. 16, 1657; 15 *Samuel*, b Jan. 9, 1659, m Sarah Newman, in 1684; 16 *Sarah*, b Jan. 22, 1661–2, m John Humiston, Sept. 10, 1685; 17 *Daniel*, b April 13, 1664, d 1700, at Milford, ae. 36 years; 18 *Mary*, b April 13, 1664, m John Ball, June 6, 1716; 19 *Elizabeth*, b Nov. 26, 1666; 20 *David*, b Nov. 14, 1668.

3. THOMAS.

THOMAS TUTTLE 2d son of William and Elizabeth Tuttle,

was born in England in 1634–5, and was brought to America by his parents in the ship Planter. He married Hannah Powell, May 21, 1661.

Children: 21 *Hannah*, b Feb. 24, 1661, m Samuel Clark, Nov. 7, 1672; 22 *Abigail*, b Jan. 17, 1663; 23 *Mary*, b June 14, 1665, d Aug. 12, 1683; 24 *Thomas Jr.*, b Oct. 27, 1667, m Mary Sanford, June 28, 1692, he d Jan. 30, 1703; 25 *John*, b Dec. 5, 1669; 26 *Esther*, b April 9, 1672, m Samuel Russell, Feb. 25, 1694; 27 *Caleb*, b Aug. 29, 1674, m Mary Hotchkiss, March 1, 1699; 28 *Joshua*, b Dec. 19, 1676, m Mary Mix, Feb 25, 1710; 29 *Martha*, b May 23, 1679, d Jan. 25, 1699, ae. 20.

4. JONATHAN.

JONATHAN, son of William and Elizabeth Tuttle, was born in Boston, and came to New Haven when a child with his parents. He married Rebecca Bell of Norwalk, Conn., and settled on a farm in what is now North Haven, and on which some of his descendants continue to reside to this day (1870). He died in 1700. Estate, £100. His wife Rebecca died May 2, 1676.

Children: 30 *Rebecca*, b Sept. 10, 1664; 31 *Mary*, b Feb. 7, 1666, m Ebenezer Frost, Oct. 4, 1704; 32 *David*, b Nov. 14, 1668; 33 *Jonathan*, b April 6, 1669; 34 *Simon*, b March 11, 1671; 35 *William*, b May 25, 1673; 36 *Nathaniel*, b Feb. 25, 1676.

5. DANIEL.

DANIEL, son of William and Elizabeth Tuttle, was a proprietor in 1685. For some cause which does not now appear, he was in 1687 put under the charge of his brother Thomas, and died in 1692, ae. 55 years, without children. He had lot 16, east side of Main-st. in Wallingford, 1670. Estate, £29.

6. JOSEPH.

JOSEPH, son of William and Elizabeth Tuttle, married Hannah, daughter of Thomas Munson, May 2, 1667. He died in Sept., 1690. She afterwards married Nathan Bradley in 1694, and died in 1695. Estate, £269. This family was of East Haven, Conn.

Children: 37 *Joseph*, b March 18, 1668, m Elizabeth Sanford, Dec. 10, 1691-2; 38 *Samuel*, b July 15, 1670, m Sarah Hart, Dec. 11, 1695; 39 *Stephen*, b May 20, 1673, m Ruth ——, settled at Woodbridge, N. J.; 40 *Joanna*, b Feb. 25, 1675, m Stephen Panbonna; 41 *Timothy*, b Sept. 30, 1678, d Nov. 21, 1678; 42 *Susannah*, b Feb. 20, 1679; 43 *Elizabeth*, b July 12, 1683; 44 *Hannah*, b May 14, 1685, d in infancy; 45 *Hannah*, b Feb. 26, 1686.

8. ELIZABETH.

ELIZABETH TUTTLE, daughter of William and Elizabeth Tuttle, married Richard Edwards of Windsor, Conn. She was the maternal ancestor of the late Gov. Henry W. Edwards, of New Haven.

Children: 46 *Mary*, b 1668; 47 *Timothy*, b May 14, 1669, m Esther Stoddard; 48 *Abigail*, b 1671; 49 *Elizabeth*, b 1675; 50 *Ann*, b 1678; 51 *Mabel*, b 1685; 52 *Cynthia* ——.

9. SIMON.

SIMON TUTTLE, son of William and Elizabeth Tuttle, married Miss Abigail, daughter of John Beach, and was among the first subscribers to the compact for the settlement of New Haven village (now Wallingford), in 1669-70, and settled there near his father Beach's land, perhaps on a portion of it. His house lot was No. 13, east side Main-st., with 8 acres of out land. He died April 16, 1719, ae. 72 years. Mrs. Abigail died Aug., 1722.

Children: 53 *Daniel*, b Nov. 11, 1680, m Ruth How, Oct. 18, 1711; 54 *Dea. Timothy*, b 1681, m 1st, Thankful Doolittle, Nov. 2, 1706, she d Nov. 23, 1728, 2d, Mary ——, 3d, Sarah Humiston, June 28, 1749, he died April 15, 1756, ae. 75; 55 *Thankful*; 56 *Rebecca*, b April 30, 1698; 57 *Jonathan*, b Sept. 18, 1701; 58 *Isaiah*, b July 10, 1704, m Susannah Doolittle, June 4, 1727; 59 *Elizabeth*, b Nov. 8, 1705; 60 *Deborah*, b Jan. 1, 1709; 61 *David*, b April 25, 1713.

11. MERCY.

MERCY TUTTLE, daughter of William and Elizabeth Tuttle, married Samuel Brown, who was among the original subscribers to the compact for the settlement of the village of Wallingford, and had assigned to him the lot on which now stands the residence of the late Moses Y. Beach, Esq.; but as he did not settle on it within the time prescribed, he lost his title, and it was assigned to John Moss. Dea. Philo Brown, of the firm of Brown, Elton & Co., of Waterbury, is a direct descendant of her. See "Bronson's Waterbury."

Children: 62 *Abigail*, b March 11, 1669, d young; 63 *Sarah*, b Aug. 8, 1672; 64 *Rachel*, b Aug. 14, 1677; 65 *Francis*, b Oct. 7, 1679; 66 *Gideon*, b July 12, 1685; 67 *Samuel*, b Oct. 29, 1699.

12. NATHANIEL.

NATHANIEL TUTTLE son of William and Elizabeth Tuttle, married Sarah How, Aug. 10, 1682. He settled in Woodbury, Conn., about 1680, where he raised a considerable family. He died Aug. 20, 1721, leaving a widow, Sarah. His descendants are somewhat numerous in Woodbury and vicinity, to this day.

Children: 68 *Mary*, bap. May, 1683, d before 1721; 69 *Ephraim*, bap. July 20, 1683, m Dinah Wheeler, Feb. 13, 1706; 70 *Temperance*, bap. Nov. 24, 1674, d Nov., 1749; 71 *Hezekiah*, m Martha Huthwith, April 11, 1711, d in 1753; 72 *Isaac*, b Feb. 3, 1698, m 1st, Prudence Wheeler, Jan. 10, 1729, she d 1730, m 2d, Mary Warner, she died Oct. 28, 1746; 73 *Anna*, d July 22, 1753.

35. WILLIAM.

WILLIAM, son of Jonathan and Rebecca Tuttle, m ———.

Children: 74 *Aaron*, b Nov. 25, 1698, m Mary Munson, Feb. 6, 1723–4; 75 *Mary*, b Aug., 1702; 76 *Susannah*, b Nov. 10, 1708; 77 *Lydia*, b Feb. 22, 1710–11; 78 *Jemima*, b Feb. 13, 1712; 79 *Hannah*, b Nov. 10, 1715; 80 *Dan*, b Aug. 1, 1718, d young; 81 *Dan*, b Aug. 30, 1722, m Abigail Frederick, Jan. 26, 1743, at Wallingford.

37. NATHANIEL.

NATHANIEL, 2d son of Jonathan and Rebecca Tuttle, married and settled in New Haven.

Children: 82 *Jonathan*, b 1701; 83 *Silence*, b 1703; 84 *Moses*, b May 8, 1704; 85 *Nathaniel*, b May 29, 1714, m Mary Todd, Jan. 16, 1737–8.

53. DANIEL.

CAPT. DANIEL TUTTLE, son of Simon and Abigail Tuttle, settled on lot 16, east side of the main street in Wallingford village, married Ruth How, Oct. 18, 1711; he died in 1748.

Children: 86 *Daniel*, b 1714, d Aug. 12, 1767, ae. 53; 87 *Jehiel*, b Aug. 7, 1717, m Hannah Hull, Aug. 31, 1742; 88 *Abiah*; 89 *Phebe*, b Jan. 8, 1719, d; 90 *Lydia*, b April 15, 1722, m Benj. Culver of Wallingford; 91 *Eunice*, b April 9, 1725, d April 12, 1726; 92 *Eunice*, b July 12, 1726, m Gideon Ives, Jr., Oct. 19, 1745; 93 *Ambrose*, b Sept. 25, 1728, m Esther Ives, May 31, 1748; 94 *Enos*, b Jan. 3, 1732, m Sarah Francis, April 21, 1757; 95 *Mary*, b Oct. 11, 1733, m Joseph Francis, Aug. 31, 1750; 96 *Phebe*, b Jan. 8, 1734, m Samuel Miles; 97 *Lois*, b March 9, 1737, m Abel Ives, June 19, 1760; 98 *Martha*, b Feb. 25, 1720, d Jan. 1, 1742.

54. TIMOTHY.

DEA. TIMOTHY TUTTLE, son of Simon and Abigail Tuttle, married Thankful Doolittle, Nov. 2, 1706. She died Nov. 23, 1728. He married 2d, Mary Rowe of New Haven, June 9, 1729; she died Jan. 22, 1747–8. He married 3d, Sarah Humiston, June 28, 1749. He died at Cheshire, April 15, 1756, æ. 76 yrs.

Children: 99 *Rachel*, b April 10, 1706, m Nathan Tyler; 100 *Ebenezer*, b May 18, 1708, d Dec. 3, 1736, ae. 28 yrs.; 101 *Ephraim*, b April 10, 1710, m Hannah Payne, Jan. 16, 1734; 102 *Mary*, b Oct. 3, 1712, m Miles Hull of Derby, Dec. 4, 1729; 103 *Gershom*, b Aug. 11, 1714, settled in Bristol, Conn., d ae. 74 yrs.; 104 *Timothy*, b Dec. 4, 1716. m Hannah Wadams of Goshen, Conn.; 105 *Abigail*, b April 11, 1719, m John Gaylord of Cheshire; 106 *Simon*, b June 12,

1721, settled in Bristol, Conn.; 107 *Moses*, b Dec. 18, 1723, settled in Cheshire; 108 *Thankful*, b Nov. 15, 1726, d Dec. 9, 1747; 109 *Mehitable*, b Nov. 15, 1730, m Andrew Clark; 110 *Ichabod*, b July 2, 1732, d Jan. 9, 1747–8.

57. JONATHAN.

JONATHAN, son of Simon and Abigail Tuttle, married Rebecca Gilbert, Dec. 8, 1724.

Child: 111 *Simon*, b Nov. 16, 1725.

58. ISAIAH.

ISAIAH, son of Simon and Abigail Tuttle, married Susanna Doolittle, June 4, 1727.

Children: 112 *Jonathan*, b May 19, 1728, settled in Wallingford; 113 *Theophilus*, b March 4, 1729, settled in Wallingford, d Nov. 17, 1787, ae. 58; 114 *Isaiah*, b Feb. 6, 1732, d in childhood; 115 *David*, b Jan. 21, 1733, d in 1765; 116 *Elizabeth*, b June 17, 1736; 117 *Sarah*, b July 13, 1738; 118 *Isaiah*, b Nov. 29, 1742, d young; 119 *Solomon*, b Aug. 19, 1746.

71. HEZEKIAH.

HEZEKIAH, son of Nathaniel and Sarah Tuttle, had a son who settled in North Haven, and has numerous descendants, some of whom reside in New Haven, Conn. (1870).

86. DANIEL.

DANIEL TUTTLE, son of Daniel and Ruth Tuttle, married Phebe ———.

Children: 120 *Zopher*, b July 19, 1743; 121 *Prudence*, b Jan. 24, 1745; 122 *Dan*, b Nov. 27, 1746; 123 *Ichabod*, b Feb. 14, 1748; 124 *Benoni*, b Sept. 30, 1749; 125 *Jabez*, b July 20, 1751; 126 *Ichabod*, b Nov. 28, 1757, d Oct. 31, 1834, ae. 77 years; 127 *Beri*, b Apr. 29, 1761, drowned May 11, 1809, ae. 47 years.

87. JEHIEL.

JEHIEL TUTTLE, son of Daniel and Ruth Tuttle, married Hannah Hull, Aug. 30, 1742.

Children: 128 *Daniel*, b Jan. 9, 1743–4; 129 *John*, b Apr. 30,

1746; 130 *Charles*, b Dec. 24, 1747; 131 *Jeremiah*, b Nov. 25, 1750; 132 *Charles*, b Jan. 26, 1753, settled at Windham, Greene Co., New York; 133 *Joel*, b July 25, 1756.

93. AMBROSE.

AMBROSE TUTTLE, son of Daniel and Ruth Tuttle, married Esther Ives, May 31, 1748. He died in 1757.

Children: 134 *Samuel*, b Dec. 22, 1748, d May 9, 1755; 135 *Ambrose*, b Oct. 11, 1752; 136 *Martha*, b Oct. 9, 1750; 137 *Benjamin*, b Sept. 5, 1754; 138 *Samuel*, b Dec. 22, 1757.

94. ENOS.

ENOS TUTTLE, son of Daniel and Ruth Tuttle, married Sarah Francis, April 21, 1757. Probably left Wallingford when a young man.

Child: 139 *Sarah*, b Feb. 19, 1758.

101. EPHRAIM.

EPHRAIM TUTTLE, son of Dea. Timothy and Thankful Tuttle, married 1st, Esther Hotchkiss, June 11, 1731. She died May, 1732, of small pox. He m 2d, Hannah Paine, Jan. 16, 1734. She died May 22, 1756, ae. 42. He m 3d, Thankful Preston, Dec. 16, 1761. He died in Cheshire, Feb 2, 1775, ae. 64 yrs.

Children: 140 *Edmund, M. D.*, b Nov. 26, 1733-4, d May 5, 1763, ae. 30 yrs.; 141 *Esther*, b Feb. 10, 1736; 142 *Ebenezer*, b Oct. 15, 1737, m Eunice ——; 143 *Ephraim*, b March 20, 1739, m 1st, Mary Hall, Aug. 2, 1754, 2d, Elizabeth Atwater; 144 *Noah*, b June 30, 1741, d July 23, 1742; 145 *Timothy*, b July 1, 1743, d young; 146 *Noah*, b Dec. 18, 1744, d June 30, 1828, at Camden, N. Y., ae. 84 yrs.; 147 *Timothy*, b May 17, 1745, went to Ohio; 148 *Hannah*, b Jan. 4, 1746-7; 149 *Lucius*, b Dec. 4, 1749, d June 27, 1846, ae. 97 yrs.; 150 *Thankful*, b March 13, 1752. By 2d marriage: 151 *Ruth*, b Jan. 3, 1761-2; 152 *Edmund*, b Dec. 30, 1764, m Sarah L. Royce, Dec. 6, 1784, he d Jan. 1, 1846, ae. 90.

103. GERSHOM.

GERSHOM TUTTLE, son of Dea. Timothy and Thankful

Tuttle, married and settled in Goshen, Conn. He died Oct. 23, 1760.

Children: 153 *Noah*, b March 26, 1742, m Ruth Beach; 154 *Mary*, b Dec. 1, 1743; 155 *Ichabod*, b June 23, 1744, was killed at Wyoming, by the Indians; 156 *Amos*, b Feb. 9, 1745; 157 *Elisha*, b Nov. 24, 1746, m Elizabeth Matthews, Feb. 20, 1772; 158 *Deliverance*, b Oct. 14, 1753, d Oct. 8, 1760; 159 *Timothy*, b Jan. 13, 1755; 160 *David*, b Dec. 26, 1756, d Oct. 10, 1760; 161 *Hannah*, b May 10, 1758; 162 *Thankful*, b May 30, 1759, m Philip Cook; 163 *Lois*, b May 21, 1760.

104. TIMOTHY.

TIMOTHY, son of Dea. Timothy and Thankful Tuttle, married Hannah Wadams Jan. 27, 1743, and settled at Goshen, Conn.

Children: 164 *Mary*, b Dec. 1, 1743, m —— Sedgwick of Cornwall Hollow; 165 *Amos*, b Feb. 4, 1745; 166 *Elisha*, b Nov. 24, 1746, d in Goshen, July 28, 1825; 167 *Ichabod*, b June 23, 1748, m Elizabeth Matthews, Feb. 20, 1772, killed by Indians at Wyoming, Pa.; 168 *Noah*, b March 26, 1752, m Ruth Beach, was hotel keeper several years in Canada; 169 *Deliverance*, b Oct. 14, 1753, d Oct. 8, 1760; 170 *Timothy*, b June 10, 1755, m Abigail ——; 171 *David*, b Dec. 26, 1756, d Oct., 1760; 172 *Hannah*, b Aug. 10, 1758; 173 *Thankful*, b May 30, 1759, m Phillip Cook of Goshen, Conn.; 174 *Lois*, b May 21, 1760.

107. MOSES.

MOSES, son of Dea. Timothy and Thankful Tuttle, married Sybil Thomas, June 2, 1746. He died in Cheshire, Jan. 17, 1809, ae. 86 yrs. She died July 16, 1804, ae. 80 yrs. Both are buried in the Episcopal yard, Cheshire.

Children: 175 *Ichabod*, b Feb 14, 1748, m Sarah Hitchcock; 176 *Sybil*, b April 15, 1749, m Amos Hitchcock, May 31, 1764, settled in Canada and died there; 177 *Sarah*, b Aug. 19, 1750, m Isaac Moss; 178 *Rebecca*, b Feb. 21, 1752, m Reuben Merriman; 179 *Moses*, b Oct. 24, 1753, settled in Prospect; 180 *Anna*, b Oct. 24, 1753; 181 *Freelove*, b April

8, 1756, m John Benham; 182 *Thaddeus*, b Aug. 18, 1757, m Cornelia Atwater; 183 *Samuel*, b April 16, 1759, m Martha Hull, settled in Vermont; 184 *Lydia*, b July 9, 1761, m Abner Doolittle of Cheshire.

112. JONATHAN.

JONATHAN TUTTLE, son of Josiah Tuttle of North Haven, married Hannah Barns, Feb. 6, 1754, and settled in the south-west corner of Wallingford, near the foot of the Blue Hills. The locality has ever since borne the name of Tuttle's farm. He died May 27, 1795, ae. 65 years. Hannah his relict died Nov. 6, 1831, ae. 97 years.

Children: 185 *Rebecca*, b Dec. 21, 1754, m Lent Hough, of Wallingford; 186 *Isaiah*, b May 5, 1757, m Sarah Yale, their children were Samuel, Jonathan, Harvey, Romantha, and Rev. Anson, all went to Ohio; 187 *Hannah*, b Jan. 2, 1760, m Bethiel Todd; 188 *Sarah*, b Dec. 18, 1762, m Reuben Jones, of Wallingford; 189 *David Justus*, b Jan. 27, 1765, m Polly Tuttle, April 29, 1790, she d Jan. 9, 1813, ae. 48; 190, *Samuel*, b 1771, m Abigail Cook, Oct. 25, 1792; 191 *Polly*, m Samuel Johnson, of Wallingford.

127. BERI.

BERI TUTTLE, son of Daniel and Phebe Tuttle, of Wallingford, was drowned while at work on the bridge at Humiston Mills, May 11, 1807, ae. 47 years. He married Charity Johnson. She died Jan. 31, 1814, ae. 52 years.

Children: 192 *Nancy*; 193 *Laura*, b 1788, m Asa Tuttle and d in Cheshire; 194 *Clarissa*; 195 *Merrit*, b 1795, m Mary, dau. of Stephen Cook; 196 *Franklin*, b 1800, d Nov. 18, 1811, ae. 11 yrs.; 197 *Ira* Esq., b June 30, 1805, m Mary, dau. of John B. Johnson Esq., d Jan. 10, 1870, ae. 64.

132. CHARLES.

CHARLES TUTTLE, son of Jehiel of Wallingford, settled at Windham, Greene Co., N. Y.

Children: 198 *Mamre*; 199 *Anna*; 200 *Charles*; 201 *Daniel Bliss*, b July, 1797, m Abigail Clark Stimpson; 202 *Sallie*; 203 *Ephraim*, d 1866.

201. DANIEL.

DANIEL BLISS, son of Charles and —— Tuttle, married Abigail Clark Stimpson.

Children: 204 *Lemuel S.*, b at Windham, Greene Co., N. Y.; 205 *Sarah B.;* 206 *Daniel;* 207 Rev. *Daniel Sylvester*, b Jan. 26, 1837, m Harriet M. Foote, he was consecrated a Bishop of the Protestant Episcopal Church of Idaho, Montana and Utah, May 1, 1867, his children were George M., b Sept. 23, 1866, and Herbert Edward, b June 14, 1869.

142. EBENEZER.

EBENEZER TUTTLE, son of Ephraim and Hannah Tuttle, married Eunice ———.

Children: 208 *Mary*, b March 12, 1761; 209 *Phebe*, b Aug. 15, 1763; 210 *Ebenezer*, b July 28; 1765; 211 *Joseph*, b Aug. 9, 1767.

143. EPHRAIM.

EPHRAIM TUTTLE, son of Ephraim and Hannah Tuttle, married 1st, Mary Hull, Aug. 20, 1764. She died in 1768. He married 2d, Elizabeth Atwater. She died in 1808. He died in Cheshire, Conn., 1811, ae. 72 years.

Child by 1st marriage: 212 *Uri*, b Oct. 31, 1765, m 1st, Peggy Morrison, she d Oct. 17, 1813, ae. 46 yrs, he m 2d, —— Stowe. By 2d marriage: 213 *Ephraim*, b Feb. 28, 1776, m Lois, dau. of Capt. David Hitchcock; 214 *Lucy*, m Gideon Walker, settled in Southington, Conn.; 215 *Mary*, b in 1769, m S. Ufford Beach, she d Feb. 1, 1854; 216 *Elizabeth*, m Nath'l Royce, of Southington, Conn.; 217 *Hannah*, m Eliasaph Preston, of Prospect, Conn.; 218 *Abigail*, m John Peck, of Homer, N. Y.; 219 *Stephen*, m Catharine Smith, and went to Burton, Ohio.

149. LUCIUS.

CAPT. LUCIUS TUTTLE, son of Ephraim and Hannah Tuttle, married Hannah, daughter of Andrew and Lowly Hull, of Cheshire. He was a prominent man in Cheshire for many years, and during the Revolution was under General Washington's command at Boston and Long Island, and himself had command of a company of his townsmen at the battle which resulted in the surrender of General Burgoyne and his army in 1777. He died at the house of his son Lucius, in Wolcott, at the age of 97 years.

Children: 220 *Andrew Hull*, b Aug. 28, 1775; 221 *Lucius*, b Aug. 7, 1776, d in Wolcott, Conn., had a family there; 222 *Betsey Ann*, b April 8, 1778, m Samuel Benham, of Cheshire; 223 *Marcus*, b March 25, 1780; 224 *Anson*, b Dec. 22, 1781, d Sept. 19, 1863, ae. 32; 225 *William B.*, b Feb. 11, 1784, d Jan. 6, 1822, ae. 38 yrs.; 226 *Hannah*, b March 24, 1785, d unm. June 9, 1846, ae. 59; 227 *Gaius*, b July 5, 1736, d ae. 67 yrs. in Cheshire; 228 *Esther*, b Dec. 30, 1792, m Levi Doolittle, and died in Cheshire.

152. EDMUND.

EDMUND TUTTLE, son of Ephraim and Thankful Tuttle, married Sarah S. Royce, Dec. 6, 1784. He died at Cheshire, Jan. 1, 1846, ae. 82 years. She died Dec. 16, 1856, ae. 89 yrs.

Children: 229 *Sybil Stella*, m John Hall, April, 1826; 230 *Lowly*, d Nov. 18, 1813, ae. 17 yrs.; 231 *Edmund*, d July 11, 1793, in infancy; 232 *Lois S.*, m James Merriman, of Southington; 233 *Nancy*, d Jan. 4, 1827, ae. 24 yrs.; 234 *Laura Ann*, d Sept. 20, 1829, ae. 23 yrs.; 235 *Myra*, m Jesse Brooks, of Cheshire; 236 *Ruth*, m John Peck, and died in Cheshire, Conn.

175. ICHABOD.

ICHABOD TUTTLE, son of Moses and Sybil Thomas Tuttle, married Sarah Hitchcock, daughter of Dan and Esther Hitchcock, of Cheshire, and was for many years owner of the farm now known as the Dickerman farm, situated about a mile and a quarter east of Cheshire village. She died Oct. 30, 1834, ae. 77 years.

Children: 237 *Dan*, m Hannah Holdreden, settled at Great Bend in Penn.; 238 *Sally*, m Ephraim Smith; 239 *Clara*, m Titus Smith; 240 *Friend*, m Eunice Linn, and died in Penn.; 241 *Susannah*, m Green Smith of Cheshire; 242 *Alfred*, d unmarried at Cheshire; 243 *Minerva*, m Ethural Bristol of

Cheshire; 244 *Ichabod*, d at Vergennes, Vermont, by his wife Elizabeth, he had Calvin, Luther and Ichabod; 245 *Benajah*, d in Vergennes, Vt.; 246 *Lavinia*, m Gaius Hitchcock of Cheshire, in 1791, he d May 27, 1862, ae. 71 years; 247 *Zephaniah*, m Betsey Hotchkiss, he d in S. C.; 248 *Sarah Julia*, m 1st, Capt. Wm. Harwood, 2d, Harry Davidson; 249 *Maria*, m 1st, Cyrus Bradley, 2d, Sheldon Lewis, of Bristol.

179. MOSES.

MOSES TUTTLE, son of Moses and Sybil Tuttle, married Damaris ——, and settled in Prospect, Conn., where he died Jan. 17, 1835, ae. 82 years. He was the honored father of Mrs. Joel Merriman, of Cheshire, and of Mrs. Benjamin Dutton Beecher, of Cheshire and Prospect, and others whose names I have been unable to ascertain. She died July 25, 1835, ae. 77 years.

Child: *Wooster*, m Mercy ——, d in Prospect, Feb. 26, 1843, ae. 65 yrs.

189. DAVID.

DAVID JUSTUS, son of Jonathan and Hannah Tuttle of Wallingford, died Jan. 9, 1813, ae. 48. Mrs. Polly Tuttle, his widow, died Sept. 22, 1836, ae. 67 years.

Children: 250 *Rebecca Hough*, b March 7, 1801, m Augustus Hitchcock; 251 *Betsey*, b Nov. 1, 1790, m John Gaylord of Wallingford; 252 *Sally*, b June 29, 1792, d Sept. 21, 1810; 253 *Harry*, b Oct. 20, 1796, m Mary Bronson of Wolcott; 254 *Julius*, b Dec 2, 1798, m Sylvia, dau. of Ambrose Tuttle of Hamden; 255 *Jesse*, b Sept. 22, 1794, res. in Wallingford; 256 *Merwin*, m Eliza Hemingway, and died at East Haven, Conn; 257 *Caroline*, m Allen Tuttle of Hamden, res. North Haven; 258 *Eliza*.

190. SAMUEL.

SAMUEL, son of Jonathan and Hannah Tuttle, married 1st, Abigail Cook. She died July 6, 1808, ae. 36. He then married Lucy ——, who died Dec, 2, 1823, ae. 56 yrs. He died Feb. 3, 1824, ae. 53 yrs. He was a man of note in Wallingford.

Children; 259 *Lucy*, b Sept. 20, 1793; 260 *Anna*, b Nov. 5, 1795; 261 *Orren*, b Jan. 18, 1801, deceased while a young man; 262 Rev. *Beri*, Baptist minister in Ohio.

195. MERRIT.

MERRIT TUTTLE, son of Beri and Charity Tuttle, married Mary, daughter of Stephen Cook, of Cheshire. He died June 20, 1844, ae. 49 years. She married Wm. Todd for her 2d husband, and died Oct. 2, 1864.

Children: 263 *Sarah;* 264 *Caroline;* 265 *Marietta;* 266 *Benajah*, killed by falling into a cider mill, Nov. 12, 1813, ae. 11 yrs.; 267 *Julia;* 268 *Ira A.*, m Maria, dau. of Hiram Bristol; 269 *Selden*, m 1st, Ellen Doolittle, April 11, 1849, 2d, Sarah L. Chatfield, Dec. 24, 1862; 270 *Henry Clay*, b June, 1832, m Cornelia Blakeslee, April 14, 1804; 271 *Merrit;* 272 *Louisa.*

212. URI.

URI TUTTLE, son of Ephraim and Mary Tuttle, married 1st, Peggy Morrison, she died; he married 2d, Catharine Stow. He died in New Haven.

Children: 273 *Henry Hopkins*, b May 18, 1794; 274 *Wm. Ames*, b Jan. 22, 1796, resides in Auburn, N. Y.; 275 *Elizabeth Mary*, b Nov. 20, 1797, m Wm. Hall; 276 *Harriet*, b April 12, 1801, m —— Smith: 277 *Jane C.*, b Sept. 17, 1803, d Aug. 17, 1805. By 2d marriage: 278 *Charles*, b Oct. 3, 1815, d Oct. 23, 1854; 279 *Jane*, b Jan. 5, 1818, d Jan. 9, 1818; 280 *Chester Allen*, b Oct. 20, 1819, d Sept. 16, 1820; 281 *Frances*, b Jan. 28, 1821, m Henry How; 282 *Frederick*, b 1822, d ae. 14 yrs.; 283 *George F.*, b Oct. 28, 1823, m Maria Antoinette, dau. of Rev. W. Brown, of New York city, a graduate of Yale College in 1818; 284 *Chester Uri*, b June 9, 1825.

213. EPHRAIM.

EPHRAIM TUTTLE, son of Ephraim and Elizabeth Tuttle, married Lois, daughter of Capt. David Hitchcock, of Cheshire, June 15, 1806. She was born Sept. 2, 1781, and died Feb. 11, 1843, ae. 62 years. He died July 4, 1860, ae. 84 years.

Children: 285 *Marus*, b March 6, 1807, m Fannie Tyon of Colchester, Conn.; 286 *Ephraim*, b Jan. 20, 1809, m Elizabeth Ives, of Middletown, Conn.; 287 *Abner*, b Jan. 27, 1811, m Hannah Beecher, of Bristol, Conn.; 288 *Henry*, b Sept. 8, 1812, m Abigail Ames, of Ohio; 289 *Edmund*, b Sept. 6, 1814, m Betsey Hubbard, of Wallingford; 290 *Peter Green*, b Sept. 7, 1816, m Mary A. Roberts; 291 *Lucy Ann*, b July 24, 1818, m Henry Lane, she d Jan. 14, 1855; 292 *David*, b May 6, 1820, d ae. 6 weeks; 293 *Joseph*, b March 26, 1822; 294 *James*, b March 26, 1822, d ae. 3 weeks; 295 *James*, b Feb. 14, 1822, m 1st, Levia Root, of Southington, Conn., 2d, Calista Darrow, of Bristol, Conn.

264 STEPHEN.

CAPT. STEPHEN TUTTLE, son of Ephraim and Elizabeth Tuttle, married Catharine Smith, of Cheshire, Conn. He went to Burton, Geauga Co., Ohio, and died there about 1866–7.

Children: 296 *Augustus F.*, res. in New Haven; 297 *Mary*, m Silas Gaylord, of Cheshire, and settled in Ohio; 298 *Elizabeth.*

227. GAIUS.

GAIUS TUTTLE, son of Capt. Lucius and Hannah Tuttle, married Bella Gaylord, of Wallingford. He was a farmer and resided about a mile and a quarter from the village of Cheshire, eastward, on the road to Meriden. He died in Cheshire, ae. 67 years.

Children: 299 *Phebe N.*, b Jan. 24, 1811, m Stephen Beecher, Aug. 8, 1844; 300 *Samuel Anson*, b Aug. 18, 1814, m 1st, Eunice Pierrepont, May 1, 1844, she d Sept. 17, 1850, ae. 29, he m 2d, Emily R. Royce, dau. of Dea. Silas Royce of Meriden, May 11, 1854.

JOTHAM.

JOTHAM TUTTLE, a descendant of Jonathan and Rebecca Tuttle, son of Nathaniel and Mary Tuttle, married Keziah Munson, and settled at Tuttle's farm, in Wallingford, where he died, ae. 66 years. His 2d wife was Elizabeth Perkins.

Children by 1st marriage: 301 *Eli*, m Asenath Perkins, and settled in Hamden; 302 *Asa*, m Laura Tuttle, and settled in Cheshire, where he d, she d in 1870; 303 *Mary;* 304 *Esther*. By 2d marriage: 305 *Manning*, went west many years ago.

TYLER.[1]

Roger, John and William Tyler, supposed brothers, were the first of the name in Wallingford. Roger Tyler married Sarah Humiston, Jan. 10, 1698. John Tyler married Phebe Beach. William and Mary Tyler were the first of the name in Wallingford.

JOHN.

JOHN TYLER, married to Abigail Hall, by Rev. Samuel Street, Jan. 14, 1694. She died Nov. 20, 1741.

Children: 1 *Esther*, b Sept. 20, 1695, m Moses Beach of Wallingford; 2 *John*, b Jan. 29, 1697; 3 *Abigail*, b Jan. 29, 1697, m Sam'l Andrews, of Wallingford; 4 *Nathan*, b Apr. 17, 1701, m Rachel ———, she died in Cheshire, Nov. 2, 1749, ae. 44 years; 5 *Lois*, b Nov. 7, 1706; 6 *Thomas*, b Nov. 26, 1708, m Lydia ———; 7 *John*, b Jan 14, 1710, m Phebe Beach, April 7, 1731; 8 *Isaac*, b Jan. 17, 1713, m Susannah Miles, Nov. 27, 1732; 9 *Joseph*, b March 21, 1716, m Mehitable ———; 10 *Experience;* 11 *Hannah*, m Macock Ward.

WILLIAM.

WILLIAM TYLER married Mary ———. She died in Wallingford, March 11, 1754. He, in company with Mr. Samuel Stanley, purchased the mills at Yalesville in 1703. He bought the interest of Mr. Stanley in 1704. From this

1 For collateral branches see Bradbury's Hist. Kennebunkport, 16, 581; Bridgeman's King's Chapel Burial Ground, 289–91; Daggett's Hist. Attleborough, Mass., 95; Eaton's Hist. Thomaston, Me., 440; Field's Hist. Haddam, Conn., 46; Heraldic Journal, III. (1867) 184; Holden's Gen. Capron Family, part 1, 191; Hudson's Hist. Lexington, Mass., 281; Savage's Gen. Dict., IV. 354–6.

date, they remained in the family until after the decease of the late Mr. Samuel Tyler, in 1822, when they were set out to his daughter Merab, whose guardian, the late Nehemiah Rice, sold them to Charles Yale Esq.

Children: 11 1-2 *Mary*, b Sept. 7, 1695, m Francis Sedgwick, Feb. 5, 1734; 12 *Sarah*, b Nov. 25, 1697; 13 *Phebe*, b Oct. 5, 1700; 14 *Samuel*, b Aug. 11, 1702, m Jerusha Sedgwick Feb. 15, 1734; 15 *Martha*, b Oct. 4, 1706, m Jacob Francis, Jan. 20, 1763; 16 *Mehitable*, b Nov. 14, 1707; 17 *Abiah*, b Nov. 10, 1708; 18 *Ephraim*, b April 18, 1713, m Elizabeth De Wolf, Feb. 13, 1734; 19 *Mehitable*, b Nov. 17, 1718, m Stephen Merwin, April 12, 1743; 20 *Asa*, b July 30, 1722.

NATHAN.

NATHAN TYLER m Rachel ———. She died at Cheshire, Nov. 25, 1749, ae. 44 years.

Children: 21 *Lois*, b May 12, 1731; 22 *Thankful*, b April 18, 1733; 23 *Rachel*, b Nov. 24, 1736; 24 *Tirzah*, b March 6, 1738; 25 *Barnabas*, b Aug. 30, 1739, d Sept. 20, 1749; 26 *Heber*, b and d Sept. 30, 1749.

6. THOMAS.

THOMAS and Lydia Tyler were of Wallingford.

Children: 27 *Elizabeth*, b Nov. 18, 1736; 28 *Reuben*, b Sept. 19, 1738; 29 *Rispie*, b Dec. 8, 1740; 30 *Joseph*, b Feb. 19, 1743, d Feb. 25, 1752; 31 *Experience*, b Aug. 18, 1745; 32 *Obedience*, b Nov. 24. 1747.

7. JOHN.

JOHN TYLER married Phebe Beach, April 7, 1731. After her decease he married Mary Doolittle, Nov. 9, 1741.

Children: 33 *Benjamin*, b Jan, 14, 1732, d Feb. 25, 1732; 34 *Benjamin*, b Feb. 23, 1733; 35 *Lydia*, b June 28, 1735; 36 *Patience*, b March 6, 1739. By 2d marriage: 37 *John*, b Aug. 15, 1742; 38 *Phebe*, b Nov. 10, 1743.

8. ISAAC.

ISAAC TYLER married Susannah Miles; she died Jan. 25,

1760. He died April 12, 1801, ae. 89 years, at Cheshire.

Children: 39 *Abraham*, b June 9, 1735; 40 *Enos*, m Obedience Smith; 41 *Abraham*, b 1738; 42 *Miles C.*; 43 *Isaac*, b March 23, 1740; 44 *Amos*; 45 *Jacob*, b March 20, 1742-3; 46 *Susannah*, b April 8, 1745; 47 *Hannah*, b July 20, 1747; 48 *Sarah*, b March 2, 1749, m Jesse, son of Stephen Welton, of Waterbury; 49 *Nathaniel*, b Oct. 9, 1753; 50 *Eunice*.

9. JOSEPH.

JOSEPH TYLER married Mehitable ———. She died Aug. 28, 1757. He died Oct., 1741, leaving an estate of £548.

Child: 51 *Sybil*, b Dec. 31, 1740, m Benjamin Cook, Aug. 28, 1757.

14. SAMUEL.

SAMUEL TYLER married Jerusha, daughter of Samuel and Ruth Sedgwick, of Hartford.

Children: 52 *Lathrop*, b June 22, 1734, he built the original mill known as Humiston Mill; 53 *Samuel*, b Dec. 14, 1735, m Damaris Atwater, April 21, 1763; 54 *Daniel*, b March 17, 1738, he built the mill in the south-east part of the town; 55 *Moses*, b March 15, 1740, d Jan. 15, 1743; 56 *Jerusha*, b July 23, 1743, d May 3, 1744; 57 *Jared*, b Nov. 5, 1744, m Keziah Rice, she died 1817, ae. 73 yrs.; 58 *Moses*, b Feb. 12, 1746, d Nov. 22, 1776, in Wallingford; 59 *Jason*, b May 23, 1749; 60 *Mary*, b 1751, m James Rice, he d in Wallingford; 61 *Jerusha*, b Jan. 4, 1754.

40. ENOS.

ENOS TYLER married Obedience Smith, who died July 28, 1771, ae. 38 years. He then married Lydia ——, and she died Oct. 27, 1744, ae. 36 years.

Children: 62 *Reuben*, b May 30, 1759; 63 *Enos*; 64 *Nathaniel*, b Jan. 22, 1761; 65 *Bede*; 66 *Sarah*; 67 *Mary*; 68 *Lydia*.

53. SAMUEL.

SAMUEL, son of Samuel and Jerusha Sedgwick Tyler, married Damaris, daughter of Phineas and Mary Atwater, April

21, 1763. He was the last male in the Tyler line that owned the mills at Yalesville, and was himself constantly employed about the mills during a long life. Bennet Jeralds Esq. has recently erected a new house on the site of the old one. The new Episcopal church at Yalesville occupies the ground on which formerly stood the large barn of Mr. Tyler. He died March 13, 1823, ae. 88 yrs. She died April 24, 1810, aged 72 yrs.

Children: 69 *Merab*, b 1763; 70 *Selina*, m Sherlock Andrews of Wallingford; 71 son, d young; 72 *Julia*, m Dr. James Gilbert of New Haven; 73 *Lavinia*, b March 14, 1781, m Harry Whittelsey of Catskill, N. Y.

54. DANIEL.

DANIEL, son of Samuel and Jerusha Tyler. He built the mills at the south-east part of the township, which are still in the possession of his descendants. He was killed by an insane person named Coles, for the crime (as the insane man claimed), of being a tory of the Revolution.

Children: 74 *Royal D.*; 75 *Samuel*, d at the south.

57. JARED.

JARED, son of Samuel and Jerusha Tyler, married Keziah Royce, July 15, 1772. He died March 17, 1816. She died Feb. 8, 1819, ae. 73. He owned and occupied a large farm at what is now Yalesville. Miles Clark is the present owner of the house in which Mr. Tyler lived.

Children: 76 *Jared Royce*, b Sept. 2, 1776, m Rhoda ——, went to Vermont, where he died; 77 *Kezia*, b April 18, 1784, m Ethelbert Benham of Cheshire, she d July 19, 1830; 78 *Joel*, b about 1774, m 1st, Esther Hough, in 1798, 2d, P. Blakeslee, he d in 1831, in Lockport, N. Y., had Jared, James, Jane and Amanda, all deceased; 79 *Elizabeth*, b 1794, m Ebenezer Allen and went to Ohio, where she d at the age of 74; 80 *Amanda*, b April 2, 1780, m Capt. Wm. Davidson of Milford, was lost at sea; 81 twins, b 1796, d early.

58. MOSES.

MOSES, son of Samuel and Jerusha Tyler, married Lois ——. She died Aug., 1809, ae. 54 yrs. He died Nov. 22, 1776, ae. 31 yrs. He was the owner of a large house which was occupied as a hotel, and stood on the ground now occupied by Mr. McKenzie's house at Yalesville. The old tavern was burned some sixty or seventy years since, with all its contents.

Children: 82 *Noble*, b 1802, d Mar. 22, 1844, ae. 42; 83 *Lois*, m Capt. John Nott of Wethersfield, both died in Wallingford; 84 *Mary*, m 1st, Silas Benham of Meriden, and had Jared Nelson Tyler Benham, an only son, she m for her 2d husband John Kirtland Esq.

78. JOEL.

JOEL TYLER, son of Jared and Keziah Tyler, was born about 1774, married Esther Hough about 1798; after her death he married Polly Blakeslee. He died in Lockport, N. Y., in Feb. or March, 1831.

76. JARED.

JARED ROYCE TYLER, son of Jared and Keziah Tyler, was born Sept. 2, 1776. He died Nov. 14, 1844, ae. 68 yrs., in Lockport, N. Y., leaving a widow, Rhoda, but had no children born to them.

80. AMANDA.

AMANDA TYLER, daughter of Jared and Keziah Tyler, was born April 2, 1780, married Capt. William Davidson, of Milford, in the year ——. He with his vessel and crew were lost while returning from the West Indies. The last heard from him was that he left the Island with his vessel heavily laden with salt, just before a severe gale. She married 2d, Abijah Carrington, in Milford, in the year ——, and died in Milford, in the year ——.

77. KEZIAH.

KEZIAH TYLER, daughter of Jared and Keziah Tyler, was born April 18, 1784, married Ethelbert Benham, of Cheshire, Conn., Oct., 1808, died July 19, 1830, in Cheshire, Conn.

79. ELIZABETH.

ELIZABETH TYLER, daughter of Jared and Keziah Tyler, was born in 1794, married Ebenezer Allen, of Bristol, at the age of 25, and died ae. 74 yrs. and 11 months. She died in Geneva, Ohio.

WHITTELSEY.[1]

JOHN.

JOHN WHITTELSEY is believed to be the first person of the name who emigrated to the United States, and the ancestor of all the Whittelseys who have lived here. He came from England about 1650, and became a tanner and shoemaker at Saybrook, Conn. The town of Saybrook, by authority of the General Court, gave to Mr. Whittelsey and Wm. Dudley the right to establish a ferry over the Connecticut river, near which he lived, in 1663. This still belongs to his descendants. He died April 15, 1704; his wife died Sept. 29, 1714. Their descendants were:

(a) *John*, settled in Saybrook; (b) *Stephen*, attorney at Saybrook; (c) *Joseph*, settled at Saybrook; (d) *Eliphalet*, settled at Wethersfield, married Mary Pratt, Dec. 1, 1702; (e) *Ebenezer*, settled at Saybrook; (f) *Jabez*, settled at Bethlem, deacon; (g) *Samuel*, settled at Wallingford, minister; (h) *Elizabeth;* (i) *Ruth.*

SAMUEL.

REV. SAMUEL WHITTELSEY was the youngest son and child of John and Ruth Dudley Whittelsey of Saybrook, and was born there in 1686, was graduated at Yale college in 1705, married Sarah, daughter of Rev. Nathan Chauncey, son of Rev. Charles Chauncey, President of Harvard College. He

---

1 For collateral branches, see Andrews' Hist. New Britain, Conn., 235, 317, 355, 376; Cothren's Hist. Woodbury, Conn., 756–65; N. E. Hist. and Gen. Reg., XX. 321; Scranton's Gen. of Scranton Family, 43; Savage's Gen. Dict., IV. 537; Whittelsey's Memorial of Whittelsey Family.

was ordained at Wallingford as colleague to Rev. Mr. Street, April 10, 1710, after having preached one year on probation. He died April 15, 1752, having nearly completed the 42d year of his ministry.[1] His widow died Oct. 23, 1767, ae. 84 yrs.

Children: 1 *Samuel*, b July 10, 1713, m Susanna Newton of Milford, Sept. 21, 1743; 2 *Lois*, b Nov. 28, 1714, m Col. Elihu Hall, Jan. 2, 1734; 3 *Chauncey*, b Oct. 8, 1717, m 1st, Elizabeth Whiting, Oct. 17, 1751, 2d, Martha Newton, Aug. 13, 1753; 4 *Sarah*, b Jan. 19, 1720, d Aug. 23, 1725; 5 *Elisha*, b Oct. 19, 1721, m Susanna Hall of New Haven, April 8, 1754; 6 *Charles*, b Jan. 16, 1723, m Lucy Hall of Cheshire, June 13, 1751; 7 *Sarah*, b Oct. 20, 1726, d Nov. 2, 1746; 8 *Katherine*, b Dec. 26, 1728, m Rev. James Dana, May 8, 1759; he was born May 10, 1735, and d Aug. 28, 1793, at New Haven; she d Aug. 18, 1812.

1. SAMUEL.

SAMUEL WHITTELSEY grad. at Yale College in 1729. He was a tutor in that college from 1732 to 1738, Master of Arts from Yale and Harvard colleges; settled in the ministry at Milford, where his virtues, piety, and good deeds shone with peculiar brightness and beauty. His life was unceasingly devoted to faithful labor in sacred things, and the advancement of religion among his people in Milford, who with commendable zeal honor his memory. His wife, to whom he was married Sept. 21, 1743, died May 10, 1803, ae. 87. He died Oct. 22, 1769.

Children: 9 *Samuel*, b Aug. 3, 1745, m Mary Hubbard, was a physician in Milford, d Oct. 22, 1776; 10 *Susanna*, b Jan. 26, 1747, m Dr. Edward Carrington of Milford, d Jan. 1, 1801; 11 *Sarah*, b Oct. 31, 1749, m John Chandler, who grad. at Yale, 1764, and was sheriff of New Haven Co., she d July 1, 1803; 12 *Royal Newton*, b Feb. 24, 1754, m Ann Woodruff of South Farms, April 20, 1775.

3. CHAUNCEY.

CHAUNCEY WHITTELSEY was graduated at Yale College,

---

1 See p 115, ante.

1738, ordained March 1, 1758, over the 1st church in New Haven; preached election sermon, May 14, 1778. President Stiles says of him, "He was an excellent classical scholar, well acquainted with the three learned languages, Latin, Greek and Hebrew, also with Geography, Mathematics, Natural Philosophy and Astronomy, with Moral Philosophy and History, and with the general Cyclopædia of an academic life; and amassed by laborious reading, a great treasure of wisdom. In Literature, he was in his day, oracular at College, for he taught with facility and success in every branch of knowledge." One of his most distinguished pupils said of him at his funeral, "I shall never forget the pathetic and earnest recommendations of early piety which he gave to us in the course of his tutorship."

It was this man of whom David Brainard said, "He had no more grace than this chair." Peabody, in his life of Brainard (p. 274) said in reference to this language, that it was "a phrase which that individual justified by his subsequent proceedings." Dr. Bacon in his historical discourses (pp. 248, 249) refutes this charge, and shows the spirit which dictated the utterance of such language. He was licensed to preach, Sept. 30, 1740. "In 1745 he resigned his office in college, and for reasons which do not appear, relinquished the design of entering the ministry, and settled in New Haven as a merchant. He continued in business ten years; during this time he was an active member of the first Church and Society. He was brought forward by his fellow citizens into public life. He represented this town in the General Assembly of the colony, and in a variety of public trusts, he discharged himself with fidelity and growing influence. He was subsequently settled as colleague with Mr. Noyes."[1] When settled in the ministry he applied himself to theological studies and the duties of the pastoral office with an ardor, zeal and assiduity equaled by few. His

---

1 See Bacon's Historical Discourses, pp. 243, 266.

affability and dignity of manner, philanthropy and integrity, joined to an accurate knowledge of men and the affairs of life, commanded esteem and veneration.[1] He married 1st, Elizabeth, daughter of Col. Whiting, and 2d, Martha Newton, a sister of his brother Samuel's wife.

Children: 13 *Chauncey*, b Oct. 27, 1746, m Lucy Wetmore, Feb. 12 1770; 14 *Samuel Joseph*, b July 13, 1749, d Aug. 3, 1751; 15 *Elisha*, b Oct. 14, 1751, d Oct. 23, 1751; 16 *Newton*, b June 1, 1754, grad. at Yale, 1773, m Beulah Fuller; 17 *Martha*, b Sept. 1, 1756, m Capt. Wm. Van Duerson, he d May 3, 1763; 18 *Elizabeth*, b July 1, 1758, d Aug. 1, 1758; 19 *Elizabeth*, b May 2, 1760, d July, 1760; 20 *John Bryan*, b June 15, 1763, d Aug. 27, 1763; 21 *Samuel*, b Feb. 10, 1763, grad. at Yale college in 1779, m Sarah Van Duerson, Dec. 10, 1788; 22 *Charles*, b Oct. 18, 1764, m Anna Cutler, Oct. 9, 1792; 23 *Susannah*, b Feb. 25, 1766, m Judge Dyer White; 24 *Bryan*, b Aug. 6, 1768, d at New Haven, Jan 9, 1835; 25 *John*, b Sept. 8, 1770, grad. at Yale college in 1791, m Ann Kerwood; 26 *Elizabeth*, b Sept. 18, 1773.

5. ELISHA.

ELISHA WHITTELSEY married Susanna Hall of New Haven, April 8, 1754. He was an attorney at Wallingford, and died at that place Feb. 25, 1808, ae. 87 yrs. She d Oct 19, 1768.

Children: 27 *Elisha*, b Jan. 1, 1755, m Sarah Jones; 28 *Susanna*, b Sept. 2, 1756, m Caleb Street; 29 *Sarah*, b Mar. 15, 1759, d June 23, 1764, in Wallingford; 30 *Mary*, b April 9, 1751, m Dr. Wm. Cook; 31 *Elizabeth*, b April 4, 1763, m Dr. Liberty Kimberly, in 1788, she d in Derby, 1827; 32 *Charles*, b Nov. 12, 1764, d May 26, 1768; 33 *Sarah*, b Dec. 6, 1766, d Nov. 8, 1774; 34 *Charles*, b Sept. 29, 1768, d Jan. 9, 1769.

12. ROGER.

ROGER NEWTON WHITTELSEY married Ann Woodruff, April 20, 1775; she was born April 5, 1756, and died March

---

1 See Dana's sermon on the Close of the 18th Century, Note B, p. 60.

7, 1825, at Litchfield, South Farms. He was a farmer, and died March 15, 1835; he was for many years a Justice of the Peace for Litchfield County.

Children: 35 *Samuel*, b Dec. 18, 1775, was a minister in New York, m Abigail Goodrich; 36 *Newton*, b Oct. 31, 1777, m Esther Robbins of Claremont, N. H.; 37 an infant son, b Dec. 29, 1779, d Jan. 7, 1780; 38 *Chauncey*, b Dec. 13, 1781, m Mary Bacon of Roxbury, Conn., Dec. 11, 1811; 39 *Susanna*, b Feb. 12, 1784, m Capt. Stephen Cogswell of New Preston, Conn.; 40 *Jabez*, b Feb. 8, 1786, m Nancy Parker of Terryville, Conn.; 41 *William*, b July 28, 1788, m Abigail Mills of Boston, Mass.; 42 *Henry*, b May 18, 1790, m Abby Ray of New York; 43 *Frederick*, b Jan. 25, 1792, m Hannah Ray of South Farms; 44 *Charles*, b Aug. 23, 1793, m Elizabeth Fuller of Avon, Conn.; 45 *Anna*, b May 28, 1795, m Dea. Chester Stone of Franklin, N. H.; 46 *Lucy*, b Oct. 10, 1797, m Stephen Cogswell Jr. of New Preston; 47 *George Washington*, b Aug. 10, 1799, m 1st, Cornelia Keeler, 2d, Elizabeth G. Boardman, res., New Milford.

13. CHAUNCEY.

CHAUNCEY WHITTELSEY married Lucy Wetmore of Middletown, Conn., Feb. 12, 1770; he graduated at Yale College in 1764, and was licensed to preach, but gave it up on account of his health, after two years; he was elected deacon, Sept. 17, 1778, and served twenty-three years; was Alderman and Collector of the Port at Middletown; his wife was an only daughter of Seth Wetmore, and her mother was a sister of Pres. Edwards.

Children: 48 *Lucy*, b Oct. 4, 1773, m Capt. Joe. Alsop, of Middletown, Conn., Nov. 5, 1797; 49 *Hannah*, b May 10, 1775; 50 *Betsey*, b May 24, 1780, m Capt. Joseph Williams, May 25, 1817: 51 *Chauncey*, b Jan. 18, 1783, m Seth Lathrop Tracy, April 14, 1818, an attorney.

16. NEWTON.

NEWTON WHITTELSEY, married Beulah Fuller, of Middletown, Conn. He graduated at Yale, in 1773. Was a merchant. He died Dec. 4, 1785, ae. 64 years.

Child: 52 *Martha*, b Nov. 6, 1785, m Julius Dunning, Nov. 20, 1808, settled in Shelby Center, N. Y.

21. SAMUEL.

SAMUEL WHITTELSEY married Sarah Van Duerson, of Vincennes, Ind., Dec. 10, 1788. She was born May 30, 1763, and died Apr., 1811, æ. 65 yrs., at Vincennes, Ind. He grad. at Yale, in 1779. He was an attorney. He died March 7, 1838, ae. 71 years.

Children: 53 *Catherine Van Duerson*, b Sept. 9, 1790, res. Carlisle, Ind.; 54 *Wm. Chauncey*, M. D., b Dec. 26, 1792, m Ann Elizabeth Rapine, Nov. 20, 1822; 55 *Samuel Gilbert*, b in 1794, d; 56 *Samuel Gilbert*, b Dec., 1796, d June, 1810; 57 *Isaac Newton*, b July 19, 1798, m A. Elizabeth Van Buntin, April 12, 1831; 58 *Eliza Lefferts*, b April 16, 1800, m Dr. James K. Ohaver, Dec. 6, 1825; 50 *Chas. Egbert*, M. D., b March 24, 1802, d Sept. 4, 1824.

22. CHARLES.

CHARLES WHITTELSEY married Ann Cutler, Oct. 9, 1792. She was born in New Haven, July 12, 1773, and died Feb. 8, 1850. He was a merchant at New Haven, and died March 12, 1828, ae 64 years.

Children: 60 *Mary Cutler*, b Aug. 12, 1793, d in New Haven, Dec. 5, 1853; 61 *Chauncey*, b Aug. 5, 1795, d Aug. 21, 1795; 62 *Susannah*, b Dec. 5, 1796, m 1st, Rev. Samuel B. Ingersoll, 2d, Wm. T. Eustice, of Boston; 63 *Charles Bryan*, b Dec. 12, 1798, m Jane B. Wilford, was a merchant in New Haven; 64 *Chauncey*, b Sept. 6, 1801, was a minister, d March 12, 1826; 65 *John Cutler*, b Nov. 1, 1803, m Eliza Waller, June 7, 1829, she was b in 1807; 66 *Henry Newton*, b Feb. 9, 1808, m Elizabeth A. Wilson, of New Haven, Nov. 30, 1837; 67 *Martha Ann*, b Oct. 13, 1811, m Rev. George Oviatt, Feb. 17, 1839, d April 5, 1811.

24. BRYAN.

BRYAN WHITTELSEY was lame from his birth. He died at New Haven, Jan. 9, 1835.

25. JOHN.

JOHN married Ann Kerwood, June 1, 1799. He grad. at Yale, 1791, was U. S. Inspector in N. Y. city. He died May 12, 1849, at New Haven.

Children: 68 *Elizabeth K.*, b May 12, 1800, d ae. 3 years; 69 *Edward*, b May 2, 1801, a merchant, d in New York, July 9, 1842; 70 *John Newton*, b Feb. 11, 1803, d in New Orleans, La., July 9, 1803; 71 *Mary Elizabeth*, b June 29, 1805, d in New Haven; 72 *Charles*, b Nov. 3, 1807, m Maria Tuthill, Nov. 3, 1837, she was b Dec. 28, 1816; 73 *John Russel*, b Oct. 10, 1809, m Martha Butler, Jan. 12, 1835, she was b March 29, 1809; 74 *Wm. Kerwood*, b Aug. 27, 1812, d at Tipton, Iowa, Sept. 15, 1849; 75 *Martha Newton*, b April 17, 1815, m Moses H. Baldwin April 23, 1839, Pittsfield, Mass.; 76 *Jane Ann*, b Feb. 2, 1818, d Sept. 20, 1825.

27. ELISHA.

ELISHA WHITTELSEY married Sarah Jones of Wallingford, Sept, 8, 1777. She was born March 30, 1758, and died Sept. 15, 1836. He was a merchant and town clerk of his native town for many years. He died greatly lamented, Sept. 16, 1822, ae. 67 years.

Children: 77 *John Hall*, b June 4, 1778, m 1st, Sally Chittenden, Dec. 14, 1798, 2d, wid. Clara Bostwick, Aug. 4, 1824; 78 *Nancy*, b March 15, 1780, m 1st, Wolcott Reynolds, 2d, John Hunt of New Haven; 79 *Henry*, b Feb. 2, 1782, m 1st, Lavinia Tyler of Wallingford, May 2, 1811, 2d, Merab Hull of Cheshire, May 12, 1828; 80 *Eunice*, b Sept. 26, 1784, d July 31, 1819, in Wallingford; 81 *Jared Potter*, b March 8, 1777, m Lydia G. Acker, Oct. 22, 1814, d Jan. 25, 1869; 82 *Lucy*, b Feb. 16, 1789, m Drake Andrews of Wallingford; 83 *Sarah*, b May 29, 1792, d Nov. 11, 1792; 84 *Peter*, b Feb. 8, 1794, m Betsey Hunt, April 16, 1823.

35. SAMUEL.

SAMUEL married Abigail Goodrich. He graduated at Yale in 1803, licensed to preach in June, 1804, ordained at New Preston, Dec. 30, 1807, settled nine years, during which time 142 were added to the church, April 30, 1817, took charge of the Deaf and Dumb Asylum at Hartford, became Principal of the Ontario Female Seminary, April, 1826, afterwards removed to the Seminary at Utica, became publisher of the Mother's Magazine, 1833, removed to New York city in 1833.[1]

Children: 85 *Samuel Goodrich*, b Nov. 8, 1809, m Anna Cook Mills; 86 a son, b March 26, 1811, d March 28, 1811; 87 *Charles Chauncey*, b Sept. 2, 1812, d April 29, 1818; 88 *Elizabeth*, b Sept. 29, 1815, d Jan. 26, 1848; 89 *Henry Martyn*, b Aug. 12, 1821, lawyer in N. Y. city; 90 *Charles Augustus*, b Oct. 20, 1823, a seaman; 91 *Emily Chauncey*, b Jan. 17, 1825, m Rev. Lucius Curtis, of Woodbury.

WILCOX.

The family of Wilcox is of Saxon origin, and was seated at Bury St. Edmonds, in the county of Suffolk, England, before the Norman Conquest. Sir John Dugdale, in his visitation of the county of Suffolk, mentions fifteen generations of this family previous to 1600. In the reign of King Edward III., Sir John Wilcox was entrusted with several important commands against the French, and had command of the cross-bowmen from Norfolk, Suffolk and Essex. Jno. Wm. Wilcox, of Bury Priory in Suffolk, an eminent Queen's counsel, is the representative of this ancient family. Sir George Lawrence Willcocks, of Brookend, County Tyrone, Ireland, is the eldest son of the late George Willcocks Esq. of Coal Island, County Tyrone, by Isabella, daughter of the Rev. Charles Caulfield. He was born in 1820, educated at Dungannon, and is a magistrate for County Tyrone. This family is a

---

1 See Cothren's Hist. of Woodbury, Conn., p. 270.

branch of the family of Willcockses of Tottenham High Cross, Middlesex, but has been settled in Ireland for about two centuries. They have been, and some branches are still members of the Society of Friends. On the old records the name is spelled both Wilcox and Wilcocks. It is derived from *William.*[1]

William Wilcox, who was chosen Lieut. Governor in the early times of the Massachusetts Colony, was the first of the name who is recorded on the list of the early officers. He was an officer of the artillery company, and died at Cambridge, November, 1653. He is there stated to have come to this country from the county of Suffolk. Nine of his descendants graduated at the New England colleges up to the year 1823.

JOHN.

JOHN WILCOX of Hartford was an original proprietor in 1639. He had a son John who accompanied him from England. This son John was born in England, and married 1st, Sarah, eldest daughter of Wm. Wadsworth, Sept. 17, 1646; 2d, Catherine, daughter of Thomas Stoughton, Jan. 18, 1650; 3d Mary ——, who died 1671; 4th, Esther, daughter of Wm. Cornwall.

Child by 1st marriage: 1 *Sarah*, b Oct. 3, 1648. By 2d marriage: 2 *John*, b Oct. 29, 1650; 3 *Thomas;* 4 *Mary*, b Nov. 13, 1654; 5 *Israel*, b June 19, 1656; 6 *Samuel*, b Nov. 9, 1658. By 3d marriage: 7 *Ephraim*, b July 9, 1672; 8 *Esther*, b Dec. 9, 1673; 9 *Mary*, b March 24, 1676. John Wilcox died May 24, 1676.

5. ISRAEL.

ISRAEL WILCOX was in Middletown in 1675; he mar-

---

1 This name has become the parent of a greater number of sirnames than any other baptismal appellation; among which may be mentioned Wilcox, Wilkes, Wilkins, Wilmot, Willis, Wilson and Williams. Gillet, and Gillot are also from the same source. In France this Christian name has produced Guillot, Guillemin, Guillemette, Villemain, etc. See *Mem. Soc. Ant. Normandie*, XIII.

ried Sarah, daughter of John Savage, March 28, 1678; he died Dec. 20, 1689. She died Feb. 8, 1724.

Children: 10 *Israel*, b Jan. 16, 1680; 11 *John*, b July 5, 1682; 12 *Samuel*, b Sept. 26, 1685; 13 *Thomas*, b July 5, 1687; 14 *Sarah*, b Nov. 30, 1689.

6. SAMUEL.

SAMUEL WILCOX of Middletown, born Nov. 9, 1658, married Abigail, daughter of Francis Whitmore, May 9, 1683; he died March 16, 1714.

Children: 15 *Samuel*, b Feb. 20, 1684; 16, 17 *Francis* and *Abigail*, b July 5, 1687, Abigail d in 1688, and her mother a fortnight after.

7. EPHRAIM.

EPHRAIM WILCOX removed to Middletown, and married, Aug. 23, 1698.

Children: 18 *Esther*, b Jan. 4, 1707; 19 *Ephraim*, b June 4, 1709; 20 *John*, b Aug. 8, ——.

20. JOHN.

JOHN WILCOX, born Aug. 8, 17—, married Hannah ———, lived in Middletown.

Children: 21 *John*, b Jan. 15, 1740, d April 25, 1823; 22 *Samuel*, b May 8, 1742, d Sept. 4, 1807; 23 *Hezekiah*, b Mar. 4, 1744, d Sept. 11, 1776; 24 *Joseph*, b March 29, 1746, d Jan. 31, 1832; 25 *Hannah*, b Jan. 28, 1748, d Feb. 19, 1826; 26 *Giles*, b Jan. 2, 1750; 27 *Simeon*, b Feb. 25, 17—, d Oct. 13, 1827; 28 *Submit*, b Dec. 5, 1754, d Aug. 16, 1803; 29 *Comfort*, b Feb. 17, 175—, m Patty Doolittle, Aug. 10, 1780; 30 *Sarah*, b Feb. 7, 1760, m Abel North, Feb. 11, 1788, and had five children.

21. JOHN.

JOHN WILCOX, son of John and Hannah, married Eunice Norton, Oct. 16, 1766.

Children: 31 *Seth*, b July 31, 1767, m Matty Bacon, Mar. 21, 1736; 32 *Jeduthan*, b Nov. 18, 1768, m Sally Fisk, May, 1793; 33 *John*, b Sept. 13, 1771, m Sybil Giles, 1795; 34

Eunice, b July 4, 1774; 35 *Jedediah*, b June 1, 1778, d Oct. 10, 1789.

22. SAMUEL.

SAMUEL WILCOX, son of John and Hannah, married 1st, Ruth Roberts, 1784, and 2d, Ruth Wood, 1796.

Child: 36 *Ruth*, b Aug. 12, 1798. After his death his widow married Thomas Scofel, Feb. 17, 1779.

23. HEZEKIAH.

HEZEKIAH WILCOX, son of John and Hannah, married Rachel Boardman, Nov. 9, 1775.

Child: 37 *Hezekiah*, b Oct. 11, 1776, d Jan. 18, 1792.

24. JOSEPH.

JOSEPH WILCOX, son of John and Hannah, married Miriam, daughter of Josiah and Sybil Bacon, Nov. 30, 1785. She was born Feb. 7, 1762. d March 19, 1825.

Children: 38 *Sarah*, b Oct. 29, 1786, d Nov. 4, 1847; 39 *Jedediah*, b Feb. 7, 1788, d 1856; 40 *Submit*, b Nov. 11, 1789; 41 *Joseph*, b Oct. 21, 1791, d Jan., 1858; 42 *Hezekiah*, b March 28, 1793; 43 *Elisha B.*, b June 20, 1795; 44 *Lavinia*, b Jan. 31, 1797, d Sept. 24, 1843; 45 *Maria* (or *Miriam*), b March 19, 1801, d March, 1847.

26. GILES.

GILES, son of John and Hannah Wilcox, married Rachel Dove, Nov. 9, 1775.

Children: 46 *Olive*, b Nov. 1, 1776, m Amos Churchill, April 21, 1796; 47 *Giles*, b Aug. 28, 1779; 48 *Sylvester*, b Feb. 14, 1782; 49 *Samuel*, b Oct. 20, 1786; 50 *Sarah*, b Nov. 30, 1788.

42. HEZEKIAH.

HEZEKIAH, son of Joseph and Miriam Wilcox, married Rama Roberts, Nov. 7, 1816. She was born Dec. 23, 1792, and died Jan. 10, 1869.

Children born in Westfield: 51 *Joseph Alston*, b Oct. 15, 1817, m Lucy Ann Bacon; 52 *Ann*, b Sept. 7, 1821, d March 7, 1826; 53 *Phebe Miranda*, b Dec. 4, 1822, m Hollister Risley; 54 *Lavinia*, b July 29, 1825, m Wm. Hall of Meriden; 55 *Hezekiah*, b Dec. 23, 1827, d Nov. 16, 1833; 56 *Henry*, b May 30, 1830, m Sarah Dunham.

43. ELISHA.

ELISHA B., son of Joseph and Miriam Wilcox, married Hepsibah ——, Jan. 26, 1818.

Children, born in Westfield: 57 *Frances Sophia*, b June 3, 1819, m Edwin Savage, Nov., 1837; 58 *Lucy Maria*, b June 15, 1820, m George Miller, Aug. 5, 1845; 59 *Hannah Jane*, b April 13, 1822; 60 *Horace Cornwall*, b Jan. 26, 1824; 61 *Julia*, b Jan. 7, 1826, m Newell H. Bowers, Sept. 2, 1846; 62 *Jedediah*, b March 4, 1827; 63 *Dennis Cornwall*, b Dec. 14, 1831; 64 *Edson*, b March 14, 1831, d Oct. 1, 1851; 65 *Hezekiah*, b Oct. 12, 1832; 66 *Edmund North*, b Aug, 7, 1836; 67 *Mary Ellen*, b Oct., 1838; 68 *Elisha Watson*, b July 27, 1840.

Israel and Jedediah Wilcox were the first of the name in Westfield, Conn.; both came from Middletown, Upper houses.

The arms of the Wilcoxes of England are, per fesse, *or* and *az*, a fesse, gules, over all a lion rampant, counterchanged. Crest: a demi lion rampant, *az*. The lion rampant indicates that he to whom the arms were granted, had gained a victory whilst in command of the army.

YALE.

THOMAS.

THOMAS YALE married Mary, daughter of Capt. Nathaniel Turner, of New Haven, in 1645. Capt. Turner was of Lynn, Mass. in 1630; he moved to New Haven in 1638. He was Captain of Mr. Lamberton's Phantom ship, which sailed from New Haven on a voyage to the old country, and was lost with all on board, Jan., 1666.

Mr. Yale came to America in 1637, with his father-in-law Gov. Eaton, his mother, brother David and sister Ann, who became the wife of Gov. Hopkins. He was a merchant at New Haven ; his house stood on the ground now owned and occupied by Yale College, in that city.

Gov. Theophilus Eaton, his step-father, having deceased, Mrs. Eaton and her son Thomas Yale, went to England, with Elihu, afterwards Gov. Yale, the distinguished donor of Yale College, accompanied by David Yale his brother, and Hannah Eaton, a daughter of the Governor. Returning to New Haven the following year, he purchased land in North Haven near the present location of the bridge (Mansfield bridge), of Gov. Eaton's estate, and settled on it in 1660. He was evidently a man of energy and business tact, and was frequently called to fill many important offices, by the citizens of New Haven. He died March 27, 1683, ae. 67 years. His wife, Mary Turner, died Oct. 15, 1704.

Children: 1 *John*, b 1646, settled in North Haven ; 2 *Thomas*, b 1647, settled in Wallingford in 1670 ; 3 *Elihu*, b April 5, 1648, donor of the College at New Haven ; 4 *Mary*, b Oct. 26, 1650 m Capt. Joseph Ives ; 5 *Nathaniel*, b Jan. 3, 1652 ; 6 *Martha*, b May 6, 1655, d Jan. 15, 1670 ; 7 *Abigail*, b May 5, 1660 ; 8 *Hannah*, b July 6, 1662, m Enos Talmage ; 9 *Elizabeth*, b Jan. 29, 1667, m Joseph Pardee, of East Haven.

2. THOMAS.

Capt. Thomas Yale, son of Thomas and Mary Yale, of New Haven, was born in that place in 1647, married Rebecca, daughter of William Gibbards, Esq., Dec. 11, 1667. She died, ———. He married 2d, Sarah, daughter of John Nash. She died May 27, 1716. He married 3d, Mary Beach, of Wallingford, July 31, 1716. He was one of the first and most active settlers in the village of Wallingford in 1670, to which place he removed that year. In 1710 he with the Rev. Samuel Street were the only surviving signers of the Plantation Covenant of Wallingford. He was a Justice of the Peace and Captain of the Train band, Surveyor of land and generally moderator of the business meetings of the town, &c.

He died Jan. 26, 1736, ae. 89 years. Mrs. Rebecca Yale was born Feb. 26, 1650.

Children: 10 *Hannah*, b July 27, 1669; 11 *Rebecca*, b Oct. 2, 1671; 12 *Elizabeth*, b July 25, 1673; 13 *Theophilus*, b Nov. 13, 1675; 14 *Thomas*, b March 20, 1678; 15 *Nathaniel*, b July 12, 1681; 16 *Mary*, b Aug. 27, 1684; 17 *John*, b Dec. 8, 1687.

NOTE TO BENHAM FAMILY.

URI BENHAM was born December 26, 1739, died April 22, 1832, at Cheshire. Lois his wife was born Oct. 16, 1747, died Dec. 26, 1827, at Cheshire.

Children: *Sarah*, b Oct. 11, 1769; *Uri*, b Oct. 23, 1771, d Oct. 23, 1826; *Lois*, b Sept. 25, 1773, d Nov. 27, 1774; *Mary Lois*, b Oct. 27, 1775; *Lent*, b March 25, 1778, d Oct. 18, 1836; *Ethelbert*, b July 14, 1780, d Jan. 26, 1849; *Amanda*, b Jan. 1, 1783; *Joseph*, b Jan. 26, 1785, d Oct, 29, 1853; *Martha*, b March 2, 1788, d March 7, 1836.

[This work has increased to such an extent that it has been found advisable to omit the Yale genealogy, for which material had been gathered. Mr. Elihu Yale, of New Haven, a few years ago published a genealogy of the family, to which the reader is referred].

ERRATA.

Page 19, line 2 from bot., for Julia Hall, read Hull, dau. of Jeremiah; p. 20, lines 9 and 12 from top, for Daniel, read David Atwater; p. 29, line 6 from top, for Freeman, read Truman; p. 41, line 8 from top, for Grange, read Geauga; p. 62, line 4 from bot., for McLean, read McCleve; p. 63, line 8 from top, for Hall, read McCleve; p. 69, line 15 from top, add, Ephraim Cook m Elizabeth Hull; p. 69, line 3 from bot., for Boone, read Boorge; p. 70, line 19 from bot., for survey, read society; p. 87, line 6 from top, for Perlina, read Pauline; p. 103, line 19 from bot., omit Horace; p. 137, line 6 from top, for Daniel, read David; p. 144, top line, for Bradley, read Moss; p. 174, line 8 from bot., for 1802, read 1809; p. 175, line 11 from top, for Ann Bull, read Ann Buel; p. 179, line 13 from top, read m 2d, Almer Hall; p. 190, line 15 from top, for Hall, read Hull; p. 196, line 14 from bot., read Mehitable; p. 206, line 13 from top, for Brothers, read Bray; p. 211, line 9 from top, for Sam'l J., read Sam'l G.; p. 212, line 12 from top, for Jonathan, read Jotham; p. 213, line 12 from bot., for Lawrence, read Lauren; p. 216, line 10 from top, for 1761, read 1781; p. 235, line 12 from bot., for Cookstown, read Coolstown; p. 236, line 14 from top, for Selekey, read Selebes; p. 280, line 21 from bot., for let, read set; p. 282, line 6 from bot., for Elizabeth, read Eliasaph; p. 294, line 17 from bot., for 1753, read 1653; p. 298, line 9 from bot., for Hall, read Hull.